John Freely was born in New York the age of seventeen, serving with and China during the last years of in New York, Boston, London, Athens and Istanbul written over thirty travel books and guides, most of them about Greece and Turkey. He is author of *Strolling Through Athens* (also Tauris Parke Paperbacks) and the bestselling *Strolling Through Istanbul*.

Tauris Parke Paperbacks is an imprint of I.B.Tauris. It is dedicated to publishing books in accessible paperback editions for the serious general reader within a wide range of categories, including biography, history, travel, art and the ancient world. The list includes select, critically acclaimed works of top quality writing by distinguished authors that continue to challenge, to inform and to inspire. These are books that possess those subtle but intrinsic elements that mark them out as something exceptional.

The colophon of Tauris Parke Paperbacks is a representation of the ancient Egyptian ibis, sacred to the god Thoth, who was himself often depicted in the form of this most elegant of birds. Thoth was credited in antiquity as the scribe of the ancient Egyptian gods and as the inventor of writing and was associated with many aspects of wisdom and learning.

THE WESTERN SHORES OF TURKEY

Discovering the Aegean and
Mediterranean Coasts

JOHN FREELY

TPP

TAURIS PARKE
PAPERBACKS

Published in 2004 by I.B. Tauris & Co Ltd
6 Salem Road, London W2 4BU
175 Fifth Avenue, New York NY 10010
www.ibtauris.com

In the United States of America and Canada distributed by
Palgrave Macmillan a division of St. Martin's Press
175 Fifth Avenue, New York NY 10010

Copyright © 1988, 2004 by John Freely
First published by John Murray (Publishers) Ltd, 1988.
Spine and back panel illustration on cover: Medusa head at Didyma

The right of John Freely to be identified as the author of this work has been
asserted by the author in accordance with the Copyright, Designs and Patent
Act 1988.

All rights reserved. Except for brief quotations in a review, this book, or any
part thereof, may not be reproduced, stored in or introduced into a retrieval
system, or transmitted, in any form or by any means, electronic, mechanical,
photocopying, recording or otherwise, without the prior written permission of
the publisher.

ISBN 1 85043 618 5
EAN 978 1 85043 618 8

A full CIP record for this book is available from the British Library
A full CIP record is available from the Library of Congress

Library of Congress Catalog Card Number: available

Printed and bound in Great Britain by MPG Books Ltd, Bodmin

CONTENTS

ILLUSTRATIONS

ACKNOWLEDGEMENTS

The author and publisher wish to thank the following for permission to reproduce photographs:

Ergun Çagatay (Plates 3, 10, and 14); Ara Güler (Plates 1, 2, 4, 5, 6, 7, 8, 9, 11, 12, 13, and 16); Şemsi Güner (Plates 18 and 22); and the Turkish Ministry of Tourism (Plates 15, 17, 19, 20, and 21).

A NOTE ON TURKISH SPELLING AND PRONUNCIATION

All letters in the Turkish alphabet have one and only one sound, and no letters are silent. Vowels have their short Continental value; i.e. *a* as in f*a*ther (the rarely used *â* sounds rather like *ay*), *e* as in g*e*t, *i* as in s*i*t, *o* as in d*o*ll, and *u* as in b*u*ll. However, *ı* (undotted) is between *i* and *u*, somewhat as the final *a* in Ann*a*, *ö* is pronounced as in German or as the *u* in f*u*rther; and *ü* as in German or as the French *u* in t*u*. Consonants are as in English except for the following: *c* as *j* in *j*am; *ç* as *ch* in *ch*urch; *g* is always hard as in *g*ive, never soft as in *g*em; *ğ* is almost silent, tending to lengthen the preceding vowel; *s* is always unvoiced as in *s*it, never like *z*; and *ş* is as *s* in *s*ugar. Turkish is very lightly accented, most often on the last syllable, but all syllables should be clearly and almost evenly articulated.

*For Jacob and Mimi Maya
and Roddy and Olga O'Connor*

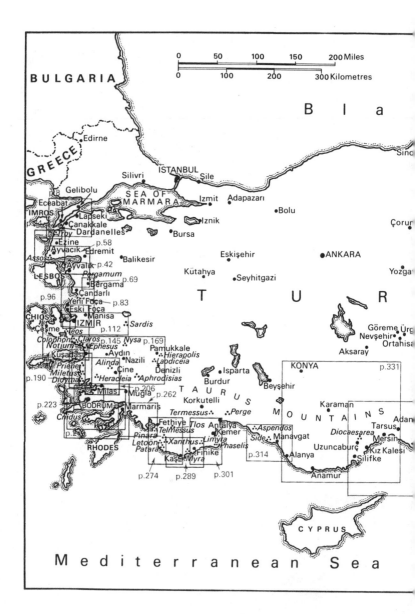

k S e a   U. S. S. R.

                                    Hopa
                                              •Artvin
Samsun   •Terme   Tirebolu   •Rize
       •   Ordu Giresun Trabzon   •Kars
•Amasya
      •Tokat   Bayburt

                                   •Erzurum   Ağrı
       •Sivas   Erzincan   Doğubayazit•
                       •

  K   E   Y
                      Bingol•   Muş   Ahlat
AYSERI   •Elâziğ   Tatvan• L.
                                        Van •Van
            •Malatya   Bitlis
                            •Diyarbakir •Siirt
        Adıyaman •Kâhta   Hakkâri
Kozan •Maraş   •Midyat
 •Kadirli   •Mardin
  ∴Karatepe Gaziantep •Urfa
 •Toprakkale   •Birecik
•Ceyhan
sis•
  •Iskenderun
 •   •Aleppo
Antakya
    p.355
         S   Y   R   I   A   I   R   A   Q

INTRODUCTION

Much of the fascination that Turkey holds for foreigners stems from the fact that it extends into two continents, for history and geography link it to both Europe and Asia. The European and Asian parts of Turkey are separated by the Bosphorus, the Sea of Marmara, and the Dardanelles, with the Black Sea bounding its shores to the north, the Aegean to the west, and the Mediterranean along the western half of its southern side. Ninety-seven per cent of Turkey's land mass is in Asia, comprising the huge subcontinent now officially called Anatolia but more generally known in former times as Asia Minor. Both names have been used since antiquity, Asia Minor in Graeco-Roman times referring to this westernmost extension of the Asian continent, while Anatolia is the Greek word for East, more literally the Land of Sunrise.

Turkey is bounded in Asia by Syria, Iraq, Iran, and Russia, and in Europe by Bulgaria and Greece. Turkey also has a maritime boundary with Greece that winds through the eastern Aegean between a series of Greek archipelagos and the Asian shore, extending from the south-eastern corner of Europe to the south-westernmost promontory of Anatolia where the waters of the Aegean and the Mediterranean merge. Thus the Anatolian subcontinent of Turkey is part of two worlds, its remote eastern marches leading into the vast timelessness of Asia, its western shores washed by the Aegean and the Mediterranean, where European civilization emerged.

I first saw the western shores of Turkey in January 1961, travelling with my wife Dolores and our three children aboard an old post-boat of the Turkish Maritime Lines, the *Tarih*, which has long since gone to its rest in a maritime graveyard along the Golden Horn. Boarding the *Tarih* in Istanbul, we embarked on a voyage that would take us along the Aegean and Mediterranean coasts of Turkey as far as Antalya, from where we returned across Anatolia by bus. The schedule and itinerary of the *Tarih* fitted in perfectly with the academic calendar at Robert College, the American school in Istanbul where I had started teaching in September 1960. Our mid-winter vacation began on the day that the *Tarih* set off on its monthly voyage around the Turkish coast from Istanbul, and it arrived in Antalya a week later, allowing us another week to make our way back to our home on the Bosphorus before the beginning of the second semester. The ship was well named, for in Turkish *Tarih* means 'history', appropriate for a vessel that each month sailed to places known in antiquity as the Thracian Chersonese, the Troad, Aeolia, Ionia, Caria, Lycia, Pamphylia, and Cilicia, one of its ports-of-call being Halicarnassus, birthplace of Herodotus, the 'father' of history.

This was the first of our many journeys along the western shores of Turkey. Some of them were made aboard more modern ships of the Turkish Maritime Lines; others on the old wooden fishing-boats known as caiques, sailing along remote stretches of the Anatolian coast; still others by land on local buses or by *dolmuş*, the public taxi that serves as the beast of burden in modern Turkey, replacing the donkey and camel of Ottoman times. Later on we acquired our own car, a second-hand Opel that has now also gone to its deserved rest in an Istanbul scrap-yard, and in this we were able to reach out-of-the-way places in Anatolia that had previously been inaccessible to us. By these means we travelled around the Aegean and Mediterranean shores of Turkey from the Dardanelles to the Syrian border. We also made our way inland along the valleys of the Hermus, the Maeander, and the Xanthus, the

three rivers along which the first Greek settlers penetrated into
Asia Minor at the end of the second millennium BC and where
they came into contact with the much older Anatolian civilizations that had preceded them. These travels took us to
virtually all of the archaeological sites in western Anatolia,
beginning with Troy and the Trojan plain, where we used
Homer's *Iliad* as our guide, and ending at Seleucia-ad-Pieria,
which in Hellenistic times was the port of Antioch, the 'fair
flower of the Orient'. *En route* we saw in turn the ruins of
Alexandria Troas and Assos, the two most important sites in
the Troad south of Troy; Pergamum, capital of the brilliant
kingdom of the Attalids; Cyme, which Strabo called 'the biggest
and best of the Aeolian cities', now almost vanished; Izmir, the
Greek Smyrna, now as in ancient times the largest seaport on
the Aegean coast of Anatolia; 'golden Sardis', capital of Lydia,
now being excavated in all of its archaic splendour; Ephesus,
shrine of the Mother Goddess, whose majestic ruins still survive
along with those of other cities of the Ionian League, most
notably Teos, Miletus, Priene, and Didyma; Aphrodisias, the
'Florence of the Hellenistic world', where Kenan Erim is now
unearthing numerous masterpieces of Graeco-Roman sculpture; the Carian cities of Heracleia-under-Latmus, Euromus,
Alinda, and Alabanda, to which we were drawn by the lure of
their romantic names and legends; Labraynda, the ancient
shrine of the Carian people, and Halicarnassus, the last capital
of the Carian kingdom, still guarded by the Crusader castle of
St. Peter at Bodrum. Further, we visited the sea-girt ruins of
Cnidus, famed for its statue of Aphrodite; Xanthus, last capital
of Lycia, whose other tomb-haunted sites we found in the
south-western corner of Anatolia, including Telmessus,
Patara, the Letoön, Myra, and Phaselis; the 'pirate coast of
Pamphylia', where we visited the port of old Antalya as well
as the ruins of Perge, Aspendos, and Side; Alanya with its
extraordinary Selcuk fortress; the succession of ruined medieval fortresses along the Cilician shore, principally those at
Anamur, Silifke, and Kız Kalesi, the Maiden's Castle; the

3

ancient sites around the eastern end of the Turkish Mediterranean coast, the most dramatic being Yılan Kalesi, the Castle of the Snake; and then finally the port of ancient Antioch in the Hatay, the Turkish province just above Syria on what was once the northern approach to Phoenicia, where our long series of journeys along the western Anatolian coast came to an end, at least for the time being. There, as we completed the odyssey that had taken us through a quarter-century of our lives, we recalled the good times and adventures we had shared with our children and old friends who had accompanied us on our Anatolian trips, remembering also the enduring friendships we had made along the way with the local people who had welcomed us into their homes and their lives. We thought with particular poignancy of our dear departed friend Cevat Şakir Kabaagaç, the Fisherman of Halicarnassus, whose stories of Bodrum life have immortalized the Aegean coast of Anatolia as it was when we first saw it in his company, an enchanted world where time seemed to have stopped somewhere between the end of antiquity and the beginning of our own era, an idyllic scene that has now in my own imagination taken on the mythic qualities of what Homer called 'the country of dreams'.

The enduring memories of these Anatolian journeys are images of a surpassingly beautiful succession of promontories, coves, and isles, with romantic ruins on every well-protected headland, an historic coast that since time immemorial has been a marchland between East and West, with nations of people passing through in their migrations and wars, leaving their imprint upon the landscape and the ways of life of those who dwell there today. The tides of history have left their traces everywhere along these shores, where Ottoman, Byzantine, Crusader, and Selcuk fortresses share the terrain with Greek and Roman temples and theatres, Carian and Lycian sarcophagi and tombs, and the mounds of ancient sites going as far back in time as the first human settlements in Anatolia toward the end of the Stone Age. Thus the western shores of

Turkey have become a palimpsest of civilizations, like a much-used canvas that has been painted over time and time again, a deeply layered scene that awaits discovery by those who travel there.

The chapters that follow are a distillation of our journeys along this ancient coast of vanished civilizations, our various voyages and drives telescoped in time just as they are interwoven in my memory. The book in one sense is meant to be an informal guide to the archaeological sites and historical monuments that one might see along the way; but it is also written with the thought that it might evoke the spirit of these places for those who are embarking upon their own odysseys along the western shores of Turkey. To help those readers in particular, I have added to each chapter maps of the area being described and its particular features, including the traditional sign ∴ for 'ancient monument'. I have inserted too at the beginning of the book a note about Turkish spelling and pronunciation, so that readers not acquainted with the language can begin to 'hear' it as they read. Also, at the end of the book I have included what I hope will be helpful practical appendices: a chronological table; a glossary of Turkish words used in the text; and a separate glossary of architectural terms. The book concludes with a bibliography and an index.

1

THE HELLESPONTINE SHORES

The western shores of Turkey begin along the Dardanelles, the ancient Hellespont, at least for travellers setting out from the imperial capital at the confluence of the Bosphorus and the Golden Horn, Istanbul. The eastern end of the Dardanelles is about 125 miles from Istanbul by sea, following a course along the European side of the Sea of Marmara. Most passenger ships leave Istanbul around noon, and so it is usually dark by the time they approach the Dardanelles, particularly in winter. That was the season when we made our first voyage aboard the *Tarih*. My first sight of the Hellespontine shores was from the flying-bridge, with lights showing from scattered hamlets off both the port and starboard bows as we drew near the entrance to the straits. One of the crewmen pointed out a large cluster of lights on the European shore, identifying it as Gelibolu. This was the town known to the Greeks as Kallipoli, the Good City, which in the West came to be called Gallipoli. It was there that we really began our first journey along the western shores of Turkey.

The harbour at Gelibolu is just a few miles downstream from the beginning of the Dardanelles, known in Turkish as the Çanakkale Boğazı.* Here the Sea of Marmara narrows at its western end into a definite channel between Europe and Asia. The Asian side of the straits was known in antiquity as the

* See the note on Turkish spelling and pronunciation on p. *ix* and the glossary of Turkish words on p. 381.

7

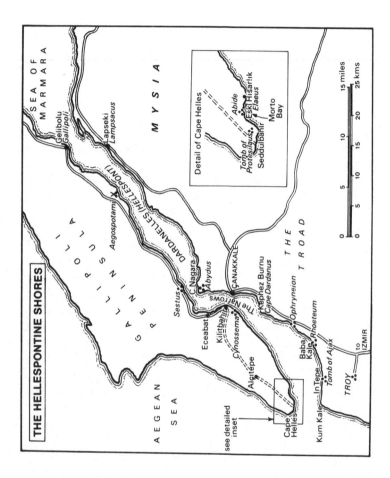

THE HELLESPONTINE SHORES

SEA OF MARMARA

Gelibolu
Gallipoli

Lapseki
Lampsacus

M Y S I A

Aegospotami

DARDANELLES (HELLESPONT)

G A L L I P O L I   P E N I N S U L A

C.Nagara

Abydos

ÇANAKKALE

Sestus

Eceabat

Kilitbahir

Cynossema

The Narrows

Kephez Burnu
Cape Dardanus

Ophryneion

T H E   T R O A D

AEGEAN SEA

Aigitepe

see detailed inset

Cape Helles

Baba Kale

Rhoeteum

Kum Kale

InTepe

Tomb of Ajax

TROY

to IZMIR

Detail of Cape Helles

Abide

Tomb of Protesilaus

Eski Hisarlık

Elaeus

Seddülbahir

Morto Bay

0   5   10   15   25 kms

0   5   10   15 miles

Troad, the land of Troy, and it forms the north-western corner of Mysia. The European shore is formed by the Gallipoli peninsula, known to the Greeks as the Thracian Chersonese, and is less than a mile wide where the straits begin at Bolayır. From there the waters of the Dardanelles follow an occasionally serpentine course of some forty miles in the general direction north-east to south-west, finally flowing west to enter the Aegean. The straits are about four to five miles wide at Bolayır, but from there westward the European and Asian shores converge to the stretch known as the Narrows, between Çanakkale and Kilitbahir, where they are less than a mile in width. Beyond the Narrows the straits diverge again to a width of about five miles before the shores converge once more so that, at the western end of the Dardanelles, they are only 4,000 yards apart.

There are numerous myths associated with the straits, the earliest being the legend of Phrixus and his sister Helle, children of Nephele, goddess of the clouds. Their father, King Athamas of Boetia, was about to sacrifice Phrixus and Helle to propitiate the gods during a time of drought, having been persuaded to do so by their evil stepmother Ino. When Nephele learned of this she flew down from the clouds to save her children, sending them off on a golden-fleeced ram given to her by Hermes. The ram carried them eastward through the heavens, but, as they soared over the first of the two straits separating Europe from Asia, Helle fell off and was drowned, after which these waters came to be known as the Hellespont, and the Greek people themselves as Hellenes. Phrixus managed to hang on as the ram carried him to the land of Colchis, where he was received with honour by King Areetes and wedded to the Princess Chalciope. As a token of gratitude for his safe arrival, Phrixus sacrificed the ram to Zeus; he then gave the golden fleece to Areetes, who hung it in a grove of oaks sacred to Ares. The golden fleece was later retrieved by Jason, son of King Cretheus of Pelion and brother of Athamas. When Jason set out on his expedition he built a ship called the *Argo*, and heroes from all over Hellas volunteered to fill the fifty seats on its rowing-benches. They came to be known as the Argonauts, the crew of the vessel that Spenser, in the *Faerie Queene*, called 'the wondred *Argo*, which ... first through the Euxine sea bore all the flower of Greece'.

Still another myth tells the story of Dardanus, a son of Zeus who was one of the ancestors of Aeneas, the mythical founder of Rome. According to tradition, Dardanus founded a town bearing his name on the Asian side of the straits, 'which was peopled first, ere Ilion [Troy] with its teeming crowds was settled in the plain'. During the Renaissance the popularity of Homer's epics revived the myth of Dardanus, so that in Europe the Hellespont was known as the Dardanelles, although in the Greek language it retained its ancient name.

On our several journeys down the Dardanelles we always spent the first night in Gelibolu, and had breakfast the following morning at a *çayevi*, or tea-house, on the waterfront before setting out on our way down the straits, either by ship or by land. The scene on the Gelibolu waterfront is lively and colourful in the morning, particularly if the fishing-fleet has been out the night before, for then the local fishermen will be hawking their catch on the dock beside their galleon-like caiques. The broad-beamed wooden hulls of these boats are painted in all the bright colours of the sun's spectrum and each vessel bears on its prow the whirling blue eye or *oculus*, the talismanic sign with which sailors in these waters have since antiquity warded off evil. And if it is a warm and sunny morning the fishermen will have spread out their nets to dry on the quay, they and their families sitting cross-legged on the cobbles to mend the billows of brilliantly tinted twine. Often one of them will make time pass as if in a dream by playing the *gayda*, the Aegean bagpipe whose wild, wailing sound evokes visions of what these straits were like when the Greeks first settled here in the dark ages of the ancient world.

The only monument in the port of Gelibolu is the ruined fortress in the inner harbour, the medieval Castle of Gallipoli.

This edifice is thought to have been erected by the emperor Philippicus Bardanes, an Armenian who ruled the Byzantine Empire from AD 711 to 713.* The Castle of Gallipoli was the key to the Hellespont throughout the Middle Ages, and as long as the Byzantines held it they controlled the western maritime approaches to Constantinople. But in 1303 Gallipoli was occupied by the Grand Army of Catalonia, a wild band of Spanish mercenaries hired by the emperor Andronicus II to help the Byzantines fight against the Turks. The Catalans used the castle as a base to ravage all of Thrace, holding out there for seven years against repeated attacks by the Byzantines and their Genoese allies. The Grand Army of Catalonia finally abandoned Gallipoli in 1310, after which the Byzantines regained the fortress. Then in 1354 this castle and another Hellespontine fortress were captured by Prince Süleyman, eldest son of Orhan Gazi, first sultan of the Ottoman Turks. Thus the Turks established their first foothold in Europe, and by the mid-fifteenth century the Ottoman Empire extended far into the Balkans and Asia Minor. Constantinople finally fell to Sultan Mehmet II on 29 May 1453, ending the long history of the Byzantine Empire, with some of the last ships of Greek refugees sailing down the Hellespont on their way to the Aegean.

After the Turkish conquest, Gallipoli became a major port-of-call for the Ottoman navy, whose warships always stopped there on their way to and from their campaigns in the Aegean. A number of Turkish mariners seem to have stayed on to live in Gallipoli after their retirement, for on the outskirts of the town there are several domed *türbe*, or mausoleums, whose inscriptions record that they were built by Ottoman captain-pashas. The most renowned of these is Piri Reis (1465–1554), the Ottoman navigator whose *Kitabı Bahriye*, or *Book of the Sea*, is the earliest Turkish geographical compendium and includes a chart of the North American coast. A statue of Piri Reis has recently been erected on the waterfront in Gelibolu, and there is a small museum related to his life and career.

* See the chronological table on pp. 373–80.

During Ottoman times the Castle of Gallipoli was also used as a prison. The most celebrated of its inmates was Shabbetai Zevi, known to history as the False Messiah. He was imprisoned there in the spring and summer of 1666, and during that time the castle became a place of pilgrimage for Jews from all over the Middle East and Europe who believed that Shabbetai was indeed the long-awaited Messiah. When these pilgrims came to see Shabbetai he received them in his cell, dressed in his medieval rabbinical robe, and told them of his apocalyptic visions; afterwards he entertained them by playing on his lute and singing old love-songs in Ladino, his favourite being a *cantada* about the tragic romance of 'Meliselda, the Emperor's beautiful daughter'. Shabbetai remained in the Castle of Gallipoli until 3 September 1666, after which he was brought to Edirne for a hearing before Sultan Mehmet IV. Thereupon he converted to Islam, eventually convincing thousands of his followers to do the same and thus creating the arcane cult whose adherents are known to the Turks as Dönme, or Turncoats. There are many Dönme still living in Turkey, principally in Istanbul and Izmir, and a number of them continue to believe that their revered Shabbetai will one day return and lead them to Paradise. For them the Castle of Gallipoli is still a sacred shrine, as evidenced by the few tattered pieces of cloth that can be seen tied to its barred windows, votive offerings of those who continue to keep faith with the lost Messiah who was once imprisoned there.

The first port-of-call on the Asian side of the straits is Lapseki, just a short distance downstream from Gelibolu. A car ferry crosses between the two towns several times a day. There is also a car ferry farther down the straits, between Eceabat and Çanakkale, so that, in driving along the shores of the Dardanelles, one has a choice of routes. During the course of our trips we have driven up and down both its European and Asian sides, as well as sailing down the straits in the *Tarih* and other vessels; and we have been able to explore most of the historic sites on both shores.

Lapseki was originally known as Lampsacus, and was a Greek colony founded in 654 BC by Phocaea and Miletus, two Ionian cities on the Aegean shore of Asia Minor. During the Graeco-Roman period Lampsacus was a more important town than Kallipoli, because the cove on which it was located made it a much better harbour for ships passing through the Hellespont. No trace remains of the ancient town, one of three places given by Xerxes, the king of Persia, to Themistocles. Xerxes presented him with 'Magnesia for his bread, Myus for his meat, and Lampsacus for his wine'.

Lampsacus was the last home of Anaxagoras, the first great philosopher to reside in Athens, where his most famous student was Pericles. Anaxagoras, born c. 500 BC in the Ionian city of Clazomenae, moved to Athens at the age of 20 and remained there until he was banished in 450 BC, convicted on charges of impiety and Medeism (being Pro-Persian). Anaxagoras then settled in Lampsacus and founded a school of philosophy, directing its activities until his death in 428 BC. After his death, the people of Lampsacus erected an altar to his memory in their market square and dedicated it to Mind and Truth. The anniversary of the death of Anaxagoras was for long afterwards celebrated in Lampsacus, and by his dying request the students of the town were always let out of school on that day.

One of the most historic sites on the Hellespont is directly across the straits from Lapseki; this is Ince Liman, the Port of the Pearl, some eight miles down the Dardanelles from Gelibolu on the European shore. The stream that flows into this cove was known to the Greeks as Aegospotami, or Goat's River, and gave its name to a decisive battle fought in 405 BC, when the Peloponnesian forces led by Lysander overwhelmed an Athenian fleet commanded by Conon and Philocles. This, the last battle of the Peloponnesian War, left Athens defeated and at the mercy of the Spartans and their allies.

The next two historic sites on the Dardanelles are Sestus and Abydus; the first is on the European shore about a mile above the Narrows, and the second on the Asian side above Cape

Nagara. Both were Greek colonies founded in the seventh century BC, Sestus by Aeolians and Abydus by Ionians from Miletus. There is virtually nothing left of Sestus, and the few stones that remain of Abydus are in an inaccessible military zone; nevertheless I could identify both sites from my classical atlas as we approached the Narrows on our first trip aboard the *Tarih*. Sestus and Abydus had always interested me because of their associations in history, literature, and legend, particularly the fabled romance of Hero and Leander. The legend tells of how Leander, a youth of Abydus, fell in love with Hero, a priestess at the Temple of Aphrodite in Sestus, and of how he swam the Hellespont nightly to see her, guided by a lamp which she placed on the European shore. But one night the lamp was extinguished in a gale and Leander lost his way, drowning in the Hellespont. When his body was washed ashore in Sestus Hero threw herself into the water in despair and lost her life too. The legend of Hero and Leander inspired Byron to swim the Hellespont at the Narrows, a feat he accomplished on 3 May 1810 when he was passing through the straits on a British schooner. Six days later Byron commemorated this crossing in his poem, 'Written After Swimming from Sestus to Abydus'. He later returned to the legend in the *Bride of Abydus*, and as the *Tarih* approached the Narrows I recalled the lines that begin the second canto:

> The winds are high on Helle's wave
> As on that night of stormy weather
> When love, who sent, forgot to save
> The young—the beautiful—the brave
> The lonely hope of Sestus' daughter

The site of Abydus is on the promontory that rises up from Cape Nagara, where the Dardanelles makes an abrupt turn as it approaches the Narrows. This cape, according to Herodotus, Strabo, and Pliny, once marked the narrowest part of the channel, but erosion of the shore around it has made this crossing a little wider than the stretch between Çanakkale and Kilitbahir. This was where Xerxes began his invasion of Greece, when the Persian army crossed from Abydus to Sestus in 480 BC on a bridge of boats built by his engineers. As Herodotus describes the scene, Xerxes held a review of his forces while seated on a throne of white marble that had been made for him by the people of Abydus, looking down upon his enormous army crossing the straits. 'And when he saw the whole of the Hellespont hidden by ships, and all the beaches and plains filled with men, he congratulated himself—and a moment later burst into tears. When his uncle Artabanus asked him why he wept, Xerxes replied, "I was thinking, and it came to my mind how pitifully short human life is—for of all those thousands of men not one will be alive in a hundred years' time"'.

Another historic crossing of the Hellespont took place here in 334 BC, when Alexander the Great began his campaign to conquer Asia. When the Macedonians reached the Hellespont, Alexander himself crossed at the Aegean end of the straits to make a pilgrimage to Troy, leaving Parmenio to lead the army across from Sestus to Abydus. A few days later Alexander rejoined his army and led them to victory over the Persians at the Battle of the Granicus, a short distance to the north-east of Lapseki.

Two villages on the European side of the Narrows look out over the most dramatic stretch of the Dardanelles, where it suddenly bends southward at Cape Nagara. The more northern one is Eceabat, the European terminus of the car ferry to Çanakkale; formerly known as Madytus, this was founded by Aeolian Greeks in the seventh century BC. Three miles to the south is the village of Kilitbahir, which is directly across from Çanakkale at the narrowest part of the straits. Kilitbahir, the Key to the Sea, takes its name from the picturesque Ottoman fortress around which it clusters, erected by Sultan Mehmet II a decade after his conquest of Constantinople. Kilitbahir consists of two defence towers connected by massive curtain walls, and its outline forms a heart-shaped enclosure facing out towards the Aegean end of the straits. Mehmet II, known to the Turks as Fatih, the Conqueror, also constructed a second fortress in Çanakkale, called Sultaniye-Bahir. The two strongholds became known in later times as the Inner Castles.

The Inner Castles were in the thick of the fighting on 18 March 1915, when the Allied navy attempted to force its way through the straits at the outset of the Gallipoli campaign. That assault was a total failure, with two British battleships and a French Dreadnought sunk by shore batteries and underwater mines, as well as two more battleships put out of action. A total of 2,750 Allied sailors lost their lives. But even before that attack the Allied high command had decided that the straits could not be forced by a fleet alone, and they had begun planning for a large-scale amphibious landing at the Aegean end of the Dardanelles, the main thrust to be made on the Gallipoli peninsula. The initial landings took place on 25 April 1915, the beginning of an eight-month battle in which more than 100,000 men of the Allied and Turkish forces lost their lives fighting over a few square miles of barren ground at the western end of the Thracian Chersonese. But the invasion too proved unsuccessful, and early in 1916 the Allies evacuated their troops from the Gallipoli peninsula, leaving the Turks in control of the Dardanelles.

On one of our journeys we drove to the site of the Gallipoli battlefield. We followed the road that at first leads down the straits from Kilitbahir and then turns inland to the crossroads at Alçıtepe, where signposts indicate the way to the various British and Commonwealth war cemeteries in the vicinity. The Cape Helles War Memorial, near the tip of the peninsula, commemorates the 35,000 British and Commonwealth servicemen who were killed in the Gallipoli campaign. Farther up the straits on the European side is the Turkish war monument at Abide, honouring the 60,000 Turks who died at Gallipoli, while elsewhere on the peninsula there is a memorial to the 9,000 French and Senegalese dead. There is also a small war museum in the village of Alçıtepe, where a local Turkish scholar has devoted his life to collecting memorabilia picked up on the battlefield. The most moving of these mementoes are letters found on the bodies of men now buried out on the deserted peninsula, some of the pages stained with blood shed when they were killed in battle.

There are reminders still of the Gallipoli campaign in Çanakkale, a sprawling mass of houses on the Asian shore at the narrowest point of the straits. Carved into the cliff face of the promontory upstream from the harbour is a huge inscription with the date 18 March 1915, commemorating the Turkish repulse of the Allied naval attack on the straits. On the hillside opposite there is a memorial to the Turkish servicemen who died in the Gallipoli campaign.

Çanakkale is not an ancient town. It dates only from the second half of the fifteenth century when Fatih built his fortress of Sultaniye-Bahir on the shore just to the south of the harbour area. Within this fortress there are a number of interesting old European cannon of the Ottoman period, some of them bearing the marks of English foundries. At the southern end of the pier there is also a military museum with exhibits relating to the Gallipoli campaign, particularly the successful defence of the straits by the Turkish navy. Another place of interest in Çanakkale is the archaeological museum; this is housed in a former Greek church in one of the back streets of the town, the building having been abandoned by its congregation in 1923 when, after the Graeco-Turkish war of 1919–23, the ethnic minorities of the two countries were exchanged. Anatolian Greeks were sent to Greece and Turks from Greece moved to Turkey. The museum has a small collection of minor antiquities found in the Troad, including votive objects, figurines, and jewellery. The most interesting of these come from a collection that once belonged to Frank Calvert, the man who led Heinrich Schliemann to Hisarlık, the true site of Homeric Troy.

Beyond Hisarlık the straits quickly expand to a width of some four miles. This makes it difficult to identify sites on the Hellespontine shores from the deck of a passing steamer like the *Tarih*, so on one of our spring vacations we hired a local fisherman named Ahmet to take us in his caique through the lower Dardanelles, starting at dawn from Çanakkale, crossing to go down the European side of the straits, and returning along the Asian shore.

Ahmet and his ancestors had been fishing in the waters of the Dardanelles since as far back as family memories extended. He was in his mid-sixties, he said, and had been a lad of about 14 when the Allied fleet tried to pass through the straits on 18 March 1915. He had watched the battle from a hilltop south of Çanakkale and saw the French Dreadnought *Bouvet* go down. After the war he and the other boatmen of Çanakkale were employed for some time in salvage operations on the Allied battleships and so he knew their sites well. On the Asian side were the *Bouvet* and the British battleships *Irresistible* and *Ocean*, all three of which went down on 18 March 1915; and along the shallows of the European shore were two more British battleships, *Majestic* and *Triumph*, sunk on 15 May of the same year. Ahmet said that the fishermen of Çanakkale still sailed out to drop their lines on these sites, for schools of fish continued to shelter in the wrecks.

After we crossed the straits, Ahmet steered his caique down along the European shore until we reached the promontory just south of Kilitbahir, the first stop on our itinerary. This cape was known to the Greeks as Cynossema, the Dog's Grave, because of a myth that Hecuba was transformed into a dog and buried here after the fall of Troy. Cynossema gave its name to a naval battle fought in the Narrows in 411 BC, in which the Athenians defeated the Spartans. The Battle of Cynossema was the last major action recorded by Thucydides in his *History of the Peloponnesian War*, for he breaks off his narrative abruptly shortly afterwards. Six more years passed before the final defeat of the Athenians at Aegospotami, just a few miles up the Hellespont from where our caique was anchored.

We then sailed down the European shore of the straits toward the Aegean, a distance of six miles, the most prominent landmark being the Turkish war memorial towering above the cliffs at Abide. The only ancient site marked on my classical atlas beyond Cynossema on the Thracian Chersonese was Elaeus, which was shown near the Aegean end of the straits. I had brought along a detailed map of the lower Dardanelles and the Trojan plain, based on the survey made by Graves and Spratt in 1840 and published in 1883 by Schliemann in one of his books on Troy. This showed that the site of Elaeus was on the promontory that formed the eastern arm of Morto Bay, the last indentation on the European shore of the straits. We went ashore there and looked for Elaeus, the westernmost of the ancient Greek towns on the Thracian Chersonese. Schliemann had found evidence of an ancient settlement here, its stones scattered around the ruined Ottoman fortress known as Eski Hisarlık, the Old Castle. However, Eski Hisarlık was one of the places where the Allies landed on 25 April 1915, and the bombardment was so intense that any ancient remnants on the site were pulverized.

Ahmet then took us over to the large tumulus on the western side of Morto Bay. Both ancient and modern travellers, including Schliemann, have sought to identify this as the Tomb of Protesilaus, the first of the Achaeans to be killed in the Trojan War. This tomb is mentioned by both Herodotus and Thucydides, and it had a renowned oracular shrine which was visited by Greek mariners who passed through the Hellespont. Alexander himself offered sacrifice there just before he crossed the Hellespont. According to his biographer Arrian, 'Alexander's purpose in performing the ceremony was to ensure better luck for himself than Protesilaus had'. After visiting the tomb, Alexander made his pilgrimage to Troy. 'It is generally believed', Arrian wrote, 'that Alexander sailed from Elaeus to the Achaean Harbour, himself at the helm of the admiral's ship, and that half way over he slaughtered a bull as an offering to Poseidon and poured wine from a golden cup into the sea to propitiate the Nereids'. (The Nereids were the daughters of the sea-god Nereus, and Greeks of an older generation still believe that they haunt bodies of water such as the Hellespont.)

Ahmet now headed the caique across the Dardanelles to the Asian side. As he did so we passed Seddülbahir, one of the two capes at the western tip of the Gallipoli peninsula, with Cape Helles still out of sight to the west. Ahmet brought us close in so that we could see the old Ottoman fortress at Seddülbahir, one of the two Outer Castles, the other fort barely visible across the way at Kum Kale on the westernmost point of the Asian shore. The Outer Castles, erected in 1659 by Mehmet Köprülü, grand vizier of Mehmet IV, were rebuilt in 1773–5 by Baron François de Tott, a Hungarian military engineer in the service of Abdül Hamit I. During the Gallipoli campaign the Outer Castles came under heavy bombardment, and today both are just ruined shells, grim reminders of the intensity of the battle here at the Aegean entrance to the Dardanelles.

As soon as we passed the ruined fort at Seddülbahir we spotted Cape Helles, the outermost tip of the Gallipoli peninsula and the site of one of the two lighthouses at the entrance to the straits. No doubt there were beacons on these capes in ancient times, for Aeschylus writes that Clytemnestra received word of the fall of Troy through the series of fire signals flashed all the way from the Hellespont to Mycenae.

After crossing the Dardanelles again to Kum Kale, which in Turkish means Sand Castle, we could see the bomb-blasted ruins of the second of the two Outer Castles, standing on the sandy Asian promontory where the Dardanelles flows into the Aegean. We could not land there, Ahmet told us, without permission from the military authorities in Çanakkale, and so we continued up the Asian shore. As we did so we had our first close-up view of the Trojan plain, which extends for miles inland between two streams that enter the Dardanelles together in a marshy estuary just to the east of Kum Kale. These streams have been identified as the Scamander and the Simoeis, two rivers which figure prominently in the *Iliad*.

About two miles up the Asian shore we passed the second of the two Heroic Tumuli on the lower Hellespont, a mound known locally as In Tepe. Early travellers attempted to identify this tumulus with the Tomb of Ajax (in Greek, Aias), son of Telamon, and it is so marked on Schliemann's map. As Homer tells the tale in the *Odyssey*, Ajax committed suicide during the siege of Troy, bitterly disappointed that the armour of Achilles had been presented to Odysseus rather than to him. There was a sanctuary of Ajax here in ancient times, for Mark Antony is known to have removed a colossal statue of the hero from his tomb on the Asian shore of the Hellespont. The statue was returned to its rightful place by Augustus after his victory over Antony and Cleopatra at Actium in 31 BC. In 1879 the tumulus was excavated by Schliemann, who dated it to the Hadrianic era, AD 117–38, but he also found evidence that the mound was probably erected on the site of an older heroon, or shrine dedicated to a hero. Close to the tumulus Schliemann discovered 'a mutilated marble statue of a warrior, draped and of a colossal size'. This was probably the cult statue of Ajax, the one removed by Antony and returned by Augustus. This sculpture has since disappeared, probably burned by local farmers to make lime for whitewash. That has been the fate of so many ancient marbles of the Graeco-Roman world.

Three miles farther up the straits we passed a promontory called Baba Kale. This has been identified as the site of Rhoeteum, which in Graeco-Roman times was one of the richest towns on the Hellespont. The Rhoeteum promontory figures in all topographical studies of the *Iliad*, for during the siege of Troy the Achaean ships would have been beached between this point and the Sigeum promontory, on the Aegean coast some two miles south of Kum Kale. Archaeological excavations have revealed that the site of Rhoeteum was inhabited continuously from c. 700 BC up until the beginning of the Christian era, but there is virtually nothing to be seen there today.

Another two miles up the coast brought us to a small cape that has been identified as the site of ancient Ophryneion, of which all that remains are some architectural fragments scattered in an old Turkish graveyard. Three miles beyond this we passed a promontory that I identified from my classical atlas as the site of ancient Dardanus. Pottery sherds found on the site range in date from the early Bronze Age to the Hellenistic period, but otherwise virtually nothing remains of what may have been the first Greek colony established on the Hellespont.

Beyond Dardanus we rounded the point known as Kephez Burnu, formerly called Cape Dardanus, and this brought us into the broad bay on the Asian shore which opens out just to the south of Çanakkale. There the Inner Castles at Kilitbahir and Çanakkale came into view at the Narrows, framing the stupendous spectacle of the Dardanelles surging past Cape Nagara through the converging continents of Europe and Asia. Then Ahmet steered the caique back into the harbour at Çanakkale, for we had completed our exploration of the shores of the lower Hellespont.

2

TROY AND THE TROJAN PLAIN

On our spring vacations we usually drove out to the western shores of Turkey via the northern coast of the Marmara and the Dardanelles, crossing the straits at either Gelibolu or Eceabat, and finally stopping for the night in Çanakkale. Then the following morning we would set off again, taking the Izmir highway from Çanakkale to our first destination, Troy, the ancient city of Priam.

The first stretch of the Çanakkale–Izmir highway leads along the Asian shore of the lower Dardanelles. This drive is particularly beautiful in the spring, with the olive-groves of Mysia giving way to the valonia oaks of the Troad as one goes down the straits, Judas-trees flowering in glorious bursts of pink and purple above the sky-blue waters of the Hellespont which here opens out to its greatest width as it approaches the Aegean. The road continues along the straits as far as Güzel Yalı, where we would often stop for a morning swim on the sandy beach that fringes the shore just north of In Tepe, and there catch our first glimpse of the Aegean out at the western end of the Dardanelles.

At Güzel Yalı the Çanakkale–Izmir highway leaves the coast and veers inland to the south-west and then south, climbing uphill through a forest of pine and valonia oak. Along the way, on knolls overlooking the Dardanelles, the highway passes a number of whitewashed monuments to nameless Turkish soldiers (they are always called *sehit*, or martyr), who died at

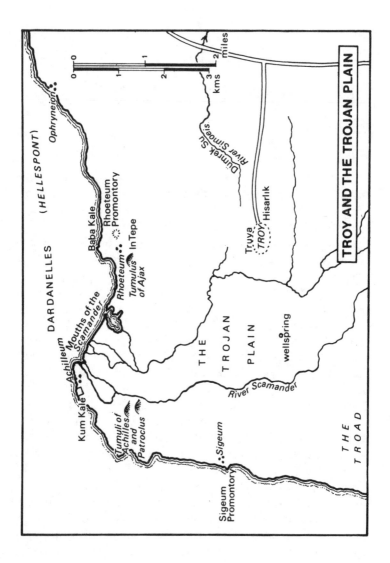

TROY AND THE TROJAN PLAIN

their guns during the Gallipoli campaign, for these are some of the artillery positions that rained explosive shells down upon the Allied fleet on 18 March 1915. The highway continues its ascent until it reaches In Tepe, a village near the tumulus of Ajax, and here, for the first time, one can look southward over the Trojan plain.

Beyond In Tepe the highway crosses the Dümrek Su, which has been identified as the River Simoeis, mentioned frequently in the *Iliad* along with the Scamander. Soon afterwards a signpost directs one along a side road to the right toward Truva, Turkish for Troy, three and a half miles to the west. The archaeological site itself is known locally as Hisarlık.

At the time of our first visit to Troy the entrance to the archaeological site was virtually untouched by tourism, possessing only a little *çayevi*, or tea-house, and a small museum housing a collection of minor objects uncovered in recent excavations. But in the past two decades the area around the entrance to Hisarlık has become commercialized. There is a large wooden model of the Trojan horse in which tourists are photographed with their heads peeping out of portholes as if they were Achaeans, with sword, shield, and crested helmet provided by the management of the Casino 'Helen and Paris', which serves its patrons 'Trojan Wine'. The Trojan Wine is actually Ada Yıldız, the Star of the Islands, a local brand bottled on the island of Bozcaada (Greek Tenedos) where most of the Achaeans hid during the stratagem of the Trojan Horse. Thus that touristic label has a remote historical basis, if only by accident.

But Troy itself, when we saw the site most recently, looked exactly as it had that warm and pellucidly clear mid-April day of our first visit in 1961, the ancient mound brooding above the windy Trojan plain, whose chequerboard of greening farmland was speckled with myriad poppies undulating in the breeze that soughed within the olive-groves and forests of valonia oak in the surrounding hills. Beyond the western limits of Asia the islands of Tenedos and Imbros were floating in the spray-flecked Aegean, there joined by the swirling waters of the Hellespont as they flowed past the last promontory of Europe. Off to the left, the cloud-plumed summit of Mount Ida soared majestically over the highlands south of the Troad, a landscape which Homer would have recognized.

As soon as we entered the excavated area we climbed to the top of the great Hisarlık mound to survey the site. At first this appears as something of an anticlimax, for the site of ancient Troy is now a scarred and cratered hill cut through by the excavations of archaeologists, most destructively by the great trench dug by Schliemann. These excavations have left behind a huge midden littered with the confused debris of three millennia of human existence, ringed with the remnants of several stages of massive defence walls and towers. Among the rubble of a theatre, gateways, temples, shrines, palaces, houses, wells, and graves, all jumbled together after successive destructions wrought by earthquakes, wars, and the erosion of fifty centuries, some definition and order is provided by a few archaeological signs, identifying and dating various structures and archaeological levels.

The first investigation at Hisarlık was made by Frank Calvert who, in the latter half of the nineteenth century, served as both American and British consul in Çanakkale, while he and his two brothers also operated a farm in the Troad. The farm included the mound at Hisarlık, and Frank Calvert made an exploratory dig there in 1865, which indicated to him that it might be the site of an ancient city. At that time the mound at Hisarlık had already been identified as the site of Ilium, the city that flourished here during the Hellenistic and Roman eras, and to which Xerxes, Alexander the Great, Julius Caesar, and others came when they made their pilgrimages to Troy. Thus it would seem that the location of the Bronze Age city of Troy was not lost when it was finally destroyed at a date calculated by both ancient and modern scholars as around 1260 BC. But proof that Hisarlık was in fact the site of ancient Troy was not provided until Heinrich Schliemann carried out his pioneering excavations, which have now led most scholars to believe that the *Iliad* was based on Greek folk memories concerning the siege of a great Bronze Age fortress-city on the Asian shore of the Hellespont, the epic itself written some five centuries later by a poet who was familiar with the topography of the site. Calvert guided Schliemann around the mound at Hisarlık in the summer of 1868, showing him the finds he had made and convincing him that this was the site of ancient Troy. As Schliemann wrote during the following year, the site 'fully agrees with the description Homer gives of Ilium and I will add that, as soon as one sets foot on the Trojan plain, the view of the beautiful hill at Hisarlık grips one with astonishment. The hill seems designed by nature to carry a great city ... there is no other place in the whole region to compare with it'.

When Schliemann made his preliminary excavations at Hisarlık in 1870, he found that the debris of centuries had accumulated on the hill to a depth of fifty feet. Since he assumed that the Troy he was looking for lay beneath this, he set out to clear the debris in one slice, and in three annual campaigns, from 1871 to 1873, employing an average of 150 workmen daily, he cut right through the mound in a great north–south trench some 130 feet wide. While digging the trench he noticed that the excavated earth did not form a homogeneous mass, but was stratified in superimposed layers which he correctly assumed were the successive settlements on the site. He named the lowermost, and presumably the oldest, Troy I. Schliemann thought he could discern seven distinct layers, of which he believed Troy II to be the Homeric city because of the wealth of jewellery he found there and called 'Priam's Treasure'.

Schliemann continued his excavations at Hisarlık, and in 1882 he was joined there by a young German archaeologist named Wilhelm Dörpfeld. Eight years later Schliemann and Dörpfeld made an important discovery in the southern sector of the mound, in the level later to be called Troy VIIa, when they unearthed a great megaron, a palatial structure divided into three rooms, with a central hall whose roof was carried on two pillars.* This megaron was so similar in plan to the royal halls at Mycenae and Tiryns that Schliemann was forced to change his mind about the archaeological dating of the various strata, and decided that the sixth layer from the bottom at Hisarlık, and not the second, was the Homeric city he sought. This view is still generally held among archaeologists. Schliemann continued to dig at Hisarlık until the summer of 1890, working on the excavations until just a few months before his death on 26 December of that year. Dörpfeld then took charge of the project, and in 1893–4 he unearthed the massive fortifications of Troy VI, thus resurrecting the fabled defence walls, towers, and gateways that would seem to have been described by Homer.

Dörpfeld concluded his excavations at Hisarlık in the summer of 1894, convinced that he and Schliemann had discovered the Homeric city there. The site was then abandoned until 1932, when a group from the University of Cincinnati began excavating under the direction of Carl W. Blegen. Blegen's group continued excavating at Troy until 1938, but their work was then interrupted by the Second World War and never again resumed, though their findings were finally published in 1950. Blegen also wrote a shorter work summarizing the researches of his group and their predecessors, entitled *Troy and the Trojans*, published in 1963. I had brought a copy along. I also carried with me copies of the *Iliad* and the *Odyssey*, in the superb translations by Richmond Lattimore, for Homer is still the best guide to Troy.

After surveying the site, we set out to identify the various levels in chronological order, beginning with Troy I. Subsequent excavations have supported Schliemann's belief that Troy I was the original settlement at Troy, and Blegen has dated its occupancy to the period 3000–2500 BC. Schliemann discovered the walls of Troy I when he dug his trench through the mound at the beginning of his excavations, and we were

---

* See the glossary of architectural terms on p. 383.

able to locate them easily, distinguished from later fortifications by the fact that they were made from piles of field stones as contrasted with the carefully worked defences of later periods. We were also able to make out the walls of several houses of Troy I, all of which were of the megaron type.

Troy II, dated 2500–2200 BC, was rebuilt on the same site after the original settlement had been destroyed by fire. By this time the settlement had expanded, so that the walls of Troy II enclosed a somewhat larger area than those of its predecessor. We were able to trace most of the circuit of the defence walls of Troy II, which are much more imposing than the earlier fortifications. As in the earlier settlement, the main gate of Troy II was in the centre of the south wall, but there were other means of entry as well, notably a propylon, or monumental gateway, on the south-west arc of the fortifications. From there a well-paved ramp of limestone slabs leads down to the Trojan plain. Troy II seems to have been one of the earliest sites to have employed town-planning, for the houses of that date unearthed within the fortifications appear to have been laid out in a grid pattern, centering on a large megaron that appears to have been a royal residence. Unfortunately a very large part of this structure was destroyed when Schliemann dug his trench. Most of the golden jewellery and other precious objects discovered by Schliemann at Troy, including 'Priam's Treasure', were found in and around this megaron, which he called the House of the City King. It was the grandeur of this megaron, together with the treasures unearthed in this part of the site, that led Schliemann originally to identify Troy II as the Homeric city. But he and Dörpfeld afterwards determined that Troy II was destroyed by fire c. 2200 BC, about a thousand years before the fall of Mycenae and the other great cities of the Bronze Age, and so it was far too early to have been the city of which Homer wrote.

There is little of note to be seen in the next three levels at Hisarlık, for which Blegen gives the following dates: Troy III (2200–2050 BC), Troy IV (2050–1900 BC), and Troy V (1900–

1800 BC). In fact the only easily identifiable remains are those of a few house walls. Dörpfeld contemptuously referred to these three levels of Hisarlık as 'miserable villages', so insignificant apparently that they were not fortified until the period of Troy V, when the settlement was enclosed within a defence wall much inferior to that of Troy II.

The most clear-cut discontinuity in the remains comes with Troy VI, which Blegen classified into three major periods, themselves further divided into eight substrata. The archaeological findings clearly indicate that Troy VI emerged in the middle of the Bronze Age, evidenced by the large number of bronze swords and other objects of real bronze found in that level, which Blegen dated to the period 1800–1300 BC. These and the pottery and other objects found in Troy VI differ markedly in character from those of the earlier levels, evidence of the arrival at Hisarlık of people with a quite different culture from those who had lived there before. A unique find establishing this difference in cultures was the skeleton of a horse, indicating that the newcomers were warriors who not only used bronze weapons but also fought on horseback or from horse-drawn chariots. That would have given them a great advantage over the indigenous people of the Troad at that time. The most striking evidence of the militant character of the new settlers is the splendid circuit of defence walls with which they ringed Troy VI, for these fortifications show a much more advanced knowledge of military engineering and architecture than the earlier city walls at Hisarlık, erected by a people who were clearly experienced in both defending and besieging walled cities. All of this and other evidence points to the settlers of Troy VI as belonging to the same culture as those who built Mycenae and the other great fortress-cities of the Mycenaean age, the Greek-speaking Hellenic people who made their first appearance in the Aegean world at the beginning of the second millennium BC and who are known to have established numerous colonies in western Anatolia during the period to which Troy VI is dated. Thus it appears that the

Trojans of the period prior to the Homeric siege of Troy were themselves Hellenes, part of the same Mycenaean culture as the Achaeans who besieged them.

According to Blegen, Troy VI was destroyed *c.* 1300 BC in a very sudden catastrophe, perhaps an exceptionally severe earthquake, as evidenced by the toppling of whole sections of the defence walls of that period. The next level at Hisarlık is divided by Blegen into three substrata, of which the first, VIIa, shows no cultural discontinuity whatsoever with Troy VI. The archaeological evidence indicates that the people who inhabited Troy VIIa rebuilt the city and its defence walls immediately after the catastrophe of *c.* 1300 BC, but less than half a century afterwards the city was destroyed once again, a disaster that Blegen dated to *c.* 1260 BC. Blegen found evidence that this second catastrophe was preceded by the erection of crude and hastily built structures just inside the defence walls, as if a shanty town was created to house people from the surrounding area of the Troad at a time of siege. This and other evidence led Blegen to identify Troy VIIa rather than Troy VI as the one described by Homer in the *Iliad*, a conclusion that is still controversial in scholarly circles. In any event, the level which Blegen calls Troy VIIa was destroyed by fire in the mid-thirteenth century BC, quite possibly by an enemy army which had besieged and sacked the town. That fate also befell Mycenae and the other great fortress-cities of the Mycenaean world at about the same time. So we felt free to imagine that the walls and other structures of Troy VIIa were those of the Homeric city and, as we wandered about the ruins, we tried to identify sites mentioned in the *Iliad*.

Beside the south entrance to the city, where the remains of a great propylon form one of the most familiar landmarks at Hisarlık, we paused on an ancient roadway leading from the citadel down on to the Trojan plain. This was the main means of entry to Troy VI and, as it was apparently rebuilt to serve the same purpose in Troy VIIa, the propylon was identified by Schliemann as the Skaian Gates. That entrance figures prominently in a number of scenes in the *Iliad*, for the Trojans passed through the Skaian Gates on their way to and from the battleground on the Trojan plain. Just inside the Skaian Gates are the remains of the Pillar House, named for the fragmentary pillar that still stands there, one of two that once supported a beam along the axis of its great hall. The Pillar House is one of the largest structures found at Hisarlık, and it quite possibly was the royal residence in Troy VI and VIIa. If so, one can identify it with the 'wonderfully built palace of Priam', the site of several dramatic episodes in the *Iliad*; and it would have been here that the very last scene was set, after the death and burial of Hector, when the Trojans 'assembled in a fair gathering and held a glorious feast within the house of Priam, king under God's hand'.

The designation and dates assigned by Blegen to the two later substrata of Troy VII were VIIb1 (1260–1190 BC) and VIIb2 (1190–1100 BC). According to Blegen, many of the inhabitants of Troy VIIa survived the catastrophe that destroyed their city *c.* 1260 BC, and soon afterwards built a new settlement on the ruins of the old one. The archaeological evidence indicates that the new defence walls followed the same course as the older ones, with the south gate located at the same place as the earlier entrance. There is no evidence of any cultural discontinuity between the second phase of Troy VII and the first one, but then, in 1190 BC, Blegen's date for the beginning of the third phase, a different type of pottery makes its appearance at Hisarlık, which he and other scholars have attributed to a new population settling on the mound. These new settlers, it is believed, came from the Balkans and, after crossing the Hellespont, seized control of Troy before some of them moved deeper into Anatolia. This third phase of Troy VII came to a close *c.* 1100 BC, when the settlement at Hisarlık was again destroyed by fire, part of a wave of destruction that brought to an end the civilization of the Bronze Age all over the Aegean and in Anatolia and marked the beginning of the dark ages of the ancient world.

After this catastrophe Hisarlık was abandoned for about four centuries. Then, c. 700 BC, the mound was populated once again, this time by Aeolian Greeks who settled there and also elsewhere in the Troad. The city they founded, which Blegen designated as Troy VIII, came to be known in Graeco-Roman times as Ilion, or in Latin as Ilium. Little is known of the history of Ilion during the Archaic period, but in later times it was venerated throughout the Greek world as being the successor of ancient Troy, known through the epic poems of Homer, and Homer may well have visited Ilion during the early years of the Aeolian settlement.

The last of the Homeric sites which we identified in our exploration of Hisarlık was the Temple of Athena, whose ruins have been found on the north-western sector of the hill. The Temple of Athena, described by Homer as being on the 'peak of the citadel', is the setting for one of the most moving scenes in the *Iliad*, where the priestess Theano leads the Trojan women in prayer, imploring the goddess to help them and promising that if she does so they will 'instantly dedicate within your shrine twelve heifers, yearlings never broken, if only you have pity on the town of Troy, and the Trojan women, and their innocent children'.

Ilion was thoroughly rebuilt during the reign of Augustus (27 BC–AD 14) and the entire top of the mound was levelled off to enlarge the sacred enclosure of Athena's temple, which was surrounded by an enormous colonnade. Another major structure erected in the Roman era was the theatre, whose remains we found just to the east of the Skaian Gates, lying across that arc of the defence walls. Schliemann determined that the theatre, which could seat 6,000, must have been adorned with a splendid colonnade in the combined Doric, Ionian, and Corinthian orders, and we found fragments of these columns as well as some of the sculptural decoration as we explored.

After we had studied the ruins of the temple and the theatre, we felt that we had completed our tour of Troy for the time being, and so we climbed back to the top of the mound, commanding a sweeping view of the entire Trojan plain, and spread out our picnic lunch in the shade of a wind-twisted valonia oak. We sat there for an hour or so, eating our lunch of bread, goat-cheese, and olives, and drinking a bottle of white wine from Tenedos, whose sea-girt silhouette we could see off to the south-west in the spray-plumed Aegean. It was a beautiful April day, the brilliant sunshine tempered by a *melteme*, the breeze that blows in from the north or north-west all along the Aegean coast of Turkey in spring and summer; and so after lunch we decided to walk out to Kum Kale, at the Aegean end of the Dardanelles, to see whether we could identify any of the Homeric sites on the windy plain of Troy, particularly the tumulus of Achilles.

We made our way down the south side of the mound and walked out through the ancient Skaian Gates, taking the same path that the people of Troy must have used when they were going to their lands in times of peace. The Great Tower of Ilion stood just beside the Skaian Gates, and as we passed through the ruined portal I recalled an incident that Homer sets there in Book III of the *Iliad*. In this scene Priam is sitting out on the tower with the old men of Troy, waiting for an impending battle between Menelaus and Paris, when suddenly they see Helen walking towards them. The old men, who had been chattering away like cicadas, lower their voices at her approach, one of them murmuring that the Trojans and Achaeans could not be blamed for fighting over such a woman, for 'terrible is her face to the likeness of immortal goddesses'. Priam calls out to Helen, telling her to sit beside him on the tower, 'to look upon your husband of time past, your friends and your people'. Then he reassures her by saying that 'I am not blaming you: to me the gods are blameworthy/who drove upon me this sorrowful war against the Achaians'.

The first Homeric site we found on the Trojan plain was the place which Schliemann refers to in his *Ilios* as the 'cavern of the three springs'. This spring served as Schliemann's water

34

source during the years he was excavating at Hisarlık, and today it is used by the local farmers to irrigate their fields. Schliemann identified this as the spring which figures so prominently in Book XXII of the *Iliad*. That book begins after the Achaeans had defeated the Trojans and driven them back within the walls of Troy, leaving Hector alone facing Achilles in single combat, standing fast 'in front of Ilion and the Skaian Gates'. But when the combat began Hector fled in terror. Achilles pursued him thrice round the walls of Troy while Priam and his people looked on in dismay from the watchtower. The principal landmark in this deadly chase is the wellspring outside the Skaian Gates, which the Trojan women used as their washing-place in happier times past, 'when there was peace, before the coming of the sons of the Achaians'. Finally, 'when for the fourth time they came around to the well-spring', Hector stopped his flight and turned to face Achilles, who killed him with a spear-thrust through his neck. Then Achilles tied Hector's corpse feet-first to the back of his chariot, dragging him away in the dust 'toward the hollow ships of the Achaians' while Priam and his people 'were taken with wailing and lamentation throughout the city'.

From the historic well-spring we headed off on the dirt track towards Kum Kale. Schliemann believed that this track followed one of the ancient roads across the Trojan plain, probably leading from Troy out to the fortress-town of Achilleum at the Asian end of the Hellespont, on the present site of Kum Kale. This would have been the 'wagon way' along which Achilles drove his chariot when he dragged Hector's corpse back to the Achaean camp. We talked of this and other scenes from the *Iliad* that are set on the Trojan plain, exhilarated that on this glorious day we were walking along one of the oldest roads in the world.

The path took us out to the northern end of the Trojan plain, walking along the right bank of the Scamander. As we walked along, I realized that we were approaching the area in which Schliemann and others place the Achaean camp, at the northern end of the Trojan plain between the Sigeum and Rhoeteum promontories, where the Scamander flows into the Hellespont. The blossoming fruit-trees and profusion of poppies and other flowers on the banks of the Scamander reminded me of the lines in Book II of the *Iliad* where Homer describes the marshalling of Agamemnon's army. 'They take up positions on the blossoming meadow of the Skamandros/thousands of them, as leaves and flowers appear in the season'.

We crossed the Scamander on a primitive bridge consisting of a line of planks slung on cables, with an upper rope to serve as a hand-hold. As I inched my way across the rapid waters of the Scamander, which was in full flood, I experienced several moments of sheer terror. When I finally reached the other side I turned back and looked at the swirling stream, which was here partially blocked by branches and other debris carried down to the mouth of the river by the force of the current. This reminded me of a dramatic scene in Book XXI of the *Iliad*, where Achilles is nearly drowned in this stream, for the river-god Skamandros is furious at him for having fouled his waters with the corpses of the Trojan warriors he has slain. The Skamandros complains to Achilles, the voice of the river-god rising 'from the depths of the eddies':

O Achilleus, your strength is greater, your acts more violent
than all men's; since always the very gods are guarding you.
If the son of Kronos has given all Trojans to your destruction,
drive them at least out of me to the plain, and there wreak
    your havoc.
For the loveliness of my waters is crammed with corpses, I
    cannot
find a channel to cast my waters into the bright sea
since I am congested with the dead men you kill so brutally.
Let me alone, then; lord of the people, I am confounded.

Achilles is saved from the Skamandros by Athena and Poseidon, who appear to him on the bank of the stream and tell him 'it is not your destiny to be killed by the river'. This sets the scene for the final battle between Achilles and Hector, who in his flight is headed off here by the 'deep whirls of the river Skamandros', running across the Trojan plain until he turns to face his relentless pursuer before the Skaian Gates.

After crossing the bridge we walked to Kum Kale. Here one of the Outer Castles stands in the sand dunes at the north-western tip of the Troad, the Hellespont opening into the Aegean just beside it. We had seen Kum Kale from our caique, but now for the first time we were looking on it close up from the landward side. Despite the beauty of the surroundings it was a desolate scene, for now we could see in detail the awesome destruction that had descended upon this area in the Gallipoli campaign, with piles of bomb-blasted debris littered around the shell of the old Ottoman fortress, rusted cannon and mortars scattered within the tangled rolls of corroded barbed wire that formed the perimeter of the ruins.

Kum Kale played an important part during the first days of the campaign. On the day the landings began, 25 April 1915, the Russian battleship *Askold* bombarded the fortress for several hours, after which a regiment of French Senegalese infantry fought their way ashore. The Senegalese captured the fortress and held it against seven counter-attacks by the Turks, and later they went over to the offensive and moved out on to the Trojan plain, establishing a perimeter that extended from the tumulus of Ajax on the Dardanelles to the tumuli of Patroclus and Achilles near the Aegean. This was the same ground that the Achaeans had taken when they began their siege of Troy more than three thousand years before. But then the Allied high command ordered the French to withdraw from their beach-head, for the assault there was intended only as a diversionary action, masking the main invasion of the Gallipoli peninsula across the straits. So the French evacuated their forces, after burying 500 black Senegalese soldiers killed in the assault, and the Turks reoccupied Kum Kale and interred their own dead in the same ground. This reminded me of how, in

Book II of the *Iliad*, the two armies agree on a brief truce to bury their dead, 'whose dark blood has been scattered beside the fair waters of the Skamandros'. Priam led the Trojans in their grim task, after which the Achaeans performed theirs, as they 'piled their own slain upon a pyre, with their hearts in sorrow,/and burned them upon the fire, and went back to their hollow vessels'.

At Kum Kale the only evidence of Achilleum that we could find was a well-preserved Roman sarcophagus, unearthed a short distance from the fortress. It was decorated in low relief with the heads of bulls draped with garlands of flowers. One of the very few references to Achilleum in antiquity is made by Herodotus, who gives a brief account of a war between that town and the Athenian colony of Sigeum in the early sixth century BC. One of those who fought for Achilleum in that battle was the lyric poet Alcaeus of Lesbos, who fled from the fighting to save his life and left his shield behind to be taken as a trophy by the victors. Alcaeus wrote of this incident in a poem addressed to his friend Melanippus at Mytilene, concluding with the lines 'now is the moment, now,/To take what happiness the gods allow'.

After exploring Kum Kale we headed south toward the Sigeum promontory, following a dirt path that must have been laid out on the ancient road connecting the towns of Achilleum and Sigeum. A walk of about three-quarters of a mile brought us finally to the tumulus of Achilles, a huge conical mound on the crest of a ridge just to the north of the Sigeum promontory, with the tumulus of Patroclus a short distance away to the south-east on the left bank of the Scamander. The tumulus of Achilles had been the goal of our long hike across the Trojan plain, and when we reached it we sat down at the base of the mound, uncorking our remaining half-bottle of Ada Yıldız and sharing the remnants of our picnic for a mid-afternoon snack. As we passed the wine bottle back and forth we considered these two Heroic Tumuli, the most familiar landmarks on the Trojan plain.

Many travellers before Schliemann's time believed that these two mounds near the Sigeum promontory were the tombs of Achilles and Patroclus. Schliemann dug exploratory shafts into both tumuli, but though he found pottery and other objects of some antiquity, including an iron sword, he did not discover any evidence of a Mycenaean burial. Nevertheless, he concluded from his reading of Homer that both heroes were buried in the same tomb, the tumulus of Achilles, and that the so-called tumulus of Patroclus must have been the burial-place of some other warrior. Schliemann's belief that Patroclus and Achilles were buried in the same tomb was based on two passages from Homer, one in the *Iliad* and the other in the *Odyssey*. The *Iliad* passage is in Book XXIII, and in it the ghost of Patroclus appears to Achilles in a dream, saying to him 'Therefore, let one single vessel, the golden two-handled/urn the lady your mother gave you, hold both our ashes'. The second passage is in the last book of the *Odyssey*, where the ghosts of Agamemnon and Achilles meet among the shades of the other departed Achaeans in 'the meadow of asphodel ... the dwelling-place of souls, the images of dead men'. There Agamemnon tells Achilles about the circumstances of his death and of how he and the other Achaean warriors had mourned for him 'for ten and seven days, alike in the day and night time', until 'on the eighteenth day we gave you to the fire, and around you slaughtered a great number of fat sheep and horn-curved cattle'. Then Agamemnon describes to Achilles how they gathered his white bones at dawn, 'together with unmixed wine and unguents', and placed them in the golden urn his mother Thetis had given him, mixing them 'with the bones of the dead Patroklus'. And finally he tells Achilles of the tumulus that he and his army erected for them:

Around them, then, we the chosen host of the Argive
spearmen, piled up a grave mound that was both great
and perfect,
on a jutting promontory by the wide Hellespont,

so that it can be seen afar out on the water
by men now alive and those to be born in the future.

We sat at the base of the mound until our wine was all gone
except for the dregs, whereupon I poured out the last few drops
on the tumulus as a libation to the ancient heroes buried there.

Then we arose to depart, for it was three o'clock and we had
a good hour's walk to make our way back to Hisarlık. We
crossed a second time the bridge over the Scamander and
walked southwards. It was just four o'clock when we passed
the Trojan well-spring by the side of the road, walking from
there across the fields to the Skaian Gates on our way back up
on to the great Hisarlık mound. There we turned to look out
once more over the windy plain of Troy, recognizing the tumuli
of Achilles and Patroclus at the Aegean end of the Dardanelles,
landmarks on the westernmost promontory of Asia since
Homeric times.

3

THE TROAD

The Troad, the land of Troy, forms the north-westernmost projection of the Asia Minor subcontinent. According to Strabo, writing at the beginning of the imperial Roman era, the Troad was the whole area governed by the nine dynasties subject to King Priam of Troy, which would have brought the southern boundary of that region down as far as the Gulf of Smyrna. But modern scholars tend to define the Troad as only the coastal region extending south from the Dardanelles to the Gulf of Edremit, the ancient Sinus Adramyttenus. A modern highway now extends right through the Troad, running south from Çanakkale beside the Trojan plain and across the foothills of Mount Ida to the Gulf of Edremit. It is a pleasant drive that always formed the first stage of our overland journeys along the Aegean coast of Turkey.

During our early years in Turkey we always travelled overland by bus or *dolmuş*, the public taxi, together with our children. This gave us little opportunity to stop off at interesting places along the way, but in later years Dolores and I acquired a second-hand car, an Opel, and this enabled us to visit places which before we had seen only in passing, and to travel to remote sites which previously we had not been able to reach. Dolores already had a driver's licence, but I had never learned to drive. So she served as chauffeur during all of our journeys in the Opel, leaving me free to study road maps and plans of archaeological sites, as well as to interrogate locals whenever

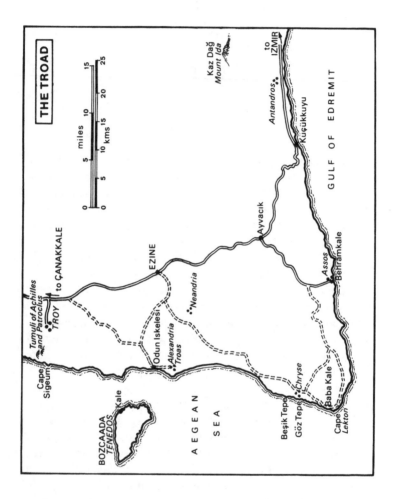

THE TROAD

miles
0 · 5 · 10 · 15
0 · 5 · 10 kms 15 · 20 · 25

Kaz Dağ
Mount Ida

to
IZMIR

Antandros

Küçükkuyu

GULF OF EDREMIT

Ayvacik

Assos
Behramkale

EZINE

Neandria

Cape
Sigeum
Tumuli of Achilles
and Patroclus
TROY

to ÇANAKKALE

Odun Iskelesi
Alexandria
Troas

Beşik Tepe
Göz Tepe
Chryse
Baba Kale
Cape
Lekton

A E G E A N

S E A

BOZCAADA
TENEDOS
Kale

we became hopelessly lost on the back roads of Anatolia.

We made our first such trip during one of my spring holidays from Robert College, driving from Istanbul to Izmir via Çanakkale. It was then that we first explored the Troad in detail, driving south from Çanakkale to Assos, with an excursion out to the Aegean coast to see Alexandria Troas. On that drive we managed to swim in three classical bodies of water on the same day; taking an early morning dip in the Hellespont at Güzel Yalı; bathing in the Scamander while having a noonday picnic among the foothills of Mount Ida; and enjoying a late afternoon swim in the Aegean at Assos.

We thought of that and other journeys along the Aegean coast as we started out from Çanakkale on our most recent drive through the Troad, passing the turn-off to Troy and heading southwards to Mount Ida. We continued south as far as Ezine, a busy market town half-way between the Dardanelles and the Gulf of Edremit. There we turned off from the Çanakkale–Izmir highway on to a side road that leads westward to the Aegean coast, a route that we had taken on our first drive in the Opel. As we drove westward we could see off to our left the distinctive peak of Çıgrı Dağı, the site of ancient Neandria, whose ruins are scattered on a mountain-top eyrie at an altitude of 1,710 feet. Neandria was founded around 600 BC, but it was abandoned two centuries later in favour of Alexandria Troas, whose site on the coast was more suitable for trade and communication with the rest of the Greek world. We had seen architectural fragments of Neandria's Archaic temple in the archaeological museum of Istanbul, but the site itself was too remote for us to visit it on those drives and so this ancient city of the Troad awaits us still.

The road from Ezine brought us to the coast at Odun Iskelesi, a tiny port just opposite the island of Bozcaada, the Greek Tenedos. Tenedos and Imbros were awarded to Turkey in the Treaty of Lausanne of 1923, after the Graeco-Turkish war that followed the First World War, although the population of the two islands remains predominantly Greek. Permission to visit Bozcaada must be obtained in advance from the military authorities in Çanakkale, but at the time of our most recent visit the officer in charge politely declined our request. So we contented ourselves with having lunch at a simple restaurant by the landing-stage in Odun Iskelesi, where boats cross over to Kale, the main town of Bozcaada, whose medieval fortress we had once seen when we passed the island aboard the *Tarih*.

Tenedos is mentioned in the *Iliad* as being sacred to Apollo Smintheus, the Mouse God, a strange form under which Apollo was worshipped on that island and also in the Troad (see p. 54). Tenedos played an important part in Agamemnon's capture of Troy, when the main force of the Achaeans lay in hiding there while their companions in the wooden horse gained entrance to the town and opened the gates for them. This episode is not in the *Iliad*, but it is mentioned in the post-Homeric epic cycles, whose chronicles are known only through late Roman and Byzantine summaries. One of these epic cycles was known to Virgil, for he gives the story of the Trojan Horse in detail in Book II of the *Aeneid*. As Aeneas begins the tale:

> Offshore there's a long island Tenedos,
> Famous and rich while Priam's kingdom lasted,
> A treacherous anchorage now, and nothing more.
> They crossed to this and hid their ships behind it
> On the bare shore beyond. We thought they'd gone ...

At the beginning of the great Greek migration to the western shores of Anatolia, a group of Aeolians established a colony on Tenedos, probably on the present site of Kale. Later the Aeolians from Tenedos founded other settlements on the Aegean coast of the Troad, gaining control of the territory known as the Tenedaean Peraea. The Aeolian islanders retained control of this coastal strip until the close of the fourth century BC, when it was given over to the new town of Alexandria Troas.

During the early Byzantine period the capital of Tenedos

was an important port, for ships sailing to Constantinople often had to stop there while waiting for favourable winds to take them through the Hellespont. Justinian built a large warehouse there to store grain from Egypt for trans-shipment to Constantinople. Later in the Byzantine era Tenedos became a pawn in the struggle between the Greeks and their enemies, as well as in internal dynastic struggles, and for considerable periods of time the island was held in turn by the Venetians and the Genoese. Then in the mid-fourteenth century it fell to the Turks, after which it became a permanent part of the Ottoman Empire. Thereafter it was known to the Turks as Bozcaada, or the Grey Island, for that is the colour which its lonely silhouette usually takes on when viewed from the mainland, even on a sunny day.

The road from Ezine to Odun Iskelesi also leads to Alexandria Troas, the most important archaeological site on the Aegean coast of Asia Minor between Troy and Assos. As we approached Alexandria Troas I looked ahead for signs of the site, which is known locally as Eski Stamboul, or Old Istanbul, and soon we were in no doubt that we had reached its outskirts, for on both sides of the road as far as we could see ahead there were extensive ruins. We stopped so that we could look around before going farther, and found that the road was flanked by a long line of huge granite sarcophagi, all of them violently displaced and broken open by tomb-robbers. We realized we were in the necropolis of Alexandria Troas, which would have been outside the walls of the city. We then climbed up on a pile of sarcophagi, which were tumbled about like giant play-blocks. From that vantage point we could see the remarkably well-preserved defence walls of the ancient city itself, whose circumference Schliemann estimated to be 'six English miles'. Their huge towers protruded above the trees, the walls extending around the ruined metropolis in a great arc and enclosing an area thought by the scholar Walter Leaf to be at least one thousand acres. All of it looked as if it had been suddenly and totally destroyed by a stupendous earthquake. The largest edifice still standing in Alexandria Troas is the enormous Roman gymnasium and baths known locally as Bal Saray, the Honey Palace. This complex of buildings and the aqueduct that conducted water to it were erected in the year AD 135 by Herodes Atticus who, a quarter of a century afterwards, built the magnificent odeion under the Athenian acropolis that still bears his name. Herodes Atticus administered the Roman Province of Asia during the reign of Hadrian, when splendid monuments like these were built all along the coast of Asia Minor.

According to Strabo, the original settlement on this site was an ancient Greek colony named Sigia. A new and far larger city was founded on the same site *c.* 310 BC by Antigonus I Monopthalmus, the One-Eyed, who succeeded Alexander the Great as king of Macedonia. The new city was called Antigonia in its founder's honour, a name that it kept only for a decade or so. In 301 BC Antigonus was defeated and killed at the Battle of Ipsus by Lysimachus, who succeeded him as king of Macedonia. Soon afterwards Lysimachus changed the name of Antigonia to Alexandria, one of fifteen cities named for Alexander by the generals who succeeded to his empire. But travellers, even in ancient times, were led by the proximity of Troy to call the city Alexandria Troas.

During the Hellenistic era it became the wealthiest and most populous city in the Troad, for its strategic position near the entrance to the Hellespont made it a convenient place for the trans-shipment of goods passing between the Aegean and points farther east. During the reign of Augustus a Roman colony was established there, a community that reached the height of its influence during the reign of Hadrian, as evidenced by the huge gymnasium and baths erected by Herodes Atticus.

By the middle of the first century AD a small group of Christians had begun to gather here, one of at least a score of such communities that formed in Asia Minor at that time. The principal evidence for the existence of these early Christian communities is in the Epistles of St. Paul and the Acts of the

Apostles, from which it is known that Paul visited Alexandria Troas at least twice on his missionary journeys, probably in the years AD 48 and 53.

Alexandria Troas was still an important town at the beginning of the Byzantine era. Coins have been found there dating from the reign of Constantine the Great, who ruled as sole emperor from AD 324 to 337. During the first year of Constantine's reign he briefly considered establishing his capital here, but the following year changed his mind in favour of the town of Byzantium on the Bosphorus, which thereafter was known as Constantinople.

Later in the Byzantine period Alexandria Troas is recorded as having the status of a bishopric, but otherwise it disappears from the pages of history throughout most of that era, along with the other ancient cities in the Troad. During the first half of the fourteenth century the Troad as a whole fell under the control of the Karası *beylik*, one of the Turkish emirates which occupied most of Anatolia at that time. Then, in 1336, the Karası *beylik* was conquered by Orhan Gazi, the first sultan of the Osmanlı Turks, and the Troad became part of their realm, soon to be known as the Ottoman Empire.

Early European travellers to the Ottoman Empire report that Alexandria Troas was totally abandoned and in ruins. When Richard Chandler visited the site in 1764 he found it completely deserted, and while looking at the ruins of a temple he was told that 'this had been lately a lurking-place of banditti; who often lay concealed here ...' The first traveller to report the site inhabited was Lechevalier, who in 1785 found a few people living there in a tiny hamlet called Talian, a corruption of Dalyan, or Fish Weir. He and other travellers recorded that the ruins at Alexandria Troas were being used as a quarry by the Ottoman government, with ancient columns being shipped away for colonnades in the imperial mosques then being built in Istanbul; sarcophagi dragged off by the local villagers to be employed as basins in street fountains; and huge granite blocks ground down by the Turkish army to make stone cannonballs. Piles of these primitive missiles still lie around the ruins and in the village of Dalyan, which we finally came to at the seaward end of the road.

Dalyan proved to be a small hamlet of wooden shacks clustering around a crescent-shaped cove with a sandy beach, all that remains of the silted-up harbour of Alexandria Troas. The cove itself presented an extraordinary sight, for on its beach lay a number of huge monoliths, all of them broken in the middle. These were obviously intended for shipment to Istanbul, probably during the second half of the sixteenth century when a number of imperial mosques were under construction there, but they had cracked while being loaded aboard ships. The villagers were now using the columns as mooring-places for their caiques, and they had constructed a primitive landing-stage out of some huge fragments of ancient walls. The scene reminded me of prints illustrating the accounts of early travellers to Asia Minor.

While at Dalyan we were shown a life-sized marble statue of a Nike, or Winged Victory, which had been discovered that morning by a local farmer while clearing his field. The farmer had smashed the statue with his axe while looking for the treasure he believed to be hidden within it, a common belief among the villagers who inhabit the ancient ruins in Asia Minor. And so the statue was lying shattered on the sandy shore of the cove, the shallow water lapping over the winged maiden's flowing robes, her blank eyes staring up into the blue Aegean sky after her long centuries of burial, a forlorn figure from the classical past now desecrated in the ramshackle modern village that had sprung up in the ruins of the ancient city.

We went back to the Çanakkale–Izmir highway and turned to the right, heading towards the Gulf of Edremit. We continued driving southward, Mount Ida looming ever larger to our left, until we reached the outskirts of Ayvacık, the largest village in the southern part of the Troad. Then from Ayvacık we took the secondary road that leads south towards the coast and

Behramkale, a seaside village on the site of ancient Assos.

As we approached Behramkale across the coastal plain we could see the acropolis of Assos rising like a truncated spire from a ridge directly above the sea. The old wooden houses of the village cling to its northern slope amidst the ruins of the ancient city, whose massive defence walls flank the site to east and west. Behramkale is separated from the plain to its north by the Tuzla Çay, believed to be the River Satnioeis of Homer's *Iliad*. We crossed the stream on a graceful hump-backed bridge with pointed arches—a span built by the Ottoman Turks when they first conquered this area early in the fourteenth century— and drove on into the upper village of Behramkale, whose unpainted wooden houses we could see arrayed in tiers up the extremely steep flank of the acropolis, with the monumental ruins of the ancient city now all around us.

The ruins of Assos were studied in 1881–3 by an American expedition sponsored by the Antiquarian Society of Boston, with J. T. Clarke directing the excavations. Most of the works of art found by Clarke's group have been on exhibit for more than a century at the Boston Museum of Fine Arts, and other antiquities are exhibited in Paris and Istanbul. As a result, Assos is well known in the West, although the site itself is visited by relatively few foreigners.

The American excavators unearthed objects on the acropolis indicating that the site was first occupied in the early Bronze Age. But Assos was probably not founded until the seventh century BC. According to Strabo, it was first settled by colonists from Methymna, principal city of Lesbos, the beautiful Greek island that lies off the western end of the Gulf of Edremit. Assos's most illustrious period was the first half of the fourth century BC, when a banker named Eubulus set himself up as ruler, not just of the city itself but of a principality which stretched from Assos to Atarneus south of the present town of Ayvalik. Eubulus was succeeded by Hermeias, a benevolent despot who came to be known as the Tyrant of Atarneus and who had studied in Athens under both Plato and Aristotle.

When he came to power in the southern Troad he decided to
establish a Platonic state there. He invited a number of scholars
from Athens to join him in Assos, most notably Aristotle,
who headed a school of philosophy in the years 347–344 BC.
Aristotle also married the Tyrant's niece and ward, Pythias,
who bore him a daughter while they lived in Assos. Aristotle
was forced to leave when Hermeias was overthrown and cru-
cified by the Persians in 344 BC. He moved to Lesbos for a year,
and worked with his student Theophrastus. During that year
Aristotle and Theophrastus began their pioneering researches
in zoology, botany, and biology, and laid the foundations for
those branches of the life sciences.

The only other person of note associated with ancient Assos
is Cleanthes, who went from there to become head of the Stoic
school of philosophy in Athens after the death of its founder,
Zeno, in 264 BC. Cleanthes was one of the first philosophers to
hold that the sun was the central body in the cosmos, an
ancient Greek concept revived in 1543 by Copernicus in his
heliocentric theory of astronomy.

The most impressive remains of Assos are its defence walls,
most of which date from the mid-fourth century BC, probably
from the time of Hermeias. Originally they were almost three
miles in circumference, and more than half the circuit is still
standing, principally on the western side. We could see these
fortifications in all their massive strength as we ascended the
acropolis, which on the seaward side is virtually a precipice.
The arduous climb is well worth the effort for the peak of the
acropolis commands a panoramic view out across the Aegean
and the Gulf of Edremit, with Lesbos rising out of the sea just
to the south.

On the peak one can see the inner line of fortifications that
were erected to defend the acropolis itself. At the centre of this
citadel are the ruins of the Temple of Athena, of which there
remains only its stylobate, or platform, and some scattered
architectural fragments, including columns and Doric capitals.
The temple is thought to have been built in the first half of the

sixth century BC, and it is the only surviving example of Doric architecture in Asia Minor. The sculptural decoration of the temple was very unusual because, in addition to the reliefs on its metopes, its architrave had sculptures as well, treated as if it were an Ionic frieze. Surviving examples are in the Boston Museum of Fine Arts, the archaeological museum in Istanbul, and the Louvre.

On the northern side of the acropolis are the impressive remains of an early Ottoman mosque, with a dome nearly thirty-four feet in diameter. This must have been built about half a century after the Turks captured Assos in 1306, for the mosque has an inscription bearing the name of Sultan Murat I who ruled from 1356 to 1389. Over the door there is a cross in relief and an inscription in Greek, indicating that the mosque was constructed from the stones of a Byzantine church. Many of these blocks look as if they were taken from the nearby ruins of the Temple of Athena.

The other remains of ancient Assos lie below the acropolis to the south, on the seaward side. There one sees the public buildings of the Hellenistic city, all of them dating from the third or second century BC; these include a large agora in the form of a porticoed market square as well as a small temple, a theatre, and a bouleterion, or senate house. This lower part of the ancient city was approached by the West Gate, which is still almost perfectly preserved in a very impressive stretch of the wall.

Outside the West Gate an ancient road passes through the necropolis where a large number of huge sarcophagi are to be seen, some of them with their massive lids still in place. Assos was renowned for its sarcophagi, which were exported to other cities in the Greek world. They were made from a local stone, much sought after for that purpose because it hastened the decomposition of the flesh of the deceased within the sarcophagus and so brought about that cleansing of the bones which in earlier times was done on a funeral pyre. According to Pliny, the word sarcophagus, which in Greek literally means 'body-eater', comes from this local Assos stone, which also, he adds, is an excellent cure for the gout.

The harbour of ancient Assos can still be seen directly below the acropolis to the south, where a small mole creates a tiny haven in which the local fishermen keep their caiques. We took a stroll out on to the mole after seeing the ruins of the ancient city, which now towered above us. It was from this harbour that Paul and his companions set sail in the year AD 53, after leaving Alexandria Troas. According to the Acts of the Apostles they travelled from Assos to Mytilene, probably stopping there at the village of Molivos, the ancient Methymna. It was an exceptionally clear day and, as we stood on the mole, we could see the uppermost houses of Molivos reflecting the late afternoon sun as if they were ablaze. A few years before, on a summer journey through the Greek islands, we had spent two weeks in Molivos, and while there had looked back across the Gulf of Edremit to see the ruins of Assos shining on their acropolis above the Asian shore, the site to which the men of Methymna had sailed to found a colony four thousand years before. But while in Molivos we spotted not a single ship crossing the straits between Lesbos and the mainland of Asia Minor, although we saw a number of caiques sailing along the shore on both sides of this very carefully monitored stretch of the international boundary between Greece and Turkey. Thus two shores, which for many centuries shared a common history and culture, are now, sadly, on separate continents, as though Europe and Asia were on different planets.

After exploring the ruins of Assos we checked in at a small hotel in the lower town, and that evening we had supper at a little restaurant by the harbour, looking at the lights of Lesbos twinkling across the straits. There we planned our journey for the following day. We intended to explore the south-westernmost corner of the Troad, including the shore opposite Lesbos and part of the Aegean coast north of the Gulf of Edremit.

Early the next morning, therefore, we drove westward from

Behramkale along the coast to Baba Kale, a tiny hamlet at the south-west tip of the Troad. The road was very primitive and gave us one of the roughest rides we have ever endured in Anatolia, but the scenery was wild and beautiful, with boulder-strewn hills plunging down to the sea in impenetrable thickets of pine, juniper, and dwarf oak, the shimmering hills of northern Lesbos only a few miles away across the straits. Finally the road brought us to Baba Kale, which proved to be a forlorn village of unpainted wooden houses on a barren headland, Cape Baba, surrounded by the crumbling walls of an old Ottoman fortress. The village and the cape take their name from a Muslim saint, in Turkish Baba, or Father, whose tomb stood for centuries on the headland. Mariners sailing close by the cape in former times would throw ashore offerings of food to the saint, and so supply the succession of hermits who cared for the Baba's tomb. In Ottoman times the cape was also called Emek Yemez Burnu, the Promontory of Do No Work, perhaps referring to the idleness of these hermits. The headland was known to Genoese and Venetian navigators as Santa Maria, but the Greeks always referred to it by its ancient name, Cape Lekton. According to Strabo, Agamemnon erected an altar to the Twelve Gods on Cape Lekton, but no trace of this has ever been found. We did discover a picturesque old Ottoman fountain, however, on the shore beside the ruined Turkish fortress, with an inscription recording that it was dedicated in 1740. This recalled to us the scene in the *Iliad* where Cape Lekton is mentioned in passing. Hera stopped there momentarily with Hypnos, the god of sleep, while on her way to observe the siege of Troy from the summit of Mount Ida. They paused briefly on 'Lekton, where they first left the water and went on/over dry land, and with their feet the top of the forest was shaken'.

Beyond Baba Kale we headed north along the Aegean coast, still on the same rock-strewn dirt road we had endured all the way from Behramkale. The road was not even shown on my map of the Troad, so I had no idea where it would take us though it appeared to be headed for the Tenedaean Peraea. About three miles north of Baba Kale we came within sight of a bay that I could identify as Ak Liman, which meant that the promontory at its far end was Göz Tepe, the site of ancient Chryse. We drove as close to the promontory as we could, until the road gave out altogether, and then walked the rest of the way carrying string bags with our picnic lunch and two bottles of Ada Yıldız wine. We made our way across the rocky ground through a wilderness of wind-blown trees and dense under-growth and finally emerged on the spine of the promontory, where we settled down on a grassy knoll under a grove of valonia oaks to enjoy our picnic.

My detailed map of the Troad showed the prominent features along the adjacent coast, with Ak Liman to the south of our knoll on Göz Tepe and to the north a stretch of craggy shore curving to a rocky headland called Beşik Tepe. This area of the Troad is way off the beaten track and far from the Trojan plain; nevertheless it has attracted a number of scholars interested in Homeric topography. J. M. Cook and others have identified Göz Tepe as the site of ancient Chryse, which is mentioned five times in Book I of the *Iliad* as a shrine of Apollo Smintheus, the Mouse God. This is a strange attribute of Apollo, who was worshipped in that form on the isle of Tenedos and at several places along the Tenedaean Peraea, and whose principal sanc-tuary in Homeric times was here at Chryse. According to Strabo, the cult of Apollo Smintheus originated among the Teucrians, a Cretan people considered by Herodotus to be the ancestors of the Trojans. When the Teucrians emigrated from Crete, they were advised by an oracle to settle in the place where they would be assailed by the 'earth-born'. As Strabo writes, the Teucrians first landed on the Aegean coast of the Troad at the future site of Chryse, where the field-mice ate up all their provisions and gnawed away at the leather straps of their weapons and utensils. The Teucrians interpreted this as a sign from Apollo, who was worshipped by the native people there, and so they settled in the Troad and erected a temple dedicated to the Mouse God at the place where they first landed. This was called the Smintheum and Strabo mentions that the temple had a wooden cult statue of Apollo, a work of the great Scopas, in which the god was represented with a mouse under his foot. The Smintheum was not in Chryse itself but at the nearby site of Hamaxitus, which Cook and other scholars have located on Beşik Tepe.

Chryse is the scene of one of the most lyrical episodes in the *Iliad*, where Homer describes the return of the maiden Chryseis to her father Chryses, priest of Apollo Smintheus at this place. Chryseis, who had been the captive mistress of Agamemnon, is carried to Chryse in a ship commanded by Odysseus. He has brought along a hecatomb of bulls and goats to be sacrificed at the Smintheum so that the Achaeans can seek atonement for having captured the daughter of Apollo's priest. I read from Richmond Lattimore's translation of this scene, the landing of the Achaean ship at Chryse, where 'Chryseis herself stepped from the sea-going vessel', after which 'Odysseus of the many designs led her to the altar', leaving the girl in her father's arms. Then I read the elegiac passage where Homer describes the hecatomb and the joyous feast that followed, verses that were particularly evocative since they recalled a scene set within view of where we were sitting on the promontory.

All day long they propitiated the god with singing,
chanting a splendid hymn to Apollo, these young Achaians,
singing to the one who works from afar, who listened in
    gladness.
Afterwards when the sun went down and the darkness
    came onward
they lay down and slept beside the ship's stern cables.
But when the young dawn showed again with her rosy
    fingers,
they put forward to sea toward the wide camp of the
    Achaians.

When I finished reading this passage we sat for a while in

this ancient place, sipping the last of our wine and basking in the late afternoon sun of a splendid April day. The Aegean sparkled below us, clusters of Judas-trees glowed pink and purple on the hillside, and the resonant tinkling of goat-bells occasionally reached us from distant pastures.

Finally we realized that we had a long trip back to Behramkale ahead of us, and that on these rough roads it was imperative that we reach the village before dark. As we started, we agreed we must return to Göz Tepe one day; and we resolved that, next time, we would find the ruins of the Smintheum. But we have not yet returned to Göz Tepe, and the site of Apollo's temple at Chryse awaits us still on this lovely but almost forgotten coast, where paeans were once sung in worship of the Mouse God.

4

THE GULF OF EDREMIT

The Troad is bounded to its south by the deep indentation of the Aegean known in antiquity as the Adramyttene Gulf. This took its name from Adramyttium, today's Edremit, at its eastern end. The bay extends all the way from the promontory at Baba Kale to the peninsula beyond Ayvalik, at the northern end of the Aeolian coast, and the two arms of the gulf almost embrace the island of Lesbos. The most panoramic view that we ever commanded over this beautiful gulf was from the acropolis at Assos when, standing on the stylobate of the Temple of Athena, we could see the whole of the gulf stretched out below us with no evidence of modern civilization in sight. The distant bow-waves of caiques far out on the Aegean could have been the trails of ancient triremes headed for the Hellespont.

After our climb to the acropolis we set out from Behramkale on our drive around the Gulf of Edremit, heading back toward Ayvacık and the main Çanakkale–Izmir highway. As we approached Ayvacık, however, we decided to turn off the bypass and pause there for a mid-morning break at a *çayevi*. Rounding the first bend on the Ayvacık road we suddenly came upon the rear of a camel caravan, which we joined when another procession of camels emerged from a side road and began following along behind us. This was our first close encounter with the Yürüks, nomadic tribal people of Anatolia, and we proceeded along with them at a camel's pace into the town. On the camel in front of us a woman was riding with

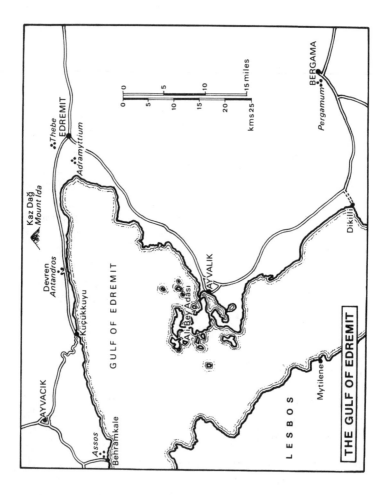

THE GULF OF EDREMIT

her baby strapped to her back and a pair of toddlers stuffed into deep wicker baskets slung from either side of the animal's hump. All her pots and pans and other belongings were festooned about her in string bags and sacks. Other children ran along beside the camels, while the men rode by on horseback, splendid bronzed figures wearing headscarves in the style of the American Indians. When we reached a bend in the road I could see Yürük herdsmen driving a huge herd of goats ahead of the caravan, which was led by a turbaned old man on a donkey. Shortly afterwards we entered Ayvacık and disengaged ourselves from the caravan to park in the town square beside an outdoor *çayevi*. There we learned that the Yürüks were gathering at a campsite outside the town, preparing for their week-long spring festival, the *panayir*, and we watched as another of their camel caravans passed through the square heading in that direction. After we had had some tea we drove out to look at the campsite, where several thousand Yürüks had set up a temporary village of black goat-hair tents, and from the deep pounding of a drum and the shrill piping of a *zurna*, or flute, we knew that the *panayir* had begun.

We parked our car by the side of the road and joined the crowd. The Yürüks immediately welcomed us to the festival, offering us food and drink, and before long we were seated in the centre of the throng, watching their beautiful folk-dances and listening to their haunting music with its echoes of the caravan life of central Asia. We stayed there the whole day. As I later drifted off to sleep in a barrack of a room at our caravanserai-like hotel, the last sounds I heard were the pounding of drums and the piping of *zurnas* outside the town. The nomads continued their celebration on into the night.

We were up and away by eight o'clock the following morning, and as we drove back to the highway we passed another camel caravan of Yürüks on their way to the *panayir*. I later learned that these *panayir* are survivals of the Greek *panegyria*, or religious holidays, which the Turkoman nomad tribes would have seen when they first made their way into

Anatolia after the Selcuk victory over the Byzantines at the Battle of Manzikert in 1071. During the next two centuries these ungovernable nomads overran much of Asia Minor and, after the downfall of the Selcuks, all of Anatolia broke up into a mosaic of about a dozen warring Turkoman *beyliks*, or emirates, which eventually were absorbed by the Ottoman Turks. When the Ottomans rose to power in Anatolia, beginning in the fourteenth century, the nomadic tribes were driven out of the settled areas and moved to the more remote regions in the south and east of the country. There they remain to this day, known to the sedentary Turks as Yürüks, or Wanderers. Today, though they no longer carry on perpetual warfare, the Yürüks live essentially the same lives as their Turkoman ancestors, spending the winters along the coastal plains of the Aegean and the Mediterranean, then migrating with their flocks up to their *yaylas*, or summer encampments, which are usually highland meadows in the Taurus or other mountains along the southern tier of Turkey. And on their way to these *yaylas* the Yürüks always pause to celebrate their spring *panayir*, congregating at Ayvacık and other old Anatolian market towns along the western shores of Turkey. The Yürüks we had seen at Ayvacık would later that week be heading up into the greening upland pastures of the Kocakatran Mountains, the range that rises above the south-eastern corner of the Troad. As the Çanakkale–Izmir highway headed eastward we could see the slate-grey peaks of this range gleaming in the morning sunshine; the highest is Kaz Dağ, or Goose Mountain, known to the Greeks as Mount Ida.

After passing the western foothills of this mountain, the highway began its descent towards the coastal plain, as the forests of pine and valonia oak gave way to vast groves of olive-trees, their silvery green leaves fluttering in the faint breeze that began to rise as we approached the sea along a sensuously beautiful gorge. Then a breathtaking scene suddenly opened up before us, with the whole of the Gulf of Edremit and its surrounding shores in view, the seaward side of the vast bay almost closed off by the blue-green mountains of Lesbos which rise precipitously out of the turquoise Aegean. We reached the gulf at the tiny hamlet of Küçükkuyu, the road then taking us eastward along the shore, passing a series of deserted sand and pebble beaches curving between pine-clad promontories. Off to our left the soaring peak of Mount Ida seemed even loftier as we passed its southern shoulder on the coastal plain, with white villages perched high on its tawny flanks above the olive-groves, looking like the mountain hamlets we had seen on voyages through the Cycladic isles of the Aegean.

The first place on our itinerary was Devren, a hamlet near the eastern corner of the Gulf of Edremit. An acropolis-like hill on the seashore near Devren has been identified as the site of ancient Antandros, and when we found the place we stopped to have a midday picnic by the sea. Virtually nothing now remains of Antandros; nevertheless the site has interesting associations in history, myth, and literature, and we talked of these while we drank a bottle of Ada Yıldız, one of a case we had bought two days before in Çanakkale.

The poet Alcaeus writes that Antandros was founded by the Lelegians, whereas Herodotus speaks of it as being Pelasgian in origin (these were two of the prehistoric peoples whom the Greeks believed to be the indigenous inhabitants of Hellas and western Asia Minor). If either is right, this indicates that Antandros was inhabited before the arrival of the Aeolian Greeks on the western shores of Anatolia early in the first millennium BC. Stephanos Byzantius, the Byzantine chronicler, states that Antandros was inhabited by the Cimmerians for more than a century, during which time the town was known as Kimmeris. Kimmeris, from the same root as the Russian 'Crimea', is one of the few place-names left behind in Asia Minor by the Cimmerians, the barbarian people from north of the Black Sea who in the mid-seventh century BC overran much of Anatolia. By the fifth century BC the town was inhabited by Aeolian Greeks from Lesbos, for the name Antandros appears in tribute lists of the period as a colony of the city of Mytilene on Lesbos. Herodotus writes that Xerxes passed through Adramyttium and Antandros on his way from Sardis to the Hellespont in 480 BC. Antandros is also mentioned by Thucydides, Xenophon, and Strabo, who reports that the Idaean peak directly above the town was called Alexandreia, named for Alexander, son of King Priam and Hecuba, better known as Paris. According to mythology, Paris spent his youth tending sheep on the slopes of Mount Ida above Antandros, and it was there that he judged the contest of beauty between Hera, Athena, and Aphrodite.

Antandros is renowned in literature as the place from which Aeneas embarked on his voyage of exile after the fall of Troy, eventually settling in Italy and founding the kingdom that would later become Rome. As Aeneas tells the tale in the *Aeneid*:

> Lordly Ilium had fallen and all Neptune's Troy lay a smoking ruin on the ground. We the exiled survivors were forced by divine command to search the world for a home in some uninhabited land. So we started to build ships below Antandros, the city by the foothills of Phrygian Ida, with no idea where destiny would take us or where we would be allowed to settle ... In tears I left my homeland's coast, its havens and the place where Troy had stood. I fared out upon the high seas, an exile with my comrades and my son, with the little Gods of our home and the Great Gods of our race.

From our cove below the acropolis of Antandros we had a clear view of Mount Ida, or Kaz Dağ, the highest peak of the range, its cloud-piercing summit rising to 5,743 feet above sea-level. The Greeks called this peak Gargaros, and Homer used it as the setting for several scenes in the *Iliad*, with both Zeus and Hera occasionally looking down from its summit to observe the battle raging on the Trojan plain. One such episode occurs in Book XIV of the *Iliad*, where Hera seduces Zeus into making love to her on the summit of Mount Ida, thus distracting him while her ally Poseidon assists the Trojans.

Mount Ida was also the setting for the love-affair between

Aphrodite and Anchises, a descendant of Dardanus who was also a second cousin of Priam. The love-child of this romance, as Homer writes in Book II of the *Iliad*, was Aeneas, 'whom Aphrodite bore to Anchises in the folds of Ida, a goddess lying in love with a mortal'. Aphrodite later bore another child on Mount Ida; this was Hermaphroditus, the bisexual offspring of her union with Hermes, who spent his childhood in a cave in the mountains cared for by the Idaean Driads.

The tales concerning Hera and Aphrodite are undoubtedly survivals of ancient myths of the Great Earth Mother, the fertility goddess who was worshipped throughout Anatolia during the Bronze Age. This primeval Anatolian deity was known by many names at various times, including Cybele, Kubaba, and Artemis, who in the Greek world took over her role as Mistress of Animals, with Hera and Aphrodite also inheriting her powers as a fertility goddess. The cult of this goddess in north-western Anatolia centered on Mount Ida, which in both the *Iliad* and in one of the Homeric Hymns to Aphrodite is called the 'Mother of Beasts'. Worship of the Earth Mother was transformed in Christian times into veneration of the Blessed Virgin, whose *panegyria* were celebrated by the Greeks of the Troad in chapels on Mount Ida up until the population exchange of 1923. It survives today in the *panayir* of the Yürüks at Ayvacık.

After lunch we left our cove below the acropolis of Antandros and continued our drive along the shore of the Gulf of Edremit. We reached the eastern end of the gulf at Akçay, a resort village on a fine sand beach. From there we continued eastward as the road headed inland through the coastal plain, and in less than a quarter of an hour we were in Edremit. We stopped for tea at an outdoor *çayevi* on the town square, which has an extraordinary rose-garden, the prettiest public park in all of Turkey. The garden was so entrancing that we lingered for at least an hour, resting our eyes on the beauties of the rose-trees and bushes that grow there in such profusion, talking as usual about the history of the place through which we were passing.

Not a trace remains of ancient Adramyttium other than the name of Edremit. The present town probably lies further inland than its predecessor, which stood at the eastern end of the Adramyttene Gulf. Even in early Ottoman times Edremit was on the shore of the gulf, or at least had a port there. At the beginning of the fourteenth century, for example, when this region was part of the Karası *beylik*, Yahsi Bey of Saruhan built a fleet of several hundred barques in Edremit, using wood cut on Mount Ida.

One of the earliest references to Adramyttium is in Xenophon's *Anabasis*, or *The March Up Country*, which chronicles the adventures of the Greek mercenaries known as the Ten Thousand on their homeward journey from Persia. This reference occurs in the last chapter of the *Anabasis*, where Xenophon describes the route taken by the remnants of the Ten Thousand after they crossed the Hellespont in 399 BC. It was the final stage in their long march across Asia. As Xenophon writes: 'Then they marched through the Troad, and after crossing Mount Ida, came first to Antandros, and then went along the coast to the plain of Thebe. They travelled from there by way of Adramyttium and Certanon to the plain of Caicus, and so reached Pergamum and Mysia'.

This route described by Xenophon was exactly the same as the one we had planned to follow from Çanakkale to Edremit, though we then would go on to Pergamum by way of Ayvalik, rather than by the inland route taken by the Ten Thousand. I was particularly fascinated by Xenophon's reference to the plain of Thebe, for that was perhaps the alluvial area through which we had driven after passing the eastern end of the gulf, just before reaching Edremit. The site of ancient Thebe has never been identified, but it is believed to have been a short distance to the north-east of the present town of Edremit. This was the place that Achilles and his Myrmidons sacked just before the beginning of the action described in the *Iliad*, and it was here that he captured Chryseis and Briseis, the two slave-girls whose possession provoked the fateful quarrel between him and Agamemnon. Briseis appears again in Book XIX of the *Iliad*, in a moving scene in which she mourns over the body of Patroclus after he has been killed in battle by Hector, recalling his kindness to her when she was captured and enslaved by Achilles. 'Therefore I weep your death without ceasing. You were kind always'.

Thebe was also the birthplace of Andromache, Hector's wife. Andromache's father, King Eëtion of Thebe, had been slain by Achilles along with her seven brothers when he and his Myrmidons sacked the town, an incident she relates to Hector in Book VI of the *Iliad*. The town is mentioned by Sappho in one of her poems, 'Andromache's Wedding', which evokes memories of a happier time in Thebe when Hector and his men came to take home his bride, 'her eyes gleaming/From Thebe the Holy ...'

After leaving Edremit we continued driving around the gulf. The highway took us along the southern shore and we had a splendid view of Mount Ida across the gulf to the north, with the mountains of Lesbos looming straight ahead of us at the western, seaward end of the bay. To our left all that we could see was an endless grove of olive-trees, extending from the coastal plain up into the foothills of the mountains beyond. This is one of the loveliest areas in all of north-western Asia Minor, and it is still spoken of with nostalgia by the old Greeks who lived here before 1923. Up until that time the Aegean coast of Asia Minor had been predominantly Greek, but afterwards it was populated largely with Turkish refugees from Thrace, the Aegean islands, and Crete. One of the ironies of this population exchange was that many of the Greeks expelled from Anatolia spoke only Turkish, while the Turkish refugees who replaced them were mostly fluent in Greek, creating a linguistic cross-current as the tides of history once again washed up on these shores and left yet another generation of exiles on each side of the international boundary.

We had lingered so long in Antandros and Edremit that it was nearly sunset by the time we reached Ayvalik, the pretty seaside town known to the Greeks as Ayvali. We drove through the town and across a causeway on to Ali Bey Adası, the largest of the isles that cluster around the Ayvalik peninsula, the south-westernmost tip of the Gulf of Edremit. We checked into a hotel on the shore facing Lesbos, choosing it because it had an outdoor restaurant embowered with vines and rosebushes. We had supper in the garden under a full moon, whose ashen light glowed on the voluptuous contours of the Lesbian mountains towering across the narrow straits only a dozen miles away, while the other isles of the archipelago sparkled like emeralds on the luminescent surface of the Aegean. It was a scene which Sappho would have recognized, and so another of her poems came to mind, a couplet that she might have written on a night like this in her island home across the straits: 'The glow and beauty of the stars are nothing near the splendid moon/ When in her roundness she burns silver about the world'.

We returned to Ayvalik and Ali Bey Adası a number of times after that, and on one of our summer visits we were pleasantly surprised to find a merry group of Greeks from Lesbos at the next table in our restaurant. By that time we had become fairly fluent in both Greek and Turkish, and so could understand the conversation and songs of our new friends as they talked and sang in both languages. Later, after they had invited us to join them, we learned that their families had lived in and around Ayvalik before the population exchange, and then in 1923 they had been resettled in Lesbos. But in recent years, political conditions permitting, they and other Greeks of the diaspora had begun to return to the Aegean coast of Turkey for summer holidays, because it had been their ancestral home and they loved it there. Our friends from Lesbos sang a number of old island folk-songs for us that evening, many of which we knew from our travels in Greece.

At the end one old man began a song that I did not recognize at once. The first line told of how 'three ships were sailing to Smyrna and Cordelio'. At that point the others joined him in the song, which I then remembered having heard once before at a *panegyri* on Lesbos, a nostalgic threnody about 'Ayvali, lovely Ayvali', and as they finished each verse they repeated the refrain. I can hear them now, as I recall Ayvalik myself:

> My eyes have never seen a village like Ayvali.
> Ask me about it, for I have been there.
> It has silver doors, golden keys,
> And beautiful girls as fresh as cool water.

5

PERGAMUM AND THE ATTALIDS

We left Ayvalik the following morning, bound for Bergama and the ruins of ancient Pergamum. As we drove south along the coastal highway the sun was just rising over the Asian hills, illuminating with its golden light the mountains of Lesbos across the straits. We drove for about half an hour, the Lesbian shore extending parallel to the Turkish coast as far as the great promontory at the south-eastern corner of the island, after which it disappears from view as the highway veers inland. This brought us eastward up the valley of the Bakır Çayı, the River Caicus of antiquity, entering the land that in Hellenistic times was the heart of the kingdom of Pergamum.

Nine miles inland from the coast we turned off the Izmir highway and drove on into Bergama, the lively Turkish market town that stands on the lower part of the site of the ancient city of Pergamum.

After passing through the centre of the town we paused to look at the extraordinary edifice known as Kızıl Avlu, the Red Court, whose ruins are just beside the town's main bridge across the Bergama Çayı, the River Selinus of antiquity. This gigantic structure consists of two tower-like circular buildings at the northern end of an enormous courtyard, much of which is still hidden under the modern houses above it, with the river flowing diagonally beneath it in a tunnel. The whole complex dates from the reign of Hadrian, AD 117–38, and from the statues still standing in its courtyard it is believed to have

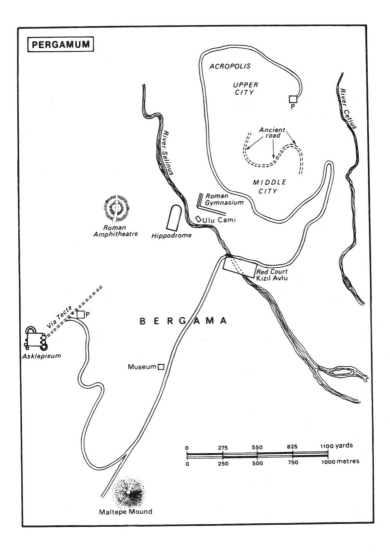

PERGAMUM

ACROPOLIS

UPPER CITY

River Cetius

River Selinus

Ancient road

MIDDLE CITY

Roman Gymnasium

Ulu Cami

Roman Amphitheatre

Hippodrome

Red Court
Kızıl Avlu

Via Tecta

P

B E R G A M A

Asklepieum

Museum

| 0 | 275 | 550 | 825 | 1100 yards |
| 0 | 250 | 500 | 750 | 1000 metres |

Maltepe Mound

been a sanctuary of the Egyptian deities Isis, Serapis, and Harpocrates. During the early Byzantine era, c. AD 400, the central hall of the structure was converted into a church dedicated to St. John the Theologian, which served as the cathedral of Pergamum, probably destroyed during the Turkish invasions of the fourteenth century. This cathedral is of importance in ecclesiastical history because Pergamum was one of the Seven Churches of Revelation. As one reads in Revelation 2: 12–13: 'And to the angel of the church in Pergamos write: These things saith he which hath the sharp sword with two edges. I know thy works, and where thou dwellest, even where Satan's throne is: and thou holdest fast my name, and hast not denied my faith, even in those days wherein Antipas was my faithful martyr, who was slain among you, where Satan dwelleth'. This reference to the throne of Satan has been interpreted by scholars to mean one of the temples dedicated to the imperial cult in Pergamum, but more probably it symbolizes the city as a seat of Roman power in Asia Minor, where Christians like Antipas had been martyred for worshipping Christ instead of the deified emperor. But the church in Pergamum overcame these adversities, and in the Byzantine era, AD 325–1453, the city had the status of a bishopric.

From the Red Court, we followed the signposts that directed us to the archaeological site of ancient Pergamum, driving along a steep, winding road that took us up close to the summit of the mountain that towers just to the north of the modern town. The road ends in a car-park just below the summit, which we reached after a short hike, emerging on the acropolis of ancient Pergamum.

Of all the ancient cities on the Aegean coast of Turkey, Pergamum has the most spectacular site, its acropolis perching on the levelled peak of a mountain 1,300 feet above the plain. This gigantic spire of rock rises precipitously from the plain on three sides, with the Selinus sweeping around the mountain to the west and the Cetius curving by it to the east, so creating the natural fortress that first attracted settlers to this superb site. The oldest pottery sherds at Pergamum date to the eighth century BC; and these remains indicate that the first settlers on the acropolis were not Greeks, but perhaps non-Hellenic people who had settled there before the great Ionian and Aeolian migrations. There are a number of myths concerning the origins of the city, which was originally called Teuthrania after its founder, King Teuthras of Mysia. Teuthras married a slave-girl from Arcadia named Auge, whose son Telephos had been fathered by Heracles. Teuthras adopted Auge's son, and Telephos eventually succeeded him as king of Teuthrania. One of the fabled exploits of Telephos was his defeat of an Achaean army led by Agamemnon, who in that version of the myth had mistakenly wandered into Mysia before he besieged Troy, probably a folk-memory of an early invasion of north-western Anatolia by the Hellenes.

The first historic reference to Pergamum is made by Xenophon in the final pages of his *Anabasis*. Aside from this Pergamum does not appear in historical sources again for more than a century, until it became a pawn in the war between Alexander's successors. When Lysimachus gained control of western Anatolia, he appointed an official named Philetaerus to be his governor at Pergamum, leaving with him a large part of his treasure. When Lysimachus was defeated and killed in 281 BC Philetaerus managed to retain his position as independent governor at Pergamum, keeping the huge sum of money that had been deposited with him and using it for his own purposes. After establishing his own kingdom, Philetaerus adorned Pergamum with temples and other public buildings, making wise loans to neighbouring rulers to maintain good relations with them, developing the Pergamene lands in the valley of the Caicus, and creating an army to defend the new state against its enemies. Philetaerus died in 263 BC and was succeeded by his nephew and adopted son, Eumenes I. The year after his succession Eumenes defeated Antiochus I in a battle near Sardis, establishing the independence of Pergamum from the Seleucid Empire founded by the Macedonian general who succeeded to Alexander's dominions in Asia, Seleucus I. During the two decades following this victory Eumenes enlarged his principality to include the whole of the Caicus valley and part of the nearby Aeolian coast. Eumenes ruled until his death in 241 BC and was succeeded by his kinsman and adopted son, Attalos I, who was the first to assume the title of king of Pergamum. Thus he formally began what came to be called the dynasty of the Attalids.

Attalos I ruled for forty-four years, and his greatest achievement was his decisive defeat of the Gauls in 230 BC, which ended the menace that these European barbarians had posed for the Hellenized people of western Asia Minor. Attalos also spent much of his long reign in warfare with the Seleucid kings of Syria, struggling for supremacy in Anatolia, but by the time of his death in 197 BC the boundaries of Pergamum were much the same as when he began his rule. Nevertheless, Attalos had entered into good relations with Rome, and when this policy was continued by his successor, Eumenes II, it soon resulted in rich benefits for the Pergamene kingdom. In 190 BC a Roman army under Scipio Africanus invaded Asia Minor and joined forces with Eumenes and his troops in order to break the power of the Seleucid Empire, then ruled by Antiochus III, the Great. Scipio and Eumenes decisively defeated Antiochus at the Battle of Magnesia early in 189 BC, after which the Romans awarded most of the former Seleucid possessions in Asia Minor to Pergamum. The territory of the Pergamene kingdom was greatly increased as a result, expanding along the Aegean coast as far south as the Maeander, and extending inland as far as the town of Iconium, the modern Konya. Pergamum reached the height of its power and prosperity under Eumenes II, who ruled until his death in 159 BC and used much of his wealth to erect temples and other splendid public buildings, including the famous library. Pergamum indeed emerged at that time as a great cultural centre, one of the focal points for the advancement of Hellenism in Asia Minor. These developments continued under Eumenes II's brother and successor, Attalos II, who ruled until 138 BC. The second Attalos is remembered today principally for the magnificent edifice which he endowed in Athens, the Stoa of Attalos, a colonnaded market building which is a fitting monument to the greatness of Pergamum during its golden age.

But the golden age of Pergamum did not long outlive Attalos II. He was succeeded by his weak and eccentric nephew, the third of the same name, and this last of the Attalids neglected affairs of state for his scientific studies, allowing his kingdom to become increasingly dominated by Rome. By that time the Romans had become so powerful that there seemed little future for an independent kingdom in Asia Minor. Thus when Attalos III died in 133 BC he left his realm and all of his possessions to the Roman people. His will was disputed by a pretender named Aristonicus, who claimed to be an illegitimate son of Eumenes II, and so the Romans had to fight a three-year war of succession before they could take over their new dominions. After the Romans put down Aristonicus they proceeded to take over the former kingdom of Pergamum, including most of it in the newly organized Province of Asia, which came into being in 129 BC, with the old capital of the Attalids honoured as a free city. The people of Pergamum rebelled briefly in 88 BC, when they joined forces with Mithridates, king of Pontus, who had created an independent realm in north-eastern Asia Minor and led a crusade to free Anatolia and Greece from Roman domination. During the climax of this revolt some 80,000 Roman colonists were slaughtered in a single day throughout Asia Minor, including many who had settled in Pergamum. But the revolt was crushed and the following year Pergamum was occupied by the Romans, ending its brief independence. Pergamum remained a rich and highly cultured city throughout the rest of the Roman period and on into the early centuries of the Christian era, but never again did it rise to the brilliance it had achieved during the golden age of the Attalids.

We began our exploration of Pergamum by walking around the acropolis, the ruins of the ancient city standing out dramatically against the distant background of the Caicus plain far below and giving the striking impression that this really was a royal capital, whose kings could survey all of the lands that they originally ruled from this impregnable eyrie. The ruins on the acropolis comprise the very oldest part of Pergamum, and during the Hellenistic period the citadel here enclosed the royal palace, the theatre, and several of the most important religious shrines, giving this quarter a sacred and ceremonial aura, in contrast to the more plebeian character of the lower city.

The oldest of the religious shrines on the acropolis is the Temple of Athena, who was worshipped as Polias Nikephorus, Bringer of Victory to the City. This temple, whose ruins stand just above the theatre, is believed to have been founded by Philetaerus himself, and thus it represents the emergence of Pergamum as a city-state at the beginning of the Attalid period. Adjoining the precincts of this temple to the north are the remains of the celebrated Library of Pergamum, founded by Eumenes II; this was also dedicated to Athena, revered as the goddess of wisdom and the patroness of learning. The Pergamene library was reputed to have had some 200,000 volumes in its collection, surpassed only by the famous library in Alexandria. The fame of the Pergamene library was a tribute to the love of learning exhibited by the Attalid kings, who were known throughout the Greek world as patrons of scholarship. Apollonius of Perge, one of the greatest mathematicians of the ancient world, studied for a time in Pergamum as a guest of Attalos I, and dedicated some of his books to him. The fate of the Pergamene library after the Attalid era is uncertain. Mark Antony promised to give it to Cleopatra after the destruction of the library at Alexandria, but it is not known whether he ever actually did so. In any event, Pergamum continued as a centre of scholarship throughout the Roman period and on into the early centuries of Christianity. Julian the Apostate studied philosophy at Pergamum in the year AD 351, a decade before he became emperor. Thus, even at that late date, the works of the ancient Greeks were still being taught in the city of the Attalids.

South of the precincts of Athena's temple are the remains of the Altar of Zeus, of which only the stepped platform survives in place. The altar was constructed by Eumenes II c. 190 BC, a time when Pergamum was at the pinnacle of its greatness, and this is what the shrine and its sculptural decoration were meant to signify. The main element in the decoration was a sculptured frieze, $7\frac{1}{2}$ feet high and 390 feet in length. It extended around the sides of the podium and up the broad stairway that led to the horseshoe-shaped altar, which was surrounded by a colonnade. The theme of this frieze was the Gigantomachy, the mythical battle between the Olympian Gods and the ancient Giants, symbolizing the triumph of Attalos I over the Gauls, and at the same time glorifying the heroic role of the Attalids as the saviours of Hellenic civilization in their struggle against barbarism. A second frieze adorned the walls inside the colonnade; this depicted the adventures of Telephos, the mythical founder of the Attalid line, establishing the divine origins of the dynasty through this son of Heracles. Remnants of these reliefs were recovered during archaeological excavations that began in 1871; they are now in the Berlin Museum, where the Altar of Zeus has been reconstructed in all of its former grandeur. These and other surviving Pergamene sculptures, most notably the Dying Gaul and the Ludovisi Gauls, are considered to be among the highest achievements of Hellenistic art.

The Altar of Zeus may have been the subject of the apocalyptic message in Revelation 2:13, where St. John speaks of 'the place where Satan has his throne'; but it is more likely that he meant just Pergamum itself, and if he had a specific place in mind it would have been the Trajaneum, the largest temple in the Roman imperial city, where both Trajan and Hadrian were honoured as deified emperors. The colossal ruins of the Trajaneum are just to the north of Athena's sanctuary on the highest level of the acropolis, standing on a vast terrace supported by a retaining wall above the theatre. The temple would have dominated the view of Pergamum as seen from the Caicus plain below, a veritable Throne of Satan.

The theatre is the most extraordinary of all the ancient structures surviving on the Pergamene acropolis. And so after exploring the rest of the acropolis we decided to sit for a while there in one of the upper tiers of the auditorium, as it were in our own private box in the grandest of all opera houses. The whole of the Caicus plain spread out before us as a backdrop. It would have been a perfect setting for Euripides' lost epic *Telephos*, which surely must have been performed in the Pergamene theatre.

The theatre at Pergamum is set into the natural contour of the mountain slope, the principal sanctuaries on the acropolis fanning out above it, with the Temple of Athena to the south and the Trajaneum to the north. The auditorium is exceptionally steep—78 rows of seats climb the slope through a height of 118 feet—and because of the lie of the land it forms an arc much more acute than is usual in Greek and Roman theatres. The orchestra extends on to a long and narrow transverse terrace, once bordered on both sides by colonnades. At the northern end of the terrace there are the remains of an Ionic Temple of Dionysos, the god of the theatre, whose festivals originally gave rise to Greek drama. The emperor Caracella (211–17) was very fond of this temple, undoubtedly because of its spectacular setting, and he had himself enshrined here as the 'New Dionysos'. The terrace connects at its southern end with the upper agora, which was the terminus of a road that led up from the lower city, so that the townspeople could enter the theatre without passing through the citadel. One can imagine, as we did, that this terrace must have been a favourite place for the Pergamenes to promenade at the end of the day, looking out over the theatre to see the palace of their king and the temples of their gods, and on the other side observing their fertile lands spread out below on the Caicus plain.

When we left we stepped down along one of the steep central aisles of the theatre and walked out on to the terrace, the same route that the townspeople would have taken after a play, passing through the upper agora and strolling downhill from there. As we went along this ancient road, we noticed the ruts worn in the cobblestones by the wagons that had used this route many centuries ago. A short walk took us to a second group of buildings that have been excavated lower down the mountain; these include the lower agora, two splendid gymnasia, a monumental public fountain, and two temples, one of them dedicated to Hera Basileia, Queen of the Gods, and the other to Demeter. The Temple of Demeter is dated by an inscription, still visible, to the reign of Attalos I, and was founded by his wife Apollonis. The cult of Demeter and her daughter Persephone, celebrated in the Eleusinian Mysteries, was in fact popular among the women of Pergamum. The Eleusinian rituals still remain mysteries, but one can sense something of their spirit from a 'Hymn to Demeter' by the poet Lasus of Hermione, evoking visions of a torch-lit nocturnal ceremony celebrated by the Pergamene women in the days of the Attalids: 'I sing of Demeter and the maiden Persephone, wife of Klymenos, leading a honey-voiced hymn in the deep mode Aeolian'.

During Roman times Pergamum's population grew to over 300,000, as the city spread out from its original mountain-top site and expanded south-south-west across the Caicus plain. Although most of Roman Pergamum is covered by the modern town of Bergama, the ruins of some of its ancient structures have been excavated by archaeologists, most notably the Red Hall, which we had visited before we went up to the acropolis, and the Asklepieum, which we now set out to see, as we drove back down the mountain road and again passed through the town.

The Asklepieum is in the south-western quarter of Bergama, approached by a turn-off to the right from the main road leading out to the Izmir highway. From the car-park at the end of the turn-off one approaches the Asklepieum along a splendid colonnaded way known in Roman times as the Via Tecta. This was once a bazaar street catering to the pilgrims and patients who came to the Asklepieum, one of the most famous shrines and therapeutic centres in the ancient world. The cult of Asklepios, the god of healing, seems to have spread here from Epidauros early in the fourth century BC, when the first sanctuary was erected on this site. The Pergamene Asklepieum was extended and rebuilt at various times in the Hellenistic and Roman periods, with the ruins one sees today mostly dating from the first half of the second century AD, when the shrine reached the height of its popularity, surpassing Epidauros as the principal therapeutic centre in the Graeco-Roman world.

The fame of the Pergamene Asklepieum during this period was largely due to the renown of the physician Galen, who was born in Pergamum in AD 129. Galen, the greatest physician and medical writer of the Roman period, received his first training in medicine at the Pergamene Asklepieum, studying philosophy as well. Galen also served his medical internship here, and among his other duties he treated the wounds of the gladiators who fought at the local arena. Later, after leaving Pergamum, Galen served as personal physician to three Roman emperors: Marcus Aurelius, Lucius Verrus, and Commodus. Galen's writings systematized all of the Greek anatomical and medical knowledge that had accumulated since the pioneering work of Hippocrates of Cos in the fifth century BC, and his treatises formed the basis for medical science from the Roman period up to the Renaissance, when he was known as the 'Prince of Physicians'.

One enters the Asklepieum through what was once the propylon courtyard, the forecourt to the monumental entrance at the end of the colonnaded street. To the left of the entrance there are two large round buildings, the first of which was the Temple of Zeus-Asklepios, and the second the main hospital, connected by a long tunnel to the sacred well in the centre of the courtyard, whose waters played an important part in the cure. The treatment in the hospital stressed good diet, mud baths, and bathing in the sacred spring, even in the depths of winter, and also psychotherapy, which included an imaginative interpretation of dreams, eighteen centuries before Freud. One of the psychic complaints recognized by Galen was lovesickness, which he believed to be the principal cause of insomnia. In one of his treatises he notes that 'the quickening of the pulse at the name of the beloved gives the clue'.

Behind the western end of the colonnaded courtyard there is a handsome Roman theatre with a seating capacity of 3,500. The Pergamene Asklepieum, like that at Epidauros, was very much a spa in the old-fashioned European sense, and while the patients awaited their recovery they were entertained by dramatic performances as well as by gladiatorial combats and other shows in the arena.

After visiting the Asklepieum, we drove back toward the centre of Bergama, stopping first at the archaeological museum. This is one of the most attractive local museums in Turkey, with an interesting collection of antiquities from all periods of ancient Pergamum, and contains a fine Hellenistic head believed to be a representation of Asklepios.

Leaving the museum, we then wandered through the old Turkish quarter of Bergama, looking at its Ottoman monuments, including mosques (one of them with the bizarre name of Kulaksız, or Earless), *hans* (inns), *hamams* (Turkish baths), and fountains, as well as a Selcuk minaret of the fourteenth century. The oldest Ottoman monument is Ulu Cami, the Great Mosque, built in 1399 by Sultan Beyazit I, who is known in Turkish as Yıldırım, or Lightning. Beyazit received this nickname because of the astonishing speed with which he moved his armies back and forth between Anatolia and the Balkans, fighting wars on both fronts at once. Gibbon wrote that the sultan's sobriquet was suitable to 'the fierce energy of his soul and rapidity of his destructive march'.

One can see monuments associated with all of the eras in Pergamum's history from the courtyard of Ulu Cami, which stands directly under the mountain on a bend of the Selinus. On the mountain slope above the mosque stand the defence walls constructed by Eumenes II; just to the north on the lower slope are the remains of a gymnasium; across the Selinus to the west lie the ruins of a Roman amphitheatre where gladiators once fought; and about a mile to the south-west, across a thicket of Turkish minarets, one can see the splendid remains of the Hellenistic Asklepieum. To complete the cultural palimpsest, Ulu Cami, one of the earliest Ottoman imperial mosques, is a reconstructed Byzantine church, probably converted to Islam soon after Sultan Orhan conquered Pergamum in 1326.

Even older layers in this palimpsest are visible from the road leading out of Bergama to the coast. These are two tumuli, Maltepe and Yığma Tepe, the first of which is to the left of the highway just opposite the turn-off to the Asklepieum, and the second about half a mile farther along to the south-east. Both of these are artificial dirt mounds, each surrounded by a stone wall and with an internal vault roofed with ashlar masonry, the Maltepe tumulus surmounted by the remnants of a monument of some kind, perhaps a statue base. The mounds were long thought to be the tombs of the ancient kings of Pergamum, but recent studies have shown that the stonework in the burial chamber at Maltepe is only of Roman date. Nevertheless, it is possible that this was originally the tomb of Auge, mother of King Telephos, the legendary founder of the Attalid dynasty. According to Pausanius, Auge, the daughter of King Aleos of Tegea, was cast out by her father when she gave birth to Telephos, the son of Heracles, but she and her child were taken in by King Teuthras of Mysia, who adopted the boy and made him his heir. As Pausanius writes, in Peter Levi's translation:

According to Heketaios, Herakles lay with Auge when he came to Tegea, and in the end she was caught with Herakles' child, and

Aleos shut her and the boy in a chest and sent them out to sea; she landed and met Teuthras, who was a powerful man in the Kaikos plain, and he loved and married her; and today Auge's monument is at Pergamos on the Kaikos, a tumulus of earth surrounded by a stone platform and surmounted by a naked woman in bronze.

So the romantic mind might conclude that the Maltepe mound is the tomb of Auge, a monument to the Arcadian princess who bore the son of a god and thus became matriarch of the dynasty that ruled Pergamum during its golden age. This myth probably perpetuates the lingering memory of some otherwise forgotten Greek migration to the Aegean coast of north-western Anatolia during the dark ages of the Hellenic world. We recalled this as we looked at the Maltepe mound against the background of the acropolis hill rising up behind the modern town of Bergama, for the ruins of Hellenistic Pergamum evoke as powerfully the brilliant culture that flourished in this place more than two thousand years ago.

6

THE AEOLIAN SHORE

After our visit to Pergamum we spent a day driving down to Izmir, visiting the sites of the ancient Aeolian cities along the coast. First we drove back to Ayvalik as far as the turn-off to Dikilli, a tiny port just opposite the south-easternmost promontory of Lesbos, for we thought that this would be a pleasant place to have breakfast. Dikilli was also an appropriate starting-point for exploring the Aeolian shore, for it is within sight of the island from which the first Greek settlers came to this coast.

The coastal region between the Adramyttene Gulf and the Gulf of Smyrna was known in antiquity as Aeolis, because the first Greeks who settled here were Aeolians. Many of them crossed over from Lesbos to the mainland at the end of the second millennium BC, starting the great population movement that led to the Hellenization of western Anatolia just prior to the beginning of recorded history in Asia Minor.

At Dikilli we stopped beside the pier at an outdoor *çayevi*, where we ordered bread, goat-cheese, and olives along with our tea, the traditional Anatolian breakfast to which we had grown accustomed during our years in Turkey. While we were eating, a car ferry from Mytilene docked at the pier and about a dozen passengers disembarked, all of them stopping at the *çayevi* for breakfast, addressing the waiter in Turkish but speaking Greek among themselves. Like the Greeks at Ayvalik, these people were all from Lesbos, and their families had lived on the Aegean coast of Asia Minor prior to 1923, many of

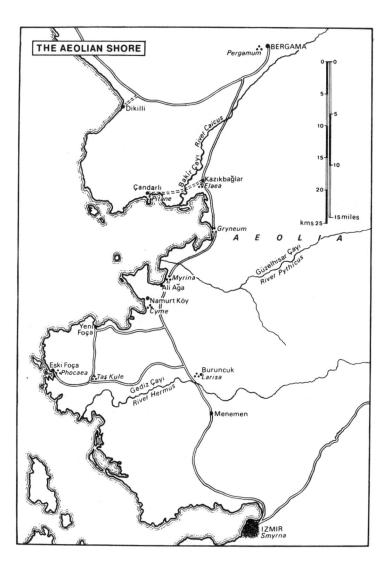

THE AEOLIAN SHORE

Pergamum ●BERGAMA

Dikilli

River Caicus

Bakir Çayı

Kazıkbağlar
Çandarlı ●*Elaea*
●*Pitane*

Gryneum

A E O L I A

Güzelhisar Çayı
River Pythicus

●*Myrina*
Ali Ağa
●*Namurt Köy*
Cyme

Yeni
Foça

Eski Foça
●*Phocaea* ●Taş Kule
Gediz Çayı
River Hermus

Buruncuk
Larisa

●Menemen

IZMIR
Smyrna

0 ⌐ 0

5

5
10

15
10

20

kms 25 ⌐ 15 miles

them now returning for the first time since that diaspora.

The great population movement that led to the first Greek settlements along this coast began *c.* 1100 BC, about a century after the collapse of Mycenaean civilization. At that time the Dorian invasion forced many of the indigenous Hellenes to flee eastward to the Aegean isles and the adjacent coast of Anatolia, the Aeolians generally settling north of the Ionians. The Aeolians originated in Thessaly, Phocis, Locris, and Boetia, and most of them landed first on Lesbos and Tenedos, then afterwards crossed to the Aegean coast of Asia Minor. According to Herodotus, the Aeolians founded a dozen colonies on the Anatolian mainland south of the Adramyttene Gulf, the most notable being Smyrna. This colony, however, they later lost to the Ionians, who had founded a dozen cities of their own on the coast and islands farther south. The colonies organized themselves into two separate confederations, each of which originally had a dozen members before Smyrna changed hands. Herodotus lists the remaining eleven Aeolian cities as Pitane, Cyme, Larisa, Neonteichon, Temnus, Cyllene, Notium, Aegiroessa, Aegae, Myrina, and Gryneum. The Ionian cities won great renown, but the Aeolian cities are known only to specialists in the history and archaeology of the area, and the names of some of them are not even mentioned by George Bean in his comprehensive *Aegean Turkey*, which we used as our guide when we first explored Aeolis. The obscurity of the Aeolian cities, as compared to the brilliance of the Ionian League, probably stems from the fact that their settlers were mostly farmers and herdsmen, while the other Greeks to their south were seafarers and merchants who came into contact with a much broader world. While the Ionians made their indelible mark on history, the Aeolians simply settled for the good life on their fertile farms. As Athenaeus writes in his *Doctors at Dinner*, the Aeolians were much 'given to wine, women, and luxurious living', and this is undoubtedly why they left no monuments on the Aegean coast in antiquity, and why their cities today have almost vanished.

84

We left the *çayevi* and drove back from Dikilli to the main highway, where we headed south toward Izmir, the ancient Smyrna, driving down the plain of the Caicus toward the Aegean. Just before reaching the coast we turned right on to a dirt road that led us westward toward Çandarlı, the site of ancient Pitane. The village which occupies the site now is named for the Çandarlı family, who monopolized the office of grand vizier of the Ottoman Empire from 1359 until 1499. Çandarlı is picturesquely situated on a long and narrow spit of a peninsula whose waist is guarded by an exceptionally well-preserved late medieval castle. The road took us as far as the castle but then ended in an impenetrable maze of village streets, so we parked the car and got out to explore on foot, to see if we would find any remnants of ancient Pitane.

Pitane was the northernmost of the towns in the Aeolian League. Its original settlement appears to have been far earlier than the Aeolian migration, for pottery sherds have been found in its necropolis dating back to the third millennium BC. The Aeolians believed that the town was founded by one of the women warriors who held command under the legendary Amazon, Queen Myrina. At the time of the Aeolian migration the town was already inhabited by the indigenous people known to the Greeks as Lelegians. The Lelegians evidently tried to regain their town after the Greeks settled there, for the Aeolians in Pitane were forced to seek help from the Ionians in Erythrae to drive out the natives. After the rise of Pergamum, Pitane and the other towns of the Aeolian League were absorbed into the Attalid kingdom, sharing its prosperity and brilliant culture. The most renowned son of Pitane during the Hellenistic period was Arcesilaus, who was head of the Platonic Academy in Athens *c.* 250 BC, and who is credited with being the first philosopher to argue both sides of a question. The most noteworthy incident in the history of Pitane during the Roman era occurred in 85 BC, the last year of the First Mithridatic War: King Mithridates himself took refuge here for a time when the city was besieged by the rebel Fimbria, who had murdered his general Flaccus and usurped command himself. But Mithridates eluded Fimbria and the Romans and escaped to Lesbos. Fimbria, afraid to return to Rome after his crime, retired to the Asklepieum in Pergamum and committed suicide there.

Very little remains of ancient Pitane, but with the aid of an archaeological map we were able to locate the sites of the theatre and the stadium. We also found one of the two harbours mentioned by Strabo in his description of Pitane, an artificial haven created by constructing a mole, now underwater, out to a tiny islet off the western side of the peninsula. The second harbour of Pitane was on the eastern side of the town, where no mole was required since ships were sheltered from the prevailing west wind by the peninsula itself. This arrangement we found at most of the ancient towns along the western shores of Turkey, for they were usually built on an easily defended promontory projecting into the sea like the little cape at Çandarlı.

After exploring the outer part of the peninsula, we walked back to look at the castle. George Bean describes this castle as Venetian, as does Freya Stark in her *Ionia, A Quest*, but the Turkish archaeologist Ekrem Akurgal, who excavated the necropolis at Pitane, believes it to be a Genoese fortress built in the thirteenth or fourteenth century. It is more likely that Akurgal is correct, for the Genoese were in control of this part of the coast during the last two centuries of the Byzantine Empire, and their strongholds here were this castle and the fortresses at Phocaea and New Phocaea.

From Çandarlı we returned to the Izmir highway and drove just a few hundred yards farther on to Kazıkbağlar, a hamlet at the head of a bay known in antiquity as the Eleatic Gulf. The gulf took its name from the ancient city of Elaea, whose few remains are to be found scattered around the fields between the highway and the sea to the west of the village. Elaea had the distinction of being the oldest Greek town on the Aeolian coast, and local tradition ascribes its foundation to Menestheus, leader of the Athenian contingent at the siege of Troy. He is supposed to have led an Ionian colony here after the Trojan War. Elaea never became a member of the Aeolian League, no doubt because the city was founded by the Ionians and remained populated by them. During its early history Elaea was of little significance, but it achieved some eminence in the Hellenistic period, when it served as the port and naval arsenal of the Pergamene kingdom, since it was located at the mouth of the River Caicus.

After Elaea the highway to Izmir took us south along the shore of the Eleatic Gulf. At the easternmost arc of the gulf we stopped just beyond the village of Yenişakran, walking out from the road to a little promontory called Temaşalık Burnu, the site of ancient Gryneum. Though this is another of the Aeolian cities, its settlement probably predated the Greek migration, since local tradition attributes its foundation to an Amazon named Gryne, one of Myrina's lieutenants. She was violated at this place by Apollo, who had a shrine and oracle here. Strabo, writing in the second half of the first century BC, describes Gryneum as having 'a temple of Apollo, an ancient oracle, and a costly fane of white marble'. Pausanius, who visited the shrine in the mid-second century AD, writes of 'Gryneum, where Apollo has a most beautiful grove of fruit-trees and other wild trees which are pleasant to smell and look upon'. It was late April when we first saw this place, and it looked just as Pausanius had described it eighteen centuries before. Wild fruit-trees and flowering Judas-trees formed a grove around the ancient shrine of Apollo, of which there remained only a few fluted column drums scattered among the grass and wild flowers. As we wandered around this sacred place we recalled how the shrine here is mentioned by Virgil in Book IV of the *Aeneid*, where Aeneas tells Queen Dido of Carthage how the oracle of 'Apollo at Gryneum, where he gives his divination by lots, has insistently commanded me to make my way to Italy's noble lands'.

After leaving Gryneum, we drove on for a short way around

the Eleatic Gulf toward the promontory at its southern end; there we stopped where the road crosses a bridge over a little river called Güzelhisar Çayı, the Stream of the Beautiful Castle. In antiquity this was known as the River Pythicus, and its original stream-bed can be seen to the south of the present watercourse, which flows into the Aegean just south of the site of ancient Myrina.

Like Pitane, Elaea, and Gryneum, Myrina was settled long before the Aeolian migration, undoubtedly inhabited by the indigenous people of the north-western Aegean coast of Anatolia. According to mythology, the town was founded not by another of Myrina's lieutenants but by the queen herself. Homer mentions the Amazon queen in Book II of the *Iliad*, where he writes of her mythical tomb outside the walls of Troy: 'This men call the Hill of the Thicket, but the immortal/gods have named it the burial ground of dancing Myrina'.

There is virtually nothing to be seen on the site of ancient Myrina, but archaeological digs on the necropolis have unearthed a large number of tombs with interesting funerary offerings dating to the Hellenistic period. The most important of these are terracotta figurines similar to the famous Tanagra statuettes. They include representations of deities, humans, and animals, as well as caricatures, theatrical masques, and comic figures. These beautiful and fascinating statuettes, which are now on exhibit in the archaeological museum in Istanbul and in the Louvre, afford a rare glimpse into the lives of those who dwelt in Myrina in ancient times.

The highway now took us along the shore of a beautiful bay that forms the southern cusp of the Eleatic Gulf, the small industrial town of Ali Ağa lying at its far end. After driving across the neck of the promontory that forms the southern arm of the gulf, we turned on to a rough dirt track that brought us to the sea again at Namurt Köy, a hamlet on a bay called Namurt Limanı, the Harbour of Nimrod. At the end of the track we found the site of ancient Cyme, which Strabo called 'the largest and best of the Aeolian cities'.

The story of Cyme's foundation is much the same as that of the Aeolian cities to its north, in that its original settlement probably took place well before the great Greek migration. Local legend has it that the town was named for its eponymous founder, the Amazon Cyme, presumably another of Queen Myrina's lieutenants. Aeolian Cyme, together with Chalcis and Eretria, founded the city of Cumae in 757 BC, the first Greek colony on the Italian mainland. The Cymaeans later founded a colony at Side on the Mediterranean coast of Asia Minor, and the ruins of that city are today one of the principal adornments of the southern Turkish shore. Cyme contributed ships to the Persian fleet in 512 BC when Darius crossed the Bosphorus on his expedition against the Scythians, and again in 480 BC when Xerxes invaded Greece, the only Aeolian city to participate in those two campaigns. But despite this, the Cymaeans were mocked by their fellow Greeks for their supposed failure to exploit their potential as a sea-power. Strabo tells several stories ridiculing the stupidity of the Cymaeans, although he does say that Cyme was the birthplace of Ephorus, an orator, philosopher, and inventor who flourished in the fourth century BC. Strabo also tells us that Cyme may have been the birthplace of both Homer and Hesiod, although this is not likely. Hesiod, in his *Works and Days*, writes that his father, Dius, was from Aeolian Cyme, and that he emigrated from there to Boetia. One wonders why Dius left the fertile lands and pleasant weather of the Aeolian coast for the harsh clime of Boetia where, as Hesiod writes of his father's life: 'He dwelt near Helicon in Ascre, a village wretched in winter, in summer oppressive, and not pleasant in any season'.

Here again, as at the other Aeolian sites we had visited, there was little of the ancient town left to be seen, other than the exiguous remains of a theatre, an Ionic temple, and the foundations of a monumental building of unknown identity. We were able, however, to identify the ancient mole of Cyme's harbour, most of it underwater. This was where the fleet of Xerxes lay at anchor during the winter of 480–479 BC, after the Persians had been defeated by the Greeks at the Battle of Salamis.

We then drove back from Namurt Köy to the main highway, which we followed for only a short way before turning off once again, heading this time for the seaside towns of Yeni Foça and Eski Foça, New and Old Phocaea. Both of these towns are situated on the huge peninsula that forms the northern arm of the Gulf of Izmir. Yeni Foça is about half-way out along the north shore of the peninsula and Eski Foça at its westernmost tip. The road brought us first to Yeni Foça, a village on a beautiful bay with a superb beach (now occupied by the Club Mediterranée).

Yeni Foça is said to stand on the site of ancient Cyllene, an obscure town of the Aeolian League about which virtually nothing is known, but this identification is doubtful. In any event, the present town of Yeni Foça is a direct descendant not of any ancient Greek colony but of the late medieval Genoese town of Foglia Nuova (New Phocaea) whose history begins in 1275 when the Byzantine emperor Michael VIII Palaeologus granted an imperial fief to two Genoese adventurers, the brothers Benedetto and Manuele Zaccaria. This fief centred on the town of Phocaea, which in antiquity had been one of the cities of the Ionian League, and also included the lucrative alum mines of the peninsula whose processed salts were in great demand for the dyeing of cloth and also as an emetic and astringent. When they received this fief the Zaccarias built a fortified enclosure on the northern shore of the peninsula to protect their alum factory there, and this soon developed into the town of Foglia Nuova. The older town came to be called Foglia Vecchia. The Zaccaria brothers also built a formidable fleet to protect their alum trade from pirates as Foglia Nuova developed into one of the richest towns in the Levant. It remained a Genoese possession until 1455, when both it and Foglia Vecchia fell to the Ottoman Turks and disappeared once more from the pages of history.

We stopped briefly to enjoy the view in Yeni Foça and then

drove on, as the road took us half-way across the peninsula and then out to its westernmost headland. There a dramatic panorama suddenly opened up before us, with Cape Malaena and Mount Mimas in view due west across the seaward end of the Gulf of Izmir. Then the road finally brought us to Eski Foça, a pleasant town clustered around a little peninsula at the inner end of an almost landlocked harbour, nearly cut off from the Aegean by a succession of promontories and offshore islets. This was the most beautiful spot we had come upon on our drive down the Aeolian coast, and so we were very pleased when we found an outdoor restaurant right on the sea, its garden terrace shaded by a gigantic plane tree of great age. We spent most of the afternoon there, taking our ease under what we came to call the Tree of Idleness.

Although Phocaea is on the Aeolian coast, it was Ionian in foundation and a member of the Ionian League. Phocaea appears to have been settled before the original Greek migration to Asia Minor, founded by colonists from the Ionian towns of Erythrae and Teos, probably in the eighth century BC. The site was obviously chosen for its excellent harbour, the finest by far on the Aeolian coast. The Phocaeans took full advantage of their superb location, and early in their history they emerged as one of the most active and venturesome maritime cities in all of Greece. Phocaea was one of the first Greek cities to send colonizing expeditions overseas, joining Miletus in the mid-eighth century BC to establish a colony on the southern shore of the Pontus at Amisus, the modern Turkish Black Sea port of Samsun, while in 654 BC the Phocaeans on their own founded Lampsacus on the Hellespont. Around 600 BC they established Massalia, the future Marseilles, with colonists from there going on to found their own daughter-colonies at Nicaea and Antipolis, the modern French Riviera towns of Nice and Antibes. Then in 560 BC the Phocaeans founded the town of Alalia in Corsica, and at the same time they established a short-lived settlement on the island of Sardinia. They even sailed out into the Atlantic and up the

Iberian coast as far as Tartassus, near present-day Cadiz.

A new age in the history of Asia Minor began in 546 BC, when Cyrus, the Persian king, defeated Croesus and captured the Lydian capital at Sardis, afterwards setting out to subdue the independent Greek cities on the Aegean coast of Asia Minor. In 544 BC a Persian army under Harpagus appeared before Phocaea and demanded the submission of the town, but the Phocaeans, after asking for a day's delay to consider the demand, abandoned the city and sailed off with all of their movable possessions to the island of Chios. There they decided to go on to Corsica, but before doing so they sailed back to Phocaea to slaughter the Persian garrison left behind by Harpagus. Swearing an oath never to return, they set sail for Corsica where most of them settled. Some of the exiles, though, overcome by longing for their native city, returned to Phocaea where they lived under Persian rule. The other Phocaeans lived in Corsica for only five years, after which a war with the Tyrrhenians and Carthaginians forced them to flee to southern Italy. They finally established a colony on the Straits of Messina, calling it Rhegium, known today as Reggio Calabria. Phocaeans from Rhegium later sailed up the west coast of Italy to found the colony of Elea, which soon became the intellectual centre of Magna Graeca and gave rise to the Eleatic school of philosophy.

In the meantime the Phocaeans who returned to their old town had to endure Persian domination until 499 BC, when they joined the other Ionian cities in the revolt led by Aristagoras, Tyrant of Miletus. By then, however, Phocaea had lost most of its adventurous spirits in the move to Corsica, and the town was able to contribute only three ships to the Ionian fleet at the Battle of Lade in 494 BC, when the Greek rebellion was crushed by the Persians. Phocaea faded into obscurity throughout most of the remainder of antiquity, emerging into prominence only twice, but on both those occasions the citizens of the town exhibited the courage and independence of their ancestors fighting against besieging Roman armies in 190 BC and again in 130 BC. On the second occasion the Phocaean resistance so provoked the Romans that the Senate ordered the town to be destroyed and its people dispersed. The citizens of Massalia, Phocaea's former colony, appealed against this harsh sentence and persuaded the Roman Senate to spare their mother city and grant clemency to its people. Thenceforth Phocaea remained in obscurity until it re-emerged in the period 1275–1455 as the Genoese town of Foglia Vecchia.

Virtually nothing remains of ancient Phocaea, and all that now survives of Foglia Vecchia is a ruined Genoese fortress on the promontory that encloses the harbour of Eski Foça to the west. As we gazed at this crumbling pile I was reminded of the words of Diogenes Laertius, which might serve as an epitaph for this once-great town: 'Phocaea is a city of moderate size, skilled in nothing but to rear brave men'.

We finally left Eski Foça late in the afternoon, driving back toward the Izmir highway on a road that took us along the central axis of the peninsula, passing the turn-off to Yeni Foça. About four miles east of Eski Foça we passed on the left an impressive rock-cut tomb known locally as Taş Kule, the Stone Tower, which is thought to date from the eighth century BC, perhaps a funerary monument of the Old Phrygian Kingdom.

After reaching the Izmir highway we headed south once again for a short way, pausing about a mile farther on at Buruncuk, a village at the foot of a steep and rocky hill. The acropolis of this hill has been identified as the site of ancient Larisa, the southernmost of the towns that formed the Aeolian League, of which there remains a very well-preserved stretch of the defence walls as well as the foundations of two temples and a palace. This is the only Aeolian city mentioned in the *Iliad*, where Homer lists among the Trojan allies 'the warlike Pelasgians who dwell around fertile Larisa'. Local tradition holds that the town was named after a daughter of one of these Pelasgian kings, of whom Strabo has this tale to tell: 'Piasus ... was ruler of the Pelasgians and fell in love with his daughter Larisa, and, having violated her, paid the penalty for his outrage; for, having observed him leaning over a cask of wine, she seized him by the legs, raised him and plunged him into the cask. Such were the ancient accounts'.

The remainder of our drive was uneventful, for there were no more ancient sites to see along the way; so we drove on as rapidly as we could to reach Izmir before dark. A short way beyond Buruncuk we crossed a bridge over the Gediz Çayı, the River Hermus of the Greeks. In ancient times the Hermus was the boundary between Aeolis and Ionia, emptying into the sea near Phocaea. But in more recent years the Hermus flowed south into the inner end of the Gulf of Izmir, where over the centuries it formed an alluvial delta that threatened to block Izmir's harbour, so that the navigable channel there today is only half a mile wide at Sancak Kalesi, at the entrance to the port. The Hermus was directed back into its ancient course in 1886, but only after its silt had caused the coastline to advance a considerable distance seaward in some places, most notably at Menemen, a former coastal town now eight miles inland. We passed Menemen as the highway curved inland through the alluvial plain of the Hermus, and then in the soft oblique light of late afternoon we suddenly saw all of Izmir before us, its seafront stretching for miles around the eastern end of the gulf. There we completed our journey along the Aeolian shore.

7

IZMIR, THE ANCIENT SMYRNA

Izmir is the third largest city in Turkey, with a population that now surpasses one million. It is far and away the most important port on the Aegean coast of Turkey, located at the head of the Gulf of Izmir, a site renowned since antiquity for its beauty.

We first saw Izmir early one morning in January 1961, when we steamed down the gulf aboard the *Tarih*, and in the years since then we have stopped there on all of our journeys along the Aegean coast. Each time we do so we stroll along the waterfront to the pier where the *Tarih* used to dock, looking back from there to see the massed houses of the city spreading out ever more widely from the ancient acropolis hill of Kadifekale, the Velvet Castle, known to the Greeks as Mount Pagus.

The Hellenistic city of Smyrna clustered around Mount Pagus, a flat-topped hill that rises up from the eastern end of the gulf and is surmounted by the ruined walls of its ancient citadel. However, the original site of ancient Smyrna lay in the north-eastern corner of the gulf, and its ruins today are covered by the seaside suburb of Bayraklı. Archaeological excavations were begun in the years 1948–51 at a site in Bayraklí called Tepekule, the project being directed by John Cook and Ekrem Akurgal. These excavations have unearthed what remains of the original city of Smyrna, and so on our most recent visit to Izmir we drove out to the archaeological site at Bayraklı, which had eluded us on our earlier journeys.

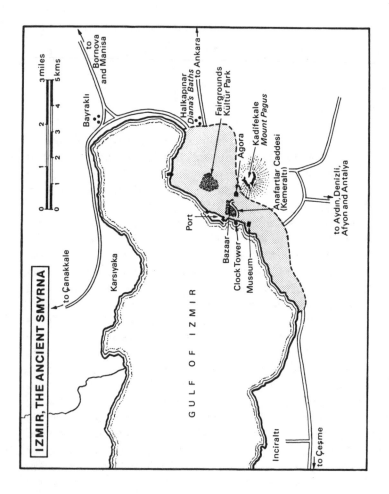

IZMIR, THE ANCIENT SMYRNA

GULF OF IZMIR

to Çanakkale

Karşıyaka

Bayraklı

to Bornova
and Manisa

Halkapınar
Diana's Baths

to Ankara

Fairgrounds
Kültür Park

Agora

Kadifekale
Mount Pagus

Port

Bazaar
Clock Tower
Museum

Anafartalar Caddesi
(Kemeraltı)

to Aydın, Denizli,
Afyon and Antalya

İnciraltı

to Çeşme

0   1   2   3 miles
0   1   2   3   4   5 kms

The excavations at Bayraklı indicate that the site was inhabited as early as the first half of the third millennium BC, the oldest strata of the settlement being contemporary with Troy I and II. Virtually nothing is known of the pre-Hellenic inhabitants of Smyrna, except that they may have been the indigenous Anatolian people whom the Greeks called Lelegians. It is even possible that Smyrna was controlled by the Hittites during the late Bronze Age, as evidenced by the Hittite carvings found on Mount Sipylos and elsewhere in the hinterland of the Gulf of Izmir. In any event, Smyrna was settled by Hellenic people at the beginning of the first millennium BC, as revealed by the large quantities of proto-geometric pottery of that period found in the dig at Bayraklı. The excavations also unearthed houses dating from the ninth to the seventh century BC, as well as an Archaic Temple of Athena, which Professor Akurgal describes as 'the earliest and finest building of the eastern Greek world in Asia Minor'. These structures would have been erected by the Ionian Greeks who, as Herodotus reported in Book I of his *Histories*, had by that time taken control of Smyrna from the Aeolians.

About 665 BC King Gyges of Lydia invaded the territory of the Ionians, putting Smyrna under siege, but the townspeople fought off the invaders. The Lydians returned in 600 BC, however, when King Alyattes invaded Ionia and took Smyrna, destroying the city and driving the survivors out into the countryside, a number of them taking refuge in Clazomenae. During the two decades that followed some of the Smyrnaeans returned to the ruined city and rebuilt their houses there. The excavations at Bayraklı indicate that by 500 BC they had restored the Temple of Athena. But the Archaic town of Smyrna never recovered its former stature, and during the classical period it was little more than a collection of villages, abandoned altogether when the new city was built on Mount Pagus at the beginning of the Hellenistic period.

The founding of the new city of Smyrna was attributed in later times by a number of ancient writers, including

Pausanius, to Alexander the Great. According to Pausanius, Alexander was out hunting on Mount Pagus when he fell asleep under a plane tree by a spring sacred to the Vengeances. The goddesses appeared to him in a dream and commanded him to build a new city on the site and to resettle the Smyrnaeans there. When his dream was reported to the Smyrnaeans they sent a delegation to the oracle at Claros, who responded that 'You shall live three and four times happy/at Pagus, across the sacred Meles'. So, according to the legend, they moved to the new site and rebuilt.

Alexander may have made a brief visit to Smyrna in the spring of 334 BC, perhaps on his way from Sardis to Ephesus. But even if Alexander did decide to rebuild Smyrna then, there was no time for him to do so on his rapid campaign, and the plan only materialized after his death when it was carried out by his successors. The foundation of the new city on Mount Pagus may have been begun by Antigonus shortly after his reign ended in 301 BC, but the project was completed by Lysimachus, probably after his conquest of Ephesus in 295 BC. The climax of this resettlement came in 288 BC, when Smyrna was made the thirteenth member of the newly revived Panionic League, a confederation of the Ionian cities originally founded early in the Archaic period. This was an honour that had been denied the city in earlier times.

Smyrna grew and flourished during the first few centuries after its refoundation on the slopes of Mount Pagus. Its population grew to more than 100,000, surpassed in Ionia only by Ephesus. During that time numerous public buildings were erected in the city by successive Hellenistic kings and Roman emperors, and these splendid monuments, set off by the natural beauty of the city's position, elicited fulsome praise from writers throughout antiquity. Strabo called it 'the most beautiful city in Ionia.'

The most detailed description of the Graeco-Roman city on the slopes of Mount Pagus is that given by the sophist and orator Aristeides Aeolis, who was born in Mysia in AD 117 and lived for much of his life in Smyrna. One of the edifices mentioned by Aristeides was a temple known as 'Dionysus Before the City', which is believed to have been on a hill near the southern gate, from where a road led to Ephesus. The earliest reference to this temple occurs in 244 BC, in connection with an attack on Smyrna by a fleet from Chios. On that day all the Smyrnaeans had gone to celebrate a *panegyri* at the sanctuary of Dionysus outside the walls, when some of them spotted the Chian ships sailing up the gulf towards their deserted city. The alarm was given, the Smyrnaeans interrupted the festival, rushed down to the shore to fight the Chians, and managed to defeat them and capture their warships. Triumphantly they returned to the sanctuary of Dionysus to continue the *panegyri*, renewing their celebration with the added joy of their victory. For centuries afterwards at the annual festival of Dionysus the men of Smyrna carried aloft one of the Chian triremes from the sea to the wine-god's sanctuary outside the walls, the high priest of the cult acting as the symbolic helmsman.

Another sanctuary in Smyrna mentioned by Aristeides and other ancient writers was the Homerion, a heroon dedicated to Homer. There was a strong tradition among ancient writers that Homer was born in Smyrna, by the banks of the River Meles, though later he dwelt in other places, most notably Chios. Pausanius writes that 'Smyrna has the river Meles with the finest water, and a cave with a spring where they say Homer wrote his poetry'. Aristeides gives a description of the Meles which has led a number of scholars to identify the Homeric river with the Halkapınar Suyu, a stream that rises in a spring now within the grounds of the Izmir water-supply station. The spring-fed source of the Halkapınar Suyu is now known locally as 'Diana's Baths', because of the discovery there of a statue of Artemis, the Roman Diana. We visited Diana's Baths after seeing Bayraklı, and were pleasantly surprised to find the source of the Meles is now a pretty, tree-shaded pool, with several Ionic column bases and other architectural fragments still visible beneath the water, perhaps the remnants of a sanctuary of Artemis. An inscription found in the spring is now in the nearby Burnabat Camii; this is believed to refer to a plague that took hold of the city in AD 165–8 during the reign of Marcus Aurelius. The fresh waters and curative powers of the river seem to have been credited with saving the city from the epidemic; as the inscription reads: 'I sing the praises of the Meles, my saviour, now that every plague and evil has ceased'.

We drove up to the top of Mount Pagus, from where one can see the whole of Izmir as well as the eastern end of the gulf and its shores. The summit is still to a large extent surrounded by the walls and towers of its medieval fortress, the Velvet Castle, still formidable-looking even though in ruins. The fortress was the focal point of the city's defences, with two lines of massive walls leading down from the citadel in great circular arcs to the shore. They enclose an area that is now the centre of modern Izmir, with the north-eastern gate leading to Aeolis and Sardis and the southern portal to Ephesus and the other cities of Ionia. The lower defence walls have vanished, and all that now remains is the citadel on Mount Pagus. Even there, only the foundations and perhaps a few of the lower courses of the walls date from the time of Lysimachus. The remainder of the fortress results from successive reconstructions by the Romans, Byzantines, and Ottoman Turks.

Hellenistic Smyrna existed as an independent city from the time of its foundation by Lysimachus in 288 BC until 129 BC, when it was included in the Roman Province of Asia. Then in 27 BC it became part of a new Roman political entity known as the League of Asia, governed by a proconsul sent annually from Rome. Smyrna enjoyed centuries of peace and progress under the mantle of the *pax Romana*, but in AD 178 the city was destroyed by the worst earthquake in its history. Aristeides had left Smyrna a few days before the earthquake, by divine guidance he said, and when he learned of the catastrophe he immediately wrote to Marcus Aurelius. The emperor wept

when he read the letter, giving orders for the work of reconstruction to begin at once, and within three years Smyrna
had been fully restored. Its citizens showed their gratitude by
erecting statues of Marcus Aurelius and Aristeides in the rebuilt
theatre.

By then there were already a substantial number of Christians living in Smyrna, the community having gathered by
the time of St. Paul's visits in the years AD 53–6. Smyrna was
one of the Seven Churches of Revelation, and its Christian
community received this apocalyptic message from St. John
the Evangelist:

> I know thy works and tribulation, and poverty, (but thou art rich)
> and I know the blasphemy of them which say they are Jews, and
> are not, but are the Smyrna synagogue of Satan. Fear none of
> those things which thou shalt suffer: behold, the devil shall cast
> some of you into prison, that ye may be tried; and ye shall have
> tribulation ten days: be thou faithful unto death, and I will give
> thee a crown of life. He that hath an ear, let him hear what the
> Spirit saith unto the churches; He that overcometh shall not be
> hurt by the second death.

The first bishop of Smyrna was St. Polycarp, who was said to
have been appointed by St. John the Apostle in the last years
of the first century AD. Bishop Eirenaios, writing c. AD 190,
remembered Polycarp well from the days of his youth in
Smyrna, reminiscing of 'how he had told about his association
with John and the rest who had seen the Lord: and as he
remembered their words, and what he had heard from them
about the Lord and about His deeds and power and about His
teachings, Polycarp used to narrate everything in conformity
with the Scriptures—as one who had received the story from
the eyewitnesses of the life of the world'. Polycarp served as
Bishop of Smyrna for more than half a century, leading the
growing Christian community there until 22 February 153,
when he suffered martyrdom for his faith, burned at the stake
in the stadium of Smyrna on orders of the Roman proconsul,
L. Statius Quadratus.

Despite further persecutions, the Christian community in Smyrna continued to grow in numbers throughout the late Roman era, and when the emperor Constantine convoked the first ecumenical council of the church at Nicaea in the year 325 the Smyrnaeans were represented by their bishop. In the ninth century Smyrna was elevated to the rank of a metropolis in the Greek Orthodox Church, a rank that it was to retain throughout the Byzantine and Ottoman Empires though it changed hands repeatedly and often bloodily.

The lower city of Smyrna was overrun during the first Arab invasion of Asia Minor in 654, but the citadel on Mount Pagus held out until this phase of the Holy War in Anatolia ended the following year. The lower town was again taken by the Arabs in their second invasion in 674–8, but once again the fortress on Mount Pagus held out until the invaders retreated eastward. Muslim armies continued to penetrate deeply into western Anatolia almost annually throughout the remainder of the eighth century. In 1078 the fortress on Mount Pagus fell at last to the Selcuks under Prince Süleyman, and remained in Turkish hands until it was recaptured by the Byzantines in 1097, at the beginning of the First Crusade. Then in 1261 the emperor Michael VIII Palaeologus entered into an alliance with Genoa, formalized in the Treaty of Nymphaeum, whereby he granted the Italians extensive concessions in the empire, including full control of Smyrna, 'a city fit for commercial use, having a good port and abounding in all goods'. The Genoese retained Smyrna until c. 1320, when it was taken from them by Umur Bey, the emir of Aydın, a Turkoman *beylik* in western Asia Minor. Pope Clement VI then appointed Martino Zaccaria captain of a flotilla of four papal galleys which in December 1344 succeeded in recapturing it once more. But on 17 January of the following year, when the Latin archbishop was celebrating a thanksgiving mass in the cathedral, a group of armed Turks broke in and captured Zaccaria, bringing his severed head back to Umur Bey as a trophy of revenge. Smyrna later passed to the Crusaders and became a fief of the Knights of St. John, whose centre of operations was the island of Rhodes. They held the city until 1403, when Tamerlane captured it after a two-week siege, putting the survivors to the sword and constructing his usual pyramid of skulls as a warning to others who might oppose him. Shortly afterwards Tamerlane returned to the East, leaving Smyrna to the emir of Aydın once again, but now a rival chieftain named Cünayet rebelled and captured the city along with a considerable territory in the hinterland. Smyrna remained in Cünayet's control until 1415, when the city was captured by the Ottoman Turks under Sultan Mehmet I. The Turks managed to make it a permanent part of their empire, defeating an attempt by the Venetians to take it from them in 1473.

When Sultan Mehmet I took Smyrna it was in ruins and virtually abandoned, but the rise of the Ottoman Empire revived the city's fortunes, and soon it became Turkey's most important port after Istanbul. During the reign of Süleyman the Magnificent (1520–66) the Turks began granting commercial concessions to European powers in order to develop their foreign trade, a policy that continued throughout the rest of Ottoman history. Sultan Murat III (1574–95) wrote to Queen Elizabeth I in encouragement of this trade, assuring her that he had issued a firman, or directive, to safeguard any of her representatives 'as shall resort hither by sea from the realm of England', who 'may lawfully come to our imperial dominions, and surely return home again, and no man shall dare to molest or trouble them'. The sultan also informed Queen Elizabeth that the English would have the same commercial privileges as 'our familiars and confederates, the French, Venetians, Polonians, and the King of Germany, with divers other neighbours about us', and that they would have the right to 'use and trade all kinds of merchandise as any other Christians, without let or disturbance of any'. This led to the incorporation of a group of English merchant-adventurers called the Levant Company, also known as the 'Company of Turkey Merchants', who in September 1581 were given a seven-year charter by the sultan which enabled them to set up trading stations in Smyrna and Istanbul. The principal products exported from Turkey by the English and other foreign merchants in Smyrna were figs, currants, carpets, and coffee, which was introduced to Europe for the first time through this trade. Thus Smyrna and its surrounding countryside became very prosperous. Richard Chandler observed when he first visited the city in 1764: 'Smyrna continues a large and flourishing city. The bay, besides numerous small-craft, is daily frequented by ships of burden from the chief ports in Europe; and the factors, who are a respectable body, at once live in affluence and acquire fortunes'.

The renewed prosperity of Smyrna also attracted Greeks from the nearby Aegean isles who once again began to settle along the western coast of Asia Minor. Other numerous minorities in Smyrna were the Armenians and Sephardic Jews, the latter having come to Turkey in large numbers in 1492 when Sultan Beyazit II invited them to the Ottoman Empire after they had been forced to leave Spain by Ferdinand and Isabella. Thus the city, which the Turks referred to as Giaour Izmir, Infidel Smyrna, became the most cosmopolitan centre in the eastern Mediterranean, the archetypal Levantine town. Chandler wrote:

> The conflux at Smyrna of people of various nations, differing in dress, in manners, in language, and in religion, is very considerable. The Turks occupy by far the greater part of the town. The other tribes live in separate quarters. The protestants and Roman catholics have their chapels, the Jews a synagogue or two, the Armenians a large and handsome church, with a burying-ground by it. The Greeks before the fire had two churches.... The factors, and other Europeans settled at Smyrna, generally intermarry with the Greeks, or even with natives of the same religion.

Greeks continued to settle along the Aegean coast of Asia Minor in increasing numbers during the latter years of the Ottoman Empire, and their numbers were relatively higher still in towns like Phocaea and Ayvalik. The predominance of the Greek population in this region led Greece to seek the annexation of Smyrna and its hinterland immediately after the First World War. Greek troops landed in Smyrna on 15 May 1919, and on 10 August 1920 the Treaty of Sèvres empowered Greece to occupy and administer Smyrna and the Ionian hinterland for a period of five years. The Greek claim to western Asia Minor was opposed by the new Turkish Nationalist movement led by Mustafa Kemal, later to be known as Atatürk. The Nationalist Turks defeated Greece in the ensuing war in Asia Minor in 1919–22, after which the Greek army was forced to evacuate its forces from Anatolia. The Turkish army triumphantly entered Smyrna on 9 September 1922, and four days later, after widespread riots, the city was destroyed by a great fire, leaving an estimated 50,000 Greeks and Armenians dead. Most of the surviving Christian population then fled Smyrna and the surrounding region, and in 1923 the remaining Greek population of Anatolia was deported in the exchange of minorities between Greece and Turkey agreed at the Treaty of Lausanne that ended the Graeco-Turkish War.

Izmir, as the city now came to be called, revived quickly after the great fire, repopulated largely by Turkish refugees from Greece and by Anatolians from villages in the interior of Asia Minor that had been destroyed during the war. In the years since then Izmir has been almost entirely rebuilt and is now a flourishing city. Only the old Turkish and Jewish quarters survive from the Levantine town of Ottoman times, and just a few fragmentary ruins remain from the Hellenistic city that was built after Alexander's dream.

The principal archaeological site surviving from Hellenistic Smyrna is the agora, which is midway between Kadifekale and the port. The present agora was originally constructed in the middle of the second century AD, destroyed by the earthquake of AD 178, and shortly afterwards restored by Faustina II, wife of Marcus Aurelius. What remains are the north and west colonnades on the courtyard level and a splendid vaulted basement on the north side. At the north-west corner of the site a small enclosure shelters two splendid sculptures in high relief, identified as Poseidon and Demeter. These reliefs were reconstructed from fragments found during excavations carried out in the years 1932–41, and are believed to have been part of a group of deities which adorned an altar to Zeus in the centre of the agora. The sculptured group here symbolizes Smyrna's two main sources of wealth: Demeter, goddess of the harvest, represents the riches of the earth, while Poseidon, god of the sea, stands for the maritime commerce that enriched the Hellenistic city. It is fascinating to think that this was the market-place of the city two thousand years ago, just a few hundred yards away from the Bazaar, the principal market area of modern Izmir.

Most of the remaining antiquities in Izmir are housed in the archaeological museum, which is presently located in Kültür Park, also known as the Izmir Fairgrounds, although it will soon be moved into a new and grander building south of Konak Meydanı. The museum has on display many of the finds made in archaeological excavations along the Aegean coast of Asia Minor in recent years, and in Smyrna itself, which is represented by a number of architectural fragments from the Archaic Temple of Athena at Bayraklı.

There are a number of other places of interest to see in Kültür Park; these include the Gallery of Painting and Sculpture, in which both Turkish and foreign artists are represented, and the Museum of Turkish Works of Art, which has changing exhibitions from the Izmir Archaeological Museum, the Ankara Ethnographical Museum and the Topkapı Sarayı Museum in Istanbul. There are also a number of outdoor theatres, where in summer there are productions of western and Turkish drama and Anatolian folk-dances. The park is in addition the site of the Izmir International Fair, a commercial exhibition held annually from 20 August until 20 September which attracts about two million visitors each year from all over the world. But even at other seasons of the year there is a general air of festivity about the Kültür Park, with outdoor cafes and restaurants around its artificial lake and within its gardens.

A boulevard leads from the south-eastern gate of the Kültür Park to Cumhuriyet Meydanı, Izmir's main seaside square, dominated by an equestrian statue of Atatürk, the father of modern Turkey. Izmir's port begins just to the left of Cumhuriyet Meydanı as one approaches the sea, extending eastward for about half a mile. The waterfront promenade continues eastward as far as Konak Meydanı, from whose pier ferries leave for the maritime suburbs around the eastern end of the Gulf of Izmir. There are outdoor cafes on the seafront where one can sit and watch the ferries and other shipping criss-crossing the eastern end of the gulf which has served as the city's harbour for more than twenty-three centuries.

The principal landmark on the Izmir waterfront is the Clock Tower on Konak Meydanı, a Moorish structure dating from 1901. Directly across the square from this stands Konak Camii, a pretty little octagonal mosque revetted in tiles, dating from 1754. The main avenue leading into the city from the Clock Tower and Konak Camii is Anafartlar Caddesi, which is better known under its old name of Kemeraltı, Under the Arches. Kemeraltı leads to the old Turkish quarter of Levantine Smyrna, as one can see from the number of minarets projecting from the crowded confines of that ancient neighbourhood. The oldest of these mosques are Hisar Camii (1598), Şadirvanaltı Camii (1636–7), Başdurak Camii (1652, restored in 1774), Kestane Pazarı Camii (mid-seventeenth century), Ali Ağa Camii (1671–2), and Haci Mehmet Ağa Camii (1672). This last mosque is also known as Kemeraltı Camii, giving its name to the main street whose most colourful stretch begins literally under the arches of its arcaded courtyard. Here one enters the Bazaar, the largest and most picturesque market-place in all of Anatolian Turkey, extending almost the entire length of Kemeraltı. From Kemeraltı Camii onwards the street is lined with shops selling every conceivable kind of produce and merchandise. Goods are also peddled from curbside barrows and by itinerant pedlars and hucksters, who add their strident cries to the clamour of the passing throng.

The oldest part of the Bazaar is at the western end of Kemeraltı, around Hisar Camii, the Mosque of the Castle. In the narrow, winding streets that lead off from the square in front of Hisar Camii one finds the oldest and most fascinating Ottoman structures in Izmir, the *hans*, huge labyrinthine structures that originally served as caravanserais and market buildings. The finest of these is the Kızlarağası Hanı, built in the second quarter of the eighteenth century by Beşir Ağa, who was chief black eunuch in Topkapı Sarayı during the reign of Sultan Mahmut I.

The old Jewish quarter is to be found at the western end of Kemeraltı, and here the gold merchants have their shops. The gold merchants and most of their neighbours are Sephardic Jews whose first language is Ladino, the medieval Spanish that their ancestors spoke when they first came to Smyrna in 1492. On one of our visits to Izmir we became acquainted with a gold merchant on this street, Jacob Benveniste, and through him we tracked down the local origins of Shabbetai Zevi, the False Messiah. This contact gave us a brief glimpse into the vanished world of Levantine Smyrna.

Shabbetai Zevi was born in Smyrna in 1626, but the local rabbis banned him from the community *c.* 1651 because of his bizarre behaviour and unorthodox religious ideas. He then wandered all over the Middle East, attracting a growing number of followers, and on 31 May 1665 in Gaza proclaimed that he was the long-awaited Messiah. News of this swept through the Jewish communities in Gaza and Jerusalem and everyone flocked to hear Shabbetai, who early in September of that year made a triumphal return to Smyrna to spread the news in his home town. There followed a dramatic confrontation with the orthodox rabbis in the local synagogue, in which Shabbetai made an extraordinary speech filled with Kabbalistic references and dramatic descriptions of his apocalyptic visions. Next he took a sacred scroll in his arms and began to sing his favourite love-song, a medieval Castilian *cantada* about 'Meliselda, the Emperor's beautiful daughter'. Then Shabbetai formally announced that he was the Messiah foretold of old, 'anointed of the God of Jacob' and redeemer of Israel, giving the date of the redemption as the fifteenth day of Sivan 5426, or 18 June 1666, just six months hence. By that time a great crowd had collected in and around the synagogue, and when they heard that Shabbetai had revealed himself as the Messiah they became delirious with joy, the news spreading quickly throughout the Jewish world of the Middle East and Europe. But by the time of the supposed redemption Shabbetai was a prisoner in the Castle of Gallipoli. Soon afterwards he renounced his mission and became a Muslim, and many of his followers joined him in his apostasy to create the cryptic sect of the Dönme, or Turncoats.

When we first met Jacob Benveniste in his gold shop we talked about Shabbetai Zevi, and he told me there were still a few Dönme living in the Jewish quarter of Izmir. They were mostly old and uneducated people who lived in total isolation from those around them, shunned by both Orthodox Jews and Muslim Turks. He also told us that they worshipped in an old house which they believed to be Shabbetai's birthplace, just down the street from the synagogue in which he had pro- claimed that he was the Messiah. We were of course very interested in seeing the house and the synagogue, so Jacob sent his young clerk Marco to show us the way, wishing us good luck in our quest as we left his shop.

Marco led us down a side street off Kemeraltı and then along a narrow alleyway ending in a wooden fence. When we reached the fence Marco pulled aside a few loose boards and motioned for us to make our way through. We found ourselves in the courtyard of a huge old Ottoman *han*, whose arcaded porticos had been converted into a slum tenement of ram- shackle wooden buildings. The courtyard and its surrounding shacks were crowded with very poorly dressed people who looked more Spanish than Turkish, and when I heard them speaking Ladino I realized that we were in the heart of the old Jewish quarter. Marco led us through the courtyard and into a labyrinth of narrow cobbled streets beyond, bringing us to a venerable building in the Byzantine style which he said was the birthplace of Shabbetai Zevi. We followed him up several flights of stairs to the top floor, and there we found a number of old people kneeling in front of a niche carved into the crumbling stone wall, all of them murmuring prayers in Ladino. Marco whispered that these were Dönme, praying to their Messiah, and we watched them in silence for a while before departing, none of them aware that we had entered or left the room.

We followed Marco again as he led us farther down the street to an ancient domed building preceded by a courtyard paved in large flagstones rutted with the marks of wagon-wheels. This was the old Portuguese synagogue, Marco said, and he led us inside and introduced us to the rabbi, a Biblical figure who greeted us in Ladino and then resumed his prayers, leaving us free to look around. As we did so I let my mind wander and tried to evoke the scene here on that extraordinary day in mid-December 1665, when Shabbetai proclaimed to the world that he was the Messiah, the news passing to the crowd outside and thence to Jerusalem and Cairo and Constantinople, through the Balkans, and on into Central Europe. Multitudes of long-suffering Jews received the word with ecstatic happiness, believing that the day of their redemption was finally at hand. In the late afternoon shadows within the synagogue I thought of Shabbetai embracing the sacred scrolls and singing of 'Meliselda, the Emperor's beautiful daughter'. Then I remembered the occasion when, years before, I had heard the echoes of that medieval Castilian love-song in the Castle of Gallipoli, where he had been imprisoned before he could redeem those who awaited him. And now I wonder whether those who believed in Shabbetai await him still, praying to their lost Messiah in his birthplace in the old Jewish quarter of Izmir.

8

ANCIENT LYDIA: THE HERMUS VALLEY AND SARDIS

Izmir is the best base from which to explore the lower valley of the Gediz Çayı, the River Hermus of antiquity. The western end of the Hermus valley once formed the borderland between Aeolis and Ionia, leading from the Aegean coast into the ancient kingdom of Lydia, whose capital was at Sardis. Now one can drive from Izmir to Sardis and return on a day-trip, and many of those exploring the western shores of Turkey do this, usually by taxi or rented car, or, as we did in years past, by bus or *dolmuş*. But with the luxury of our own car we decided to make the trip in a more leisurely manner, allowing a day each for the ride up the Hermus and back and a full day on the archaeological site at Sardis.

We decided to drive to Sardis via Manisa, for there are many points of interest along that route. The road from Izmir to Manisa heads inland from the eastern end of the gulf, passing through the town of Bornova. Bornova was once the suburban residence for most of the British community in Ottoman Smyrna, which largely developed from the trading station that the Levant Company established on the Smyrnaic Gulf after it obtained its charter from Sultan Murat in 1581. The Anglican church of this community still functions in Bornova, a survival from Elizabethan England in distant Turkey.

After passing through Bornova, the road ascends to the Sabuncu Pass between Yamanlar Dağı and Mount Sipylos, whose summit towers just to the east of the road at an altitude

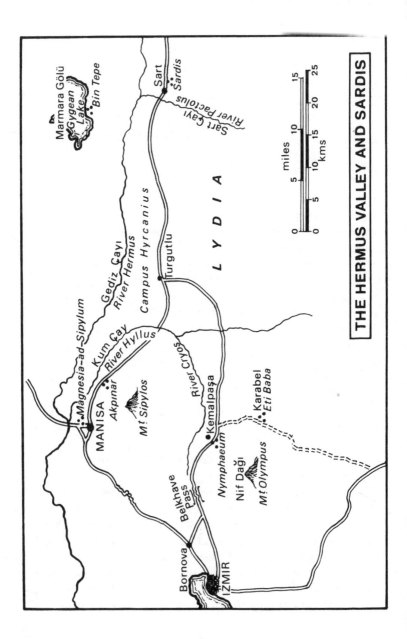

THE HERMUS VALLEY AND SARDIS

of 4,900 feet. Then the road curves around the northern slope of Mount Sipylos and down into the valley of the Hermus, where one comes to the large town of Manisa, standing near the confluence of the Gediz Çayı and the Kum Çay, the ancient River Hyllus.

Manisa takes its name from the ancient city of Magnesia-ad-Sipylum, the addendum distinguishing it from Magnesia-ad-Maeandrum in the valley of the Maeander to the south. According to tradition, both these cities were founded by settlers from Magnesia in north-eastern Greece, Magnetes, who migrated to north-western Asia Minor after fighting in Agamemnon's army at the siege of Troy. Magnesia-ad-Sipylum became Manisa to the Turks, who attacked the city from c. 1275 until the citadel finally fell to the Saruhan tribe of Turkomans in 1313. Manisa served as capital of the Saruhan *beylik* until 1390, when the city was captured by Beyazit I on one of his lightning campaigns. The Ottomans lost Manisa temporarily after Beyazit's defeat by Tamerlane at the Battle of Ankara in 1403, after which the city reverted to the Saruhan emirs until 1415, when it was recaptured by Sultan Mehmet I. Thereafter it became one of the most important provincial capitals in Anatolia, and several of the royal Ottoman princes served there in turn as governor before succeeding to the throne, including the future sultan Mehmet II, the conqueror of Constantinople. As a result, the Ottoman royal family endowed Manisa with a number of fine mosques and other buildings, in addition to those erected earlier by the Saruhan emirs.

The oldest Islamic structure in Manisa is Ilyas Bey Mescidi, a small mosque built in 1363 by one of the Saruhan emirs. A much larger edifice was erected three years later by Isak Bey, the eldest son and successor of Ilyas Bey; this is Ulu Camii—the Great Mosque—which is built on the site of an early Byzantine church, perhaps the original Cathedral of Magnesia-ad-Sipylum. The oldest Ottoman mosque in Manisa is Hatuniye Camii, which was founded in 1490 by Hüsnü Şah Hatun, a wife of Sultan Beyazit II. Another mosque in Manisa built by a member of the Ottoman royal family is Sultan Camii, erected in 1572 by Ayşe Hafize Sultan, a wife of Sultan Selim II, whose pious foundation also included a *medrese*, or theological school, and a *timarhane*, an institution that served as both hospital and lunatic asylum.

Just to the south of Sultan Camii is the Muradiye, the most splendid of all the mosques in Manisa; this was built in 1583–6 for Murat III, who had served here as provincial governor before becoming sultan in 1574. The mosque was designed by Sinan, the greatest of all Ottoman architects, and the actual construction was carried out by one of his assistants, Mehmet Ağa, who later designed and erected the famous Blue Mosque in Istanbul for Sultan Ahmet I. Mehmet Ağa also built the other structures in the pious foundation of the Muradiye, including a *medrese* and an *imaret*, or soup kitchen, which served the staff of the mosque and its associated institutions, and also gave free food twice a day to the paupers of the town. The *medrese* is now used to house the archaeological museum of Manisa, which exhibits antiquities found at various sites in Lydia, most notably at Sardis.

After leaving the Muradiye, we drove out of Manisa for a short way to examine a remarkable rock formation at the base of Mount Sipylos. The rock, which was discovered by H. T. Bossert only half a century ago, has been identified as the figure of 'weeping Niobe' mentioned by several ancient writers, including Homer, Sophocles, Ovid, and Pausanius. This figure is supposed to represent the mourning Niobe, wife of Amphion, king of Thebes, whose children were killed by Apollo and Artemis because of the jealousy of their mother Leto. According to one version of the myth, Mount Sipylos itself is named after one of Niobe's dead sons. Other rock formations, carvings, and topographical features on the mountain are associated with Niobe's father, the legendary King Tantalos of Phrygia, and her brother Pelops, after whom the Peloponnesus is named.

We now drove on towards Sardis, as the road took us over

1 The defence walls of Troy VI, perhaps part of the city described in Homer's *Iliad*

2 The Hellenistic theatre on the acropolis of ancient Pergamum, with the modern town of Bergama on the plain below

3 Izmir's Bazaar, one of the oldest market-places in Turkey

4 The Hellenistic Temple of Artemis at Sardis,
the ancient capital of Lydia

5 A coffee-house in the village of Geyre, built from the ruins
of ancient Aphrodisias

6 (right) A Roman basilica in
Ephesus, converted into the
Church of the Blessed Virgin
in the fourth century

7 (above) The Embolos, or Colonnaded Way, one of the main streets of ancient Ephesus

8 (below) A colonnade of the Roman agora at Aphrodisias

10 The classical Temple of Athena Polias at Priene, which bears the name of Alexander the Great among its founders

9 (left) The Roman odeion at Aphrodisias, with the Hellenistic Temple of Aphrodite in the background

11 The Graeco-Roman theatre at Miletus, looking down on the silted-up Theatre Harbour

12 The Hellenistic Temple of Apollo Branchidae at Didyma, site of one of
the most famous oracles in Asia Minor

the northern flank of Mount Sipylos. We stopped about four miles east of Manisa at a place called Akpınar, climbing up the hillside to the right of the road to find the relief known as Taş Süret, the Stone Figure. This carving is more than thirty feet high, and though it is badly eroded it is still possible to make out the shape of a female figure seated upon a throne. Scholars have for long suggested that the Taş Süret is a work of the Hittites, and a hieroglyphic inscription on the relief has just recently been identified as being in the Hittite language. The Taş Süret is undoubtedly the figure that Pausanius described as being 'the most ancient of all statues of the Mother of the Gods', the Hittite fertility goddess that the Phrygians later worshipped as Kubaba and the Greeks later still as Cybele and Artemis. This deity was known by different names; on Mount Ida in the Troad she was called the Idaean Mother, whereas here on Mount Sipylos she was the Sipylene Mother.

From the Taş Süret we continued along the valley of the Hermus. The great plain here, to the east of the confluence of the Hermus and Hyllus rivers, was known in antiquity as the Campus Hyrcanius. According to Strabo, the plain received this name during the Persian era, when settlers were brought here from Hyrcania, on the south-east shore of the Caspian Sea. The Battle of Magnesia took place out on the Hyrcanian plain one rainy day in January of the year 189 BC, when the Romans and their Pergamene allies defeated the forces of Antiochus III, ending forever Seleucid rule in Asia Minor.

At Turgutlu we joined the main Izmir–Ankara highway, which follows the same course as the ancient road that led in from the Aegean coast to central Anatolia, a thoroughfare that has been in use since the days of the Hittite Empire. During the Persian era this was a branch of the Royal Road, the main highway of which led from Ephesus to Sardis and thence to the imperial capital at Susa, in Iran. 'At intervals all along the road are recognized stations', Herodotus writes, 'with excellent inns, and the road itself is safe to travel by, as it never leaves inhabited country'.

Beyond Turgutlu the highway led us on eastward along the middle reaches of the Hermus valley, a region that Homer refers to in the *Iliad* as 'lovely Maeonia', known in later times as the Plain of Sardis. As we crossed the plain the eroded acropolis hill of Sardis came into view on the western ramparts of Boz Dağları, the Grey Mountains, the range known of old as Mount Tmolus. Then finally we crossed the Sart Çayı, once called the Pactolus, where we came to the village of Sart, the site of ancient Sardis.

There was no hotel in Sart, but we were able to rent a room in a village house, buying food for our meals in the local *bakkal*, or grocery shop. Then as soon as we were settled we set off to explore the archaeological site, walking south along the east bank of the Pactolus for about a thousand yards. This brought us to the ruins of the Temple of Artemis, the most renowned edifice surviving from the capital of ancient Lydia.

The region that later came to be known as Lydia had its centre in the Hermus valley south of the Gygean Lake, known today as Marmara Gölü, whose southern shore is less than four miles north of Sardis. This region is known as Bin Tepe, the Thousand Hills, where the kings of ancient Lydia are buried. Excavations in the Bin Tepe area have unearthed evidence of human occupation going back to *c.* 2500 BC, though the oldest settlement at Sardis itself seems to be no earlier than *c.* 1500 BC. Hittite tablets record that King Tudhaliyas IV (1250–1220 BC) led several campaigns in far western Anatolia against a nation called the Assuwa, who are believed to be the ancient Sardian tribe known as the Asias, after whom, according to Herodotus, the entire continent of Asia was named. These are the people whom Homer calls the Maeonians, who fought as allies of King Priam in the defence of Troy, coming from 'the Gygean Lake beneath Mount Tmolus'. Hittite archives of the same period also refer to a powerful seafaring people known as the Akhiyawa, now generally identified as the Achaeans, and indeed sherds of imported Mycenaean pottery of the thirteenth century BC found at Sardis indicate a possible Greek conquest of the Lydian capital at about the same time as the fall of Homeric Troy. Pottery sherds of a later date suggest that the Achaeans may have occupied the city throughout the period 1200–900 BC, and perhaps for two centuries after that. This would accord with Greek tradition, which holds that the first Hellenes to rule at Sardis were the Heraclidae, the sons of Heracles, who supplanted a dynasty that had originated before the Trojan War in the time of the Maeonians.

According to Herodotus, the Heraclidae ruled in Sardis from *c.* 1185 BC to 680 BC, when they were succeeded by the Mermnadae, descendants of a Lydian tribe of that name. The first of the Mermnadae was Gyges (*c.* 680–652 BC), who seized power from Candaules, the last of the Heraclidae. Under Gyges the Lydian kingdom began its rise to greatness, for he was apparently the first to exploit the gold that was washed down from Mount Tmolus by the Pactolus, minting it for the world's first coins. The invention of coinage further added to the already considerable wealth of the Lydians, allowing them to develop their widespread trade, which extended from central Anatolia to the Aegean coast and beyond into the eastern Mediterranean, all of it passing through Sardis, which became the richest city of its time. Lydia emerged as the dominant power in western Anatolia under Gyges, for by his time the Phrygian kingdom had been destroyed by the Cimmerian invasions. Gyges began his reign by attacking the Ionian cities, an aggressive policy that was followed by his successors: Ardys (651–625 BC), Sadyattes (625–619 BC), Alyattes (609–560 BC), and initially by Croesus (560–546 BC), the last of the Mermnadae, under whom the Lydian kingdom reached the pinnacle of its greatness, the golden age of Sardis.

Early on in his reign, however, Croesus abandoned the aggressive Lydian policy towards the Asian Greeks, and instead he entered into a treaty of peace and friendship with the Ionian cities. The terms agreed to by the Ionians were not harsh; they swore to pay an annual tribute to Croesus and to supply troops to his army when he was on campaign. Otherwise they were not occupied by Lydian garrisons nor did they have royal governors; indeed Miletus had complete freedom. Croesus was very generous to the Greeks; he sent fabulous treasures to the shrine of Apollo at Delphi, gave money to the Spartans, and helped Ephesus restore its Artemision. The Ionian cities shared in the extraordinary prosperity of Sardis during this period, an unprecedented economic boom in which the Asian Greeks acted as middle-men in the lucrative trade between the eastern Mediterranean world and the vast realm of Croesus.

However, when Lydia was at the height of its power and prosperity Croesus made the mistake of attacking King Cyrus of Persia, whose expanding kingdom he feared as a threat to his own empire. In the spring of 546 BC Croesus led his army across the River Halys to attack the forces of Cyrus and, after an indecisive battle, he withdrew to Sardis to spend the winter there, disbanding his mercenaries. But Cyrus was not content to wait out the winter, and in October he made a surprise attack and defeated the Lydians on the Sardian plain, besieged Sardis, and captured the citadel after a two-week siege. This was the end of the Lydian kingdom. Croesus ended his days a prisoner of Cyrus, as Herodotus eloquently tells in Book I of his *Histories*.

After his conquest of Lydia, Cyrus sent his generals to subjugate the Greek cities in Asia Minor, and the region was thenceforth ruled by a Persian satrap in Sardis. The Ionians rebelled against Persian rule in 499 BC, attacking Sardis and setting fire to the city. Within five years though the Persians put down the revolt, ending the campaign by defeating the Ionian fleet at the Battle of Lade in 494 BC. Thereafter western Asia Minor remained under Persian rule until 334 BC, when Alexander the Great conquered the subcontinent at the beginning of his campaign and occupied Sardis without a struggle shortly after his victory at the Battle of the Granicus. After Alexander's death Lydia became part of the Seleucid Empire; then, following the Battle of Magnesia, it was awarded to the kingdom of Pergamum, becoming part of the Roman Province of Asia in 129 BC. Sardis remained as prosperous under Roman rule as it had been under the Persians, when it had been the western terminus of the Royal Road. Along with the other cities of western Asia Minor, Sardis reached its peak under the Romans in the second century AD, when its population exceeded 100,000 as the city expanded out over the Sardian plain. During the reign of Diocletian (285–305), Sardis became capital of the Roman province of Lydia and seat of the proconsul, retaining that distinction up until the reorganization of Asia Minor in the medieval Byzantine era.

During the early Byzantine period Sardis developed as an important centre of Christianity, another of the Seven Churches of Revelation. As St. John the Evangelist wrote 'to the angel of the church in Sardis: He who holds the seven spirits of God and the seven stars speaks as follows: I know your deeds, that you have a name and that you live, and you are dead. For I have not found any of your works completed in the face of my God ...' It is believed that the Evangelist's words were addressed to St. Clement, who according to tradition was the first bishop of Sardis.

Sardis was still a considerable city during the early centuries of the Byzantine era, but in 616 it was totally destroyed by the Sassanid king Chosroes II and never fully recovered. From that time on it was reduced to the status of a provincial town, having lost forever its ancient splendour. During the medieval period Sardis and most other cities of Asia Minor almost disappeared from the pages of history, mentioned only by an occasional chronicler. Then in 1425 it became a permanent part of the Ottoman Empire, diminished to the status of a *kaza*, a mere local administrative centre in the province of Aydın. When Richard Chandler visited it in 1765 he reported that it had degenerated to a 'miserable village' surrounded by the wreckage of its illustrious past, its most conspicuous monument being the edifice now identified as the Temple of Artemis.

The first systematic excavation of this temple was carried

out in 1910–14 by H. C. Butler and the Princeton Expedition; this was followed over forty years later by the Harvard-Cornell Archaeological Exploration, a project initiated in 1958 by George M. A. Hanfmann and continuing to the present day. The early excavators assumed that they were unearthing the Temple of Cybele, mentioned by Herodotus and other ancient writers, but inscriptions soon indicated that it was actually dedicated to Artemis. The Harvard-Cornell archaeologists have since discovered a shrine and an altar of Cybele elsewhere in Sardis, and it appears that both goddesses were worshipped in the city. The original shrine of Artemis on this site was an altar to the goddess that may have been erected in the Archaic period (c. 680–480 BC), perhaps during the reign of the Mermnadae kings. Early in the third century BC, under the Seleucids, construction began on the first phase of an Ionic temple to Artemis incorporating this altar, which formed the western end of the sanctuary. During the second building phase, which took place c. 175–150 BC, work was begun on the erection of a peristasis, or outer colonnade, with eight columns along each of the ends and twenty on each side, counting corner columns twice. This colonnade and other additions and changes were completed in the third building phase, which was carried out in the mid-second century AD, during the reign of Antoninus Pius (138–61). During this final phase the cella was divided into two halves by an internal cross-wall, with the western half still sacred to Artemis, but the eastern half now dedicated to the late empress Faustina, who was deified after her death in AD 141. The Harvard-Cornell expedition has now cleared the temple and its immediate vicinity, establishing the plan of the edifice and the various stages of its construction; a number of column drums in the colonnade have been re-erected, and two of the columns now stand to their full height, capped with their superb Ionic capitals. They make a marvellous sight when viewed against the background of the ancient acropolis hill on its spur of Mount Tmolus.

After visiting the temple we walked eastward to ascend the

acropolis hill, on which stand the ruins of the citadel of ancient Sardis. The ascent to the acropolis is somewhat perilous at times, and as we inched our way up the narrow path on the final approach to the citadel I was reminded of Herodotus' description of the conquest of Sardis in 546 BC, when he says that the final Persian assault was made on 'a section of the central stronghold so precipitous as to be almost inaccessible'. We finally made our way to the summit, where we commanded a panoramic view of Sardis and the surrounding countryside. The ruins on the acropolis hill include the remnants of a palace of the Archaic period, undoubtedly the imperial residence of the Mermnadae dynasty, beginning with Gyges and continuing down to the reign of Croesus.

After spending an hour exploring the ruins on the acropolis, we made our way back toward the village of Sart, passing the Temple of Artemis and walking along the east bank of the Pactolus. As we approached Sart we passed through the archaeological zone known as Pactolus North, where excavations have unearthed the site of the Lydian gold-refinery, dated to the reign of Croesus. An altar of Cybele, found on this site, is believed to have been an integral part of the gold-refinery. The dedication of a shrine to Cybele here may be a testimony to her role as a mountain goddess, the protectress of the Lydian gold sources on Mount Tmolus, washed down to the Sardian plain by the Pactolus. This ancient gold-refinery and its shrine of Cybele reminded me of a poem written in the late seventh century BC by Alcman, who may have been born here in Sardis, though he later moved to Sparta:

Ancient Sardis, abode of my fathers, had I been reared in you I should have been a maund-bearer unto Cybele or beaten pretty tambours as one of her gilded eunuchs; but instead my name is Alcman and my home Sparta, town of prize-tripods, and the lore I know is of the Muses of Helicon, who have made me a greater king even than Gyges, son of Dascylus.

A major undertaking of the Harvard-Cornell archaeological programme has been to explore the area just to the east of

Sart, particularly on the north side of the highway after it leads out of the village. There an enormous Roman civic centre has been excavated. This was erected following a catastrophic earthquake in A D 17, the building project and numerous reconstructions continuing throughout the remainder of the Roman period and on into the early centuries of the Byzantine era. The eastern half of the complex was designed as a great gymnasium, while the western half consisted of its associated baths and athletic facilities. The central core of this complex, the Marble Court, is now in the process of reconstruction, with its monumental two-storeyed arcade gracing the eastern propylon of the courtyard, where one passed from the palaestra, or exercise yard, into the bathing establishment. Most of the eastern half of the gymnasium is taken up by the palaestra, the huge area of which is surrounded by a colonnade, now also in the process of reconstruction, together with a long suite of three rooms at its southern end apparently used originally as a series of dressing-chambers or lecture-halls. The southern side of the gymnasium was converted in early Byzantine times into a row of vaulted shops, facing a similar arcade on the other side of the avenue which comprised the westernmost stretch of the Royal Road between Susa and Sardis. The quarter of the ancient city south of the highway here is known as the Lydian Market Area, since this appears to have been the agora, or market-place, of Sardis. The major structure unearthed in this area is called the House of Bronzes, from the large number of bronze objects found here, some of them dating to the early Byzantine era.

One of the most interesting discoveries made by the Harvard-Cornell team is the ancient Sardis synagogue, which in late Roman times occupied the long apsidal area in the gymnasium just south of the palaestra and adjoining the main highway. This is the largest ancient synagogue known, and its size and grandeur are a testimony to the prosperity of the Jews in Sardis during Roman times and to their eminent position in the city. Construction of the synagogue seems to date to the years

AD 220–50, with renovations as late as the fourth or fifth century A D. Evidence of a much older synagogue in Sardis is given by the Jewish historian Josephus, who quotes decrees of Julius Caesar and Augustus guaranteeing the Jews of Sardis the right, which they had apparently long held, of meeting in worship together in their own congregation.

By the time we finished our exploration of the synagogue and the other ruins east of Sart the sun had set, and so we returned to our room in the village, having a simple supper there and then retiring for the night. The next morning we took one last look at the site of ancient Sardis and then set out to explore Bin Tepe, the Thousand Hills, making a detour there on our way back to Izmir.

We drove along the highway towards Izmir for about three and a half miles and then turned right on to a dirt road leading to Marmara Gölü, known in antiquity as the Gygean Lake. As we approached Marmara Gölü we turned right on to another dirt road that led into the heart of the Bin Tepe area, where we could now see some of the hundred or so conical tumuli that rise up from the landscape just south of the lake, the burial mounds of the kings and nobles of ancient Lydia. The three most prominent of these mounds have been identified as the tombs of Alyattes, Gyges, and Ardys, three of the five kings of the Mermnadae dynasty. The largest and easternmost of these is the tomb of Alyattes, which is 377 feet in diameter and 226 feet high, with the king's burial chamber, looted in antiquity, located near the centre of the mound at ground level. Herodotus considered this tumulus to be 'the greatest work of human hands in the world, apart from the Egyptian and the Babylonian'. After describing the construction of the tumulus, Herodotus writes that 'It was raised by the joint labour of the tradesmen, craftsmen, and prostitutes, and on top of it there survived to my own day five stone pillars with inscriptions cut in them to show the amount of work done by each class. Calculation revealed that the prostitutes' share was the largest. Working girls in Lydia prostitute themselves without exception to collect money for their dowries, and continue the practice until they marry, choosing their own husbands ... Apart from the fact that they prostitute their own daughters, the Lydian way of life is not unlike our own ...'

From Bin Tepe we drove back to the main highway, where we headed west once again towards Izmir. This route took us along the Hermus valley past Turgutlu to the turn-off to Manisa. Here we followed the direct route back toward Izmir, leaving the Hermus valley and entering the valley of the Nif Çayı, known in antiquity as the Cryos, the Cold River. This stretch of the highway passes south of Mount Sipylos and north of Nif Dağı, one of the nineteen peaks known in antiquity as Mount Olympus, its summit rising to 4,900 feet, exactly the same height as the Sipylene peak. We arrived by this road at the small town of Kemalpaşa, midway between the peaks of Olympus and Sipylos, where we stopped for lunch at a little kebab *lokanta* and talking about the last two monuments we would see on the journey from Sardis to Izmir, in the vicinity of Kemalpaşa.

The first of these monuments was a ruined Byzantine palace standing in a vineyard just to the right of the road beyond the town. It is virtually all that remains of the ancient town of Nymphaeum, which in Turkish became simply Nif, giving its name to the Nif Çayı and Nif Dağı. The palace of Nymphaeum was built by the emperor Andronicus II Comnenos during his short reign, 1183–5. During the Latin occupation of Constantinople, 1204–61, when the Byzantine capital was shifted to Nicaea, Nymphaeum became one of the favourite imperial residences. The town gave its name to the historic Treaty of Nymphaeum, signed in March 1261, just a few months before the Byzantines recaptured Constantinople. This was the pact (see p. 102) by which the emperor Michael VIII Palaeologus granted various territories and commercial rights to the Genoese in return for their military and diplomatic support of the Byzantine empire. The Genoese were difficult allies, seizing imperial territory on the Aegean coast of Asia Minor as well as the isles of Chios and Lesbos, but they fought alongside the Greeks in their last struggle against the Ottomans, battling valiantly on the walls of Constantinople when the capital was besieged and captured by the Turks in 1453. The palace of Nymphaeum is one of the last relics of Byzantium in this part of Asia Minor, evoking memories of that vanished medieval empire in which the ancient culture of the Hellenes survived for more than a thousand years after it had all but vanished in Greece itself.

The second of the two monuments in the vicinity of Kemalpaşa is the famous rock-carving known in Turkish as Eti Baba, or Father Hittite. This is to be found in Karabel, the Black Pass, through which runs a tributary of the Nif Çayı that flows between Nif Dağı and the next range to the east, Mahmut Dağı, known in antiquity as Mount Drakon. The Karabel Pass is just four miles south of the Izmir highway from Kemalpaşa, approached by a road that follows the course of the ancient way from Ephesus to Sardis and Phocaea. The carving is visible above the road to the left as one drives south from Kemalpaşa, a panel about eight feet high cut into a rocky cliff of Mount Drakon. The figure represents a marching warrior wearing a short tunic or kilt, a short-sleeved vest, and a conical headdress, with boots upturned at the toes. He holds a spear in his right hand and in his left a bow. There is also a faint hieroglyphic inscription that has been identified as Hittite. The carving is similar to carvings found in and around Hattusha and may represent the Hittite weather-god, Teshuba; it is thought to date from the period of the New Empire, c. 1500–1200 BC, but is of particular interest because it is mentioned by Herodotus, who believed it to be a figure of the pharaoh Sesostris, although it is not clear which one for there were three Egyptian rulers of that name during the twentieth and nineteenth centuries BC. The Eti Baba carving was rediscovered by European scholars c. 1840, and in 1875 a second figure, badly damaged but resembling the first, was found about 220 yards away in the Karabel Pass. This latter has since been removed for preservallon and study. It too is mentioned by Herodotus, who believed it to be a second figure of Sesostris.

We now drove back to the main highway at Kemalpaşa, heading once again towards Izmir. The highway took us over the Belkahve Pass, at an altitude of 2,625 feet, and soon we could see the late afternoon sun shining on the waters of the Gulf of Izmir. We then passed through the outskirts of the city and, within ten minutes, were back at our hotel on the waterfront, so completing a journey that had taken us into the heart of ancient Lydia.

9

THE NORTHERN IONIAN SHORE

The Ionian shore of Asia Minor is the most beautiful and historic region of all western Anatolia. In antiquity Ionia was the coastal region south of Aeolis and west of Caria. As Strabo wrote, 'the bounds of the Ionian coast extend from the Poseidium of the Milesians, and from the Carian frontiers, as far as Phocaea and the Hermus River, which latter is the limit of the Ionian seaboard'.

Throughout antiquity writers praised the beauties of Ionia and the pleasantness of its climate. Herodotus wrote in Book I of his *Histories*: 'These Ionians ... had the good fortune to establish their settlements in a region which enjoys a better climate than any other we know of. It does not resemble what is found further north, where there is an excess of cold and wet, or further south, where the weather is both too hot and too dry'. And Pausanius said: 'Ionia enjoys the finest of climates and its sanctuaries are unmatched in the world ... The wonders of Ionia are numerous, and not too much short of the wonders of Greece itself.'

This region took its name during the Ionian migrations, which are believed to have reached the Aegean coast of Asia Minor and its offshore islands *c.* 1050–1000 BC, shortly after the Aeolian population movement that founded the Hellenic cities on the same shore between the Adramyttene and Hermaic Gulfs. Some of these places were already inhabited when the Greeks first arrived. The Lelegians were living in the

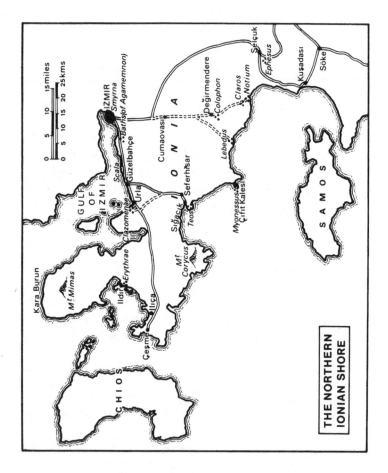

THE NORTHERN
IONIAN SHORE

region south of the Troad as far down as the Hermaic Gulf; inland to the west dwelt the Lydians and the Phrygians; and in the region just to the south were the Carians. Nor were the Aeolians and the Ionians even the first Hellenes to settle in western Anatolia, for legends tell of soldiers from Agamemnon's army moving there after the siege of Troy, and archaeological excavations have unearthed evidence of Mycenaean settlements along the Aegean coast of Asia Minor. In any event, the Ionian colonies soon organized themselves into a confederation called the Panionic League, which comprised the Aegean islands of Chios and Samos and ten cities on the mainland opposite them: Phocaea, Clazomenae, Erythrae, Teos, Lebedus, Colophon, Ephesus, Priene, Myus, and Miletus. These twelve city-states, also called the Dodecapolis, had their religious centre at the Panionium, on the mainland opposite Samos, and excluded all others from being members. Smyrna, which was originally Aeolian, was taken over soon after its foundation by Ionians from Colophon; nevertheless the city was not made a member of the Ionian League until the third century BC, when the confederation was long past the days of its glory.

We travelled through Ionia many times on our journeys along the western shores of Turkey, and visited the sites of all ten of the mainland cities of the Dodecapolis, together with Chios and Samos visible just across their narrow Aegean straits. Using Izmir as our base, we saw first the ancient sites on the northern Ionian shore, which comprises the enormous hydra-headed peninsula that projects out towards Chios and forms the southern arm of the Hermaic Gulf. Then we drove down to Selçuk, a town on the Maeander forty-five miles south of Izmir, which we used as a base to see Ephesus and the other cities on the southern Ionian shore, on the coast opposite Samos.

On our most recent journey we followed the Ionian coast from Izmir west and then south, starting out by driving westward along the gulf towards Çeşme, the Turkish port opposite

Chios. Our trip began just after sunrise on a superb mild-April day, the weather for our Ionian journey promising to be as pleasant as Herodotus and Pausanius had led us to believe. After leaving the outskirts of Izmir we passed on our right the coastal plain on which Inciraltı Airport is laid out, and on our left we looked up at Kızıl Dağ, the Red Mountain, whose summit rises to 3,500 feet, with a cluster of peaks at its northern ramparts known as the Three Sisters and a pair of crags near its western end called the Two Brothers. The Two Brothers, which rise to 2,900 feet, are used by the people of Izmir to forecast their weather, for if the twin peaks are free of clouds in the morning it will be a clear day, but if they are cloud-shrouded it is sure to rain. The Two Brothers rose into an absolutely clear sky as we approached them along the southern shore of the Gulf of Izmir, and as we drove along we remembered how beautiful these Ionian shores had appeared to us when we saw them for the first time, from the deck of the *Tarih* in January 1961. The weather had been just as superb then, despite the season, for it was one of those halcyon days that the Aegean world enjoys for a fortnight or so in mid-winter every year. One of the first to describe this blissful weather was the Ionian poet Simonides of Keos, writing in the late seventh century BC.

> As when in the winter moons God stills
> weather a space of fourteen days,
> and winds sleep in the season, and men have named it
> sacred to the breeding of the bright halcyon.

The halcyon was a mythical bird, identified with the king-fisher, who the ancients believed nested on the Aegean at the time of the winter solstice. For this the gods calmed the winds and brought an unseasonal period of good weather, the halcyon days. Alcman, who would have known the Ionian coast from his early days in Sardis, also wrote of the fabled bird, but associated it with spring, and as we drove along the Gulf of Izmir I recalled also his poem, 'The Halcyons'.

No more, O maiden voices, sweet as honey, soft as love is,
No more my limbs sustain me—A halcyon on the wing
Flying o'er the foam flowers in the halcyon coveys,
Would I were, and knew not care, the sea-blue bird of spring!

About six miles out of Izmir, where the approach road to
Inciraltı Airport leads off to the right, a signpost directed us
down a road to the left to the Baths of Agamemnon, a bathing
establishment fed by sulfurous springs that rise in and around
a small stream that flows down from Kızıl Dağ just to the west
of the Three Sisters. These springs, which were known in
antiquity as the Agamemnion, have long been famous for their
therapeutic powers, though not a trace remains of the ancient
baths and healing shrine that were located here. According
to mythology, the baths took their name from the fact that
Agamemnon's army were directed there by an oracle after
they were defeated by King Telephos of Mysia. The wounded
Achaeans were healed after bathing in the waters of the springs
and, as a token of their gratitude, they hung up on the walls
of the baths the helmets of the Mysian warriors that they were
bringing home as trophies after their battle with Telephos. In
later times a shrine of Asklepios was dedicated here, and
Aristeides Aeolis, the orator and sophist of Smyrna, writes that
the healing god 'first began to give oracles at the hot waters'.
Aristeides spent much time at the Agamemnion trying to cure
his many maladies. While there he may have met Galen, the
physician from the Asklepieum at Pergamum, who came to
Smyrna in AD 149 to study with two local doctors. For Galen
wrote a three-volume work on the chest and lungs, which
would undoubtedly have led him to visit the Agamemnion.
Aristeides writes that the local physicians brought him to the
springs of the Agamemnion for treatment to ease his breathing,
and it was at this shrine that he began to receive instructions
from the god Asklepios through dreams and visions. At the
Agamemnion he also had dreams in which the goddess Isis
appeared to him, on one occasion telling him to sacrifice two

geese for her. He went into Smyrna for this purpose, and when he reached the poultry shop he found that the owner had set aside the last two geese for him, for Isis had appeared to this man as well, telling him that Aristeides was on his way to purchase them. Isis also sent two of her sacred geese to accompany Aristeides on his walk back from Smyrna to the Agamemnion, and as we left the baths we amused ourselves by picturing the sophist walking down the road with the holy birds waddling along either side of him.

Back on the main highway we drove westward again towards Çeşme and stopped next at Clazomenae. A short way before the turn-off for Clazomenae we reached the seaside village of Scala, where we stopped briefly for sentimental reasons. This was the birthplace of George Seferiades, better known as Seferis, one of the great poets of modern Greece and winner of the Nobel Prize for Literature in 1963. Seferis was born in Scala on 29 February 1900 and lived there and in Izmir until 1914, when his family moved to Europe. Seferis returned to his childhood home in 1950, visiting the ancient Ionian cities while he was there. This visit made a deep impression on him, which he describes in his memoirs and in several of his poems, most notably in this strophe from 'Memory II':

> Even now I remember:
> he was journeying to Ionian coasts, to empty shells of theatres,
> where only the lizard glides over dry stones,
> and I asked him: 'Will they ever be full again?'
> And he answered me: 'Perhaps at the hour of death',
> And he ran across the orchestra howling.
> 'Let me hear my brother!'

After this pause at Scala we continued until we came to the beginning of a huge peninsula projecting northwards into the Gulf of Izmir, and there we took a side road to the right which brought us to Urla Iskelesi, a village opposite a long narrow islet connected to the mainland by a causeway. This was the site of ancient Clazomenae, renowned as the birthplace of the philosopher Anaxagoras. There is virtually nothing left of the ancient city, and the few remnants that exist are out on the islet which is closed to the public since there is a tuberculosis hospital and quarantine station there. So we contented ourselves with a walk along the shore while we identified the principal features of Clazomenae from an archaeological map.

According to Pausanius, Clazomenae was first settled during the Ionian migration, its colonists mostly from the Peloponnesus; these people settled first on the mainland, later moving over to the island for fear of the Persians. However, it now appears that the site was inhabited before the Greek migrations, for archaeologists have unearthed pre-Hellenic pottery sherds on the low hill between Urla Iskelesi and the causeway leading out to the island. Archaeologists have also discovered the remains of an Archaic Greek city on the mainland, with its acropolis on the low eminence just south of Urla Iskelesi. This is where the Ionian city was situated before the townspeople moved out to the island, probably late in the Archaic period. The most distinctive objects found in these excavations are the Clazomenaean terracotta sarcophagi with painted decorations, of which a few examples are on display in the Izmir Archaeological Museum. More than a hundred of these sarcophagi have been found along the shore around Urla Iskelesi, most of them dating to the sixth century BC; thus it appears that the Clazomenaeans used the site of their original city as a necropolis after they moved out to the islet.

We returned to the main highway at Urla, where we headed westward towards Çeşme once again across the base of the peninsula on which Clazomenae is located. Then, after passing the gulf to its west, the highway took us across the base of the enormous peninsula that forms the western arm of the Hermaic Gulf, Mount Mimas towering above its northern promontory. This brought us to the western end of the great peninsular land mass that projects out towards Chios, which we could now see just across the straits; and there, at land's end, we drove into Çeşme.

Çeşme is a pleasant coastal town with a small port from which there is a ferry service out to Chios. The port is dominated by a picturesque Genoese fortress, probably dating from the late thirteenth century. This fortress played a major role in the Battle of Çeşme on 5 July 1770 when a Russian fleet virtually annihilated the Ottoman navy, which was trapped in this little harbour and blown up.

In recent years Çeşme has become a popular summer resort, with several excellent beaches and yacht anchorages on its surrounding coast—most notably the bathing facilities at Ilıca, and the Altın Yunus marina and holiday village on Ildır Bay, across the peninsula to the west of the town.

Çeşme is also a convenient base for visiting the ruins of the city of Erythrae, another member of the Ionian League. The ruins lie eleven miles up the coast beyond Ilıca, approached by a rough track that leads to the seaside hamlet of Ildır. The most impressive of them is the long stretch of well-preserved defence walls, the ancient city looking out across the straits towards Chios, formerly its nearest neighbour in the Ionian League.

Erythrae's foundation was somewhat different from that of the other Ionian cities. Legend holds that it was first settled by an expedition from Crete, the colonists also including Lycians, Carians, and Pamphylians, with Ionians joining them later under a son of King Kodros of Athens. According to one legend, the city was named for its founder, Erythros, 'the Red', who was a son of Rhadamanthys, brother of the legendary King Minos of Crete.

Since Herodotus writes that the Erythraeans and Chians spoke a similar dialect, they probably had a common origin. Nevertheless, the Erythraeans and the Chians fought one another in several wars during the Archaic period, when Erythrae appears to have been one of the strongest military powers among the Ionian states. One of these disputes concerned the possession of a sacred image of Heracles, which was found floating in the straits between Chios and Erythrae. The people on both sides naturally struggled to pull it to their own shore. At that moment, according to Pausanius, a blind fisherman of Erythrae had a dream in which it was revealed to him that the women of the city would have to cut off their hair and plait it into a rope to pull the image to their side of the straits. The free women of Erythrae refused to do this, but the Thracian slave-women who were living there agreed. Their hair was thereupon cut off and made into a rope, which the townspeople put successfully to use. The image was then housed in a shrine called the Heracleion, and the only women allowed to enter it were the Thracian slaves whose rope of plaited hair was still exhibited there when Pausanius visited the shrine in the second century A D.

Erythrae was also famous for its sibyl, a prophetess whose name was Hierophile. After the famous sibyl at Cumae, Hierophile was the most renowned prophetess in the ancient world, and a number of places claimed to be her home, but the Erythraeans said that she had been born in a cave on the nearby mountain of Corycus. Mount Corycus is mentioned in one of the Homeric Hymns, where the poet describes the seascape around this western promontory of Ionia where Erythrae was founded: 'Chios, brightest of all the isles that lie in the sea, and craggy Mimas and the heights of Corycus and gleaming Claros and the sheer hill of Aesagea ...'

From Erythrae we drove back to Izmir, passing Kızıl Dağ and its clustered peaks, with the Two Brothers to the west and to the east the Three Sisters. As we approached the city I turned back and saw that the sun was setting behind the Two Brothers, which were as clear of clouds as when we had begun our journey that morning, and as twilight slowly came I recalled the words that Seferis had written of this scene after his return to Ionia in 1950: '... the sun sinks below the rock of the Two Brothers. The twilight spreads over the sky and the sea like the colours of an inexhaustible love'.

The next morning we again started off very early, once more headed westward along the gulf, pleased that the cloudless peaks of the Two Brothers promised another day of good weather. After passing Scala and Güzelbahçe, the Beautiful Garden, we turned left to take the road that crosses the base of the great peninsula that juts out west of Izmir. This brought us to Seferhisar, where we took a side road out to Sığacık, a little port with a picturesque Genoese fortress. The road goes on for a short way to the fine beach at the northern end of the little peninsula that has now been taken over by NATO for its staff. But we turned left on to a dirt road that led us south to the ruins of ancient Teos, which lies in the middle of the peninsula between its north and south ports. We drove our car as far as we could go and then began to wander among the ruins, which include the acropolis and its Archaic defence walls, a theatre, an odeion, the Temple of Dionysus, and the Hellenistic fortifications, which form an unusual rectangular outline between the acropolis and the southern harbour. We found a comfortable spot within the Temple of Dionysus and spread out a picnic in the shade of the olive-grove that has entwined itself among the ruins, embowering the whole site of ancient Teos.

The Ionians were not the first Greeks to settle in Teos, nor were those who dwelt there in the early years of the city solely Hellenes. According to Pausanius, 'Teos was settled by Minyans from Orchomenus ... Here as well the Carians and the Greeks had mingled. Opikos ... brought Ionians from Teos, though without any plan to disturb the Orchomenians or the people of the place. Then not many years afterwards men came from Athens and Boetia ... and the people of Teos accepted them as fellow citizens'.

From early on in their history the Teans appear to have prospered, and they established a number of overseas colonies, also joining with other Greek cities in founding the trading port of Naucratis on the Nile delta. Around 600 BC the philosopher Thales of Miletus suggested that the Ionian cities should strengthen the Dodecapolis by establishing a central government with its capital at Teos. However, the Ionians prized their freedom and individuality too much to implement this proposal, and so they never presented a united front against their enemies. After the conquest of Sardis in 546 BC, Cyrus of Persia sent Harpagus the Mede to subjugate the Greek cities of Asia Minor, first taking Phocaea and then Teos. The Teans followed the example of the Phocaeans and fled by sea rather than surrender to the Persians. The Tean exiles then settled in Thrace, where they founded the city of Abdera. This was to be the birthplace of Democritus, the first physicist to formulate an atomic theory, and also of the philosopher Protagoras, who wrote that 'Man is the measure of all things'. But many of the Teans later returned to their native city, and the spirit of Teos seems to have revived with the return of the exiles, for the city contributed seventeen ships to the unsuccessful Ionian expedition against the Persians at the Battle of Lade in 494 BC, more than any other mainland town except Miletus.

One of the Teans who fled to Abdera was the poet Anacreon, who was born in Teos c. 560 BC. After Anacreon established his reputation as a poet he was invited by Polycrates of Samos to tutor his son, also becoming the tyrant's boon companion. When Polycrates was killed by the Persians, c. 524 BC, Anacreon returned to Abdera, but soon afterwards he was invited to Athens by Hipparchus, eldest son of the tyrant Peisistratus. Anacreon finally returned to Teos in his last years, and died there c. 483 BC at the age of 87, choking on a grape-pip while drinking raisin wine. According to Pausanius, Anacreon was honoured with a monument on the Athenian acropolis, 'the statue representing him singing in his cups'. Pausanius also writes that Anacreon was 'the first poet excepting Sappho of Lesbos to make his main theme love'. So we drank a toast in the Temple of Dionysus to the memory of Anacreon, recalling one of the Tean's poems: 'Bring water, lad, bring wine, bring me garlands of flowers; aye, bring them thither; for I would try a bout with love'.

We wandered for a while in the temple, for it was deliciously cool in the shade of the olive-grove that had overgrown the sanctuary. The Temple of Dionysus was the largest structure ever dedicated to the wine-god in the ancient world, with its peripteral colonnade of six by eleven columns standing on a stylobate measuring 60 feet by 115 feet. This Ionic temple was designed by the architect Hermogenes of Priene and completed early in the second century BC, with considerable reconstruction and restoration in the second century AD. There must have been an earlier temple of the wine-god at Teos, though no trace of it has been found on the site of the present sanctuary, because in the third century BC the city was the home of the renowned Artists of Dionysus, a guild of itinerant actors and musicians who performed at festivals throughout the Greek world.

We now walked down to what was once the southern harbour of Teos, called Geraesticus by the Greeks; in 190 BC this was the scene of one of the most important naval battles in the Hellenistic period, when the Romans and their Rhodian allies defeated the forces of the Seleucid king, Antiochus III. After this Antiochus suffered a second and even more decisive defeat at the Battle of Magnesia early in the following year. This resulted in the downfall of the Seleucid Empire in Asia Minor and eventually led to the formation of the Roman Province of Asia, after which Teos never again played an important part in history.

After seeing the ruins at Teos we decided to make an excursion to Myonnesus, Mouse Island, an ancient site some ten miles down the coast south of Sığacık. It is possible to drive there over a rough track that goes as far south as Doğanbey, from whence one can hike to the site, but a much better approach is to hire a boat in Sığacık, if one is available, for then one can just sit back and enjoy the coastal scenery *en route*.

Myonnesus, which in Turkish is known as Çıfıt Kalesi, the Jew's Castle, is a miniature Gibraltar, consisting of a sheer rocky crag 190 feet in height jutting out of the sea just north of the promontory which forms the southernmost point of the coastline south of Teos. The crag, known to the Greeks as Cape Macris, is connected to the mainland by an ancient causeway which can still be seen underwater. In ancient times this was a lair of pirates, and in 190 BC some corsairs from here attacked the Roman supply ships just prior to the naval battle off Teos. The Roman fleet pursued the pirates back to Myonnesus, but they were not able to get at them for fear of rocks being thrown down on their ships from the cliffs above. All that remains on the sea-girt rock of Myonnesus are some ancient walls, and there is virtually nothing left of the city which must have been located just opposite the islet on the mainland. Myonnesus is mentioned as a city as early as *c.* 500 BC by the historian Hecataeus of Miletus, and in the third century BC it was for a time the home of the Artists of Dionysus after they were evicted from Chios. According to Pliny, Myonnesus was once a fairly prosperous town, but it ceased to exist in his own time, and now it has been abandoned for so long that the elements have eroded its remnants to the point that it appears as a natural part of the landscape.

From Myonnesus we returned to Sığacık and then to Izmir. The following day our destinations were the sites of Colophon, Claros, Notium, and Lebedus, which we approached by taking the highway that leads from Izmir to Selçuk, and then, after nine miles, turning south on to a secondary road. Then, twelve miles out of Izmir, we came to Değirmendere, the Valley of the Mill, a village near the site of ancient Colophon.

There is little left of Colophon except for a few stretches of Hellenistic defence walls on the hills around Değirmendere. The ancient city was built on three of these hills, whose peaks formed the apexes of a triangular fortification studded with a dozen fortified watch-towers. Virtually nothing remains of the city that was once surrounded by these walls, so that we had to use our imagination to evoke a picture of what Colophon was like in the days of its glory.

Although Colophon was a member of the Ionian League, its original settlers were not Ionians. According to archaeologists, the Mycenaeans first established a colony on this site, which seems to have been inhabited continuously from the end of the Bronze Age on into the historical period. One local tradition holds that the first permanent settlers here were Cretans, with Thebans who had been driven out of Greece by the Achaeans later joining the colony. Another tradition, probably based on a later Hellenic migration, holds that Colophon was founded by an expedition of Ionians from Pylos, who afterwards went on to take Smyrna from the Aeolians. The principal source for this is the Colophonian poet Mimnermus, who flourished in Smyrna c. 600 BC, writing perhaps a century after that city was captured by his fellow Ionians from Colophon. As Mimnermus writes of that expedition, 'After leaving Pylos, the lofty city of Neleus, we came in our voyage to the long-wished-for Asia, and settled at Colophon, and hastening then from the river Astëeis, by the will of God we took Aeolian Smyrna'.

Mimnermus was one of several poets for whom Colophon was celebrated, and there is also a tradition that Homer lived here at one point in his life. Another renowned Colophonian poet was Xenophanes, who won even greater fame as a philosopher. Xenophanes was born in the city of Colophon c. 570 BC and fled from there to southern Italy at the time of the Persian invasion in 546 BC, eventually settling in the Phocaean colony of Elea, where he founded the Eleatic school of philosophy.

Xenophanes and Mimnermus are among the several ancient sources who write of the military prowess of Colophon, which was famous for its cavalry and for its warrior dogs who were trained for battle as well as for guard-duty. The military might of Colophon and its sea-borne commerce made it one of the wealthiest and most powerful cities of the Dodecapolis. But this wealth also softened the once-tough sinews of the Colophonians, leading them into a decadent life-style that eventually resulted in their downfall, conquered first by the Lydians and then by a Persian army commanded by Harpagus the Mede. The voluptuous ways of the Colophonians are eloquently described by Xenophanes in his poem 'Gay Days in Asiatic Colophon', written after the city had lost its freedom and he was living in exile: 'They had acquired useless luxuries in Lydia while still free of her odious tyranny; paraded to the market-place in sea-purple robes, often in bright swarms of a thousand. They were proud and pleased with their elaborate coiffures, and hid their body odours with rare perfumes'.

Xenophanes wrote with sadness of his birthplace just before he died in southern Italy at the age of 92: 'Three score and seven years have crossed my careworn soul up and down the land of Hellas, and there were then five and twenty years from my birth'. And one can sense the nostalgia in the old poet's soul as he reflects on his long exile: 'Such things should be said beside the fire in wintertime when a man reclines full-fed on a soft couch drinking sweet wine and munching chick peas, such things as who and whence art thou? And how old are thou, good sir? And what age was thou when the Mede appeared?'

After leaving Colophon we drove on to the site of ancient Claros, ten miles beyond Değirmendere, where we found the Temple of Apollo in a river valley about a hundred yards to the left of the road. Since the temple is below the level of the local water-table, the ruins are kept visible only by constant pumping, making the site all the more impressive in its half-submerged state. One notices in particular the gigantic fragments of the huge cult statue of Apollo; the large number of massive column drums; the great altar table nearly sixty-five feet long; and the subterranean chamber where the oracle delivered his messages in verse after drinking from the secret fountain which was at the core of this shrine.

The Clarian Temple of Apollo dates from the late fifth or early sixth century B C, and is one of the very few Doric monuments in Ionia. But the shrine is far older, for it is mentioned in one of the Homeric Hymns to Artemis: 'Muse, sing of Artemis, sister

of the Far Darter, the virgin who delights in arrows, who was
fostered with Apollo. She waters her horses from Meles deep
in reeds, and swiftly drives her all-golden chariot from Smyrna
to vine-clad Claros where Apollo, god of the silver bow, sits
waiting ...'

We now drove down to the sea some two miles beyond
Claros, to the site of ancient Notium. The ruins of Notium are
extensive, spreading across the peaks and slopes of the two
hills to the right of the beach as one faces inland. They include
the ruins of a Temple of Athena and two other sanctuaries, as
well as an agora, a senate house, a theatre, and some remnants
of a defence wall which was originally two and a half miles in
length, all of them poorly preserved. Notium was originally an
Aeolian colony but throughout antiquity it was always the
port for Colophon and for long periods in their history the two
cities formed part of one civic unit, which belonged to the
Panionic League. Later, with the growth of the local sea-borne
commerce, much of the population moved down to the port,
which came to be called New Colophon, while the inland city
was then known as Old Colophon. From that time on the name
Notium fell into disuse and disappears from history, as indeed
would the names of New and Old Colophon themselves, as
these towns eventually declined apace with the growing
importance as a seaport of Ephesus.

From Notium we drove back towards Izmir, passing the sites
of Claros and Colophon and continuing as far as Cumaovası,
where we found a rough track leading down to the sea and
the village of Ürkmez. As the track approached Ürkmez we saw
some ruins to our left on the Kısık peninsula, and we parked
our car to walk in that direction to the site of Lebedus.

Lebedus was the smallest and least significant city in the
Panionic League, making virtually no mark in history and
producing no remarkable men, though it continued in existence from the beginning of the first millennium BC up until
the medieval Byzantine period. Lebedus was for a time the
residential centre for the Artists of Dionysus, and it is in this

connection that the city is mentioned by Strabo: 'The Dionysiac artists (who travel about) ... migrated to Lebedus, and the Lebedians were glad to receive them, on account of their scanty population'. All that is left of Lebedus are some ruined fortifications on the acropolis hill, fragments of the sea-wall that once ringed the Kısık peninsula, and the remnants of five watch-towers that still stand.

We sat for a while looking out across the Aegean to see Samos and Mount Mycale almost enclosing the great gulf to the south, the eastern reaches of what in antiquity was known as the Icarian Sea. The promontory of the mainland reaching out towards Samos was known in antiquity as Cape Mycale, and it was here that the Ionians built the Panionium, the shrine where each year they celebrated their common festival, the Panionia. Every fourth year the Ionians also celebrated at an even greater festival on Delos, and as we sat on the ruined sea-walls of Lebedus I recalled a passage from the Homeric Hymn to Delian Apollo, which evokes a vision of what life was like among the Ionians in their golden age.

> Yet in Delos do you most delight your heart; for the long-robed Ionians gather in your honour with their children and shy wives. Mindful, they delight you with boxing and dancing and song, so often as they hold their gathering. A man would say they are deathless and ageing if he should come upon the Ionians so met together. For he would see the graces of them all, and would be pleased in heart gazing at the well-girded women and the men with their swift ships and great renown.

10

EPHESUS AND THE MOTHER
GODDESS

By the time we left Lebedus and started back to the main
highway it was late in the afternoon. At the highway we turned
south and headed for Selçuk, the town that now occupies the
site of ancient Ephesus. As we drove along in the lengthening
shadows I checked our route on both the Turkish road-map
and my classical atlas. The first landmark I recognized was a
ruined Byzantine fortress on a crag to the right of the road
thirty-five miles out of Izmir. This romantic ruin, known to the
Turks as Keçikalesi, or the Goat's Castle, was built early in the
thirteenth century by the Lascarids, the dynasty who ruled the
Byzantine Empire from Nicaea during the Latin occupation of
Constantinople, 1204–61. During the last two centuries of
Byzantine rule in Asia Minor this fortress guarded the approach
to Ephesus along the valley of the Cayster, the river known
today as the Küçük Menderes, which flows from the Colophonian plain into the Aegean at the head of the enormous
gulf north of Cape Mycale and Samos, once the heart of ancient
Ionia.

We arrived at Selçuk shortly after sunset, driving through
the town and out towards the Tusan Motel, which is near the
entrance to the archaeological site at Ephesus. Above Selçuk I
could see the medieval citadel brooding on the Ayasuluk hill,
and below it to the south on the Kuşadası road we passed the
sacred precincts of the Artemision. The road then led us past
the northern end of Panayir Dağı, the Greek Mount Pion, and

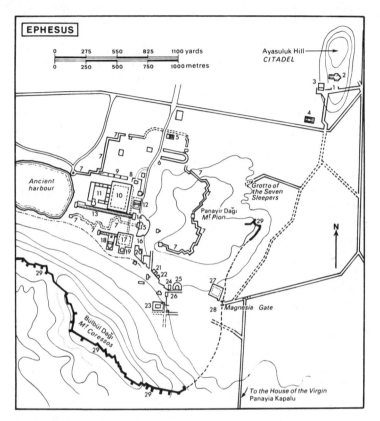

Key to Plan of Ephesus

1 Gate of Persecution
2 Church of St. John
3 Isa Bey Camii
4 Artemision
5 Gymnasium of Vedius
6 Stadium
7 Byzantine defence walls
8 Proconsul's Palace (Byzantine Baths)
9 Church of the Blessed Virgin
10 Portico Verulanus
11 Baths of Constantius
12 Gymnasium of the Theatre
13 Arcadiane
14 Fountain
15 Theatre
16 Marble Way (Street of the Curetes)
17 Commercial agora or marketplace
18 Temple of Serapis
19 Library of Celsus
20 Baths of Scholastica
21 Temple of Hadrian
22 Nymphaion of Trajan
23 Temple of Domitian
24 Prytaneion
25 Odeion
26 State Agora
27 East Gymnasium
28 Magnesia Gate
29 Hellenistic defence walls

at the turn-off to the left beyond the hill we came to the motel. After we had checked in, we walked down the side road a short way and stopped at the entrance to the archaeological site, which extends around the western and southern sides of Mount Pion and up the lower slopes of Mount Coressos, known in Turkish as Bülbül Dağı, the Mountain of the Nightingales. There were nightingales that evening in Ephesus, serenading one another somewhere within the deserted valley, their resonant arias calling across the vast ruins of the ghost city that was now disappearing from our sight in the deepening indigo of twilight. We had come to Ephesus once again, as we always did on our journeys along the Ionian coast, almost as if we were on a pilgrimage.

According to Strabo, the area around Ephesus was inhabited by both Carians and Lelegians at the time the first Ionian settlement was being established by an expedition led by Androclus, a son of King Kodros of Athens. Strabo says that Androclus drove out the Carians and Lelegians, after which the Ionians apparently took over the shrine of the Great Earth Mother which these Anatolian people had held sacred since at least as far back as the late Bronze Age, the latter half of the second millennium BC. The temple of this ancient Anatolian goddess was the magnet that attracted pilgrims and settlers to Ephesus, for this was sacred ground even before the Ionian migration.

The original Ionian settlement at Ephesus stood on the shore by the lower northern slope of Mount Pion, for at that time the sea penetrated inland as far as the Ayasuluk hill. Under Croesus the Lydians forced the Ephesians to leave their strongly fortified port and move inland to a new site near the Artemision. Then early in the fourth century BC the site of Ephesus was changed once again, when Lysimachus re-established it on what was then the sea-coast, where the ruins of the Graeco-Roman city are to be seen today.

Ephesus reached its prime during the imperial Roman era, when its citizens proudly proclaimed that their city was the 'First and Greatest Metropolis in Asia'. Strabo, whose career spanned the first half-century of that era, wrote that 'the city by the advantages which it affords, daily improves and is the largest mart in Asia within the Taurus'. By then Ephesus had surpassed Smyrna as the busiest port on the Aegean coast of Anatolia, and was also the most important commercial and financial centre in the Asian dominions of Rome. Its population reached 400,000 at its peak in the second century A D. Ephesus also attracted pilgrims from all over the Graeco-Roman world, including a number of emperors, beginning with Augustus, all of whom came to pay homage to Artemis Ephesia, 'she whom all Asia and the world worship'.

During the latter half of the first century A D Ephesus became a centre for the new Christian faith that would replace the old pagan religion of the Graeco-Roman world. This new religion developed at first principally among the Jewish community there, with Paul making numerous conversions among the Jews as well as among the Greek populace during his two visits to Ephesus, the first in AD 52 and the second beginning two years after that. There is also a tradition that St. John the Apostle lived out his last years in Ephesus along with the Blessed Virgin. There has been much discussion as to whether John the Apostle is here being confused with St. John the Theologian who, according to local tradition, is buried on the Ayasuluk hill where a small church was dedicated to him in the second century. This church was replaced in the year 535 by a huge cathedral erected by the emperor Justinian, the impressive ruins of which are still visible above the town of Selçuk.

Ephesus continued to flourish under the mantle of the *pax Romana* until the middle of the third century A D, but in 262 the city was attacked by the Ostrogoths who destroyed the Artemision and inflicted considerable damage on the quarter next to the harbour. The Artemision was partially restored on a smaller scale during the reign of Diocletian (285–305), and it remained in use until 392 when Theodosius I published an edict closing down all of the pagan shrines in the empire. The temple was then destroyed in 401 by a fanatical mob led by the patriarch John Chrysostom, who saw this as the final triumph of Christianity over paganism. By that time a large public building in Ephesus had been converted into a church dedicated to the Virgin Mary, and so the belief in Christ and the veneration of his Blessed Mother replaced the worship of Artemis and the other deities of the Graeco-Roman world, although some continued to pay homage to the older gods for at least a century afterwards.

During the medieval Byzantine era Ephesus shared the same fate as the other towns of Asia Minor, enduring invasions by the Persians, Arabs, and Turks, who held the city from c. 1190 to 1196. These centuries of almost continual warfare took their toll on Ephesus, ultimately destroying the magnificent Roman city of late antiquity, and gradually transforming it into a smaller and more modest Byzantine town. Byzantine Ephesus initially had two centres, one comprising the harbour quarter and the other situated on the hill above the present town of Selçuk, both of them enclosed by defence walls. But by the end of the Byzantine period in Asia Minor the harbour in Ephesus had been silted up so completely that ships could no longer dock there. The harbour quarter was then abandoned and the townspeople thereafter lived only on the citadel hill to the north. This hill was known to the Greeks as Haghios Theologos, after the cathedral of St. John the Theologian erected by Justinian. The Venetians and Genoese who traded there changed Theologos in their tongue into Altoluogo, which the Turks later altered to Ayasuluk, and this is the name by which Ephesus was known in later Ottoman times.

Ephesus finally fell to the Turks on 24 October 1204, becoming part of the Aydınoğlu *beylik*, which included the whole of the Cayster and Maeander valleys. Ephesus revived under the Aydınoğlu emirs, and the high point in the resurgence of the town was reached in 1374–5 with the erection of the Isa Bey Camii, the enormous mosque that stands at the foot of the Ayasuluk hill, just below the Church of St. John. Ephesus

148

remained in the hands of the Aydınoğlu Turks until 1390, when Sultan Beyazit I captured the town in the campaign in which he conquered all of the *beyliks* in western Anatolia and added them to the Ottoman Empire. After Beyazit's defeat by Tamerlane at Ankara in 1402, Ephesus was restored to the Aydınoğlu, ruled by Musa Bey, son of the emir Isa. Tamerlane himself visited Ephesus twice during the following months, before and after his capture of Smyrna, and then, having restored the Turkoman emirs to their *beyliks* in western Anatolia, he marched off with his hordes to the East. Eventually the Ottoman Turks succeeded in regaining all of western Anatolia that had been lost after the Battle of Ankara, and finally, in 1425, they recaptured Ephesus, which became a permanent part of their dominions for the remaining five centuries of the Ottoman Empire.

After its restoration to the Ottoman Empire, Ephesus became a local administrative centre called a *kaza*, the seat of a *kadi*, or judge, who upheld the sultan's laws and dispensed his justice. The population of the town in the mid-fifteenth century appears to have been about 2,000. There were a total of 481 houses divided into 24 quarters, three of them inhabited by Greeks and the others by Turks, all dwelling on the citadel hill at Ayasuluk. The Ottoman town, though small, appears to have prospered at first, for a government mint was built at Ayasuluk, along with a small mosque, a theological school, and a free soup-kitchen. The great mosque of Isa Bey also remained in good repair. But towards the end of the sixteenth century Ephesus began an irrevocable decline. No doubt because its harbour had been silted up for so long, it was now bypassed by the main trade routes through western Anatolia and Smyrna replaced it as the principal port of the region. Evliya Çelebi, writing in the mid-seventeenth century, describes Ephesus as having only about a hundred houses with earthen roofs, along with a mosque, a public bath, and a caravanserai for travellers. The whole region about Ephesus was in decline as well, for the silted-up delta of the Cayster had become a malarial swamp. Murderous bandits used to lie there in wait to waylay passers-by, as the English traveller Covel reported in 1670. Richard Chandler visited the site twice during 1764–5, writing that he had searched for the Artemision, but 'to as little purpose as the travellers who had preceded us ... We now seek in vain for the temple; the city is prostrate; and the goddess gone'.

The Artemision eluded discovery for more than a century after Chandler's visit. The first archaeological excavations of ancient Ephesus were begun in 1863 by John Turtle Wood in a project sponsored by the British Museum. After searching for more than six years, Wood finally unearthed part of the marble pavement of the temple on the last day of 1869; the stylobate which supported the colonnade had been buried beneath nearly twenty feet of soil. Wood continued excavating the site until 1874, but even then he had not cleared the temple to its lowest levels. This task was accomplished by D. G. Hogarth who, resuming the excavations for the British Museum on 30 October 1904, in the next two seasons unearthed the temple to its foundations and determined the various periods of its construction as well as recovering many of the architectural members and works of art, including precious dedicatory offerings. A team of Austrian archaeologists also began excavating at Ephesus in 1895 and, with interruptions for the First and Second World Wars, their successors continue working on the site to this day. These archaeological excavations have been paralleled by restoration work on a number of important structures in both the ancient and the medieval sites, so that one can once more see some of the great edifices of Ephesus in something of their former splendour.

We began our tour where Ephesus itself had its beginnings, at the Artemision. We started out from the motel after an early breakfast, walking back almost a mile toward Selçuk until we came to the site of the temple, just to the left of the road below the Ayasuluk hill. The Artemision is a mournful sight, just a single reconstructed column standing beside the excavation pit along with foundation stones and architectural members, all half-submerged in water. And so we had to exercise our imagination to evoke an image of this great temple in the days of its fame, when it was one of the Seven Wonders of the Ancient World.

The earliest shrine of Artemis discovered on this site is an altar dated to *c.* 700 BC. The first full-scale temple here seems to have been erected in the second quarter of the sixth century BC, at about the same time as the Heraion in Samos. The Archaic Artemision was destroyed in 356 BC when a madman named Herostratus set fire to the temple to make his name immortal. The Ephesians soon afterwards began to rebuild the Artemision on a scale at least as grand as the original. According to Pliny, it was 120 years abuilding, covering an area of 220 feet by 425 feet, more than three and a half times larger than the Parthenon in Athens. It contained 127 columns, of which 36, bearing sculptures in relief, stood at the front of the sanctuary: truly one of the wonders of the world, and awe-inspiring even in its present desolation.

From the Artemision we retraced our steps to the Tusan Motel, in order to pick up a picnic lunch. Then we walked to the main area of the archaeological site and began our exploration of the Graeco-Roman city, which is still partially surrounded by the remnants of its Hellenistic walls on the slopes of the hills above.

The road from Smyrna reached Ephesus at the present entrance to the archaeological site, and from there it joined the main avenue of the ancient city, extending along the western flank of Mount Pion as far as the valley between that eminence and Mount Coressos. The path from the entrance to the archaeological zone joins this ancient avenue just beyond the first of the two monumental Roman structures that one passes on the left; this is the Gymnasium of Vedius, erected in the mid-second century AD. The second, even vaster structure is the stadium, erected during the reign of Nero (AD 54–68). A short distance beyond the stadium the pathway passes a complex known until recent years as the Byzantine Baths, this has now been identified as the Palace of the Proconsul of Asia, probably dating from the reign of Diocletian.

Just beyond the proconsul's palace a side path to the right leads westward to the harbour, which was about half a mile distant. This took us to a long and exceedingly narrow Roman basilica, a market building which in the second half of the fourth century AD was converted into a church dedicated to the Blessed Virgin and served as the original cathedral of Ephesus. The Third Ecumenical Council was convened here in 413 by Theodosius II, and the church was also the site of the infamous 'Robber Council' of 449 which the Orthodox Church condemned as heretical.

After visiting the church we explored the area just to its south, a vast field of ruins originally known as the Baths of Constantius, erected in the mid-fourth century AD. The baths were themselves only a small part of the most enormous complex of public buildings in Ephesus. This complex covered an area of 550 yards by 330 yards and comprised, besides the baths themselves, the Harbour Gymnasium, and an enormous palaestra called the Portico Verulanus, which alone took up an area of 220 yards on each side, far larger than any other public building in the city.

We now came to the main east-west road to Ephesus, the Arcadiane, a great colonnaded avenue leading from the harbour to the theatre and one of the most splendid sights in all of Asia Minor. This beautiful promenade took its name from the emperor Arcadius (395–408), during whose reign it took its present form. Double colonnades flanked covered porticoes with mosaic pavements on both sides, monumental gateways stood at both ends, and a hundred street-lamps in two rows illuminated the avenue for those who strolled there in the evening. Shops opened off from both sides of the avenue, along which were ranged on either side honorific columns and commemorative statues including four large pedestals bearing figures of the Four Evangelists.

We walked eastward along the full length of the Arcadiane, some 650 yards, passing at its far end on the left a large public building identified as the Gymnasium of the Theatre. This brought us to the theatre itself, an extremely impressive structure built into the lower western slope of Mount Pion, forming the most distinctive landmark in Ephesus. Once inside the theatre, we climbed up to the top tier of seats and found a comfortable place to spread out our picnic, with a sweeping view of the whole of the ancient city.

The theatre dates originally from early in the Hellenistic period, with extensive additions and reconstruction in the imperial Roman era. The horseshoe-shaped cavea extends through an arc of two hundred and twenty degrees, with a diameter of 495 feet, its uppermost tier nearly 100 feet above the orchestra. The seats are arranged in three tiers of increasing steepness, divided by rising radial stairways into eleven wedge-shaped sections called cunei. Additional stairways divide each of the top sections in two, the tiers separated from one another by circumferential walkways called diazomata, and the middle arc at the top is adorned with a colonnade. Originally, the actors in the Greek theatre performed in the skene, or scene building, of which the core remains in the structure that closes the arc of the cavea. This is the ruin of the monumental Roman stage building, originally an ornate structure in three storeys, in front of which the broad stage itself was raised well above the level of the orchestra on three rows of Doric columns, whose remnants are still *in situ.*

Looking down on the orchestra, as we finished the last of our wine, we could picture some of the scenes that had been played out there: performances of ancient Greek drama, mimes, and pantomimes; athletic events; celebrations of religious festivals; and mass demonstrations of the townspeople such as the one described in the Acts of the Apostles, where the silversmiths protested against the missionary activities of St. Paul, crying out 'Great is the goddess Artemis of the Ephesians!' According to a contemporary Syriac chronicle, the climactic moment in the triumph of Christianity over paganism in Ephesus took place in the theatre, where St. John the Theologian converted a multitude assembled by the 'procurator', the Roman governor. Clive Foss, in his *Ephesus After Antiquity*, paraphrases the Syriac account, ending with this description of the mass conversion:

> The procurator called an assembly of the people to confirm the conversion and discuss the fate of the idol-worshippers: as was the custom, the meeting took place in the Theater, where the ruler sat on his throne. Meanwhile the priests of Artemis blew horns and opened the gates of the Temple, where a multitude assembled. St. John, standing on the highest, or easternmost, row of seats in the Theater, blessed the Ephesians and baptized some 40,000 of them.

This mass conversion of the Ephesians by St. John would have taken place in the closing years of the first century AD, soon after the Theologian returned to Ephesus in AD 96. But an inscription of AD 104, found in the theatre by John Turtle Wood, indicates that the ancient rites of Artemis were then still being observed by the Ephesians in all their pomp and splendour. The inscription, found on a dedicatory offering to the goddess, described a ceremony that took place annually on the birthday of Artemis, 25 May according to the modern calendar. On the morning of that day a procession began at the Artemision, with the eunuch priests called Megabyzi leading the way and holding aloft a sacred image of the goddess. The procession reached the city at the Magnesia Gate, where it was met by all of the Ephebes, the young athletes in training, who from there formed a guard of honour for the goddess as her sacred image was carried to the theatre. There the principal festivities were celebrated, and at the conclusion of the ceremonies the Ephebes again formed a guard of honour as the Megabyzi headed the procession to escort the image on its return journey to the Artemision, leaving the city through the Coressos Gate. When Wood read this inscription he knew that the Artemision for which he had been searching vainly was outside Ephesus on the road that ringed Mount Pion to the north between the Coressos and Magnesia Gates, and his theory proved to be correct. It led to his discovery of the Temple of Artemis on 31 December 1869.

When we left the theatre, we turned to the left to continue along the main north-south street of Ephesus; this is generally known as the Marble Way, although some call it the Street of the Curetes, after an order of Ephesian priests. This part of the street was paved in marble in the fifth century A D by a wealthy Ephesian named Eutropius, creating a thoroughfare that was reserved for wheeled vehicles. Pedestrians used the raised porticoes that flanked the avenue.

A short stroll along the Marble Way brought us to the eastern end of the main commercial agora, a vast area stretching off to the right, ringed with the stumps of the columns that had formed its periphery, more than a hundred yards along each of its sides. Just as the theatre was the focal point of the cultural life of Ephesus, so was the agora the centre of its commercial world, for this was the place where much of the enormous volume of goods that passed through the city was bought and sold when the city was the principal port and entrepôt in Asia Minor. The agora was principally a food, produce, and cattle market, though on occasion it served as a place of public assembly. This market-place was founded in the Hellenistic period, with additions in the imperial Roman era. The double Doric colonnade in two storeys that forms the eastern side of the agora was erected during the reign of Nero, while the southern entrance is dated by an inscription to the year 4–3 BC. A large square off the south-east corner of the agora was once the sacred enclosure of a temple dedicated to the Egyptian god Serapis, with an inscription recording that it was also dedicated to the deified Caracella (211–17).

Just beyond that south-east corner, to the right of the Marble Way at its far end, we came to the Library of Celsus, now being splendidly restored. Inscriptions in both Greek and Latin record that the edifice was founded in A D 110 by the consul Gaius Julius Aquila in honour of his father, Gaius Celsus Polemaenus, a Roman senator and proconsul of Asia, and was dedicated as his funerary monument. The library, which was completed in AD 135, stood at the western end of a marble courtyard, its main floor approached by a flight of nine steps, once flanked by statues of Celsus. The reconstructed façade of the library, which is one of the glories of Ephesus, has as its principal members two pairs of columns supporting beams on each of its two storeys, and the three entrances are flanked by four niches containing figures personifying the virtues of Celsus— Manliness, Good Will, Wisdom, and Knowledge—copies of which now replace the originals. The library itself consisted of two towering chambers with a two-tiered gallery containing the rectangular niches in which some 12,000 books were stored, with the semicircular niche on the main floor facing the central portal probably containing a statue of Athena. The locked tomb of Celsus is located directly below this niche, his skeleton still intact inside his lead coffin, his remains having somehow escaped the catastrophes that ruined his beautiful library.

The Marble Way came to an end at the intersection, just beyond the agora and the Library of Celsus, with another street named the Embolos, or Colonnaded Way, which led from that point up through the valley between Mount Pion and Mount Coressos. The Embolos was the main street of Ephesus and the centre of the city during the imperial Roman era, flanked by some of its most important buildings, as well as by arcaded shops, monumental fountains, and honorific statues.

One of the colonnades that gave the Embolos its name extended along the left side of the avenue at its eastern end, just opposite the forecourt of the Library of Celsus. At the far end of the courtyard, just before the first side street leading off to the left, stood the public latrines, which apparently were adjacent to a brothel. The complex of buildings across the side street from the latrines is the Baths of Scholastica, the largest public bath-house in central Ephesus. The bath-house was founded by a Christian lady named Scholastica, who rebuilt this edifice lavishly in the latter years of the fourth century A D. A plinth within the baths bears a headless statue of a seated female figure identified as Scholastica herself, with an inscription praising her piety and generosity.

Directly in front of the baths, on the left side of the Embolos as one walks eastward, stands the Temple of Hadrian, the most beautiful structure in all of Ephesus, particularly its reconstructed porch. It consists of two pairs of columns framing the arched entrance to the porch, the architrave decorated with a superb relief in which the central figure, forming the keystone of the arch, is a bust of Tyche, the goddess of fortune and protectress of the city. An inscription over the architrave records that the temple was built by an Ephesian named P. Quintillius and dedicated to the deified emperor Hadrian (AD 117–38). The temple was restored during the fourth century A D, at which time a figurative relief was added to the upper zone of the walls in the porch together with the lunette opposite the entrance depicting a naked maiden emerging from a foliate scroll. The figures in the relief, which are copies of the originals in the archaeological museum of Selçuk, are thought to date from the third century A D; among the scenes represented here is one depicting the founding of Ephesus, with Androclus killing a wild boar whose presence revealed the site advised by the Delphic oracle.

The most recent excavations at Ephesus are on the hillside opposite the Temple of Hadrian, where a whole residential quarter of the late antique city has been unearthed on the lower slope of Mount Coressos. This seems to have been a very prosperous neighbourhood, the most luxurious dwellings consisting of a series of rooms arrayed around a peristyle court. Some of the villas still preserve their marble and mosaic floors and large sections of their walls decorated with gaily painted frescoes. This elegant quarter was still flourishing as late as AD 616, when it was destroyed in the Persian invasion led by Chosroes II.

After looking at this residential quarter, we returned to the

Embolos and continued walking eastward, passing on the left a side street that led to the upper tier of the theatre. Beyond that intersection, on the left, we passed the monumental Nymphaion of Trajan, a grandiose fountain whose façade has been partially reassembled. An inscription records that the fountain was erected in the years AD 102–4 by an Ephesian named T. Claudius Aristion, who dedicated it to the emperor Trajan (98–117). The pool of the fountain was surmounted by a colossal statue of Trajan, and statues of other emperors, gods, and heroes stood in niches around him. All of these were destroyed in some great catastrophe in late antiquity, and now fragments of the emperor's colossal statue lie along the side of the Embolos by his fountain. They include a giant right hand and a fragment of the globe that it once held, symbolizing the world that Trajan ruled as 'Emperor and God'.

Continuing on past the intersection, we followed the Embolos as far as the Gate of Hercules, which in antiquity formed the end of the avenue for vehicular traffic; the rest of the way was used by pedestrians only. The gate takes its name from the two figures in relief of Hercules on its western side, where he is shown wearing the pelt of the Nemean Lion. These pillars date from the second century AD, but they originally stood elsewhere and were erected here only in the sixth century. Beyond the gateway on the left side of the Embolos there are two minor monuments. The first of these, the Hydreion, consisted of a pool preceded by four columns, which have recently been re-erected. These columns were once surmounted by statues of the Tetrarchs, the Roman Emperors of the East and West and their two Caesars; this was an arrangement instituted by Diocletian in AD 286, when he became Emperor of the East, choosing Maximian as Emperor of the West, with Galerius and Constantius Chlorus serving as their Caesars. Just beyond the Hydreion is a funerary monument with an inscription dedicating it to 'Caius Memmius, son of Caius, grandson of Sulla, the Saviour'. The inscription here refers to Sulla's capture of Ephesus in 84 BC, 'saving' the city from those who had sided with Mithridates in his revolt against Rome.

This brings one to a large square once dominated at its south end by the Temple of Domitian (AD 81–96), of which there remains only the platform of the sanctuary, some column bases, and fragmentary reliefs from the altar of the deified emperor. Within the sanctuary there stood a colossal cult statue of the emperor—four times larger than life—but when Domitian was assassinated in the year AD 96 this sculpture was toppled by a mob and smashed to pieces on the ground where many of its fragments still lie. The monstrous head and an arm are preserved in the Izmir Archaeological Museum.

The north end of the square opposite the Temple of Domitian marks the beginning of a street known as Clivus Sacer, the Sacred Way, which leads eastward to what was once the government centre of Roman Ephesus. The street took its name from the fact that it was the route for the processions in which the sacred image of Artemis was carried through the city to the theatre after entering the Magnesia Gate. The street was also held sacred because it led to the shrine of Hestia Boulea; this was housed within the Prytaneion, the town hall of the autonomous city of Ephesus, whose ruins are just past the colonnade along the left side of the first stretch of the Sacred Way. The shrine of Hestia Boulea was in a small room behind the main chamber of the Prytaneion, and in there the sacred flame of the cult was kept perpetually burning in the sacred hearth of the sanctuary. Hestia, whose name in Greek means Hearth, was the goddess of the hearth and its sacred fire, and as such she was the patroness of the family, the tribe, and ultimately of the city. This is a cult that must go back to the very early days of the Greek race. According to mythology, Hestia was one of the children of Chronos and Rhea, a sister of Zeus, but in Ephesus she seems to have become identified with the ancient Anatolian fertility goddess, for several statues of Artemis were found within the Prytaneion and its shrine of the sacred hearth, apparently buried there in late antiquity after the worship of the old pagan deities had been forbidden by the edict of Theodosius.

Just beyond the Prytaneion, on the left side of the Sacred Way, there is another temple, now covered by the ruins of private houses from late antiquity. This temple was erected in 27 BC for Augustus, who dedicated it to the city of Rome and to the deified Julius Caesar, his adoptive father. Beyond this on the same side of the street is a small theatre, formerly called the Odeion, with a seating capacity of about 400; apparently this served as the bouleterion, or senate house, although it may also have been used for musical performances and ceremonial gatherings.

The right side of the Sacred Way was formed by the portico known as the Basilica; this in turn formed the northern stoa of the State Agora, a vast public square laid out and constructed during the reign of Augustus (27 BC–AD 14). This whole area has now been excavated and its foundations cleared, revealing in its western half the platform of a Temple of Isis. A portrait bust of Mark Antony was found within the temple, indicating that it may have been founded when he and Cleopatra visited Ephesus together in the winter of 32–31 BC.

A necropolis has been unearthed in recent excavations near the south-east corner of the State Agora, revealing tombs dating back to the sixth century BC. Across on the other side of the State Agora there is a monumental Roman fountain; this was originally built in the second century AD, but an inscription records that it was completely restored during the joint reign of the emperors Constantine II and Constans (337–50). This fountain served as the distribution point for the water brought into Ephesus on an aqueduct built during the reign of Augustus, erected by an Ephesian named Sextillius Pollio. The ruins at the north-east corner of the agora were a private bathhouse, built in the fifth century AD by a wealthy Ephesian named Varius.

There is an interesting structure some 200 yards to the south-east of the upper end of the Sacred Way, on the other side of the Selçuk road. The rotunda there was excavated by John Turtle Wood while he was searching for the Artemision, and the figures of a cross and a buffalo led him to believe that he had discovered the tomb of St. Luke. However, modern archaeologists have rejected this theory, identifying the rotunda as a heroon of the first century AD, converted into a Christian chapel in the Byzantine era. As for St. Luke, although there is a tradition that he may have died in Ephesus, the generally accepted belief is that he spent his last days in Bithynia and was buried there.

We continued walking eastward beyond the State Agora, heading towards the last ruins on that side of Ephesus; these have been identified as the East Gymnasium, erected in the second century AD. This was one of six large gymnasia that operated in Ephesus during the imperial Roman era, giving one some idea of how large a population the city had at that time. In addition to the exercise-rooms, gymnastic facilities, and baths it also had a market area with shops and a tavern, catering to the travellers who entered the city at the adjacent Magnesia Gate. The ruins of the Magnesia Gate can be seen just across the Selçuk road from the East Gymnasium. This gate took its name from the fact that it was the terminus for the road from Magnesia-ad-Maeandrum; and it was also the point at which the processional way entered the city, used when the sacred image of Artemis was carried through Ephesus during the celebration of her festival.

The Magnesia Gate and the Coressos Gate were the two main entrances through the defence walls of Hellenistic Ephesus. Just to the south of the Magnesia Gate one can see the eastern end of the Hellenistic walls that run along the slopes of Mount Coressos, extending a distance of some two and a half miles and originally stretching as far as the ancient harbour. The tower that anchored the walls at their seaward end can still be seen on a hilltop above the old harbour; this was known as the Prison of St. Paul, from a tradition that Paul was confined there during his imprisonment in Ephesus in AD 54–7.

just beyond the East Gymnasium a dirt road leads back to Selçuk, following the course of the ancient processional way between the Artemision and the Magnesia Gate. About two-thirds of the way along this road a path leads off to the left around a shoulder of Mount Pion, on whose northern slope stand a large necropolis and the remains of an early Christian basilica in and around a cave on the hillside. This is the Grotto of the Seven Sleepers of Ephesus, one of the most fascinating places in the ancient city and the subject, as it is, of a legend.

According to the legend, the cave is the tomb of seven Christian youths martyred during the reign of the emperor Decius, AD 149–51, when they were sealed up in the cavern by Roman soldiers and presumed dead. But the youths were only slumbering, and two centuries later they awoke, as the legend goes, and one of them went into Ephesus to buy food. The miracle became known throughout the empire and the medieval world, and Theodosius II himself made a pilgrimage to see the Seven Sleepers in their cave before they died natural deaths some time afterwards. The legend became as popular with Muslims as with Christians, appearing in the Koran; and in the Arab version of the tale the Seven Sleepers are always accompanied by their faithful dog, Katmir, who ascended with them into Paradise. The legend made the Grotto of the Seven Sleepers such a popular shrine that many pilgrims were after-wards buried there. Inscriptions indicate that it continued as a Christian sanctuary and necropolis until late in the fifteenth century. Accounts of medieval pilgrims indicate that the graves of St. Timothy and Mary Magdalene were also believed to be in the immediate vicinity of the cave. The tradition that Mary Magdalene spent her last years in Ephesus can be traced back to Gregory of Tours (AD 538–94), and in 1952 it was lent some credence by the French archaeologist Louis Massignon, who claimed that he had identified her tomb at the entrance to the grotto.

After viewing the Grotto of the Seven Sleepers, we retraced

our steps to the dirt track that leads from the Magnesia Gate to Selçuk, and soon we reached the Kuşadası road once again. There we crossed the road and took the path that leads up to the citadel on the Ayasuluk hill, past the Artemision. Then a short distance above the temple we came to Isa Bey Camii, the great mosque of Ephesus.

Isa Bey, who built this superb mosque in 1374–5, was a grandson of the emir Aydın, founder of the Aydınoğlu dynasty. Prior to that time the Aydınoğlu Turks in Ayasuluk had used the former Church of St. John as their principal mosque. The new mosque of Isa Bey, which was dedicated on 5 January 1375, was the first monumental structure to be erected in Ephesus since Justinian built the Church of St. John 840 years before, and it was the last building on a large scale ever to be put up in the town. Isa Bey Camii is a fine example of the Islamic architecture of the *beylik* period, a monument to the culture of the Aydınoğlu Turks, who flourished here in western Anatolia in the last century before the rise of the Ottoman Empire.

After leaving Isa Bey Camii, we climbed up the steep path that leads to the ruined medieval town of Ayasuluk, entering its lower enclosure through what was once the main gateway in the lower defence walls. This gate and the walls of which it is a part were constructed during the medieval Byzantine period, making considerable use of material from more ancient structures. Fragmentary reliefs above its arched entrance have been identified as scenes from the *Iliad* and include the deaths of Patroclus and Hector. These led an early traveller to call this the Gate of Persecution.

We passed through the gate and walked up a short way to the Church of St. John. During recent years this, the principal Christian monument in Ephesus, has been thoroughly studied by archaeologists, who have restored the building so that one can make out the plan of Justinian's great cathedral erected in 535. The church was preceded on its western side by a large atrium, from where the congregation passed to the nave through the exonarthex and the narthex, the outer and inner vestibules. The church itself is a cruciform basilica with four domes along its longitudinal axis and a pair flanking the central dome to form the arm of the cross. The structure was built in brick except for the marble piers that supported the dome, and was 213 feet wide across the transept and 525 feet in length, including the atrium and the semi-circular apse which was covered by a semi-dome. The floor of the nave was paved in marble, of which large sections have been restored, and the domes, semi-dome, and upper walls were undoubtedly decorated with mosaics and fresco paintings, as in the surviving churches of Byzantium. But the very heart of this edifice, and its reason for existing, was the sacred grave of St. John, enshrined beneath the pavement before the high altar and under the central dome—the goal of the multitudes who flocked to Ephesus during the Middle Ages.

The tomb was reached by a flight of six steps leading down from the nave, where one entered a small chapel containing the grave of St. John and three very precious relics: a fragment of the True Cross, a seamless garment woven by the Blessed Virgin which she wore during her last years in Ephesus, and the original manuscript of the Book of Revelations written by the Theologian himself. According to the popular belief among the pilgrims St. John was not really dead, but eternally sleeping in his grave here in Ephesus, where he would awaken only at the Second Coming of Christ. This belief seems to have been perpetuated by the local monks, as attested by Jordanus Catalanus who made a pilgrimage to Ephesus *c.* 1330: 'As I heard from a certain monk, who was there and heard it with his own ears, from hour to hour, a very loud sound is heard there, as of a man snoring'. Pilgrims were also led to believe that the grave of St. John exuded a fine dust, which they called manna, and to which they attributed magical and curative powers.

After leaving the Church of St. John, we made our way up into the citadel that crowns the Ayasuluk hill. This imposing fortress was probably built in the medieval Byzantine period when Ephesus had shrunk to the status of a small town, its people huddling for protection within this citadel as invading armies swept across the plains below. The town of Ayasuluk experienced a revival under the Lascarids, the dynasty that ruled in Nicaea from 1204 to 1261, giving rise to the Byzantine renaissance. One of the major figures of that cultural revival, Nicephorus Blemmydes (1197–1272), spent the last quarter-century of his life at a monastery in Ephesus, pouring out scholarly works on science and the humanities, a truly Renaissance man whose ideas would be influential in the intellectual regeneration that spread from Byzantium to the West in the following two centuries.

After exploring the citadel, we walked down into Selçuk and visited the archaeological museum there. The most interesting exhibits are two statues of Artemis Ephesia that were found in the Prytaneion, both of them dating from the middle imperial Roman era. The statues portray the goddess as Artemis Poly-mastros, a fertility goddess with numerous pendant breasts, the ancient Earth-Mother of Anatolia, as she also appears in other sculptures elsewhere in the museum.

When we had completed our visit to the museum we drove off to see the reputed House of the Blessed Virgin, known in Turkish as Meryemana. Meryemana is at Panayia Kapalu, five miles south of Selçuk, approached by a road that leads off to the right from the Aydın highway about half a mile from the town. The shrine at Panayia Kapalu is an ancient house where the Blessed Virgin is supposed to have spent the last years of her life when she dwelt in Ephesus in the company of St. John. The site of the house was revealed in a dream to Catherine Emmerich (1775–1824), an invalid German nun who never left her native Germany, but who gave a description from her vision that enabled the Lazarist Fathers of Izmir to locate this old stone dwelling in the wooded hills above Ephesus. It is just possible that this structure may date from the early Christian era, though there is no proof. In any event the House of the Virgin, as it is now called, was officially declared a shrine of the Roman Catholic Church in 1896, and since then it has become an extremely popular place of pilgrimage, attracting not only Christians but also non-Christians, including Muslim Turks, and a number of cures have been attributed to the Virgin by those who pray there for her intercession. On 26 July 1967 the house at Panayia Kapalu received a visit from Pope Paul VI, which made headline news around the world, and afterwards the pontiff granted a plenary indulgence to pilgrims who visited the shrine there. Thus Ephesus is once again the site of a world-famous shrine, with the Blessed Virgin now the object of veneration instead of Artemis, who herself replaced Cybele, the Phrygian deity who in turn developed from the far more ancient Anatolian fertility-goddess, the Great Earth-Mother, whose worship goes back to the beginning of civilization in Asia Minor.

After visiting Panayia Kapalu, we strolled about in the verdant woods above the shrine, pausing on a knoll that commanded a panoramic view of the countryside around Ephesus. Just a short distance to the west we could see the ruins of a Roman aqueduct crossing a valley between two ridges in the foothills of Mount Coressos, and I identified this as Arvalia, which some scholars have held to be Ortygia, the place in Greek mythology where Leto gave birth to Artemis. As one reads in the Homeric Hymn to Delian Apollo: 'Rejoice, blessed Leto, for you bear glorious children, the lord Apollo and Artemis who delights in arrows; her in Ortygia and him in rocky Delos ...'

The ancient festival celebrating the birth of Artemis survived into modern times as a *panegyri* of the Orthodox Church, which the local Greeks in the village of Kirkince observed each year on 15 August, the feast-day of the Assumption of the Blessed Virgin. Now that custom has ended too, discontinued since 1923 after the population exchange, and the birthday of Artemis, the virgin goddess, is no longer celebrated in her birthplace. But another holy lady has taken her place, as we were reminded when we walked back past the shrine at

Panayia Kapalu. A group of nuns on pilgrimage were singing a hymn to the Blessed Virgin, evoking visions of the ancient Anatolian goddess who once graced Ephesus with her divine presence.

11

THE MAEANDER VALLEY
AND APHRODISIAS

The morning after visiting Panayia Kapalu we set out on a two-day journey up the Maeander valley, our principal objective being the site of ancient Aphrodisias. After that we would resume our trip down the Aegean shore.

We drove toward Selçuk and turned right on to the Izmir–Aydın highway, which took us south for a short way before heading eastward along the Büyük Menderes, the River Maeander of antiquity, whose windings have given rise to the word 'meandering'. About three miles out of Selçuk we passed the ruins of a Roman aqueduct, built in the last decade of the reign of Augustus, the years AD 4–14. Then at Ortaklar, some thirteen miles from Selçuk, we turned right on to the road to Söke, our first diversion of the day. Two miles farther along we came to the site of Magnesia-ad-Maeandrum, whose fragmentary ruins flank the road, with the foundations of several monumental structures just to the right of where we parked our car. These ruins seemed totally out of place here beside a modern highway, survivors as they are from a completely different age in the history of the planet.

According to tradition, Magnesia-ad-Maeandrum was founded at the same time as Magnesia-ad-Sipylum, both of them settled by soldiers from Agamemnon's army after the Trojan War. These were the only important towns established inland from the Aegean coast at the time of the Hellenic migration to Anatolia at the end of the second millennium BC.

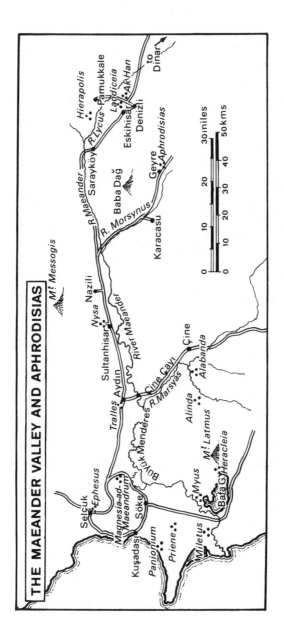

THE MAEANDER VALLEY AND APHRODISIAS

Magnesia ad Sipylum was founded in the valley of the Hermus and Magnesia-ad-Maeandrum here in the valley of the Maeander. This gave the Greeks access to the two great rivers that flowed into the sea from the heartland of Anatolia, and opened up the subcontinent to their trade and commerce.

Although Magnesia-ad-Maeandrum was in Ionia, its founders were Aeolians, and another tradition holds that, in their wanderings from the original Magnesia, they went first to Delphi, then to Crete, and then finally crossed the Aegean to Asia Minor, and thus their descendants could claim in an inscription that this was the first town in Anatolia to be established by the Greeks. Magnesia was originally located at the confluence of the Maeander and the Lethaeus, one of its tributaries, but in 398 BC it was moved to its present location by Thibron who, at Pergamum, succeeded Xenophon as commander of the Ten Thousand. The new site was chosen because it lay in the fertile valley of the Maeander on the eastern side of Mount Thorax, strategically located on an ancient thoroughfare called the Southern Highway which, according to Strabo, was 'a kind of common road used constantly by all who travel from Ephesus towards the east'. The new site also possessed a very ancient shrine of the Anatolian fertility goddess, whom the Greeks worshipped here under the name of Artemis Leucophryne, Of the White Brow. Late in the third century BC the Magnetes built a large temple dedicated to Artemis Leucophryne on the site of this shrine, and its foundations can still be seen to the west of the modern highway, beyond the ruins of the Byzantine defence walls. This was designed by Hermogenes, who also built the Temple of Dionysus at Teos, and Strabo writes that it was the third largest temple in Asia, surpassed only by the sanctuaries at Ephesus and Didyma. However, he believed that the Temple of Artemis Leucophryne was superior to that of Artemis Ephesia 'in the fine proportion of the skill exhibited in the structure of the enclosure'.

The new temple by Hermogenes seems to have been erected

following an extraordinary epiphany of Artemis shortly before 220 BC when the present structure was begun. The towns-people sent news of this to the shrine of Apollo at Delphi, whereupon the oracle there declared that Magnesia-ad-Mae-andrum and its environs were sacred ground. This led the Magnetes to institute a great quadrennial festival called the Leucophryna, inviting people from all over the Greek world, and an inscription found in the agora records the acceptance of some seventy cities. The celebration of this festival would have been held in the sanctuary of Artemis and also in the theatre, whose site we found at the foot of the hill to the south of the temple, though little is left of its structure.

Before we left Magnesia we recalled that two famous figures in the ancient Greek world met their end here, Polycrates of Samos and Themistocles of Athens. Polycrates was killed in Magnesia c. 524 BC by the Persian nobleman Oroetes, who had lured him here on the promise of giving him a rich treasure. This story is told by Herodotus in Book III of his *Histories*, where he writes that Polycrates 'sailed for Magnesia, where he met his end in dreadful contrast with his distinction and high ambition. For apart from the lords of Syracuse, no other petty king in the Greek world can be compared with Polycrates for magnificence. Somehow or other—the precise manner need not be told—Oroetes had him murdered and the dead body hung on a cross'. Themistocles died in Magnesia by his own hand in 466 BC, thus resolving the crisis of conscience that confronted him when his host Xerxes asked him to take action against his fellow Greeks. As Plutarch writes:

At any rate he decided that his best course was to end his life in a manner that was worthy of it, and so after offering sacrifice to the gods he called his friends together, clasped their hands and bade them farewell. Then, according to the generally accepted theory, he drank bull's blood, or as others say, a swift poison, and died in the sixty-fifth year of his life, most of which he spent in politics and wars, in government and in command. It is said that when the king learned of the manner of his death and the reasons for it, he admired Themistocles more than ever and continued to show kindness both to his friends and family.

After leaving Magnesia, we drove back to the Izmir–Aydın highway and headed eastward once again up the Maeander valley, which is here bounded to its north by Mount Messogis. Strabo follows this same route in his description of the Maeander valley between Magnesia and Tralles, the site of which is now occupied by the modern town of Aydın. As he writes: 'After Magnesia is the road to Tralles; travellers have on the left hand Messogis, and on the right hand ... the plain of the Maeander, which is occupied in common by Lydians, Carians, Ionians, Milesians, Mysians, and the Aeolians of Mysia'.

After a drive of nineteen miles past the turn-off to Söke we came to Aydın, a large market town on the northern side of the Maeander valley. Once known as Güzel Hisar, the Beautiful Castle, the town takes its modern name from the fact that, in the fourteenth century, it was the capital of the Aydınoğlu *beylik*, the Turkoman principality that flourished in this part of Asia Minor before the rise of the Ottoman Empire. There are no monuments in the town surviving from the Aydınoğlu era, but from the Ottoman period there are several structures: the Cihanoğlu Camii, dating from 1768; Bey Camii and Ramazan Camii, both built in the sixteenth century; and an eighteenth-century *medrese* constructed from the ruins of ancient buildings in Tralles. In the upper part of the town a pair of towers flanks Zindan Kapı, once the entrance to the citadel of Byzantine Tralles. This quarter would have been the birthplace of Anthemius of Tralles, one of the great mathematicians and physicists of late antiquity, who in 532 was appointed by Justinian to design the new cathedral of Haghia Sophia in Constantinople. The fragmentary ruins of Tralles are on the flat-topped acropolis hill above the modern town, but this site is a military zone and cannot be visited without permission. So after a brief visit to the town we drove on.

Nineteen miles beyond Aydın we turned left off the highway into Sultanhisar, a little village at the foot of Mount Messogis. From the village a drive of about a mile and a quarter along a dirt road brought us to the site of ancient Nysa, where we spent an hour or so exploring the ruins. Here we let Strabo act as our guide, for he had studied at Nysa and knew the town well. His description of its topography is still remarkably accurate though written two thousand years ago:

Nysa is situated near Mount Messogis, for the most part lying upon its slopes; and it is a double city, so to speak, for it is divided by a torrential stream that forms a gorge, which at one place has a bridge over it, joining the two cities, and at another it is adorned with an amphitheatre, with a hidden underground passage for the torrential waters. Near the theatre are two heights, below one of which is the gymnasium of youths; and below the other is the market-place and the gymnasium for older persons.

The setting of Nysa is quite striking, with the overgrown ruins set astride the wild gorge running down from the slopes of Mount Messogis. It is just as Strabo describes it—a double city—bisected by the torrential stream which in winter and early spring flows down the gorge from the mountain, with a bridge crossing it at one point, a long tunnel canalizing the flood waters for a long part of its course, and an amphitheatre constructed above the torrent, an ingenious engineering feat which thus joined the two halves of the river-riven town. The most prominent of the surviving structures is the theatre, which is made particularly picturesque by the grove of olive-trees that has taken root among its tiers of seats. The library is the best-preserved building of its type in Asia Minor; like all of the other extant structures in Nysa it dates from the Roman period.

From Nysa we returned to the highway and continued eastward up the Maeander valley, with the snow-capped summit of Baba Dağ, the Father's Mountain, looming ahead and to the right, its peak 7,570 feet above sea-level. Soon we passed Nazilli, another large market town at the foot of the hills on the northern side of the valley. Then, fifteen miles past the turn-off to Nazili, we turned right on to a road signposted for Karacasu, which would bring us along the banks of the Akçay, the ancient River Morsynus, as we headed for the ruins of Aphrodisias.

The site of Aphrodisias is some twenty-five miles up the valley of the Morsynus at Geyre. Geyre was one of the prettiest and most picturesque villages in this part of Anatolia, and much of its charm stemmed from the extraordinary way in which the Turkish community seemed to have grown out of the ancient city of Aphrodisias, with fragments of Graeco-Roman architectural members forming part of the modern houses. But, unfortunately, the widening scope of the archaeological excavations, which began in 1961 under the direction of Professor Kenan Erim of New York University, have made it necessary to relocate the villagers of Geyre to a new site, which is about a mile and a quarter to the west of the Byzantine defence walls of the ancient city. This has made old Geyre somewhat less picturesque, but it has allowed Professor Erim to begin resurrecting Aphrodisias in all its glory, one of the most exciting and rewarding archaeological projects in all of Turkey. Some of the beautiful works of sculpture unearthed by Professor Erim are now housed in a new museum in Aphrodisias, while others are preserved around the site itself. This is one of the most extraordinary collections of ancient sculpture in existence and, after seeing it, one realizes why Aphrodisias is called the Florence of the Graeco-Roman world, a centre of art here in the remote hills of ancient Caria.

The archaeological excavations at Aphrodisias have uncovered pottery sherds from the beginning of the third millennium BC, the early Bronze Age, and some finds even date back to the fourth millennium BC, the latter part of the Chalcolithic, or Copper Age. According to Stephanus of Byzantium, one of the earliest names of Aphrodisias was Ninoë, after the semi-legendary Babylonian king Ninus; however it more probably derives from the Akkadian name for Ishtar, the fertility goddess of Nineveh and Babylon, who was one of the predecessors of the Greek goddess of love, 'golden Aphrodite ... who stirs up sweet passions in the gods and subdues the tribes of mortal men'. The earliest evidence for a shrine of Ishtar-Ninoë-Aphrodite here dates to the sixth or fifth century BC, but there does not seem to have been a town-sized settlement until the second century BC. The emergence of Aphrodisias as a town at that time seems to have been followed within a century by the construction of the present Temple of Aphrodite. This appears to have been a turning-point in the history of the town, for then its shrine became clearly identified with the Greek goddess of love rather than with the earlier Anatolian fertility goddess. The identification with Aphrodite, known in Latin as Venus, was of particular importance later when Roman rule was established in Asia Minor, for the goddess of love was the mother of Aeneas, the legendary founder of Rome. According to Appian, writing in the second century AD, the oracle at Delphi advised the Roman dictator Sulla to make offerings to the shrine of Aphrodite at Aphrodisias whereupon, in 81 BC, he donated a golden crown and a Carian double axe. Inscriptions on the Archive Wall of the theatre building record the donation of a golden Eros by Julius Caesar, whose family claimed direct descent from Venus. In 39 BC Octavian, the future Augustus, while still triumvir, referred to Aphrodisias as 'one city in all of Asia I have selected as my own', and it remained a favourite of his after he became emperor in 27 BC and indeed throughout his reign. The privileged position of Aphrodisias in the Roman Empire is also attested by a number of letters from emperors of the second and third century AD, most of which are inscribed on the Archive Wall. During the Roman period the Temple of Aphrodite at Aphrodisias became a very important shrine, attracting growing numbers of pilgrims from all over the Graeco-Roman world. As a result monumental structures were built in Aphrodisias and the city adorned with splendid sculptures; local sculptors in fact also exported their works to Rome and else where in the eastern Mediterranean. This success of Aphrodisian sculpture was made possible by the proximity of a rich source of marble on the slopes of Baba Dağ, with quarries only a mile from the city. The exceptionally high artistic quality of the local statues suggests that master sculptors moved to Aphrodisias from Pergamum after the end of the Attalid dynasty in 133 BC. They gave a tremendous impetus to Aphrodisian sculpture, which reached its peak in the second century AD and continued at an exceptionally high level right down to the end of antiquity. The town also had a number of renowned scholars and writers, of whom the most notable was Alexander of Aphrodisias who flourished late in the second century AD, and whose commentaries on Aristotle were very popular in Europe during the Renaissance.

The status of Aphrodisias changed in the mid-third century AD, when it ceased to be an autonomous city and became capital of a Roman province that included both Caria and Phrygia. However, that province was reduced subsequently, during the reign of Diocletian (284–305), to a province that comprised only Caria. After the adoption of Christianity by Constantine the Great in the year 325 Aphrodisias became the seat of an archbishopric; nevertheless, the worship of Aphrodite continued in the city until it was stamped out by the anti-pagan edicts of Theodosius I (379–95). Later, in the sixth century the name of Aphrodisias was changed to Stavropolis, the City of the Cross, as a final measure to eradicate all memory of the pagan goddess of love. But as time went on this name went out of use and the town was generally referred to as Caria, a name which in the Turkish tongue eventually became Geyre, the village that grew up in the ruins of ancient Aphrodisias.

After visiting the new museum in the main square of old Geyre, we walked toward the centre of Aphrodisias, which is still surrounded by large stretches of its Byzantine defence walls, a circuit more than two miles in circumference. At the western end of the village we came to the Tetrapylon, an elaborately sculptured monumental gateway that originally had four rows of four columns. Part of the pediment is still in place between a pair of spirally fluted monoliths. This handsome gateway was erected in the mid-second century A D, and may have been part of an ornamental approach to the Temple of Aphrodite whose own propylon was just a hundred yards to the west.

We now walked over to the Temple of Aphrodite, the most romantic monument in Aphrodisias, its peripteral colonnade having withstood for two thousand years the force of earthquakes and the onslaught of invading armies that destroyed the city of which it was once the heart.

The earliest sanctuary of Aphrodite on this site is believed to date from the sixth century B C. The principal evidence for this is a colossal Archaic statue of Aphrodite found in 1962 immediately to the south of the temenos, or temple precinct, undoubtedly the cult figure that once stood within the sanctuary. Many smaller replicas of this statue have been found in several places around the eastern Mediterranean, including a large number in Rome. They give one some idea of how popular and widespread the cult of Carian Aphrodite was in Graeco-Roman times. The present edifice is believed to date from the late second or early first century B C. It was originally designed as an Ionic temple with a peristyle of thirteen columns along the sides and eight at the ends, with the cella, or inner sanctuary, preceded by a pronaos, or porch. Fourteen of the columns are still standing, all but one of them complete with their Ionic capitals, and two groups still support fragments of the architrave. The apsidal structure at the eastern end of the sanctuary dates from the fifth century A D, when the temple was converted into a Christian basilica.

Just to the south of the temple there is a complex of ruins unearthed in 1962. The first of the monuments to be uncovered in this complex was the odeion, an elegant little theatre with nine rows of seats divided into five cunei, the ends of the tiers adorned with lions' legs. This dates to the second century A D and is one of the best-preserved structures of its type in Asia Minor. The odeion had a capacity of 1,700 and would have been used for concerts, musical comedies, ballet, pantomime, lectures, political discussions, and meetings of the senate and town council. The floor of the auditorium was covered with a mosaic pavement and the stage building was adorned with sculptured reliefs and statuary, while a backstage corridor opened on to a porticoed square lined with portrait statues of prominent Aphrodisians; many of these works of art were found during the excavations and are now on exhibit in the local museum. Adjoining the odeion to the west is a circular heroon dedicated to a prominent but unknown Aphrodisian; in the centre of this stood an ornate sarcophagus with sculptures in low relief, now in the museum. Beyond the odeion to the west is a complex centering on a courtyard with a lovely peristyle of blue marble columns and a triconch hall to the east; this is thought to have been the residence of the bishop of Aphrodisias in early Byzantine times.

South of the odeion and the bishop's palace are the remains of the vast agora, an unexcavated area that is overgrown with grass and brambles, brilliant with wild flowers and blossoming fruit-trees at the time of our mid-April visit. A splendid colonnade complete with capitals and architrave stands nobly in a poplar grove, evoking the vanished grandeur of Roman Aphrodisias.

Another large complex of ruins has been excavated just south of the agora. The westernmost of the structures unearthed here has been identified as the Baths of Hadrian, dating from the second century A D. This comprises two pairs of large galleries on either side of a huge central hall, the calidarium or steam-room; the chamber to the south of this was the tepidarium, a room of intermediate temperature which served as the anteroom to the baths; and the chamber to the east was the apoditarium, a reception hall and dressing-room, where a number of beautiful sculptures were found in 1965. Adjoining the Baths of Hadrian to the east is the Portico of Tiberius, whose splendid Ionic colonnade has now been partially restored. Adjoining the south-west corner of this portico is a long and narrrow basilica consisting of a large nave and two side aisles, the whole structure extending southward for over one hundred yards. Both the basilica and the Portico of Tiberius are believed to date from the first century AD.

At the eastern end of the Portico of Tiberius there is a monumental structure known as the Agora Gate complex. This structure, which dates from the late second century AD, appears to have been an elaborate gateway with a massive two-storeyed columnar façade, flanked by projecting towers with barrel vaults surmounted by colonnaded upper storeys. Inscriptions indicate that the Agora Gate complex was converted into a fountain-house in the fifth century AD.

A short way to the north-east of the Agora Gate another complex of ruins has been unearthed in recent years. This has been identified as the Sebasteion, a word derived from the Greek 'Sebastos', which is equivalent to the Latin 'Augustus'. It is a shrine devoted to the cult of the deified Augustus-Sebastos and his successors in the Julio-Claudian line. The Sebasteion consists of two parallel porticoes about ninety yards in length along the east-west axis, the north and south porticoes separated by a fifteen-yard-wide area that may have been a processional avenue. A propylon stands at its western end, and to the east is a platform that may have been a shrine to the deified imperial line. The south portico was designed in three superimposed rows of half-columns, the lower one Doric, the middle Ionic, and the upper Corinthian, with large panels decorated in relief in the intercolumniations of the second and third storeys. The north portico was of essentially the same design, but with subtle differences in its façade. Investigations indicate that the Sebasteion was built in the first century AD, starting in the reign of Tiberius (14–37) and continuing through those of Claudius (41–54) and Nero (54–68).

Another impressive complex of ruins has been excavated

south of the Agora Gate complex, the most notable monument being a large theatre unearthed from the eastern slope of an eminence known as the Acropolis. The theatre dates from the second half of the first century BC. It had seats for about 8,000 spectators, the horseshoe-shaped cavea designed with two or three diazomata divided into nine cunei, and twenty-seven rows of seats still survive in excellent condition below the preserved diazoma. Extensive remodelling of the orchestra and stage building was carried out toward the end of the second century AD. The main objective of this reconstruction was apparently to deepen the pit of the orchestra and to separate it from the first row of seats, so as to protect the spectators during gladiatorial combats and animal hunts and baitings. The core of the stage building consisted of six vaulted chambers identified by inscriptions as dressing-rooms for the actors and performers, with a congeries of dungeon rooms and corridors below which were used as storage areas and for the confinement of wild animals kept for hunts and baitings.

The most exciting find made in the excavation of the theatre was that of an archive of inscriptions on the wall of the north parados, one of the corridors connecting the cavea and the stage building. This Archive Wall, as it is now called, contains numerous historical inscriptions made in the first half of the third century AD, and records decrees, letters, and events dating back to the middle of the first century BC. They include letters from the emperors Trajan, Hadrian, Commodus, Septimius Severus, Caracella, Severus Alexander, and Gordion III, all of them referring to the favoured status granted to Aphrodisias by the Romans. Here and elsewhere in the excavations beautiful works of sculpture were found among the ruins, in this case along with a fresco representing the Archangel Michael, a rare example of the painted art of the early Byzantine era.

Excavations around the theatre have unearthed a large area immediately to its east, and a complex of ruins just to the south of that area. The large area east of the theatre had a circular foundation at its centre, apparently an altar, and its periphery was formed by a rectangular colonnade, which led to its being called the Tetrasoon, or four-porticoed piazza. It is believed that the Tetrasoon was used as a market-place and shopping mall, and was perhaps built in the fourth century A D after the older agora to the north-west had been permanently flooded by a rising of the local water-table. Adjoining the Tetrasoon to the south is a structure identified as the Theatre Baths, originally constructed in the late second or early third century A D. Two notable units of the baths that have been excavated so far are an enormous domed chamber of circular plan, which served as the calidarium of the baths, and a beautiful hall in the form of a basilica, adorned with marble paving and an exquisite colonnade of blue-grey Corinthian columns. This basilica-hall may have been an extension of the Tetrasoon market piazza, with cubicles in its side aisles perhaps housing shops and tavernas.

The acropolis hill on which the theatre was built is one of two mounds, both of them artificial, which stand within Aphrodisias. The other is Pekmez Hüyük, which stands just a few hundred yards to the east within the village. Excavations on these mounds have shown that both of them were inhabited as far back as the early Bronze Age and even the late Copper Age. (A very recent find within the Pekmez mound has been dated to c. 5800 BC, in the latter part of the neolithic period, or New Stone Age.)

We completed our tour of Aphrodisias at the stadium, which is on the northern side of the archaeological site. This is one of the largest and best-preserved stadia surviving from the Graeco-Roman world. The stadium is 290 yards long and 55 yards across at its widest point, and it terminates at two circular ends to east and west. There are about thirty tiers of benches, with a seating capacity of some 30,000. The stadium was built in the first or second century A D, and was used principally for athletic events and games. However, on occasion it was the scene of musical performances, theatrical productions, political meetings, religious festivals, and contests in poetry and singing, as well as a unique competition in sculpture, evidence of the high esteem in which that art was held in Aphrodisias.

As several gnarled old olive-trees had taken root along the top tier of the stadium, we found a place in the dappled shade of one of them and had our lunch there looking out over the ruins of Aphrodisias. The setting of the ancient city is superb, standing at the head of the valley in which the Morsynus rises. Mount Cadmus towers majestically to the east, while to the north one can see the distant summits of Mount Tmolus towering over the peaks and ridges of the Messogis range. Aphrodisias is one of the loveliest sites in Anatolia, and seeing it that April day made us realize why Augustus preferred this among all the cities he ruled in Asia Minor.

It was mid-afternoon when we left, and the beauty of the April day made our departure an even more reluctant one, but our schedule was inexorable and forced us to move on. We drove back from Geyre to the main highway, after which we turned right and once again headed eastwards up the valley of the Maeander. Then, twenty-five miles past the turn-off to Aphrodisias, the highway turned abruptly south and brought us to Sarayköy, as we crossed the Maeander just below the Çürüksu, the River Lycus of antiquity. We had completed our journey up the valley of the Maeander and were now heading south-east along the valley of the Lycus to Denizli, one of the great crossroads of western Anatolia, where highways lead off to Caria, Lydia, Phrygia, and Lycia.

Denizli was originally known as Ladik, a corruption of the Greek Laodiceia whose inhabitants had been moved there during the Selcuk period from the ancient town which was some six miles farther to the north. During the period of the Aydınoğlu *beylik* and in early Ottoman times this was an important market-town, famed for its Ladik carpets, which can still be found here and in Istanbul's Covered Bazaar. The earliest description of Laodiceia-Denizli under Turkish rule is by the famous Arab traveller Ibn Battuta, who visited the town in 1336 and wrote of its 'splendid gardens, perennial streams, and gushing springs. Its bazaars are very fine and in them are manufactured cotton fabrics edged with gold embroidery. Most of the artisans there are Greek women, who are subject to the Muslims and pay dues to the Sultan'. Ibn Battuta also noted that there was a slave-market in the town, where buyers could come 'to purchase beautiful Greek girls and put them out to prostitution and each girl has to pay a regular share to her master. The girls go into the bath-house along with the men'.

Denizli is now a large market town that has become a centre for tourists visiting Pamukkale, or Cotton Castle, an extraordinary natural phenomenon which is to be seen on the cliffs of the Lycus some twelve miles to the north on the site of ancient Hierapolis; but there is nothing to see in Denizli itself, because whatever old Aydınoğlu or Ottoman monuments it might have had were destroyed in the frequent earthquakes that have shaken the region.

About five and a half miles out of Denizli we crossed the Lycus, after which we traversed the northern side of the valley and approached the foothills of Çal Dağ on the other side. As we did so we came within view of Pamukkale, one of the most extraordinary sights in all of Anatolia, its incredibly eroded and calcium-encrusted cliff-face a dazzling chalk-white phantasmagora of stalactites and stalagmites, with vaporous water pouring down its sides through a widening succession of scallop-shell and petal-like pools surfaced in glistening limestone. And atop this plateau was the final goal of our long drive up the valley of the Maeander, the ruins of ancient Hierapolis.

Hierapolis, the Holy City, is undoubtedly so named because of the many temples that once stood there. Hierapolis was founded in the first quarter of the second century BC by Pergamum, probably by King Eumenes II. Apart from the necropolis, there is hardly anything left of the Hellenistic city, and virtually all of the surviving monuments are from the Roman period when Hierapolis was an extremely popular resort. The first buildings which we saw on our arrival were the huge Roman baths, ponderous edifices dating from the second century A D. One of the baths is now used to store the sculptures and other antiquities discovered in recent excavations, and perhaps in the future it will be opened as a museum.

After parking by the baths we checked in at the Turizm Hotel, which is built around the Sacred Pool, where we had a swim before exploring the ruins of Hierapolis. There cannot be another hotel in the world that has a swimming-pool like this: it winds around the hotel courtyard, bounded by a very pretty garden of rose bushes, hibiscus, oleanders, mulberry trees, cedar trees, and cypresses, and on its bottom we could see fluted columns and Corinthian capitals from the Roman portico that stood nearby, looking like the submerged ruins of an enchanted palace.

When we set out to explore the ruins we began with those behind the hotel, which are the remains of a monumental fountain of the fourth century A D. Behind the fountain are the ruins of a Temple of Apollo, the only one of the city's many sanctuaries that has survived. The upper parts of the building are from the imperial Roman era, but the foundations are from the Pergamene period, probably part of the original temple built by Eumenes II. The god of the Underworld was also worshipped here in a cave sanctuary called the Plutonium, the atmosphere of which was said by Strabo to be deadly poisonous though 'the eunuchs of Cybele, however, are immune, to the extent that they can approach the orifice and look in, and even penetrate for some distance, though not necessarily without holding their breath'. The entrance to the Plutonium is an arched opening on the south side of the Temple of Apollo, a grotto known locally as the Place of Evil Spirits, where occasionally one sees the bodies of birds or small animals that have strayed into the cave and been killed by the deadly vapours within.

We now strolled along the main thoroughfare of ancient Hierapolis, which is a colonnaded street extending for about a mile and a quarter parallel to the edge of the plateau and passing between the Temple of Apollo and the Sacred Pool. This grand avenue had monumental propylae at both ends but only the northern one remains largely intact; it comprises a triple arch flanked by a pair of round towers, and an inscription on the gateway records that it was erected in AD 84 in honour of the emperor Domitian.

On the hillside behind the hotel is the theatre, a splendid Roman structure that has recently been restored. Some of the sculptures with which the building was once adorned are now stored in the Roman baths; one of the reliefs there is a scene representing the emperor Septimius Severus, and thus the theatre is dated to the period of his reign, AD 193–211. Many of the other reliefs are scenes from the life of Dionysus, including a Dionysian procession, a festival that would have had its climax here in the theatre of Hierapolis when the feast-day of the wine-god was celebrated.

After visiting the theatre we walked behind it to explore the Roman defence walls, which extend around the city in an irregular semicircle as far as the edge of the cliff. Outside the city walls to the east, approached by a portal known as the Gate of Hadrian, is the necropolis of the ancient city; some 1,200 tombs have been unearthed here in recent excavations, the oldest dating back to the time of the original Pergamene town. Within the area of the necropolis there is also a Christian basilica of the fifth century AD. On a hill to the north of the necropolis a martyrium of the fifth century AD has been identified as the tomb of Philip the Apostle. Although no evidence of a burial has been unearthed on the site, Christian tradition holds that St. Philip spent his last years in Hierapolis, suffering martyrdom here c. AD 80.

After leaving the necropolis we returned to the theatre and sat in one of its upper tiers to look at the approaching sunset, which in the wonderland of Pamukkale was quite sensational. After the sun had set we returned to the hotel, where we had supper outside on the terrace overlooking the Sacred Pool. The following morning we would retrace our journey back along the Maeander valley, pausing first for a brief excursion in the Lycus valley and a stop in ancient Laodiceia.

The next day, after descending from the plateau, we drove back across the valley and crossed the Lycus once again. We then rejoined the main highway that connects Denizli and Dinar and turned left on a brief excursion up the Lycus for about a mile and a quarter to its confluence with the Cadmus, known in Turkish as Gök Pınar Suyu, the Stream of the Sky-blue Pine. There, on the left side of the highway, we stopped to see the object of our diversion, the Selcuk caravanserai known as Ak Han. An inscription over the doorway of Ak Han records that it was founded on 19 July 1254 by the Selcuk sultan Izzedin Kaykavus II, who ruled from 1246 to 1283. These caravanserais were wayside inns where travellers could remain without charge for three days, one of the amenities of Anatolian travel in the days of the Sultanate of Rum as the Selcuk realm was called. There are fifty of these caravanserais still standing along the highways of central Anatolia, all of them built in the thirteenth century when the Sultanate of Rum was at the height of its power.

From Ak Han we once again headed for Denizli. Then after about half a mile we turned right off the highway on to the old road to Pamukkale, which is now the approach to the site of ancient Laodiceia. About a mile down this road we came to the village of Eskihisar, the Old Castle, the name by which Laodiceia came to be known in Turkish times after its people had abandoned the town and allowed it to fall into ruins. We passed Eskihisar and came to the site of Laodiceia itself, whose ruins are scattered over a bare hilltop bounded by two tributaries of the Lycus, the Asopus to the north-west and the Caprus to the south-east. The road brought us around the southern side of the hill and we stopped midway along the side bordered by the Asopus, surveying the ruins we were about to explore.

Laodiceia was founded in the second quarter of the third

century B C by the Seleucid king Antiochus II Theos who named it for his wife Laodicea (though he divorced her in 253 BC). The city that he founded here is more accurately known as Laodiceia-ad-Lycum, since there were many other towns named Laodiceia founded by the Seleucid kings, including five established by Seleucus I Nicator (312–281 BC), the founder of the dynasty.

Laodiceia is known in the history of Christianity as another of the Seven Churches of Revelation. As the Evangelist wrote in the seventh letter of the Book of Revelation: 'To the angel of the church at Laodiceia: These are the words of the Amen, the faithful and true witness, the prime source of all God's creation: I know all your ways; you are neither hot nor cold. How I wish you were either hot or cold! But because you are lukewarm, neither hot nor cold, I will spit you out of my mouth ...'

Laodiceia continued to flourish throughout late antiquity, but in the year AD 494 it was destroyed in a catastrophic earthquake from which it never fully recovered. In 1094 Laodiceia was further severely damaged when it was captured by the Selcuks, and though the Byzantines recovered the town three years later, during the Fourth Crusade, it was sacked repeatedly during the remaining years of Greek rule in Asia Minor until it was finally abandoned altogether, leaving the ruins that one sees today. These include the remains of an Ionic temple, a large Greek theatre, a smaller Roman theatre, an odeion, a gymnasium, a stadium, and an aqueduct, as well as some fragmentary remnants of the defence walls that once encircled the town.

We resumed our journey back to Selçuk, soon passing through Denizli and heading westward along the Maeander valley. As we drove we caught occasional glimpses of the Maeander, as it undulated its way inexorably through to the Aegean between colonnades of poplars and birches, its fertile soil still nurturing the farms along its verdant banks, as it has since the first Hellenic-Carian towns were founded in this valley before the dawn of history. We thought of this as we drove on in the late afternoon through the beautiful countryside where Caria and Lydia merge into Ionia.

Just after sunset we reached Selçuk, where we checked in once more at the Tusan Motel, the ruins of Ephesus silent about us in the elegiac twilight.

12

MILETUS AND THE VANISHED
SPLENDOURS OF IONIA

Once again, during the midnight hours, we heard nightingales singing to one another in the ruins of Ephesus. In the morning we made an early start for Kuşadası, planning to have breakfast there before beginning our tour of the southern Ionian shore.

The Kuşadası road brought us down the alluvial plain of the Cayster to the sea, some three miles west of Ephesus, after which it turned south and took us across a headland to one of the most beautiful bays on the Aegean coast of Turkey. In late medieval times this was called the Gulf of Scala Nova. The bay is formed by two promontories: the one to the north is called Kuşadası or the Isle of Birds. That name in Turkish times was given to the little town around the port, which on its southern side is enclosed by a causeway terminating in a ruined Genoese fortress. Kuşadası has in recent years become a major port-of-call for foreign cruise-liners, most of whose passengers go from there on day-trips to Ephesus, and it has also developed into one of the most important yachting centres on the Aegean coast of Turkey, with a marina handling some 400 vessels. This had changed Kuşadası from a quiet old fishing village into a bustling modern tourist resort, but the crowds of foreign travellers have not spoiled its charm. So it was with great pleasure that we sat down for breakfast that April morning at our favourite restaurant in Kuşadası, on the quay beside the pier, where a ferry was just about to leave for the Greek island of Samos.

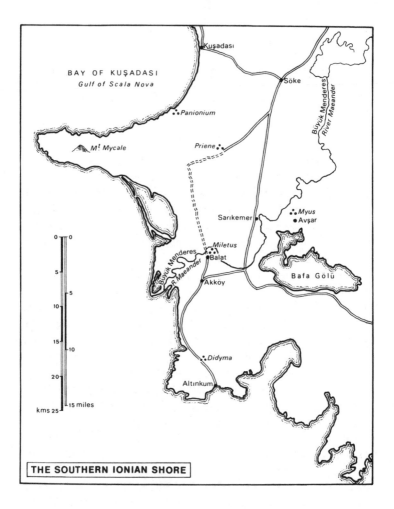

BAY OF KUŞADASI
Gulf of Scala Nova

Kuşadası

Söke

Büyük Menderes
River Maeander

••*Panionium*

M.ᵗ *Mycale*

Priene ••

•*Myus*
•Avşar

Sarıkemer

Büyük Menderes
R. Maeander

Miletus
▪Balat

Akköy

Bafa Gölü

••*Didyma*

Altınkum

kms 25 ⌐15 miles

THE SOUTHERN IONIAN SHORE

The original Greek name for Kuşadası was Phygela, one of three little ports on the coast around Ephesus, the other two being Neapolis and Panormus. As the harbour of Ephesus itself began to silt up in late antiquity, Phygela became its principal port, and later served as an important naval base in the Byzantine Empire. With the signing of the Treaty of Nymphaeum in 1261, Phygela became the property of the Genoese, who called it Scala Nova, the New Port, the same name as was also applied to the surrounding gulf. After the Turkish conquest of the town, at the beginning of the fourteenth century, its name was changed to Kuşadası, probably because of the sea-birds that nest on the island-like promontory that forms the northern arm of the port. Despite this long history, the only antiquities to be seen in Kuşadası are the Genoese fortress at the end of the causeway, which probably dates to the late thirteenth century, and the Okuz Mehmet Paşa Hanı, a seventeenth-century Ottoman caravanserai that now serves as a luxury hotel run by the Club Mediterranée.

Kuşadası is an ideal base for seeing the sites on the Aegean coast below Izmir, but we decided to spend the night in Söke, an inland town seventeen miles farther to the south, because it was closer to the sites on the southern Ionian shore that we were going to visit over the next two days.

Söke is a very lively and very Turkish market town, always busy with farmers coming in from their lands on the alluvial delta of the Maeander, which finally winds its way out to the Aegean south of Cape Mycale. We checked into a little hotel in the centre of Söke, went next door to a *bakkal* to buy some food and wine for lunch, and then we were off, heading for the southern Ionian shore.

We drove south from Söke across the plain of the Maeander, with the great massif of Mount Mycale looming above us just to the west and extending literally from the roadside in a great arc out to Cape Mycale, cutting off our view of Samos as soon as we passed under its north-eastern shoulder. About four and a half miles out of Söke we passed the ruins of a Roman aqueduct. Then another four and a half miles farther along we turned off on to a dirt road that brought us in past the flank of Mount Mycale to the very pretty village of Güllü Bahçe, the Rosy Garden. We parked our car there and walked up the path that leads to the site of ancient Priene.

Priene is the most superbly situated of all the ancient Ionian cities, standing on a tiered terrace of Mount Mycale well above the Maeander plain with an enormous spire-like crag of the mountain jutting up directly behind it to a jagged peak 1,275 feet high. And the ruins themselves are like no other site along the western shores of Turkey, quintessentially Greek as contrasted to Roman Ephesus. On the mid-April day of our last visit to Priene, when we spent the entire afternoon there alone, getting to know the place again after an absence of almost ten years, the mottled stones of the early Hellenistic city looked as if they had suddenly collapsed in one catastrophic moment, with fallen walls and columns scattered among the fresh spring grass and blossoming wild flowers.

Priene was founded in the great Ionian migration at the beginning of the first millennium BC, though it was established on its present site below Mount Mycale only in the mid-fourth century BC. The original site of Priene has never been found, probably buried deep beneath the soil near the ancient mouth of the Maeander. The entire topography of this coastal region has changed enormously since Priene was first built on its present site, for the whole of the lower Maeander valley is an alluvial delta and the Aegean in ancient times penetrated well past Mount Mycale, which was originally a sea-girt promontory, with Miletus standing on what was once the next cape to the south. Both of these maritime Ionian cities are now stranded far inland.

Throughout antiquity Priene had much the same history as the other Ionian cities in this region. Yet Priene remained a small town, hemmed in as it was by powerful neighbours, the Ephesians to the north and the Milesians to the south, and its population never exceeded the 5,000 or so that it numbered when it was founded. Thus Priene did not undergo the great building programme in the imperial age experienced by places like Ephesus, which is largely a Roman city, and the ruins one sees today on the slope of Mount Mycale are essentially those of a Greek town of the late classical and early Hellenistic periods.

Priene is by far the finest extant example of a Hellenistic town planned on the Hippodamian model; in the style, that is, of Hippodamus of Miletus, who in the mid-fifth century BC became the world's first known city-planner. He laid out Greek towns on a rectangular grid with straight streets intersecting at right angles in the modern manner, rather than in the labyrinthine way of ancient and medieval settlements. The city faces mostly south, with a cliff of Mount Mycale at its back. The main avenues run east-west and the side streets rise from south to north on steps from one to another of the four tiers of this natural shelf above the Maeander plain. The defence wall rings the periphery of this shelf from the cliff on either side, and another wall encloses the more gradually sloping southern side of the citadel on the mountain high above. Up there a garrison was on round-the-clock duty for periods of two months at a time. An aqueduct brought water across the Maeander plain from the north, passing through the walls to a reservoir in the north-eastern corner of the city from where it was distributed within a system of earthenware pipes to public fountains throughout the town. The defence wall was also penetrated by three gates, one to the north-east, a second to the south-east, and a third to the west, opening on to the main avenue of the city where the principal public buildings of Priene were located.

We entered the city through the remains of the north-east gate, and once inside we oriented ourselves with a map of the archaeological site. A path inside the gateway led us to one of the main east-west avenues of Priene and we walked half-way along this to the theatre, whose cavea is built into the hillside on the northern side of the street. This is one of the finest extant theatres of the early Hellenistic world, and though it was somewhat modified in the Roman era it remains as typically Greek as the rest of Priene.

The civic centre of Priene was just to the south of the theatre, and its principal edifices faced one another across the main east-west avenue, with the agora and the Temple of Zeus Olympios to the south and the Sacred Stoa to the north, the eastern end of the portico opening on to the bouleterion and the prytaneion. The bouleterion, or council chamber, is one of the best-preserved and most distinctive structures in Priene, with rectilinear tiers of seats rising from three sides of the almost square room, the remains of an altar still standing in the centre. Adjoining the bouleterion to the east is the prytaneion, or senate, in an inner chamber of which was the shrine of Hestia, where the sacred flame of the tribe, originally lit at the hearth of the goddess in Athens, was kept perpetually burning.

Just to the west of the civic centre are the remains of the Temple of Athena Polias, the oldest and most famous edifice in Priene, begun in the third quarter of the fourth century BC and originally bearing the name of Alexander the Great as its founder. The temple was designed by Pytheos, architect of the world-famed Mausoleum at Halicarnassus. According to Vitruvius, this edifice, which he called 'the Ionic fane of Minerva which is at Priene', was described by Pytheos in a lost work on architecture as the archetype of the Ionic temple, and it thereafter served as a model of its type. The temple was a peripteral structure of the Ionic order, with eleven columns along its sides and six at the ends, counting corner columns twice. It also had a pair of columns *in antis* (that is, between projecting piers) in the front and rear porches, the pronaos and the opisthodomos, with the latter serving as a treasury. One passed through the pronaos into the cella, or inner sanctuary, at the rear of which there was a large cult statue of Athena Polias, which Pausanius thought one of the most remarkable sights in Ionia. In recent years five columns of the north colonnade have been re-erected, giving Athena's sanctuary a stirring grandeur it had previously lost when in total ruins.

After visiting the Temple of Athena, we looked around the archaeological site at some of the structures farther from the civic centre: the Temple of Demeter, on the hillside to the north-west; the gymnasium and the stadium just inside the city walls at their southernmost arc; and a shrine of Cybele just inside the West Gate, evidence that the worship of the ancient Anatolian fertility goddess still continued in Priene in the Hellenistic period. Another small building just inside the West Gate has been identified tentatively as a shrine of Alexander the Great, as evidenced by a statuette of the deified emperor found there during the archaeological excavations that began in 1896. It has even been suggested that this building served as Alexander's residence during his visit to Priene in 334 BC, when he endowed the Temple of Athena Polias.

We returned to the theatre and enjoyed our picnic at the centre of the uppermost tier which gave us a sweeping view of the ruins and the surrounding plain of the Maeander. Then we departed from Priene with great regret, for it is one of our favourite places in all of Turkey. After a last lingering look around the ruins we walked back to our car in Güllü Bahce, from where we drove back to the main road and returned to Söke. There we made an early night of it, because at dawn the next day we planned to begin the last leg of our journey along the Ionian shore.

The next morning we left Söke shortly after sunrise, to enable us to drive down to Miletus and Didyma, stopping at Myus on the way. It promised to be yet another glorious April day, the Maeander valley brilliant with wild flowers and blossoming fruit-trees, the water of the river glinting in the morning sunlight as we approached its sinuous course obliquely, passing the turn-off to Priene as we drove by Mount Mycale and continued south across the delta. Then we passed a great bend in the river and stopped at the village of Sarıkemer, from where a road leads to the site of ancient Myus.

The road from Sarıkemer to Myus was too rough for our car, so we engaged a local farmer to take us there in his jeep, a drive of about three and a half miles. This took us past Avşar, a village on one of the two little lakes that are all that remain of the great gulf that once penetrated the coast of Asia Minor as far as here, when Myus was on the Aegean shore. Then we finally came to the site of ancient Myus itself, of which there remains only the foundations of an Ionic temple, some archaic walls, and the ruins of a Byzantine fortress. We remained there for only half an hour, just long enough to walk around the ruins and to review the history of the ancient town. Myus was once a member of the Panionic League though in its latter years it was the least significant member of the Dodecapolis.

According to Pausanius, Myus was founded by a party of Ionians under Kyaretos, a son of King Kodros of Athens. The city they established was one of the most important ports in Ionia, with some 200 Greek warships anchoring there in 499 BC at the beginning of the Ionian Revolt against the Persians. The city was already in decline by then, though, for at the Battle of Lade in 494 BC Myus contributed only three ships, as many as half-abandoned Phocaea: these were the smallest contingents in the Ionian fleet. The decline was due to the silting-up of the port of Myus with mud carried down by the Maeander, transforming the area into a malarial marsh. Thereupon, as Strabo writes: 'The people from Myus withdrew to Miletus with everything they could carry, including the images of the gods; in my time there was nothing left at Myus but a white stone temple of Dionysus'.

Our driver now took us back to Avşar, whence we drove back in our own car to the highway. There we headed south across the Maeander delta once again, and now we could see the northernmost hills of Caria beyond the southern end of the valley. As we approached the Carian hills we crossed a bridge over the Maeander, which here curves westward on its final approach to the Aegean. Then just beyond the bridge we turned right on to a side road that leads along the left bank of the Maeander to Akköy, a drive of three and a half miles, and there we turned right to drive another three miles or so to Balat, the site of ancient Miletus.

Miletus always evokes a feeling of desolation which somehow goes beyond the inevitable sadness that one feels when wandering about among ancient ruins, and the feeling is accentuated here because in its time this was the greatest city in the Greek world, though it is now utterly marooned in the midst of the alluvial delta that has left it four or five miles from the sea it once ruled. But something of the vanished grandeur of Miletus survives, particularly in the sombre magnificence of its ruined theatre which looks out over what was once one of the four harbours of an ancient city which the Milesians proudly called 'the first settled in Ionia, and the mother of many and great cities in the Pontus and Egypt, and in various other parts of the world'.

Miletus is probably the oldest of all the Ionian cities, for archaeological excavations have revealed evidence of human habitation going back to at least the sixteenth century BC. The first settlers appear to have been Minoans from Crete, part of the thalassocracy, or maritime empire, that the Great Island developed throughout the eastern Mediterranean in the first half of the second millennium BC. Greek tradition credited the establishment of this thalassocracy to King Minos, the semi-legendary founder of the Minoan dynasty on Crete. When Minos gained supremacy on Crete he defeated his brother Sarpedon, who left the Great Island with his followers and settled along the south-western coast of Asia Minor. He founded the Lycian race, as one tradition has it. According to Strabo, the Cretans who settled at Miletus were led by Sarpedon, and they named their new colony after their native city of Milatos on Crete, with the Ionians settling there later under the leadership of Neleus, another son of King Kodros of Athens.

These traditions have been confirmed by archaeological

onaavations on the promontory just south of the theatre, which reveal evidence for a Cretan settlement that seems to have been taken over by the Mycenaeans in the late Bronze Age, *c.* 1400 BC. This would have been about the same time that the Mycenaeans became the dominant power on Crete itself, ending the Minoan era on the Great Island. Scholars have also in recent years deciphered correspondence between the Hittite emperors and the kings of the Achaeans where reference is made to a Greek-controlled city on the south-west coast of Asia Minor known as Millawata or Millawanda, and this has been identified as Mycenaean Miletus, then known as Milwatos.

Although both Cretans and Mycenaeans dwelt at Miletus in the late Bronze Age they were probably there to establish trading-stations rather than to settle in a permanent colony, and the indigenous Carians undoubtedly formed the bulk of the population. But when the Ionians established their colony at Miletus, at the beginning of the first millennium BC, they came to stay, killing all of the male Carians and taking the Carian women as their wives, so that from then on Miletus was a Greek city. This reminded me of the chilling lines in Book I of the *Histories* of Herodotus, where he writes of how the Ionian settlers 'took no women with them but married Carian girls, whose parents they had killed. The fact that these women were forced into marriage after the murder of their fathers, husbands, and sons, was the origin of the law, established by oath and passed down to their female descendants, forbidding them to sit at table with their husbands or to address them by name. It was at Miletus that this took place'.

Miletus was one of the original members of the Panionic League, and throughout its history one of the leading members of the Dodecapolis. During its early years Miletus greatly surpassed all of the other Ionian cities in its maritime commerce, founding its first colonies in the eighth century BC on the Anatolian shores of the Pontus. During the following two centuries Miletus established a far greater number of colonies than any other state in the Greek world, including more than thirty in what is now the Black Sea and its approaches in the Dardanelles and the Sea of Marmara. The Milesians also had a privileged position at Naucratis, the great emporium on the Nile founded *c.* 610 BC by the Greeks, building there a trading-station called Milesionteichos, or Fort Miletus.

The same dynamism of the Milesians that gave rise to their commercial enterprises and numerous colonies also burst forth in an extraordinary outpouring of intellectual creativity, beginning early in the sixth century BC and continuing into the classical period. This cultural flowering produced the first physicists: Thales, Anaximander, and Anaximenes; the historian Hecataeus; the city-planner Hippodamus; the poets Timotheus and Phocylides; and the orator Aeschines. The city produced still another figure of renown in late antiquity; this was Isidorus of Miletus, a distinguished mathematician who succeeded Anthemius of Tralles as architect of Justinian's Haghia Sophia, completing the great cathedral in Constantinople in the year AD 537.

Miletus played a leading role in the Ionian Revolt against the Persians that began in 499 BC. The last battle in this revolt was that fought in 494 BC off the islet of Lade, just outside the harbour of Miletus which had been besieged by the Persians throughout the war. There a fleet of 600 Persian warships defeated an Ionian force of 353 triremes, after which the victors renewed the siege of Miletus and soon captured the city, burning it to the ground and enslaving its surviving population. This catastrophe deeply shocked the Athenians, as Herodotus records in a moving passage. 'The Athenians ... showed their profound distress at the capture of Miletus in a number of ways, and, in particular, when Phrynichus produced his play, *The Capture of Miletus*, the audience in the theatre burst into tears. The author was fined a thousand drachmas for reminding them of a catastrophe which touched them so closely, and they forbade anyone ever to put the play on the stage again'.

But Miletus endured, and the survivors who were not carried

off to Persia must have made their way back to the site of their ruined city, for by the middle of the fifth century BC it was a flourishing port and commercial centre once again, as evidenced by the fact that, in the Delian Confederacy, the Milesians contributed only slightly less than the Ephesians. The city was rebuilt according to the designs of Hippodamus, the Milesian architect, who laid it out on the rectangular grid pattern that became the archetype for city-planning in the modern world. Even so, the golden age of Miletus was over, and during the remainder of antiquity it had much the same history as the other Ionian cities. In late antiquity, indeed, Miletus went into decline, for by then the Maeander had silted up the Latmian Gulf and pushed the shoreline westward beyond the city so that by the early Byzantine period the Milesians had to ship their commerce down the river to reach the sea.

The ruins that one sees today at Miletus all date from after the reconstruction of the city in the mid-fifth century BC, and many of the edifices are considerably later than the Hippodamian rebuilding. The theatre in its present form dates to *c.* AD 100, replacing an earlier theatre that may have been erected when the city was rebuilt after the Persian sack. The present structure is one of the finest extant examples of a Graeco-Roman theatre, designed for an audience of over 15,000. The spectators in the theatre would have looked out over one of the three harbours on the western side of the Miletus promontory, the fourth being directly across the waist of the city on its eastern side, about 550 yards distant. The other two harbours were just to the north and south of the theatre on the western side of the promontory, the deepest and most important of them being the northernmost, the Lion Port. From our seat in the top tier of the theatre we could discern the outlines of the four ancient harbours, after which we used an archaeological map to identify the other surviving structures of the ancient city.

Looking across the silted-up Theatre Harbour to the end of

the promontory on that side we saw the West Agora, built late in the Hellenistic period; just to the south of that were the foundations of a Temple of Athena, dedicated in the fifth century BC; and then directly south of this the most prominent monument was the stadium, built *c.* 150 BC; while east of that across the narrow waist of the promontory was the vast porticoed square known as the South Agora, with a processional way leading northward to the inner end of the Lion Port, passing the bouleterion. We climbed down from our seat in the theatre to look more closely at these structures and others around the Lion Port, including the Harbour Stoa, the Harbour Monument, and the Delphinium, the principal sanctuary in Miletus. The Delphinium was dedicated to Apollo Delphinus, the Dolphin God, an appropriate patron deity for a city whose wealth and renown came from the sea. The oldest parts of this shrine are four altars dating from the sixth century BC; these were part of the Archaic Delphinium, which was re-erected here when the city was rebuilt after it was sacked by the Persians.

As we looked at the Lion Port I was reminded that St. Paul stopped here in April of the year AD 57 while on his way back to Jerusalem. In Miletus Paul sent word to his friends in Ephesus to join him, and after speaking with them for the last time he bade them an emotional farewell, a scene movingly described in Acts 20: 17–38. Paul then took leave of his Ephesian friends and boarded his ship, probably here in the Lion Port, sailing off via Cos and Rhodes to Patara, and from there to Tyre.

We then walked out along the northern side of the Lion Port, passing the ruins of Roman baths dating from the early imperial age. This brought us out along the lower slopes of the eminence known as Humay Tepe, the northern spur of the Miletus promontory. On that bright April day it was covered with myriad irises, their brilliant colours contrasting vividly with the grey stones of the ghost city over which they cast their blue-purple mantle. Then we came to what had been the mouth of the port, where the figures of two talismanic lions still stand, guarding the main harbour of Miletus though almost buried in the alluvial earth that marooned this once great city.

From the Lion Port we returned to the main area of the site, spending some time in the little museum there. Then we visited Ilyas Bey Camii, just to the south of the South Agora. This handsome mosque is the last surviving monument of the Turkish town of Balat, a corruption of the Greek Palatia, or Palace, the name by which the ruins of ancient Miletus became known in the late Byzantine period when this area was conquered by the Menteşeoğlu, a Turkoman tribe. The mosque in Balat was built in 1404 by Ilyas Bey, who had been restored as emir of the Menteşeoğlu *beylik* soon after Tamerlane's victory over Beyazit I at the Battle of Ankara. Ilyas Bey Camii is one of the most distinguished mosques of the *beylik* period still standing in Anatolia, with a dome nearly forty-six feet in diameter. Unfortunately, this handsome edifice is no longer used as a mosque, for Balat was abandoned after being severely damaged in an earthquake in 1955, and the villagers were resettled some three miles to the south in the hamlet of Akköy.

We drove south after leaving Miletus, and headed for the site of ancient Didyma. After we passed Akköy the road curved westward to bring us along the Aegean shore, which is here fringed with a succession of pretty sand beaches. Then the road curved back inland to bring us to the village that has grown up around the ruins of Didyma, which consist solely of the colossal Temple of Apollo Branchidae, one of the most magnificent sights in all of Asia Minor, its gigantic shattered columns shining in the brilliant sunshine of late afternoon.

The name Didyma appears to be Carian in origin, as evidenced by similar place-names that have survived farther to the south in Caria. And the name Branchidae derives from the family who served as hereditary priests in the Archaic period, descendants of a semi-legendary figure called Branchus who was given oracular powers when Apollo fell in love with him here. According to Strabo, the oracular shrine of Apollo at

Didyma predated the Ionian settlement, so that the Greeks who colonized Miletus probably took over an existing Carian shrine. The Milesians subsequently linked their city to the shrine of Apollo Branchidae with a Sacred Road flanked by huge statues in the Egyptian style, now in the British Museum. The first Temple of Apollo at Didyma was erected at the beginning of the sixth century BC, and was a small structure at the end of the Sacred Road. Then in the mid-sixth century BC a much larger Temple of Apollo was constructed there, apparently on the same grandiose scale as the Archaic Artemision at Ephesus, with Croesus, whose mother was a Carian, contributing generously and depositing a large quantity of gold in its treasury. The Branchidae at Didyma was one of several oracles Croesus consulted before embarking on his ill-fated campaign against Cyrus, but what advice he was given is not recorded.

According to Strabo, the Archaic Temple of Apollo was destroyed in 479 BC by Xerxes, an act of vengeance against the Greeks when he returned to Asia Minor after his defeat at the Battle of Plataea. At that time the priests of Apollo's shrine, the Branchidae, surrendered the temple treasury to Xerxes, after which they and their families marched off with the Persian army to escape retribution from their fellow Greeks; they finally settled in Sogdiana. Alexander's army found the descendants of the Branchidae living in Sogdiana when they arrived there in 327 BC, and the exiled Greeks greeted the Macedonians as liberators. But Alexander, after conferring with his men, wreaked on them the vengeance of Apollo for the treachery of their ancestors: he had them all slaughtered.

The temple at Didyma was founded a second time early in the Hellenistic era by King Seleucus I of Syria. The Hellenistic Didymaion, which was five centuries in the building and never fully completed, was designed on an even grander scale than its predecessor. It ranked in fact as the third-largest edifice in the ancient Greek world, surpassed in size only by the Artemision at Ephesus and the Heraion at Samos. Though in ruins, enough of the structure remains for one to make out easily its design and structure. The temple is of the Ionic order and its plan is 'dipteral decastyle', that is, a sanctuary surrounded by a double row of columns numbering 10 each at the front and back and 21 along the sides, and with 12 more in the pronaos (front porch), making a total of 120. Between the pronaos and the cella there is an antechamber with two Corinthian columns; from there three doors open on to a flight of steps leading down to the cella, which can also be reached from the pronaos by two sloping tunnels. The cella is unroofed and like a great open courtyard, with walls over seventy feet in height. At the rear end of the cella one can see the foundations of a small Ionic sanctuary which probably housed the sacred cult statue of Apollo, a work in bronze by the noted sculptor Kanachos; this was looted by Xerxes when he destroyed the Archaic Didymaion, and subsequently brought back from Ecbatana in 300 BC by Seleucus I.

The ruins of Didyma are not as desolate as those of Miletus, for the magnificent Temple of Apollo Branchidae stands dramatically in the midst of a cheerful village constructed partly from the ruins of the Hellenistic sanctuary. The temple was particularly beautiful at the time of our last visit, the colossal ruins washed by the soft pastels of approaching sunset, the great jagged columns casting faintly purple shadows across the ancient shrine, evoking once again the vanished splendours of Ionia.

13

THE CARIAN HILLS

After leaving Didyma we drove south for about two miles to the road's end at Altınkum, a seaside hamlet where we spent the night at a little *pension* on the beach. We rose early and drove back along the same road, passing the ruins of the Didymaion, even more beautiful in the morning sunlight. We retraced our route until we reached the main highway again where we had left it before turning off to Miletus; there we turned right and drove south once more across the Maeander valley, heading towards the Carian hills.

The Carians, who inhabited these highlands in antiquity, were believed by the Greeks to have originated in the Aegean islands, probably in the days of the Minoan thalassocracy, and to have moved over to south-western Asia Minor long before the Hellenic migrations. The Carians were renowned warriors, fighting as mercenaries for the various city-states of Greece as well as for the Persians and Egyptians. Although the Ionian and Dorian migrations occupied the coastal regions, the Carians remained independent of the Greeks, though as time went on they became increasingly Hellenized. During the Archaic period the Carian towns had organized themselves into a national federation that met regularly at a place on the River Marsyas which Herodotus calls the White Pillars, with their religious centre at the Temple of Zeus Carius in Mylasa. But after the Persian capture of Sardis in 546 BC, Cyrus sent an army into Caria under Harpagus, who soon conquered the

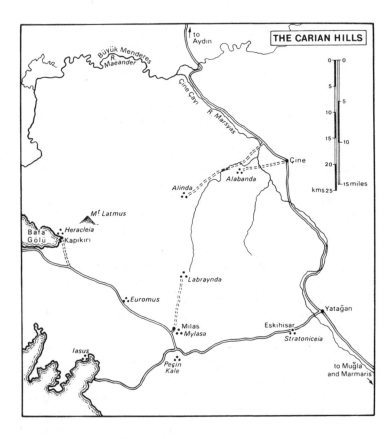

THE CARIAN HILLS

to Aydın

Büyük Menderes
R.
Maeander

Çine Çayı
R. Marsyas

Çine

Alinda   Alabanda

0   0

5

10   5

15

20   10

kms 25   15 miles

Mᵗ Latmus

Bafa
Gölü   Heracleia
          Kapıkırı

Labraynda

Euromus

Yatağan

Milas
Mylasa   Eskihisar
                Stratoniceia

Iasus

Peçin
Kale

to Muğla
and Marmaris

region. The Carians joined with their Greek neighbours to the north in the Ionian Revolt of 499–494 BC, but they were defeated by the Persians in a great battle near the White Pillars, after which they made an heroic but unsuccessful last stand at their national shrine in Labraynda.

Caria then became a satrapy of the vast Persian Empire, with its capital at Mylasa. There a local dynasty took control and established Caria as a virtually independent power by the beginning of the fourth century BC. The most renowned member of this dynasty was Mausolus, who ruled as king of Caria from 377 BC to 353 BC, transferring his capital from Mylasa to Halicarnassus. When Mausolus died he was buried in Halicarnassus in a magnificent sepulchre known as the Mausoleum, one of the Seven Wonders of the Ancient World, erected for him by his widow Artemisia, who was also his sister. The kingdom created by Mausolus lasted little more than two decades after his death. It came to an end soon after Alexander the Great captured Halicarnassus in 333 BC, thus closing the most illustrious period in the history of Caria.

We reached the Carian hills at the southern edge of the Maeander valley, where the highway turns abruptly eastward to begin its gradual ascent into the highlands above the coastal plain. The road then veers toward the south-east when it reaches the shores of Bafa Gölü. This shallow lake lies under the western flank of Beşparmak Dağı, the ancient Mount Latmus, whose main peak rises to a height of 4,485 feet above sea-level. This brought us to one of our favourite spots in all of Anatolia, a little restaurant beside the lake in an olive-grove, which we had discovered on our first journey through Caria twenty years before when looking for the site of Heracleia-under-Latmus. We stopped to have lunch at our usual table there, down on the beach in the shade of the olive-grove; and from there, in a wildly romantic setting, we looked across the lake to the massive western ramparts of Mount Latmus on the opposite shore, where the mysterious ruins of Heracleia beckoned to us once again.

The murky and brackish waters of Lake Bafa are the land-locked remains of the Latmian Gulf, the deep indentation of the sea that once cut in between Cape Mycale to the north and the Milesian promontory to the south, with Heracleia situated near the elongated end of the bay and directly under the massif of Mount Latmus. Heracleia was originally known as Latmus, named for the great mountain that towered above it. The town was captured by Mausolus early in his reign, whereupon he changed its name to Heracleia in keeping with his programme to Hellenize Caria. The town thereafter was called Heracleia-under-Latmus to distinguish it from the many other places in the Greek world also named for Heracles. Strabo describes the town in his survey of the coast of Asia Minor, after his description of the Milesian shore: 'Next follows the Gulf of Latmus, on which is situated Heracleia-under-Latmus, as it is called, a small town with a shelter for vessels. It formerly had the same name as the mountain above ... At a small distance further, after crossing a small river near Latmus, there is to be seen in a cave the sepulchre of Endymion'.

The story of Endymion is a deeply layered myth that has always haunted this mountain. Several versions are woven together by Pausanius, who says that Endymion was a son of Aethlios, a son of Zeus who was the first king of Aleia. But a local version of the myth at Heracleia is much simpler and more beautiful. In this version Endymion is a local shepherd youth who fell asleep in a cave one evening while grazing his flock on the slopes of Mount Latmus; Selene, goddess of the Moon, saw him there in her bright light and fell in love with him, lying down beside him in the Latmian grotto. When Zeus learned of this he decided that Endymion should never wake but should slumber on in perpetual youth. While he dreamed Selene made love with him and in time bore him fifty daughters. The myth seems to have lingered on into Christian times, when Endymion was venerated locally as a Christian saint, one of many holy men who were attracted to this magic mountain. According to tradition the Christian anchorites who took refuge on Mount Latmus in early Byzantine times discovered an ancient tomb with a sarcophagus which they took to be the sepulchre of Endymion, which thereafter they converted into a shrine. Every year on the day that the cult of Endymion was celebrated here the local monks would open the lid of the sarcophagus inside the shrine, whereupon the skeleton within invariably emitted a strange humming sound. This they interpreted as Endymion's attempt to communicate to man the name of God, which he had learned from Selene while they slept together in the Latmian cave. In recent years a cave sanctuary has been discovered among the ruins of Heracleia-under-Latmus, and scholars have identified this as the sepulchre of Endymion mentioned by Strabo. Although there is no sarcophagus within the shrine, many other sarcophagi lie scattered around the site of the ancient city, further adding to the haunting romance of this enchanted place.

When we first visited Heracleia the only way to reach the site was by boat across the lake, but in recent years a rough dirt road has been laid out from the village at the eastern end of Bafa Gölü. There one can hire a jeep for the six-mile ride to the site, which is occupied by the picturesque hamlet of Kapıkırı. But at the time of our last visit we decided to travel out to Heracleia as we had first done twenty years before, hiring a fisherman near our restaurant to take us across the lake in his old caique. The voyage took us past several islets and promontories covered with the ruins of half-submerged churches and monasteries of the Byzantine period, when Latmus was an important monastic centre. We landed at a white sand beach on an island connected to the mainland by an ancient causeway. The shore around us was covered with fallen columns and other architectural members, and also with sarcophagi scattered about on the strand and in the shallow waters offshore from the necropolis on the promontory to our right. Above that towered the well-preserved cella walls of a sanctuary identified as the Temple of Athena. We walked up from the beach to look at the site of the lower city, where the tiny hamlet of Kapıkırı has been built unobtrusively among the ruins, most of the houses constructed from the remnants of ancient edifices. The most impressive structures here are the great Hellenistic defence walls, probably dating from the time of Mausolus. Their lower stretch encloses the ancient town along the shore, climbing from there up the mountain on both sides to a height of 1,600 feet and, on the summit, enclosing two enceintes that would have been used as a citadel in times of siege, with a third walled enclosure on the adjacent crag to the south-east. The principal monuments of the ancient town are scattered in and around Kapıkırı: the Temple of Athena on the promontory above the beach; the agora in the centre of the village and the bouleterion behind that; higher up on the hill the theatre and a nymphaion, or monumental fountain; and a Byzantine castle standing on another promontory above the southernmost tip of the city, with the necropolis on the little peninsula that juts into the lake below. The ruins on the lower slopes of Mount Latmus date principally from the reign of Mausolus and the early Hellenistic period that followed, when Heracleia and the other towns in the region were undergoing the transition from Carian to Hellenic culture, so that the structures whose remnants one sees today are essentially those of an ancient Greek city.

We walked out from the village by a path that leads to the Byzantine castle on the right, stopping half-way along at the ruins of an unidentified temple beside which is the cave shrine of Endymion. This unusual structure is built into a narrow hollow in the rock-face behind, enclosed by a cross-wall which once had a colonnade in front, with the stumps of two columns still evident within the sanctuary itself. The sight of this grotto inevitably evokes the romantic myth with which it is associated and the first lines of Keats' *Endymion*:

> A thing of beauty is a joy forever:
> Its loveliness increases; it will never
> Pass into nothingness; but will keep

A bower quiet for us, and a sleep
Full of sweet dreams, and health, and quiet breathing.

After visiting Heracleia, we returned across the lake and then drove on to our next destination, the ancient Carian city of Euromus. From the restaurant on Bafa Gölü, the highway took us twelve miles past the eastern end of the lake, and then south-east along a valley that led deeper into the Carian hills. Finally we stopped when we saw a signpost identifying the site of Euromus, which is a short distance to the left of the highway.

We parked our car by the side of the road and headed through the vast olive-grove that embowers the site, carrying along some fragments of bread and cheese and a half-bottle of wine we had brought with us from the restaurant because we had wanted to savour the last of our lunch here celebrating our return to Euromus. We walked until we came within sight of the Temple of Zeus, the principal monument of the ancient city, and then we sat with our backs against the trunk of an enormous olive-tree of great age, which had probably been growing here when Euromus was still a flourishing Carian town and not just a romantic ruin. But the site of the ruined temple was indeed romantic, standing alone and serene in the midst of the olive-grove, with a gnarled old olive-tree entwined around one of its mottled columns as if embracing it. Then we filled two plastic tumblers with wine and drank to Jim and Carla Lovett, with whom we had first discovered this temple twenty years before. In those days there was no archaeological sign to identify Euromus, and we had been searching for the site for some time before we saw the temple standing in all its glory in this remote olive-grove. The Lovetts and we ourselves had sat down together under this same old olive-tree. We had been there for only a few moments when two old Turkish shepherdesses joined us, sitting down by the olive-tree and generously sharing with us their lunch of bread, goat-cheese, and olives, though they politely declined our wine. Then Jim Lovett turned to one of the women and asked her if she knew how old the temple was, and now, two decades later, Dolores and I recalled her reply. '*Eski! Cok, cok eski!*', she had replied, shaking her head in wonderment, 'It is old, very, very old!' '*Evet!*' added the other old shepherdess, shaking her head as well, 'Yes, it is very old, it was standing here when we were just children.'

Euromus, one of the principal cities of ancient Caria, controlled the whole plain leading inland from the eastern end of the Latmian Gulf south-west as far as the approaches to Mylasa. The Temple of Zeus is by far the best-preserved edifice that has survived from the ancient city, with sixteen of its columns still standing along with their connecting architrave. The temple is of the Corinthian order and dates from the second century AD; its peripteral colonnade originally had eleven columns along the sides and five at the ends, with a second row of columns behind the first row in the front porch, or pronaos, and with five more *in antis* in the opisthodomus, the recessed porch to the rear of the temple. Twelve of the surviving columns have tablets with dedicatory inscriptions, recording that seven of them were presented by the state physician and magistrate Menecrates and his daughter Tryphaena, and the other five by the magistrate Leo Quintus. Three of the columns were left unfluted, indicating that the temple was never fully completed. Recent archaeological work has unearthed an altar in front of the temple to the east, and an inscription has been deciphered recording that the sanctuary was dedicated to Zeus Lepsynus, a unique epithet for the god that is not Greek but presumably Carian.

The Temple of Zeus was outside the bounds of the city proper, which was to the north of the sanctuary. Its periphery is traceable to a large extent through the defence walls that once encircled it; their principal remnant is a well-preserved round-tower. The sturdy walls, which date to the early Hellenistic period, enclosed an area estimated by George Bean to be a quarter of a square mile. The only other surviving structures of Euromus, all of them very poorly preserved, are the theatre, of which only five tiers of seats are visible in the hillside above the temple; and the agora, a market square surrounded on all four sides by a portico of which only a few stumps of columns still remain *in situ*; all else is so fragmentary as to be unidentifiable.

We now headed on to Milas, site of ancient Mylasa, a drive of some seven miles. Soon we could see the town at the far end of the long and narrow plain, and behind it the great flat-topped rock known as Peçin Kale, rising abruptly from the floor of a transverse valley to a height of some 700 feet. Apparently this was the original site of Mylasa, which was moved down to its present location in the valley only in the third century BC.

We drove on into the centre of Milas and checked in at the Park Hotel, where we would be staying for two nights while we explored the hill-towns of ancient Caria. Then we set out to see the antiquities in Milas and its environs.

The first monument we looked for was the Temple of Zeus Osogos; this has vanished except for a stretch of its polygonal precinct wall, which George Bean has identified about 330 yards to the west of the Park Hotel, near 'the Güveç Dede Turbesi, in the quarter of Haci Ilyas'. Using Bean's map of ancient Mylasa in his *Turkey Beyond the Maeander* we were able to find the site of the temple which in fact was just beyond the tomb of Güveç Dede, a Muslim saint whose name in English literally means 'Grandfather Casserole'. The Temple of Zeus Osogos is mentioned by Pausanius as being one of only three in the Greek world where there was a salt-water spring not far from the sea; the others are the Erechtheion on the Athenian acropolis and the Temple of Horse Poseidon in Mantineia. This salt-spring is also mentioned by other ancient writers, including Theophrastus who attributed it to the frequency of earthquakes in this region.

The remnant of another ancient temple stands in the centre of Milas on the eastern slope of Hisarbaşı Tepe, whose summit is marked by the Belidiye, the Town Hall. In a garden there we found all that remains of the temple itself, a single fluted column complete with its Corinthian capital, which was at that moment surmounted by a stork in its nest, a common sight in Anatolia. The column stands on a well-preserved stepped podium about eleven feet high, to which a stone stairway gave access up until recent years. There is a panel on the column where the dedicatory inscription would have been recorded, but this has long since been effaced. Nevertheless, the temple is undoubtedly one of those mentioned by Strabo in his description of ancient Mylasa, probably the one dedicated to 'Carian Jupiter, common to all the Carians'.

Richard Chandler, one of the first European travellers to write about this column, remarks that two other columns of the temple were standing until not long before his visit in 1765. Chandler's description is interesting because, just prior to his inspection of the column, he had visited the site of the former Temple of Augustus and Rome, now vanished; this stood opposite the present Orta Okul, the Middle School, which is on the side street around the corner from the Park Hotel. Chandler reports that there were six columns of that temple still standing, but he was unable to gain admission to the house that stood on the site, for the Turkish gentleman who owned it told him that 'there was his harem, or the apartment of his women, which was an obstacle not to be surmounted'.

Besides this column, George Bean also identified the whole of the eastern end of the precinct wall of the temple. It extends for a hundred yards along the bank of the canal that parallels the main street of Milas a short distance to the east. We crossed the canal and then turned left to follow the main street on that side as it brought us to the most picturesque sight in Milas, a perfectly preserved Roman gateway spanning the modern road. This is Baltalı Kapı, the Gate of the Axe, and it dates from the late first century BC, probably erected when the city was rebuilt after the sack of Mylasa by Labienus in 40 BC. The gate takes its name from the double-bladed axe on the keystone of the arch on the northern side of the portal. The Greek name for this double axe is 'labrys', and it was the symbol of divine royalty in Minoan Crete and apparently also in Caria, probably originating from the days when the Carians dwelt on the Cycladic isles in the thalassocracy of Minos. This gate would then have been the beginning of the Sacred Way that led from Mylasa to Labraynda, where the Carians had their great shrine of Zeus Labrayndus, the god of the double-axe, which we were to visit later.

The most remarkable monument in the immediate vicinity of Milas is the Roman tomb known in Turkish as Gümüşkesen, which is on the outskirts of the town just to the right of the road leading to the west. This is a splendid funerary monument probably dating from the same period as Baltalı Kapı, erected just before the beginning of the Christian era. The Turkish name of the tomb means the Silver Purse, and results from the hoary legend that a treasure is buried there, the silver having supposedly been poured into its subterranean hiding-place through the curious funnel-shaped hole in the top of the burial-chamber. The tomb is an exceedingly handsome structure on two storeys, with the massive burial chamber forming the lower level. The tomb itself is entered by a door on the western side, while above this there is a superb Corinthian porch with a fluted colonnade with square piers on the corners and between them pairs of oval columns, the whole surmounted by a pyramidal roof of ingenious construction. William Bell Dinsmoor in *The Architecture of Ancient Greece* suggests that the design of this tomb was based on that of the Mausoleum in Halicarnassus.

After seeing Gümüşkesen we drove back to the centre of Milas, where we hired a driver with a Land-rover to take us the eight miles to Labraynda, for we had been told that the road was too rough for our car. The road proved indeed to be quite primitive, as we jolted along up into the rugged hills north of Milas, following the course of the ancient Sacred Way. Finally we reached ancient Labraynda, whose majestic ruins stand serenely alone on the terraces of its exceedingly steep site high up among the pine-clad Carian hills, not a soul around to disturb its sanctity. The shrine was dedicated to Zeus Stratius, God of the Hosts, an epithet venerating Zeus as the leader of the Carian people. According to Herodotus, 'The Carians were the only people we know of who sacrifice to Zeus Stratius', and he describes the god's shrine at Labraynda as being in a 'great grove of sacred plane-trees dedicated to Zeus'. There are indeed a few venerable plane trees shading the site, along with an olive-grove and some dwarf pines whose aromatic scent was like incense in this ancient hilltop shrine.

Labraynda was excavated by a Swedish expedition in the years 1948–53, and their reports have identified the surviving edifices on the site and established their architectural history. They found that the earliest shrine on this site, a temple dedicated to Zeus, was erected in the fifth century BC, whereas the present Temple of Zeus and the other surviving buildings of the sanctuary date to the reigns of Mausolus (377–353 BC) and his brother Idrieus (351–344 BC). A dedicatory inscription found on the site records that the present Temple of Zeus was dedicated by Idrieus, but undoubtedly he was just carrying through to completion a programme initiated by Mausolus, who obviously wanted to revive the shrine of the great God of Hosts as the spiritual centre of his resurgent Carian kingdom. The temple erected by Idrieus, which includes the earlier fifth-century temple in its structure, had at its core a cella with a pronaos and a very shallow opisthodomus with two columns *in antis.* It also had a peripteral colonnade with eight columns along each of its sides and five on the ends, designed in the Ionic order. The platform of the temple has been cleared by the Swedish archaeologists, who erected along its periphery a number of fluted columns of the colonnade, thus accentuating the outline of the structure, so that one can trace the pronaos, the cella, and the very shallow opisthodomus. The great cult statue of Zeus Labrayndus would have stood at the rear of the cella, a work in marble based on the famous Pheidian chryselephantine statue of Zeus at Olympia. The head of the cult statue that once stood in the temple at Labraynda is now in the Boston Museum of Fine Arts, where it is identified as a head of Carian Zeus.

The best-preserved structure at Labraynda is the edifice just behind the Temple of Zeus and to its left. This is the so-called First Andron, also dedicated by Idrieus, which stands to its full height apart from the roof, a complete doorway opening from its colonnaded porch to the large interior room. This splendid monument, the best-preserved structure of its type in Asia Minor, would have been used to house the king and his retinue when they came to the shrine to celebrate the great Carian festival of Zeus Labrayndus, and at the conclusion of the religious ceremonies in the temple the celebrants would have come here to partake of a royal banquet, with the guests afterwards going to their rooms in one of the 'terrace houses' whose remains can be seen along the south side of the temple. Directly behind the temple there are the foundations of a building that used to house the priests of Zeus; and just to the south of the terrace houses are two other androns. The one that is closest to the temple, and virtually identical to the First Andron, is identified by an inscription as a foundation of Mausolus himself.

The eastern end of the sanctuary precincts beyond the temple terrace has not been excavated, but it is believed that a great palace stood there, probably built by Mausolus as the royal residence of the king of Caria who, from here, would have surveyed one of the most beautiful regions of his domains and the great national shrine of the Carian people. As we stood on the temple terrace at the end of our tour of Labraynda, I recalled that this was the place where the Carians had made their last stand against the Persians during the Ionian Revolt of 499–494 BC, a stirring tale told by Herodotus in Book V of his *Histories*.

The sun was setting when we left Labraynda, and by the time we returned to the Park Hotel in Milas it was twilight. We had dinner in a little kebab restaurant in Milas, a very pleasant experience, as dining out always is in Anatolia, no matter how humble the restaurant, for the food is good, the atmosphere pleasant, and the local people invariably friendly and hospitable to foreigners.

After dinner we took a stroll around the town to look at some of the Turkish monuments of Milas which, in the fourteenth century, was the capital of the Menteşeoğlu *beylik*. There are three fourteenth-century mosques in Milas remaining from the time of the Menteşeoğlu; these are Orhan Bey Camii; Haci Ilyas Cami; and Ulu Cami, the Great Mosque. The oldest Ottoman edifice in Milas is Firuz Ağa Camii, founded in 1394.

The following day we made a long excursion deep into the Carian hills, first going eastward from Milas to the crossroads-town of Yatağan, and then driving northward from there to Çine. Our first stop was at Eskihisar, some twenty-two miles east of Milas, a small village on the site of ancient Stratoniceia. There we visited the interesting little local museum and then toured the ruins of Stratoniceia which surround the village.

The Hellenistic city of Stratoniceia was founded by the Seleucid king Antiochus I (281–261 BC). He named it after his wife, Stratonice, who had previously been married to his father, Seleucus I. But Stratoniceia was merely the refoundation of a much older Carian town named Chrysaoris, or Golden Sword. This name came from a nearby sanctuary administered by the town, the Temple of Zeus Chrysaoreus, the God of the Golden Sword. This temple was the spiritual centre of a federation of towns called the Chrysaoric League, first mentioned in an inscription of 267 BC, which was probably a revival of the old Carian federation.

We drove on to Yatağan and turned north on the highway that leads to Aydın, heading for Çine. Here our route took us along the wildly beautiful gorge of the Çine Cayı, the Marsyas of antiquity. This river is named for the satyr Marsyas, whose ill fate it was to challenge Apollo to a contest, claiming that he could play the flute better than the god of music. Apollo accepted the challenge, but on condition that the victor could

218

do whatever he wished with the vanquished, and that Athena should act as judge. After they had both played the flute Athena decided that Apollo was the winner, whereupon he flayed Marsyas alive, and as the satyr screamed out in agony all of Phrygia wept for him, as Ovid tells the tale:

> The spirits of the countryside and the fauns who haunt the woods wept for him; and so did his brothers, the satyrs, and nymphs and all who tended woolly sheep and horned cattle on those mountains—and Olympus, dear to him now wept as well. The fertile earth grew wet as she received and drank up the tears that fell and became soaked to the veins in her depths. She formed of them a stream which she sent up into the open air. From this source a river, the clearest in all Phrygia, rushes down between its sloping banks into the sea. And it bears the name of Marsyas.

We finally arrived in Çine, where we stopped at an outdoor restaurant to have lunch before setting off for Alabanda. We had stopped at this restaurant for the first time nearly twenty years before, and we were pleased to see that the place had lost none of its unique charm in the interim. We enjoyed lunch in a garden embowered with wisteria vines once again in full bloom, with a view down the Marsyas valley to the northern Carian hills. The only change I noticed in the restaurant was its garden wall, which was now made of concrete blocks, whereas at the time of our last visit it had been constructed entirely from empty bottles of *raki*, the potent national drink of Turkey. That anise-flavoured liqueur turns white when mixed with water, so that those who are addicted refer to it fondly as Lion's Milk.

After lunch we drove south from Çine for four miles along a rough dirt road to the hamlet of Araphisar, the Arab Castle, which stands on the site of ancient Alabanda. This is one of the most charming sights in all of Anatolia, with the humble little village, constructed largely from bits and pieces of antiquity, nestling peacefully among the monumental ruins of the ancient Carian city. As we wandered through the village

an old man bade us welcome from the door of his ramshackle
house which was framed by two fluted marble columns, the
plinth above carved with a long inscription in ancient Greek
placed into the wall upside down. In his garden was a well-
head fashioned from a Corinthian column—the picturesque
present constructed from the ruins of the past as elsewhere in
this broken-down paradise of Araphisar.

Alabanda is twice mentioned briefly by Herodotus in his
Histories, both times in connection with Xerxes' invasion of
Greece in 480 BC. Thereafter it is not mentioned again in
historical sources until the third century BC, when it is listed
among the cities of the Chrysaoric League. Strabo lists Alabanda as one of the three principal cities in the interior of
Caria in his time, along with Mylasa and Stratoniceia. He also
remarks that the townspeople were known for their sybaritic
ways, that 'Alabanda is a city of people who live in luxury and
debauchery, containing many singing girls who play the harp'.

After leaving Alabanda we returned to the main highway
and drove on toward Aydın for a few miles; and then we turned
off on another rough dirt road which led us westward to the
village of Karpuzlu. From there we walked up to the site of
ancient Alinda, whose ruins are on the eastern slopes of
Latmus, with Heracleia off on the opposite side of this
enchanted mountain.

The ruins of Alinda are among the finest in Caria, hardly
surpassed in splendour even by those at Labraynda, and yet
the site has never been excavated by archaeologists, which
perhaps adds to the romance of the place. The steep hill upon
which Alinda is built appears to have an altitude of some
650 feet, with its defence walls anchored on the summit and
extending around in a serrated arc to enclose a terraced area
stretching down the more gradual southern slope. The theatre
is directly below the summit and faces down to the south,
while below that is a monumental market building attached
to the adjacent agora. Across to the north-west of the acropolis
we could see a second walled enclosure at an even higher

altitude, connected to the main citadel of Alinda by a curtain-wall that extended along the saddle between the two peaks. It has been suggested that this second enclosure contained a royal palace, in which case it would have been the residence of Queen Ada, the last ruler of Caria. Ada succeeded as ruler after the deaths of Mausolus and Artemisia, her brother and sister, and of her brother Idrieus. She was deposed however in 340 BC by her brother Pixodarus, and subsequently maintained her independence from him in her mountain fastness here in Alinda, from where she made contact with Alexander the Great after he captured Miletus in 334 BC. Ada adopted Alexander as her son and helped him in his siege of Halicarnassus. As a result, when the Macedonians finally took that city she was reinstated as queen of Caria and ruled until her death a few years later. After that her realm reverted to the Greeks.

This remote mountain fastness on the eastern slopes of Latmus was thus the last stronghold of the Carian people, who thereafter virtually disappear from history. The name of Ada is still remembered here in the city where she preserved her independence, for the uneducated old *bekçi* who showed us around the site mentioned her name with great respect, almost as if she were still reigning. As we stood on the citadel of Alinda he pointed out the extent of her realm—extending from the majestic peak of Latmus and the other hills around us down to the distant Aegean shore—the ancient kingdom of Caria.

14

BODRUM,
THE ANCIENT HALICARNASSUS

The following morning, after breakfast at a *çayevi* in the centre
of the town, we took one last stroll to the Temple of Zeus
Carius, noting that the stork was still there in its nest atop the
Corinthian column, perched on the capital as patiently as a
medieval stylite. Strangely satisfied with this wonderfully
bizarre sight, we got into our Opel and headed for the Carian
shore.

We drove southwards from Milas once again, towards the
crossroads below the great table-rock at Peçin Kale. I first
heard of Peçin Kale from George Bean himself, when I met him
at a dinner party in Istanbul in the mid-1960s, and later I read
his description of the site in *Turkey Beyond the Maeander*. Peçin
Kale was inhabited as early as 2000 BC and, according to Bean,
it was the original site of Mylasa and the first capital of the
Carian kingdom. The most extensive remains at Peçin Kale are
those of the great fortress that dominates the plain below, a
structure originally erected by the Byzantines and later taken
in turn by the Menteşeoğlu and then the Ottoman Turks. There
are two edifices in Peçin Kale remaining from the time of the
Menteşeoğlu, the Ahmet Gazi Medresesi and the Orhan Bey
Camii, both built in 1375.

At the crossroads below Peçin Kale we turned right on to
the new highway that leads south-westward along the Myndus
peninsula towards Bodrum. Then, eleven miles out of Milas
we turned right on to a side road leading to Güllük, five and a

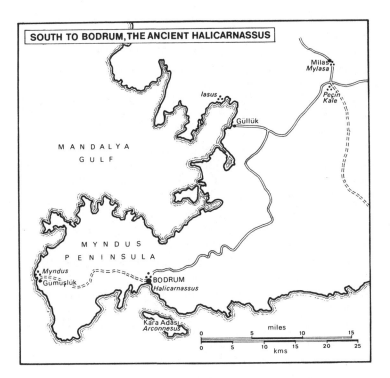

SOUTH TO BODRUM, THE ANCIENT HALICARNASSUS

Milas
Mylasa

Peçin
Kale

Iasus

Güllük

MANDALYA
GULF

MYNDUS
PENINSULA

Myndus
Gümüşlük

BODRUM
Halicarnassus

Kara Adası
Arconnesus

miles
0   5   10   15

0   5   10   15   20   25
kms

half miles away, a little port town at the eastern end of the Mandalya Gulf.

Güllük is a pleasant village clustering around its semicircular port. We had not been there for years, but the village seemed not at all spoiled by the great wave of tourism that has deluged so many seaside towns in Turkey. We were also pleased that our old hotel was still standing on the northern promontory of the port, and so we checked in and were given a room with a balcony overlooking the harbour. Almost immediately we had a drink on the balcony to celebrate our return, for we had first visited Güllük twenty years before while travelling around the Turkish coast with our children and some friends from Robert College, our group renting this entire hotel for three days. We arrived then on the eve of Çocuk Bayram, the Children's Holiday, a joyous festival which is held throughout Turkey annually on 23 April, but we had kept the party going for another two days here in our hotel and on the quay outside.

As soon as we finished our drinks we went to a *bakkal* and bought some food and wine for a picnic lunch. Then we hired a caique to take us across the head of the Mandalya Gulf to the site of ancient Iasus, which is on the promontory that forms the eastern side of an almost land-locked cove called Asin Liman. We landed at the village which lies at the inner end of the deeply indented port, and from there made our way up to the top of the acropolis hill.

According to tradition, the first Greek settlers at Iasus were from Argos, but when they arrived they were attacked by the indigenous Carians. As a result, the Argives had to call for help from their fellow Greeks at Miletus, who sent reinforcements led by a son of King Kodros of Athens. Consequently the colony at Iasus became Ionian, whereas the other settlements in south-western Asia Minor, most notably Halicarnassus, remained Dorian.

Italian archaeologists under Professor Doro Levi began excavating Iasus in 1960, a project that still continues. Their excavations reveal that the oldest part of the site is on the summit of the acropolis hill, now occupied by the ruins of a Byzantine fortress. Objects found around the fortress have been dated as far back as the early Bronze Age, the end of the third millennium BC, making this one of the oldest sites on the south-western coast of Anatolia. Remnants of a very early ring-wall have been unearthed beneath the fortress, perhaps the fortifications of the pre-Hellenic settlement which was here when the first Greek colonists arrived in about the ninth century BC. Part of the residential quarter of ancient Iasus has been found just to the south of the theatre, where one can see a section of a walled street and the numerous houses that flanked it; the wall itself dates to the fifth century BC, but pottery sherds have been found here dating back through the Archaic period to the Mycenaean era.

The civic centre of Iasus was in the area just to the north of the theatre, where the Italian archaeologists have discovered the remains of the agora; an odeion that may have been the meeting-place of the bouleterion; and a structure believed to have been the palaestra of a gymnasium-baths complex. An inscribed stone let into a wall of the gymnasium records the dedication of a temple to Artemis Astias, apparently an amal-gamation of an old Carian deity with the Greek goddess of the hunt. This temple is known to have been of the type called hypaethral, meaning that the cella was unroofed. But the cult statue of Artemis Astias that stood there was protected from the elements nonetheless for local tradition held that neither rain nor snow ever fell within the sanctuary, which was shielded from the elements by the goddess to whom it was dedicated.

The city of Iasus was confined almost entirely to the prom-ontory, with only the defence walls and necropolis situated on the mainland. The most prominent structure in the necropolis is a newly discovered mausoleum; this is just north of the village next to a stretch of Roman aqueduct, where a temple-like funerary monument has been re-erected on its stepped base and podium. This splendid tomb, unique in Caria, dates from the Roman period, but the identity of the person buried there is unknown.

Among the objects excavated by the Italian archaeologists are coins of Iasus, some of which depict the delightful legend of a local youth who was befriended by a dolphin, an incident mentioned by both Aelian and Pliny. According to Pliny, the incident that gave rise to this legend occurred not long before Alexander passed through Iasus, just prior to the Macedonian siege of Halicarnassus in 334 BC. Alexander was so charmed by the story that he took the youth along with him on his campaign into Asia, and afterwards, as Pliny writes, he 'made the boy head of the priesthood of Poseidon at Babylon, interpreting the dolphin's affection as a sign of the deity's favour'.

On our way back to Güllük we looked out for dolphins in the Gulf of Mandalya but none were visible that day. We saw them elsewhere, though, on our journeys along the Aegean coast of Turkey, and when we did we always thought of that boy from Iasus and his dolphin friend, who are shown on the coins of the ancient city swimming happily together off the Carian shore.

Early the following morning we started off for Bodrum, driving back to the main highway and then turning south. This used to be a long and arduous drive, as the old road wound its sinuous way down the spine of the Myndus peninsula along an endless succession of wild gorges; but the new highway now cuts a direct swathe through the rugged Carian hills and brings one to Bodrum more quickly and more comfortably. Yet we missed the adventure of our earlier rides along the old road, usually in a crowded bus or *dolmuş*, craning our necks as we careened around yet another perilous hairpin turn, until finally we were rewarded with one of the most spectacular views in all of Turkey, the white Aegean town of Bodrum clustering in tiers around the graceful arc of its harbour, the magnificent Crusader castle of St. Peter towering beside it on its sea-girt promontory.

We were staying at a little *pension* down by the harbour.

After we checked in we walked down to have lunch at one of the restaurants on the quay, sitting out on a shaded deck right over the water, the shimmering marine light undulating on the sea-blue awning above us. As we dined on lobster and white wine we could see the castle of St. Peter mirrored in the still waters of the port, along with the white houses along the periphery of the harbour and the gleaming hulls of the yachts and fishing-boats tied up along the quay, an occasional caique making its way out past the breakwaters into the open sea beyond where the turquoise mountains of Cos loomed off to the south-west. Over on the inner breakwater by the castle we could see a group of Turkish fishermen sitting cross-legged on the sea-wall beside their caiques as they mended their nets, one or another of their number occasionally breaking into song, the soul-stirring ululations of the Anatolian melodies echoing across the water towards the Hellenic world just in sight out on the Aegean. We were well and truly back in Bodrum, known to the Greeks as Halicarnassus, and the birthplace of Herodotus.

Herodotus first mentions the city towards the end of Book I of his *Histories*, where after describing the Ionian League he writes about the Doric League just to its south, a confederation to which his native city once belonged:

> Something similar can be seen in the case of the Dorian Pentapolis (or Hexapolis, as it used to be), where the Dorians are careful to exclude their neighbours from the use of their temple, the Triopium, and even went so far as to put a ban upon some of their own body who failed to observe the proprieties in regard to it. It used to be customary at the Games of the Triopian Apollo to give bronze tripods as prizes, and the winners were not allowed to take them away, but were required to dedicate them on the spot to the god. This ancient custom was openly defied by a Halicarnassian called Agasides, who, after winning his tripod, took it home and fastened it up on the wall of his house. In punishment for this offense the five cities of Lindus, Ialyssus, Camirus, Cos, and Cnidus excluded Halicarnassus (which was the sixth) from the temple privileges.

The six states of the original Hexapolis had been founded in the Dorian migration to the south-eastern Aegean isles and the mainland of Asia Minor just across from them; this is believed to have begun early in the first millennium BC, after the Aeolian and Ionian migrations which had Hellenized the region just to the north. The Dorians first established colonies on Cos and at the three Rhodian towns of Lindus, Ialyssus, and Camirus, afterwards crossing to Asia Minor to establish settlements at Cnidus and Halicarnassus. A detailed account of the stages of this third and last population movement from Greece to the eastern Aegean world is given by Strabo, who quotes Homer to support his belief that the settlers were Aeolian rather than Dorian.

Herodotus was born in Halicarnassus c. 484 BC. According to a Byzantine source, the *Suda*, he was from a prominent Halicarnassian family, and in his youth accompanied them into exile in Samos 'because of the despot Lygdamis'. This was the dynast Lygdamis II, grandson of Queen Artemisia I, ancestress of Mausolus and his sister-wife Artemisia II. Herodotus appears to have been closely related to the family of Queen Artemisia, whose father, Lygdamis I, seems to have established the Halicarnassian dynasty. When Xerxes invaded Greece in 480 BC Artemisia I commanded a Carian contingent in the Persian fleet, and their audacious exploits were described by Herodotus in Book VII of his *Histories*: 'They were the most famous in the fleet, after the contingent from Sidon, and not one of the confederate commanders gave Xerxes sounder advice than she did'. And as Herodotus quotes Xerxes after watching Artemisia at the Battle of Salamis: 'My men have turned into women, my women into men'.

Herodotus would have known Artemisia when he was a youth in Halicarnassus, although by then the city was ruled by her grandson, Lygdamis II. The tyrannical rule of Lygdamis II forced Herodotus and his family to flee from Halicarnassus and seek exile in Samos. Afterwards he moved on to Athens, where he lived during the brilliant period of Pericles, also travelling widely throughout the known world at that time. Herodotus returned to Halicarnassus at some time prior to 454 BC and joined in the overthrow of the tyranny there, but he apparently fell into political disfavour in the town and so emigrated to the Athenian colony of Thurii in southern Italy. He seems to have returned to Athens at least once after settling in Italy, probably c. 430 BC. Then he must have returned to Thurii, where he is believed to have lived out his last days because, in early editions of his book, that town is given as his place of residence. But in later times he was known as Herodotus of Halicarnassus, the 'Father of History'. As he wrote at the very beginning of his *Histories*, where he stated the theme of his life's work: 'Herodotus of Halicarnassus, his researches are here put down to preserve the memory of the past by putting on record the astonishing achievements both of our own and other peoples, and more particularly to show how they came into conflict'.

The greatest period in the history of Halicarnassus came during the reign of Mausolus (377–354 BC). During his reign Mausolus made Halicarnassus the capital of a Hellenized Caria, transporting there the people from six of the Lelegian towns on the Myndus peninsula and thereby increasing the city's population by a factor of four or five. Mausolus was well-established in his new capital by 367 BC, and before the end of his reign he ruled from here over a kingdom that included all of Caria and considerable portions of Ionia and Lycia, as well as the islands of Rhodes, Cos, and Chios. Mausolus enclosed his capital at Halicarnassus with a great circuit of powerful defence walls studded with watch-towers at regular intervals, along with three separately walled citadels; one of these enceintes was on the ancient acropolis hill at the north-western angle of the land-walls; the second was on the promontory at Salmacis, which formed the western horn of the crescent-shaped walled port; and the third was the 'King's Castle,' on the offshore islet of Arconnesus. Mausolus also adorned Halicarnassus with splendid edifices to suit its new role as capital of the Carian kingdom, erecting a royal palace, several temples, a theatre, an agora, and other public buildings, and also beginning work on his great funerary monument, the Mausoleum.

A new era in the history of Halicarnassus began in 334 BC, when the city fell to Alexander the Great after the most difficult battle by far that the Macedonians had fought up to that point in their Asian campaign. In fact, two fortresses in the city were still holding out when Alexander and the main body of the army marched on, leaving these pockets of resistance to be reduced within the following year by Queen Ada and the Macedonian troops left behind to garrison Halicarnassus. That city became part of Alexander's empire on Ada's death.

After Alexander's own death in 323 BC, Halicarnassus passed in turn to the Ptolemies of Egypt, the Seleucids of Syria, and then to Rome, becoming part of the Roman Province of Asia in 129 BC. It survived as a Graeco-Roman city up until AD 654–5, but then it was sacked and totally destroyed in the great Arab invasion of Asia Minor led by Muawiyah. Halicarnassus never recovered from that catastrophe, which was followed by other invasions throughout the seventh and eighth centuries, so that the city literally disappeared from history during the latter period of Byzantine rule in Anatolia.

A new period began for it early in the fifteenth century, however, by which time the town was known as Bodrum to the Menteşeoğlu Turks who then controlled the Carian coast. Another power in the region was the Order of St. John. In 1310 the Knights Hospitallers of St. John had conquered Rhodes and built a great fortress there, giving them control of the waters off the south-western corner of Asia Minor, where the Aegean merges with the Mediterranean. Philebert de Naillac, who was master of the Hospitallers from 1396 to 1421, decided after the fall of Smyrna in 1402 to use Bodrum as the Order's base of operations in Asia Minor. Therefore, some time before 1408, the Knights of St. John began to build a fortress, dedicating it to St. Peter. The castle, built largely from the ruins of the

Mausoleum, was for more than a century afterwards a salient of Christian Europe thrust into the maritime frontiers of the increasingly powerful Ottoman Empire, and it enabled the Hospitallers to control coastal shipping between the Aegean and the Mediterranean, serving also as a refuge for Christian slaves who escaped from captivity in Anatolia and enabling them to make their way to freedom in Europe.

The castle of St. Peter remained in the possession of the Hospitallers up until 1522, when Rhodes was captured by Süleyman the Magnificent. Thereupon Rhodes and Bodrum became part of the Ottoman Empire, while the Knights Hospitallers of St. John were forced to move their headquarters to Malta, leaving the Turks in full control of south-western Anatolia and its coastal waters.

Travellers to Bodrum had long reported that many fragments of the ancient Mausoleum were to be seen built into the walls of the castle of St. Peter. In June 1844 Charles Alison stopped off at Bodrum at the request of Stratford Canning, British ambassador to the Sublime Porte, who instructed him to report on what sculptures of the Mausoleum were visible in the walls of the fortress. Alison's report led Canning to request permission from the Ottoman government to remove these sculptures to England, and in 1846 Sultan Abdül Mecit graciously granted his request. Canning sent an expedition to Bodrum to remove the sculptures, which were carried off to England in a British warship. The marbles, which included thirteen of the original seventeen slabs of an Amazonomachy, a battle between Greeks and Amazons, were exhibited in the Mausoleum Room of the British Museum along with more sculptures obtained by Sir Charles Newton in his excavations at Bodrum in 1856–9 (another expedition sponsored by Canning). During his excavations Newton succeeded in finding the site of the Mausoleum itself, a discovery he described in his *Travels and Discoveries in the Levant*. I used his book myself on this trip as a guide to the antiquities of Bodrum and Cnidus.

After lunch we walked around the periphery of the harbour

to visit the castle of St. Peter, which has now been converted into a museum, a unique and extraordinary monument to the last days of Crusader warfare on the western shores of Turkey. As we approached the castle I noted from Newton's description that 'it is built on the rocky extremity at the eastern side of the harbour. This rock, which is about 400 feet square, was in antiquity the site of an acropolis, and according to Pliny was once an island. Before his time it became united to the mainland by a rocky isthmus'. This makes it seem probable that the castle was built on the site of the citadel first erected there by Mausolus, which was one of the two forts that held out after Alexander's departure from Halicarnassus.

Passing through the outer gate of the fortress, we entered the north fosse, where Ottoman cannon and ancient architectural and sculptural fragments are displayed. From there we passed through a courtyard and into the west fosse, with the wall of the citadel to our left and the counterscarp to our right. From the top of the counterscarp we crossed by a footbridge and made our way into the outer bayle, or citadel. Set into the walls and over the gateway we could see a large number of architectural fragments and reliefs from the Mausoleum, as well as Christian reliefs and escutcheons bearing the arms of the various grand masters of the Hospitallers and commanders of the fortress. Then, immediately to the right on entering the outer bayle, we came to the Chapel of the Knights. This now houses part of the Bodrum Museum's collection of antiquities, including some Mycenaean pottery and a portion of the frieze from the Mausoleum. A stairway beside the chapel leads up to the two buildings that house the remainder of the museum's collection, the Carian Hall and the Hall of Underwater Archaeology.

The Carian Hall, as its name implies, houses antiquities from ancient Halicarnassus and other Carian sites. Its most recent and exciting acquisition is a relief from the Mausoleum, which was discovered built into the castle. The fascinating exhibits in the second hall are some of the finds from the pioneering work in underwater archaeology by Professor George Bass and his colleagues, a group now under the aegis of the Institute for Nautical Archaeology headed by Dr. Donald Frey. This group has explored ancient shipwrecks all around the south-western coast of Anatolia, adding a new and extraordinarily interesting dimension to the archaeology of the western shores.

After visiting the museum we explored the inner bayle of the citadel. Here one is surrounded by the towers of the various nations of the Hospitallers: the French and Italian Towers on the uppermost level of the citadel, the English Tower at the far corner of the lower level, and the German and Snake Towers (the latter probably belonging to the French and Catalans) along the north wall of the inner fortress, beyond which are the great bastions of the outer wall. We walked over to the English Tower, and as we did so I read from Newton's description:

> This tower was probably erected by Englishmen, as the arms of Edward IV, and of the different branches of the Plantagenet family, together with many other coats, are sculptured in a row over the door. Scattered about the castle are the arms of its successive captains, ranging from 1437 to 1522, when the garrison surrendered to the Turks. Among these is the name of a well-known English knight, Sir Thomas Sheffield, with the date 1514. The arms of another Englishman, John Kendal, who was Turcopolier, 1477–1500, may be seen under the royal arms, on the tower at the south-east angle.

The Turcopolier was commander of the light-armed militia called Turcopoles, a word of Byzantine origin for children of Turkish or Saracen fathers and Greek mothers. There are references to such a militia of Turcopoles serving the emperor of Byzantium, undoubtedly made up of youths of mixed parentage born in the Anatolian marchlands of the empire during the Turkish invasions, and they would have been a natural source of recruits for the Knights Hospitallers here in the castle.

The English Tower was built entirely by contributions from Englishmen; the funds would have been raised by Philebert de

Naillac during his visit to England c. 1409, when he received the support of King Henry IV. (The royal coat-of-arms identified by Newton as belonging to Edward IV is actually that of Henry IV.) The origins of the English Tower are commemorated by these royal arms which appear over the huge lion on the west wall, and also below a smaller lion on the north wall; over the north entrance there is a long line showing the arms of the principal contributors to the building, with twenty-three of them flanking the arms of the king and three below. Six coats-of-arms besides those of Henry IV belong to the royal family, and among the others fourteen belong to Knights of the Garter. These are identified in the excellent little guide entitled *Bodrum Castle and its Knights*, by Evelyn Lyle Kalças, who points out that all the warriors mentioned by Shakespeare, in the address of King Henry V to the Earl of Westmoreland before the Battle of Agincourt in 1415, are represented at Bodrum:

> Then shall our names,
> Familiar in their mouths as household words,
> Harry the King, Bedford and Exeter,
> Warwick and Talbot, Salisbury and Gloster,
> Be in their flowing cups freshly remembered.

After visiting the castle, we walked back to the western harbour to see the site of the ancient Mausoleum, which is at the centre of the village about 650 feet in from the middle arc of the western harbour. The most recent excavations on the site have been made by a group headed by the Danish archaeologist Jeppeson, which has cleared a large area of the foundations of the Mausoleum, originally unearthed by Newton.

These archaeological excavations, together with descriptions of the monument by ancient writers, particularly Pliny, have led to a number of attempts to restore the Mausoleum conjecturally. The architects of the Mausoleum were Pythius and Satyrus, who wrote a book about their masterpiece that was known to Vitruvius, but this has since been lost. Pythius, who built the Temple of Athena at Priene at about the same time, also sculptured the quadriga, or four-horse chariot, that surmounted the monument. According to Pliny, the lower part of the structure consisted of the high basement, or podium, which was set into foundations estimated by W.B. Dinsmoor, in *The Architecture of Ancient Greece*, to measure 108 feet by 127 feet. Above this stood a peristyle of thirty-six columns, which Dinsmoor and others have arranged with eleven on the sides and nine on the ends. Above the portico there was a pyramidal roof of twenty-four steps, surmounted by the quadriga. The Mausoleum was also adorned with three sculptured friezes, the placement of which is a matter of some controversy; these represented an Amazonomachy, a Centauromachy, and a scene with charioteers. The sculptors are named by Pliny as Bryaxis, Leochares, Timotheus, and Scopas, each of whom is believed to have worked on one side of the monument. Scopas made the sculptures on the east face, which would have been the front of the Mausoleum. The British Museum has sculptures from all three of these friezes, as well as other statues discovered by Newton, including the colossal figures identified as those of Mausolus and Artemisia which may have stood in the quadriga surmounting the Mausoleum.

Aside from the Mausoleum foundations and the fragments of its structures built into the walls of the castle, virtually nothing remains of Carian Halicarnassus other than some scanty remains of the land-walls built by Mausolus. And so, after looking at the castle and the site of the Mausoleum, we spent the remainder of the afternoon just strolling through the village itself. Bodrum is the prettiest community on the western shores of Turkey, its tiers of whitewashed cubistic houses arrayed chock-a-block just like the Greek island towns in the Aegean to the west, all of them once having been part of the same world and still partaking of the same atmosphere even though they are now separated by an international boundary.

The first modern author to write about the Aegean quality of Bodrum life was Cevat Şakir Kabaağaç, known to Turks as Halikarnas Balıkçısı, the Fisherman of Halicarnassus. We thought of Cevat as we sat down for a drink in a cafe on the harbour, for he is a legend in Bodrum, and just being here reminded us of a wonderful evening we spent with him years ago in Izmir talking about his beloved Halicarnassus.

We had been introduced to Cevat by his sister, Aliye Berger-Boronai, who was one of our closest friends in Istanbul. Aliye had told us how Cevat had been exiled to Bodrum in 1908, convicted of murdering his father in a crime of passion, the two of them having been in love with the same woman. Cevat had just graduated from Oxford, and he brought his books with him when he was sent off to Bodrum, which was then just a sleepy fishing-village almost totally cut off from the modern world. He found a little house in the village and made a way of life for himself with the local fishermen, reading and writing in his spare time, eventually winning a national reputation for his stories about the people of Bodrum, particularly about how their lives and folklore perpetuated the spirit and philosophy of the people who had lived along the Aegean coast of Anatolia since antiquity. I had talked about this with Cevat when I met him in Izmir, and I asked him if he would contribute an essay on this theme to a literary magazine that I was then editing in Istanbul, the *Golden Horn*. Cevat graciously consented to do so, and while we drank Brandy Alexanders together that evening he wrote out for me an essay called 'Laughing Tombstones', which was based on epitaphs that he had translated from tombstones in the old graveyard in Bodrum. There was nothing profound in Cevat's essay or in the epitaphs, just his feeling that these last expressions of farewell represented the irrepressible joy in life that the Aegean people had always manifested and still do today in Bodrum. So, as we lifted our glasses to Cevat's memory, I quoted a few of the epitaphs he had written for me:

A pity to good-hearted Ismail Efendi, whose death caused great sadness among his friends. Having caught the illness of love at the age of seventy, he took the bit between his teeth and dashed full gallop to paradise.

Stopping his ears with his fingers, Judge Mehmet hied off from this beautiful world, leaving his wife's cackling and his mother-in-law's gabbling.

(*On a wayside tomb*): Oh passerby, spare me your prayers, but please don't steal my tombstone!

I could have died as well without a doctor as with the quack that friends had set upon me.

I have swerved away from you for a long time. But in soil, air, cloud, rain, plant, flower, butterfly or bird, I am always with you.

(*On a tombstone with the relief of three trees: an almond, a cypress, and a peach-tree*): I've planted these trees so that people might know my fate. I loved an almond-eyed, cypress-tall maiden, and bade farewell to this beautiful world without savouring her peaches.

Those of us who knew the Fisherman of Halicarnassus find his presence still lingering in Bodrum, even though he has now departed from this world. His remains are buried elsewhere, and no free-spirited epitaph is written on his tombstone. And so, while we spoke of him in the cafe that evening, down on the old harbour where he had spent the happiest days of his life, I chose as his epitaph these lines written in the fourth century BC by Kallimachus of Kyrene in memory of his beloved friend, the poet Heracleitus of Halicarnassus:

They brought me news of your death, Heracleitus, and I wept for you, remembering how often we watched the sun setting as we talked. Dear Halicarnassian friend, you lie elsewhere now and are mere ashes; yet your songs—your nightingales—will live forever. And never will the underworld, destroying everything, touch you with its ugly hand.

15

THE CERAMIC GULF

On one of our spring trips to Bodrum we explored the shores and islands of the Ceramic Gulf, known in Turkish as Gökova Körfezi. This is the great indentation where the sea cuts deeply into Anatolia between the Myndus and the Dorian peninsulas, the two enormous extrusions of Asia Minor that reach out into the Aegean on either side of the Greek island of Cos. On several of our voyages along the Aegean coast we had steamed across the head of this gulf, which takes its name from the ancient town of Ceramus, and on a number of occasions we had driven by its eastern end when travelling by bus or car between Izmir and Marmaris. But the Ceramic Gulf itself had eluded us until that spring trip to Bodrum, when we explored its beautiful shores and islands by caique. That is really the only way to see most of this remote south-western coast of Turkey.

After driving to Bodrum on that trip we walked down to the harbour, looking for a caique to take us on an overnight journey up the Ceramic Gulf. We had been given an intro-duction to an old captain named Hüseyin, who had taken a number of our friends out on cruises in his caique, the *Hürriyet*. We found the *Hürriyet* right away, recognizing Hüseyin from the many photographs of him that had been snapped by friends from Robert College while on joyous voyages aboard his caique. After exchanging greetings he agreed to take us on the journey we had planned. We decided to start the next morning at five, for we wanted to stop along the way at Ceramus before

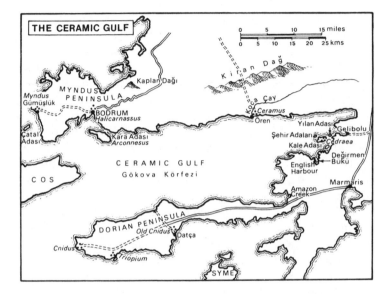

THE CERAMIC GULF

0 5 10 15 miles
0 5 10 15 20 25 kms

Kiran Dağ

Myndus
Gümüşlük
MYNDUS
PENINSULA
Kaplan Dağı
Koca Çay
Ceramus
Ören
Çatal
Adası
BODRUM
Halicarnassus
Yılan Adası
Gelibolu
Şehir Adaları
Cedraea
Kara Adası
Arconnesus
Kale Adası
Değirmen
Bükü
English
Harbour
CERAMIC GULF
Gökova Körfezi
COS
Amazon
Creek
Marmaris
DORIAN PENINSULA
Old Cnidus
Datça
Cnidus
Triopium
SYME

opending the night on one of the islands at the head of the gulf. Then we walked back to our *pension*, stopping off at a *bakkal* to buy food for our two-day journey.

We were down at the harbour the next morning well before sunrise, to find Hüseyin waiting for us on the *Hürriyet*. He bade us good morning and helped us aboard with our supplies, which included a case of local white wine and two bottles of *raki* for our captain, whose Homeric capacity had become legendary among our friends at Robert College. Then, once we were aboard, Hüseyin cast off and steered the *Hürriyet* out of the harbour, as he headed up the gulf, passing between the mainland and Kara Adası, the Black Island, known to the Greeks as Arconnesus. Then we headed eastward along the coast of the Myndus peninsula, as the lemon light of false dawn tinted the horizon towards which we were sailing. We were finally exploring the Ceramic Gulf.

The gulf is some fifty-five miles in length, measuring eastward from an imaginary line joining Bodrum and Cnidus (on the Dorian peninsula). Such a line would pass close by the easternmost promontory of Cos, now behind us in the pre-dawn blue haze to the south-west. After passing Kara Adası, we sailed by a beautiful procession of pine-clad promontories, jutting out from the rugged coastal foothills of Kiran Dağ, the mountain that forms the spine of the Myndus peninsula, with the first golden rays of the rising sun lighting up the peak of Kaplan Dağı, the Tiger's Mountain, known in antiquity as Mount Lide. That long massif now loomed above the northern shore of the gulf near its eastern end. I could see from my map that the site of Ceramus was on the coast about thirty miles east of Bodrum as the eagle flies, where a break in the mountain wall allows a stream known as the Koca Çay to flow down into the gulf through an alluvial plain. We landed there in the bay of Ören, a village whose name, 'Ruins', it takes from the nearby site of Ceramus. After Hüseyin had tied up the caique, Dolores and I went ashore and walked out to the site of the ancient city about a mile from our landing-place.

Ceramus was an ancient Carian city, a member of the Chrysaoric League, but despite its fairly substantial size virtually nothing of note happened there, and its history was identical to that of most of the other insignificant towns in the region. Ceramus was not included in the synoecism instituted by Mausolus *c.* 360 BC, when six other towns on the Myndus peninsula were incorporated within the new Carian capital at Halicarnassus. Probably this was because it was too far to the east. Ceramus had a neighbouring town called Bargassa, on the shore of the gulf to the west, but this has not been identified. The evidence for this is Strabo's description of the coast between Cnidus and Halicarnassus: 'Next after Cnidus are Ceramus and Bargassa, small towns overlooking the sea'.

Up until fairly recent times Ceramus was still surrounded by its ancient defence walls, but most of these have now been demolished by the locals to build houses and field-walls. We were however able to find one short stretch of wall still standing to a few courses, with the arch of a gateway remaining in place. The principal edifices of ancient Ceramus have suffered the same depredation, and only pathetic ruins of its two temples now remain. One of these is outside the village on a hill called Bakıcak, where the discovery of a stone inscribed with the *labrys*, the double-axe, has led to the identification of this edifice as the Temple of Zeus Chrysaoreus, the God of the Golden Sword. In 1932 the local farmers found nearby the head of a *kouros*, an Archaic statue of a god-like young man, the archetypal representation of Apollo. This is now in the Izmir museum. The youthful god appears together with the God of the Golden Sword on coins of Ceramus, and is probably the survival of an earlier Carian deity whose cult was amalgamated with Zeus when Mausolus Hellenized his kingdom *c.* 360 BC.

There are the remains of a second temple about 440 yards to the east of Ceramus, at a place called Kurşunlu Yapı, the Place with Lead. The temple there, which was of the Corinthian order, has been so completely vandalized that it is now just a sorry ruin, whereas in not too recent times it was still a grand sight The temple walls were decorated with plaques framed in wreath-like borders enclosing inscriptions; one of these, translated by George Bean, reads 'With good fortune, I the pious priest Marcus Aurelius Chrysantas, zealously and open-handedly performed my duties towards the gods and other priests, together with my wife Aurelia Euphrosyne'.

After exploring the ruins of Ceramus we returned to the caique, where Hüseyin was waiting for us. As soon as we were aboard our captain cast off, manoeuvering us out of the bay of Ören and heading up the gulf once again. As soon as we were well underway we opened our parcels of supplies and laid out a picnic on the fantail of the caique, Dolores and myself drinking wine with our lunch while Hüseyin had his customary *raki*. When our glasses were full Hüseyin wished us good health, '*Şerifinize!*', while we echoed his wish and also drank to the pleasure of his company on this splendid journey.

Just eastward of Ceramus the gulf narrows abruptly, as the Dorian peninsula widens out from its extremely narrow waist in a great shoulder to the north. Thus the width of the gulf contracts from fifteen miles to just six miles. Then over the course of the next six miles the gulf narrows again to a width of three miles as one approaches its easternmost inlet. As we neared the inlet Hüseyin headed the caique towards the shore of the Dorian peninsula, where a small archipelago now came into view. Hüseyin identified this as Şehir Adaları, the Islands of the City, so named because of the ruins of the ancient city that stand on the largest and southernmost of the isles. Hüseyin pointed this out as we approached it, calling it Kale Adası, the Island of the Castle, while the smaller isle just to its north he said was Yılan Adası, the Island of the Snake. Hüseyin steered the caique through the narrow passage between these isles and then turned south around the northernmost promontory of Kale Adası into the large bay beyond, which almost cuts the island in two. So he brought us into an almost completely land-locked cove, where we were suddenly surrounded by the ruins of ancient Cedreae. It is one of the most enchanting sights on these shores, a ghost city set in the midst of some of the most beautiful maritime scenery one can ever look upon. After Hüseyin had anchored the *Hürriyet* we waded ashore and just stood there for a while looking at the extraordinary scene, resting our eyes on the beauty of the setting while we reviewed what we knew of the history of this fascinating place, for we seemed to have passed through a warp in time on to another planet in a different age.

Cedreae was an ancient Carian town, though its name in Greek derived from that of the cedar tree. Nothing is known of the history of the ancient Carian town, and the first appearance of Cedreae is in the classical period, when it was a member of the Delian Confederacy. During the Peloponnesian War Cedreae was an ally of Athens, and this in 405–404 BC led the Spartan commander Lysander to attack the city on two occasions. The first attack was unsuccessful, but when Lysander took Cedreae on the second attempt he sacked the town, selling the surviving townspeople into slavery. This is recorded by Xenophon in his *Hellenica*, where he refers to the people of Cedreae as 'half-barbarian', indicating that the native stock, who were probably Lelegians, had not yet been completely Hellenized. Soon afterwards Cedreae fell under the control of Rhodes, becoming part of the island's possessions on the nearby shore of Asia Minor, the so-called Rhodian Peraea. Cedreae became completely Hellenized as a result, for it was in effect a Rhodian city and participated fully in the culture of the island as a member of the Rhodian Peraea, which continued in existence up until the Roman period.

The ruins of ancient Cedreae occupy the eastern half of Kale Adası, which is about 880 yards in length, divided into two almost equal halves by the deep inlet of the bay. The city proper is on the eastern end of the island, where the fortification wall that ringed the town can still be seen along the shore, studded with several fine watch-towers, some of them still standing. We walked through the site and discovered the very well-preserved but heavily overgrown ruins of the theatre, as well as the remains of a Doric temple that has been identified as a sanctuary of Apollo; this was evidently converted into a Christian church in the early Byzantine period, indicating that Cedreae still had a substantial population at that time, although it was undoubtedly ruined during the Persian and Arab invasions and thereafter abandoned. Wandering through the heavily overgrown ruins, we also came upon the remnants of what appeared to be the agora, where the feeling that we were intruding upon a ghost city deepened, giving the place an almost haunted atmosphere.

After exploring the ruins we walked back and wandered around on the other side of the island. There we located with our map of the island the small cove that in recent times has come to be known as Cleopatra's Beach. This name derives from an unsubstantiated story that Antony had sand from Egypt transported here to create a more beautiful beach for Cleopatra. Whatever the truth of the story, the beach is a very pretty one, and we enjoyed a late afternoon swim there after which we basked on Cleopatra's sand in the delicious sunshine of yet another glorious April day. Then we returned to the *Hürriyet* to have a brief nap before supper, with Hüseyin setting up his grill on the beach and cooking some fish he had caught an hour before, a great feast that we washed down with considerable quantities of wine while our captain finished off his daily bottle of *raki*. Dolores and I then returned to our bunks below, while Hüseyin bedded down on an old mattress in the wheel-house, his *raki* bottle beside his pillow.

The following morning Hüseyin took us across to look at the necropolis on the mainland opposite the islands, where a number of sarcophagi lie scattered amid a profusion of plundered tombs and grave-sites. Cedreae was only one of three cities that existed here in antiquity, all of them members of the Rhodian Peraea during the Hellenistic period, with Kallipolis at the head of the bay just to the north of the islands, and Idyma at the very end of the Ceramic Gulf near the present town of Gökova. Hüseyin offered to guide us to these sites, but we regretfully refused for it was time for us to start heading back to Bodrum. So we started on our return journey, passing once again through the channel between Castle and Snake Islands. As we did so we took one last, lingering look back at the bewitching ruins of Cedreae, wondering if we would ever return to this enchanted place, which still haunts me on the far horizon of my memory.

The first part of our return voyage took us along the south-eastern shore of the Ceramic Gulf, a surpassingly beautiful coast, where we explored the pine-embowered fiord known as Değirmen Bükü, probing into a little land-locked cove called the English Harbour, then stopping in another cove for an early lunch of roast goat at a simple seaside restaurant. After lunch we continued to follow the shore of this hydra-headed peninsula which forms the boundary between the Aegean and Mediterranean coasts of Turkey, its land mass breaking off to the south-west in the Loryma peninsula and to the west in the Dorian peninsula. This serrated shore then curves dramatically in a great bend to the south, to where the Dorian peninsula narrows down to its slender neck. We passed Yedi Adalar, the Seven Isles, then rounded yet another pine-clad promontory to explore the inlet known as Amazon Creek, drawn there mostly by the glamour of its strange name. Then, since the sun was already well past the meridian, we headed straight across the Ceramic Gulf to Bodrum, finally arriving back in the harbour in the deepest indigo of twilight with the old castle of St. Peter looking like an ideal setting for a production of Hamlet.

On the way back to Bodrum we had agreed with Hüseyin that, early the following morning, we would set off on another journey, this time a day-trip out to Gümüşlük, a little port at the western end of the Myndus peninsula, where we wanted to look for the site of ancient Myndus.

An hour or so after dawn, therefore, we went down to the harbour and found Hüseyin ready again and waiting aboard the *Hürriyet*. This time he headed out towards the channel between Cos and the south-westernmost bulge of the Myndus peninsula, keeping well north of the international boundary and steering a course between the mainland and the little offshore archipelago called Çatal Adası. This brought us to the westernmost point of the peninsula, with the Greek island of Kalymnos due west on the horizon. There Hüseyin steered us into the calm waters of Gümüşlük, a pleasant little port on an almost land-locked cove. We docked at a quay near the seaward end of the harbour, the port of ancient Myndus.

Myndus was one of the eight towns that existed on this peninsula in ancient times, all of them originally populated by the indigenous Anatolian people whom the Greeks called Lelegians. Besides Myndus, these towns were, from west to east along the peninsula: Uranium, Termera, Telmissus, Madnassa, Side, Pedasa, and Syangela. Syangela was east of Halicarnassus, a Dorian Greek city, while all the other towns lay between there and Myndus, which was originally some two miles to the south-east of Gümüşlük, on a hilltop site at Boğaz-kale.

During the second quarter of the fourth century BC, the people of all of these Lelegian towns, except Syangela and Myndus, were resettled by Mausolus in his new capital at Halicarnassus. At the same time the people of Myndus were resettled on the present site of Gümüşlük, where Mausolus fortified a large area around the cove, with the line of fortifications also including the peninsula that forms the western side of the harbour. Large parts of the defence walls erected by Mausolus were still standing a century ago, but since then the fortifications have virtually disappeared, being used in the usual way as a quarry by the local people for building houses and field-walls. Almost all of the other structures of ancient Myndus have disappeared as well, and for the same reason, leaving as the only substantial remnant a ruined basilica in what was once the centre of the walled town, about 500 yards north of the village centre.

We explored the site at Myndus for an hour or so, tracing what remained of the defence walls. Then we strolled down to the fine beach of Gümüşlük and had a swim, after which we picnicked on the strand and enjoyed a cat-nap in the dappled shade of an aromatic grove of stunted pines. We then walked back to the port and found Hüseyin in a restaurant by the quay, where he was enjoying the last remnants of a plate of fried fish and a large bottle of *raki*, which he had half-finished. Hüseyin took the bottle with him as we boarded the caique, setting it down by the tiller as he steered us out of the harbour at Gümüşlük on our journey back to Bodrum. As soon as we rounded the southern cape and headed into the Ceramic Gulf we had the sun at our backs for the rest of the homeward voyage, so we finished off a bottle of wine that we had left over from lunch while we rested our eyes on the superb maritime scenery, and Hüseyin occasionally crooned old Anatolian love-songs. Our captain seemed supremely happy and completely in his element, and so were we, and the sight of him swigging on his *raki* bottle, as we passed our own wine bottle back and forth, occasionally doused by a wind-blown splash of salty spray, put me in mind of a poem by Archilochus of Paros, who flourished in the mid-seventh century BC: 'Come, go then with a cup along the swift ship and draw wine from the hollow tuns, draining the red wine to the lees; for we no more than any other man can stay sober on this watch'.

And in that splendid state we returned to Bodrum.

16

CNIDUS AND THE
SOUTHERN SHORE OF CARIA

We returned to Bodrum again at the beginning of my school vacation in early June of that year. Between spring and summer vacations we made arrangements with Hüseyin to embark on another voyage aboard the *Hürriyet*, sailing from Bodrum all along the Carian and Lycian shores to Antalya.

This time we decided to travel to Bodrum by bus. A friend agreed to drive our Opel from Istanbul to Antalya, where we would pick it up after we arrived on the *Hürriyet*; from there we would be able to drive on for the remainder of our trip along the Mediterranean coast. We arrived in Bodrum at twilight on the first day of our vacation, exhausted after the long bus-ride down from Istanbul, but as we walked down to the harbour and found Hüseyin waiting for us aboard his caique, we revived, eager to embark.

We were down on the quay early the following morning, on what promised to be a typical June day on the Aegean coast, not a cloud in the sky and the heat of the sun tempered by the first stirrings of the *melteme*, the prevailing northerly breeze. Then, after our bags and provisions were aboard, Hüseyin cast off and headed south across the Ceramic Gulf toward the tip of the Dorian peninsula and the Cnidian promontory.

The direct distance from Bodrum to the promontory at Cnidus is about eighteen miles. But we travelled farther than this while crossing the Ceramic Gulf, for Hüseyin had to veer eastward so as not to cross the international boundary, which

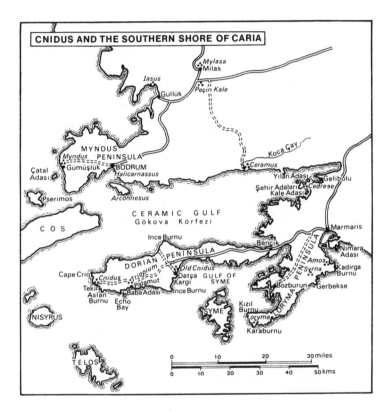

CNIDUS AND THE SOUTHERN SHORE OF CARIA

Iasus

Mylasa
Milas

Güllük

Peçin Kale

Koca Çay

MYNDUS PENINSULA

Myndus

Çatal Adası

Gümüşlük

BODRUM

Halicarnassus

Ceramus

Yılan Adası

Gelibolu

Şehir Adaları

Cedreae

Kale Adası

Pserimos

Arconnesus

CERAMIC GULF

Gökova Körfezi

Marmaris

Nimara Adası

COS

Ince Burnu

Bencik

Amos

DORIAN PENINSULA

ORYMA PENINSULA

Syrna

Kadirga Burnu

Cape Crio

Cnidus

Triopium

Old Cnidus

Datça

Kargı

GULF OF SYME

Bozburun

Gerbekse

Tekir

Palamut

Aslan Burnu

Baba Adası

Ince Burnu

Echo Bay

Kızıl Burnu

SYME

NISYRUS

Locryma

Karaburnu

| 0 | 10 | 20 | 30 miles |

| 0 | 10 | 20 | 30 | 40 | 50 kms |

TELOS

curves in around the island of Cos between the Myndus and Dorian peninsulas. After passing the eastern end of Cos we approached Cape Crio, the western tip of the lizard-like Dorian peninsula, which is some thirty miles in length from Cape Crio to the extremely narrow neck where it almost breaks off from the Loryma peninsula to the south. The Dorian peninsula, so-called because of the Peloponnesian origins of the first Hellenic settlers of Cnidus, is at no point more than eight miles in width and in most places much narrower. This led the Cnidians, soon after the fall of Sardis in 546 BC, to begin digging a canal across the neck of their peninsula, to isolate their city from the mainland as a defence against the Persian army led by Harpagus. But their efforts were doomed to failure, as Herodotus reports, for many of their workmen were injured in the project, and when the Cnidians consulted the oracle at Delphi they were given this advice in iambic verse: 'Do not cut off the isthmus; do not dig./Zeus would have made an island, had he willed it'. Thereupon, as Herodotus writes, 'Having received their answer, the Cnidians stopped digging, and surrendered without a struggle on the approach of Harpagus and his army'.

We finally rounded Cape Crio, a bold and rocky headland with a lighthouse on its peak, connected to the end of the peninsula by an isthmus only about a hundred yards wide. After we had rounded the cape Hüseyin brought us into the little harbour on the southern side of the isthmus, where we anchored off the tiny hamlet of Tekir. This is the base for the American archaeologists excavating Cnidus, the site of which is principally on the mainland just to the east of the isthmus.

The western end of the Dorian peninsula was known in antiquity as the Triopium promontory, named for the Argive hero Triopas who in one tradition is held to be the founder of the original Hellenic settlement here, although Herodotus says that the first settlers were from Lacedaemon (Sparta). The original site of Cnidus was half-way along the Dorian peninsula, near what is now the coastal village of Datça. The Cnidians abandoned that city c. 360 BC and moved to a new location at the western end of the peninsula, undoubtedly because it was better suited for both defence and commerce. That is the present archaeological site.

The Cnidians were renowned mariners, sailing their ships all over the eastern Mediterranean in search of trade and joining other Greek cities in establishing an emporium at Naucratis on the Nile c. 610 BC. These enterprises made Cnidus one of the most prosperous cities in the Greek world during the Archaic period, with its citizens building two splendid edifices at Delphi; one of these was a *lesche*, or assembly-room, with frescoes by the great painter Polygnotos; and the other was a treasury to house their dedicatory offerings to Apollo. Since the Cnidian treasury at Delphi was built shortly before the fall of Sardis in 546 BC, and Cnidus was taken by the Persians less than two years afterwards, some people said that the Cnidians had brought the catastrophe upon themselves by their ostentatious display of wealth.

Although the shrine of Triopian Apollo was on Cnidian territory, the principal deity of Cnidus was not Apollo but Aphrodite. According to Pausanius, she was worshipped here as Aphrodite Euploia, the Goddess of Good Sailing, an appropriate name for the patron deity of a sea-girt maritime city such as Cnidus. This temple was probably built soon after the Cnidians moved their city to the new site near Cape Crio in the mid-fourth century BC, in which case the cult statue of the goddess in her sanctuary would have been the famous nude figure of Aphrodite done by Praxiteles. This work, believed to be the first monumental free-standing statue of a nude woman, is thought to have been modelled on the sculptor's mistress, the beautiful courtesan Phryne. Apparently the people of Cos, who had also moved their city to a new site at about the same time as the Cnidians, had ordered a statue of Aphrodite from Praxiteles but they rejected the nude figure that he sent and asked for a clothed representation of the goddess instead. The people of Cnidus thereupon accepted the nude statue of the goddess of love, and they thereby immortalized their city, for this figure of Cnidian Aphrodite became famous throughout the Graeco-Roman world. As Charles Newton noted in his diary in 1858, when he was excavating at Cnidus:

> If Halicarnassus could boast of its Mausoleum, and Rhodes of its bronze Colossus, the little state of Cnidus could point with just pride to its statue of Aphrodite, the masterpiece, in exchange for which Nicomedes, king of Bithynia, offered to redeem the whole public debt of the city, and which, under the Roman Empire, attained so great a celebrity that the *dilettanti* of all countries were attracted to Cnidus solely for the sake of seeing this famous work.

One of these pilgrimages to Cnidus in Roman times was described by the author known as Pseudo-Lucian in a work called *Amores*, in which he tells of an admirer so overcome by the beauty of Aphrodite that he sneaked into the sanctuary at night and embraced her. She ever afterwards bore a dark stain on one of her inner thighs where he had kissed it passionately.

The American archaeological team, directed by Professor Iris Love, has recently unearthed the circular base of a Temple of Aphrodite; they have also found a marble fragment inscribed with the first four letters of the name Praxiteles and the first three of Aphrodite, making it certain that this is where the famous statue of the goddess of love stood. Less certain by far is Professor Love's claim to have discovered the head in the basement of the British Museum, one of the many sculptures that Charles Newton shipped back to England from his excavations at Cnidus in 1857–8. The authorities at the museum insist that the rather battered head is that of Persephone, which Newton discovered in a sanctuary dedicated to her and her mother Demeter and attributed to the Praxitelean school rather than to the great sculptor himself.

After we had landed we explored the ruins of Cnidus, using a map of the archaeological site. The cove where we had anchored was identified on this map as the South Harbour, which would have been used by the commercial vessels that put in at Cnidus. The smaller haven on the other side of the narrow isthmus is called the Trireme Harbour. The ancient city actually flanked these two harbours and the isthmus that separated them, with houses and a defence wall on the Cape Crio promontory as well as on the mainland, where the greater part of Cnidus was located, including all of its important edifices, separated from the rest of the peninsula by a defence wall anchored by a citadel on the acropolis hill to the north-east. The first of these edifices that we visited was the renowned Temple of Aphrodite Euploia. The American archaeologists discovered this in 1969 in the north-western corner of the city at the point at which the defence walls come down to the sea about 250 yards north of the Trireme Harbour. This was a round temple with a circular colonnade of eighteen Doric columns, standing on a stepped base that was approached from the east where there was an altar dedicated to Aphrodite Euploia. Her statue presumably stood in the centre of the sanctuary.

One famous structure of ancient Cnidus that has eluded excavation is the observatory of the renowned astronomer and mathematician Eudoxus. Eudoxus of Cnidus, who flourished in the first half of the fourth century BC, was one of the most influential thinkers in the history of ancient Greek science and mathematics. He was a student of Plato and, together with Theaetetus, is considered one of the founders of geometry, Euclid's work being largely a compilation of their theorems. Eudoxus was also the first to apply mathematics to the study of astronomy, and his theory of epicycles formed the basis for Aristotle's model of the cosmos, which was passed on to Europe and was not abandoned until after the acceptance of the new heliocentric theory of Copernicus, published in 1543.

Having explored the main archaeological site we walked out to look at the necropolis of the ancient city, which is outside the walls immediately to the east. This necropolis was first explored by Charles Newton, who was led on 'with the vague hope of stumbling on the tomb of the Cnidian astronomer Eudoxus, as Cicero found that of Archimedes amid the *dumeta* of the Necropolis at Syracuse'. Newton did not find the tomb of Eudoxus, but he did discover a charming sanctuary dedicated to the local hero Antigonus, with an inscription indicating that the sacred enclosure stood by the roadside outside the city, and included a gymnasium, a palaestra, and an altar 'where poets might recite their compositions'.

This sanctuary and many of the tombs of the necropolis were situated beside the road that led from Cnidus to the mainland at Physcus, the modern town of Marmaris. This modern road from Marmaris to Cnidus follows the same course as the ancient road, passing through Datça, the site of old Cnidus, a total distance of 66 miles. Until very recently this was just a rough track, and its great length, plus the isolation of the site and the lack of hotels and restaurants, had kept us like most other travellers from visiting the place, though we had seen it from the deck of the *Tarih* in January 1961 when it looked like the most remote spot on the western shores of Turkey. Even today, when the roads in the south of Turkey have greatly improved, the most convenient and pleasurable way to see coastal sites like Cnidus is to go there by sea, as we were doing now with Hüseyin in his caique, for places like this are more a part of the Aegean than they are of Anatolia, and are linked to the maritime world rather than to the subcontinent from which they are cut off by the Taurus mountains.

After exploring the necropolis we returned to the harbour where we had a swim before having supper at a little *lokanta* in Tekir. Then, since it was a warm night, we bedded down in sleeping-bags on the deck of the *Hürriyet*, lulled to sleep by the sound of the sea slapping on her hull, beneath which I could hear the deeper tone of the wild Aegean surging by the promontory on Cape Crio.

We rose at dawn the next morning and climbed up to the peak of the promontory on Cape Crio and out to the lighthouse on the headland. From there we had a sweeping view of the seascape and the capes and islands around us: the Myndus peninsula on the north side of the Ceramic Gulf; west of that the long and mountainous outline of Cos; then the tiny isles of Nisyrus and Telos, to the west-south-west and south, respectively; off to the east-south-east the somewhat larger isle of Syme; and, barely discernible far off on the south-eastern horizon, the pale blue mountains of Rhodes. As we looked out on this stunning maritime scene, and saw a caique sailing northward in the wind-tossed waters of the Aegean between Cape Crio and Nisyrus—a scene that has not changed since antiquity—I was reminded that these distant Greek isles had sent contingents of ships and men to join Agamemnon's forces in the siege of Troy. Nireus of Syme, 'the most beautiful man who came under Ilion', commanded three warships from that island and Nisyrus, while the men of Cos and the other isles to the south-west came in a flotilla of thirty vessels led by Pheidippos and Antiphos, grandsons of Heracles. When Xerxes invaded Greece in 480 BC, the men of Nisyrus rowed in one of the five ships commanded by Artemisia I, queen of Caria. During the last years of the Crusades these islands belonged to the Knights Hospitallers of St. John, outposts of Christian Europe on the maritime frontiers of the unending war with the Saracens and Turks. Now these lonely isles are on a frontier once again, lying up against the international boundary between Greece and Turkey, although from our perch on Cape Crio the promontories and isles around us all seemed to be part of the same Aegean world.

As soon as we returned from Cape Crio Hüseyin was ready to cast off. We left Cnidus, heading eastward up the southern coast of the Dorian peninsula. Then, some five miles from Cape Crio, we passed Aslan Burnu, Lion Point, named for the Lion Tomb that Newton discovered there during his excavations of Cnidus. The remnants of this huge monument, which originally was more than 120 feet in height, can still be seen on top of the promontory. The lion itself is now in the British Museum. Newton believed that the tomb was a funerary monument erected by the Athenians after the naval battle that took place off Cnidus in 394 BC, when Conon decisively defeated the Lacedaemonians.

Some four miles beyond Aslan Burnu we rounded another promontory and entered Echo Bay; there we passed between the islet known as Baba Adası and Palamut, where there is a small port with a few *pensions* and restaurants. According to George Bean, this is the site of Triopium, an ancient town founded at about the same time as old Cnidus, the site of Datça. Both are thought to date from the time of the Dorian migration early in the first millennium BC.

There is a fine sand beach at Palamut, but although we were tempted to pause there we decided to press on to Datça before we stopped for lunch, sailing across towards the south-east-ernmost promontory of the Dorian peninsula at Ince Burnu whose lighthouse we could now see ahead. The Dorian peninsula reaches its greatest width at that point, measuring ten miles north from Ince Burnu to another cape of the same name on the Ceramic Gulf. The peninsula narrows sharply as one proceeds eastward, only a mile and a half in width beyond Datça, then widens somewhat before it reaches its narrowest point at Bencik, where it is not much more than half a mile across. Immediately after that it joins the Loryma peninsula in a great extrusion of the Anatolian coast.

After passing Ince Burnu, the Cape of the Pearl, we turned northward to follow the coast of the Dorian peninsula, which there cuts sharply back as it narrows to its waist north-east of Datça. About three miles north of Ince Burnu the coast projects out in a broad headland called Kuru Burnu, which to its south encloses a large and beautiful bay known as Kargi. After passing this we rounded Kuru Burnu and came within sight of Datça, heading in to the southernmost of its two harbours, which are separated by a causeway connecting the mainland to a little islet called Ata Ada. As soon as we had tied up, Dolores and I went ashore, while Hüseyin remained aboard to tinker with his engine, taking a long swig from his *raki* bottle as he settled down to work. In the meanwhile Dolores and I walked around the village for a while, amazed to see how this once remote and sleepy little hamlet had developed into a tourist resort, with cafes, restaurants, motels, and even a holiday village. As we sat down for lunch at a restaurant on the harbour, we felt a little nostalgic for the good old days when we had had places like this all to ourselves.

After lunch we headed out across the Gulf of Doris toward the Loryma peninsula, bound for the little port of Bozburun, our course swerving in toward the mainland to keep us clear of the international boundary line which curves in around the Greek island of Syme. In mid-passage we were equidistant from Syme and the Dorian and Loryma peninsulas, a marine landscape of surpassing beauty; then, as we approached the Loryma peninsula, we entered the great gulf formed by the two dragon-headed peninsulas ending in the capes called Bozburun and Kızıl Burnu. This brought us into the mile-long bay that forms the harbour of Bozburun, a pleasant seaside village at the end of the Loryma peninsula.

We spent the night at Bozburun, eating at a restaurant in the port and then bedding down on the deck of the caique. We were up at dawn, and after a breakfast of tea, bread, and cheese at a çayevi in the village we were on our way once again, sailing out of the Gulf of Syme and then rounding Kızıl Burnu, bringing us out around the western end of the Loryma peninsula, with Syme once again off our starboard bow. Then we rounded Karaburnu, the south-westernmost point in Asia Minor, where we turned eastward to follow the seaward coast of the Loryma peninsula with Rhodes now off our starboard bow. This is one of the grandest sights on the western shores of Turkey, as one sails through from the Aegean to the Mediterranean between one of the most beautiful of all the Grecian isles and this last magnificent rampart of the Anatolian subcontinent. Pindar must once have looked upon this scene, probably from the Rhodian town of Ialysus, for he catches its grandeur in one of his odes, and as we passed through the strait I recalled his lines: 'Sea-girt Rhodes, child of Aphrodite and bride of Helios ... nigh to a promontory of spacious Asia'.

The Loryma peninsula for several centuries formed the threshold to the dominions that Rhodes acquired across the way in Asia Minor, the Rhodian Peraea. These Asian dominions had originally belonged separately to the three Rhodian cities of Ialysus, Camirus, and Lindus, but when they joined to form a united island state in 408 BC their territory in Asia Minor was combined together as the Rhodian Peraea. The Rhodian Peraea originally comprised the Loryma peninsula and the contiguous area in both directions along the Aegean and Mediterranean coasts, but when the power of Rhodes reached its peak in the Hellenistic era the island's possessions in Asia Minor expanded to include all of Lycia except its deep mountainous interior and the whole of Caria south of the Maeander. But by the beginning of the imperial Roman era the Rhodian Peraea had diminished to the Loryma peninsula and the coast on either side, extending from the Ceramic Gulf to the Gulf of Glaucus, known in Turkish as Fethiye Körfezi.

George Bean has identified a number of sites in the Loryma peninsula that were once part of the Rhodian Peraea. The first of these sites that we came to on the Asian promontory opposite Rhodes was Loryma, which gave its name to the whole peninsula. Its ruins are situated on the western shore of Bozuk Bükü, a bay some two miles north-east of Karaburnu. As we approached the entrance to the bay we could see the impressive citadel of ancient Loryma on the headland to the left, which George Bean describes as 'an elongated enclosure some 350 yards in length by 30 in width, with a fine wall 8 feet thick ... undoubtedly of Rhodian construction'. He also reports that there are nine ruined rectangular watch-towers along the sides and a pair of round-towers at the ends, the one to the east now vanished. There is no sign of any building in the interior of the citadel, which was a fortress rather than a walled town. The residential quarter of Loryma was probably situated on the shore of the gulf to its north where some fragmentary ruins are still to be seen. Bean found inscriptions on the rocks outside the citadel recording that the acropolis was sacred to Zeus Atabyrius, a name under which the king of the gods was worshipped only by the Rhodians.

After entering the bay we sailed around the inner side of the headland and anchored under the citadel. Hüseyin stayed aboard the caique while Dolores and I went ashore for a delicious meal of fried fish that had been caught in the bay just a few hours before. After lunch, as we sat back and enjoyed the view, I recalled that even this remote bay has some historical association: it is mentioned by Thucydides in connection with the last phase of the naval battle fought off Cnidus in 412 BC, when the Athenian fleet stopped here before it sailed on to Samos.

About two miles beyond Loryma on the east coast of the peninsula we passed the opening of the beautiful fiord-like cove at Serçe, where we were tempted to stop for a swim. But it was too soon for lunch, so we sailed on until we anchored in the cove at Gerbekse, somewhat more than half-way up the Loryma peninsula. George Bean describes the ruins at Gerbekse as those of a small Byzantine trading-station; he also gives directions to the site of ancient Syrna, one of the towns of the Rhodian Peraea, which is to be found in the hills above the cove at the village of Bayır, a hike of about an hour and a half. Syrna is named after a daughter of one of the semi-mythical kings of ancient Caria, who gave her the Loryma peninsula when she married Podaleirus, a son of Asclepius. Podaleirus and his brother Machaon had commanded a contingent of thirty ships in Agamemnon's fleet at the siege of Troy, and afterwards he wandered off to Caria, where he met Syrna. The story of Podaleirus had always fascinated me—all the more so now that I had come to the town he had founded for his Carian princess—because it is so obviously a folk-memory of the wanderings of some of the Greek warriors along the Anatolian coast after their long campaign at Troy.

Three and a half miles farther along we rounded the easternmost point of the Loryma peninsula at Kadirga Burnu, the

Cape of the Galley, where a lighthouse stands to guide nocturnal mariners on their approach to the great bay at Marmaris
toward which we were now headed. After passing the lighthouse we sailed by the bay known as Kadirga Liman, and
then, about a mile and a quarter beyond that we passed
another headland and came to the large bay called Kumlu
Bükü. After crossing the bay we sailed close by the promontory
on its far side, known locally as Hisarburnu, the Cape of the
Castle. The little cape took its name from the citadel on the
acropolis hill above, which George Bean has identified as the
site of ancient Amos, another of the towns of the Rhodian
Peraea. We could see a tower of the citadel atop the acropolis
hill, which Bean says is 'encircled by a wall 6 feet thick,
standing up to 10 or 12 feet in height'. He also describes the
remains of a small theatre and a little temple, which was
probably dedicated to Apollo Samnios, the principal deity of
Amos.

After passing the Hisarburnu promontory we headed due
north as we approached the twin entrances to Marmaris
Liman, the Bay of Marmaris, where Hüseyin took us through
the eastern strait which passes between Keçi Adası and Nimara
Adası. This brought us into the great Bay of Marmaris, the
most magnificent harbour on the western shores of Turkey.

17

FROM CARIA TO LYCIA

The harbour at Marmaris, by far the largest on the southern coast, is some four miles wide and nearly two miles in length from its twin entrances to the point where its shores converge to an apex at the northern end of the gulf. Its rugged frieze of pine-clad mountains, which form its periphery, give it more the appearance of a fiord than an Aegean port. The old town of Marmaris stands on a promontory at the inner end of the gulf and beyond it a long line of hotels and holiday villages extends out along the superb beach that fringes the western shore. These new buildings now reach as far as the entrance to the harbour on that side, and as we passed that way in the *Hürriyet* we were amazed at how much the town had grown since we first saw it from the deck of the *Tarih* in January 1961.

When we first saw Marmaris it was a picturesque and broken-down village of old stone houses clustering around the crumbling fortress at the head of the gulf. The town was still largely in ruins after the earthquake that had levelled it in the summer of 1957. We visited Marmaris several times in the two decades that followed, coming overland from Muğla by bus or car, passing through some of the most beautiful hill-country in all of south-western Turkey and emerging from the mountains to a magnificent view of the sea where the road winds down to the coast at the head of the plain from which emerge the Dorian and Loryma peninsulas. Through these two

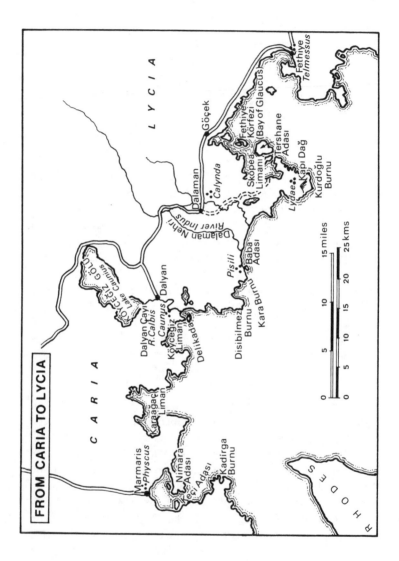

FROM CARIA TO LYCIA

CARIA

LYCIA

Marmaris
Physcus
Nimara Adası
Keçi Adası
Kadirga Burnu

Karağaç Liman
GÖCEK GÖLÜ
O Lâe
Ceaunus
Dalyan Çayı
R. Calbis
Caunus
Köyceğiz Liman
Delikada
Disibilmez Burnu
Kara Burnu
Pisili
Baba Adası

Dalyan

River Indus
Dalaman Nehri

Dalaman

Calynda

Göçek

Skopea Limanı
Fethiye Körfezi
Bay of Glaucus
Fethiye
Tershane Adası
Lydae
Kapı Dağ
Kurdoğlu Burnu

Fethiye
Telmessus

RHODES

0   5   10   15 miles

0   5   10   15   20   25 kms

decades we saw Marmaris slowly recover from the earthquake, and the many years of stagnation which had preceded that catastrophe. The town began to prosper and develop into a major centre of tourism, the embarkation point for ferries crossing to Rhodes, and a major port-of-call for cruise-ships and yachts travelling on the scenic sea voyage along the southern Turkish coast—known in travel brochures as Mavi Yol, the Blue Journey—which we ourselves were now making in our own modest way. But when we sailed into Marmaris aboard the *Hürriyet*, after an absence of five years, we were astonished at how the old fishermen's houses on the promontory had been replaced by modern hotels, and the romantic fortress restored to picture-postcard prettiness. The once-picturesque old town was now engulfed in a wave of modern tourism, with a yacht marina replacing the little caique port of the local fishing-fleet, and with a Riviera-like esplanade lined with motels, restaurants, cafes, souvenir shops, and travel agencies. We looked in vain for the simple little *çayevi* where we used to stop years ago when embarking on a caique voyage across to Rhodes. The romantic old town of our earlier voyages was gone for good, and only the stunning beauty of the great bay and its surrounding mountains remained to remind us that this was indeed the old Marmaris.

The city, standing on the site of ancient Physcus, was the most important of all those in the Rhodian Peraea, which became a deme, or district, of Lindos in the mid-fourth century BC. The acropolis hill of Physcus was not on the promontory where the fortress now stands, but on a much higher and more defensible hill over a mile to the north. That place is called Asar Tepe, and there are still the remains there of Hellenistic fortifications as well as fragmentary ruins of earlier periods first recorded by Newton when he was excavating Halicarnassus and Cnidus. Other than these nothing remains of ancient Physcus, and the only ancient monument in Marmaris is the old castle on the promontory, a medieval fortress completely rebuilt by Süleyman the Magnificent in 1522 when

Marmaris served as the principal base for his conquest of Rhodes.

We remained in Marmaris for only one night. Dolores and I treated ourselves to a little luxury by booking into a deluxe hotel, taking steaming-hot showers and drinking ice-cold martinis before enjoying supper outside on the terrace. From there the Bay of Marmaris looked even more magnificent under the luminous splendour of a full moon.

Early next morning saw us back aboard the *Hürriyet*. Hüseyin steered the caique out of the harbour through the east channel and then, as soon as we were clear of Nimara Adası, we headed south-eastward through the outer waters of Marmaris Liman. This was necessary to keep clear of the restricted military zone around Karaağaç Liman. The prohibited area extends some two and a half miles out to sea from the opening of the bay and the two promontories that flank it: Turnali Burnu to the west and the western cape of Kızıl Burnu to the east. Once clear of the military zone we turned in toward the next bay to the east, Köyceğiz Liman, heading for the long sandy beach and the tiny islet of Delikada on its north-east side. This is also called Dalyan because of the fish-weirs (in Turkish, *dalyan*) that the locals use to catch fish in the Dalyan Çayı, the stream that meanders down to the sea from Lake Köyceğiz a short distance inland. This lake was called Caunius in antiquity and the river the Calbis. On its way to the sea, according to Strabo, it flowed by the city of Caunus, whose ruins we were now going to visit.

Caunus was probably once on the mouth of the Calbis, but silt carried down by the river has now left the ruins of the ancient city some two and a half miles from the sea. Hüseyin took us there in his dinghy, a motor-powered rubber raft, after anchoring the *Hürriyet* off Delikada. (Caunus can now also be reached by road, approached by a turn-off to the village of Dalyan from the coastal highway between Marmaris and Fethiye.) The most prominent feature on the site is the fortified acropolis hill, which towers on a crag some 500 feet above a hairpin turn of the river. The most striking sight at Caunus, however, is the series of rock-hewn Lycian tombs cut into the sheer face of the cliff to the north of the acropolis, their façades carved in the form of miniature Greek temples, a city of the dead looking down on what had been the living city of the Caunians.

The ruins of the ancient city lie to the north-east of the acropolis hill and cluster around the little shallow lake that was once the harbour of Caunus. A long stretch of its western defence wall still stands, its oldest part dating from the reign of Mausolus. At the foot of the acropolis to the west is the attractive Greek theatre which faces to the south-west over the site of the ancient harbour, with the other surviving edifices arrayed to its right and below down to the shores of the lake. These include a stoa, baths, a palaestra, a water reservoir, a nymphaion, and the ruins of four temples, most of them dating from the Roman period. The most interesting is a newly excavated structure by the harbour; this forms three-quarters of a circle, with a colonnade standing on the uppermost of two concentric steps that formed the periphery of the curved part of the structure. The Turkish archaeologists who discovered this unique structure, Professors Baki Ögün and Umit Serdaroğlu, have tentatively suggested that it may have been an outdoor swimming-pool, the only structure of its type ever discovered in Anatolia.

Though most of what survives dates from the Roman period, Caunus is one of the oldest towns on this coast, a transitional area between Caria and Lycia that was undoubtedly inhabited before the Greek migrations. As Herodotus writes:

The Caunians I believe myself to be of native stock, though by their own account they came originally from Crete. As to dialect they have come to resemble the Carians—or the Carians them, for I cannot say definitely which way round it should be; but in their way of life they are very different from the Carians, and indeed from everyone else; for they think it is the finest thing in the world for men, women, or children to organize large drinking parties of friends of similar age. Again, having decided on one occasion to reject certain cults which had been established amongst them, and to worship only their own ancestral gods, all but the boys put on their armour and went as far as the boundary of Calynda, striking the air with their spears and saying that they were driving out the foreign gods.

Later we headed southward in the *Hürriyet* along what Strabo calls 'the great bend of the Carian coast opposite to Rhodes'. Seven miles south of Delikada we came to the southernmost promontory of that coast, Disibilmez Burnu, which lies directly opposite the north-westernmost promontory of Rhodes, twenty-five miles from the city of the Knights Hospitallers. After rounding that cape we turned eastward with the coast bending in that direction and, after passing a deeply indented bay, sailed by Kara Burnu and then the lighthouse on Baba Adası, on whose summit a ruined brick pyramid stands as a landmark for passing mariners. There Hüseyin changed course to the south-east, taking us directly across the great bight in the Anatolian coast that extends in a shallow arc from Kara Burnu to Kurdoğlu Burnu, ten miles away.

Half-way along that stretch I could see from my chart that we were passing the mouth of the Dalaman Nehri, known in antiquity as the River Indus. This river, which is more than a hundred miles long, flows into the sea about three miles to the east of Kara Burnu. On the west bank at its mouth there is an extensive medieval ruin that George Bean has identified as Pisili, mentioned in the Italian portolanos as Prepia. Pisili is mentioned by Strabo as being between Caunus and Calynda, the next town to the east, whose site Bean had identified a short distance to the east of Dalaman where the new international airport is located. According to Herodotus, Calynda contributed a warship to Xerxes in 480 BC, and it was this trireme that Queen Artemisia of Caria rammed at the Battle of Salamis, sinking this vessel from her own flotilla to save herself from the Greeks and to impress the Persian king.

After rounding Kurdoğlu Burnu we turned northwards into Fethiye Körfezi, known in antiquity as the Bay of Glaucus. This gulf took its name from Glaucus, the hero who, with Sarpedon, commanded the Lycian contingent among the Anatolian allies of King Priam who fought in the defence of Troy. As Homer writes in the last lines of Book II of the *Iliad*: 'Sarpedon with unfaulted Glaucus was lord of the Lycians/ from Lycia far away, and the whirling waters of Xanthus'.

We had now passed from Caria into Lycia and, as we sailed up the Gulf of Fethiye, we talked about the hero from whom it took its ancient name. He was a grandson of Bellerophon, whose myth is a folk-memory of the earliest history of the Lycians, a people whose origins otherwise remain shrouded in mystery. The myth of Bellerophon probably perpetuates the adventures of the first Hellenic hero to make his way down into Lycia in the late Bronze Age, carving out for himself a kingdom in the years before the great Greek expedition against the fortress-city at Hisarlık on the Hellespont, when his successors and other local rulers in Anatolia would have allied themselves with Priam against the Achaeans. As for the native Lycians themselves, the Greek tradition for their origin is recorded by Herodotus (in Book I of his *Histories*):

The Lycians come originally from Crete, which in ancient times was occupied entirely by non-Greek peoples. The two sons of Europa, Sarpedon and Minos, fought for the throne, and the victorious Minos expelled Sarpedon and his party. The exiles sailed for Asia and landed on Milyan territory, Milyas being the ancient name of the country where the Lycians live today, though it is occupied by the Solymoi. During the reign of Sarpedon, the Lycians were known as the Termilae, the name they had brought with them from Crete—and which is still in use among their neighbours; but after Lycus, son of Pandion, had been driven out of Athens by *his* brother, Aegus, and had taken refuge with Sarpedon among the Termilae, in the course of time they adopted his name and came to be called Lycians. In their manners they somewhat resemble the Carians.

This Sarpedon, mentioned by Herodotus, is traditionally dated to the second half of the fifteenth century BC, when his brother Minos was ruling in Crete; the other Sarpedon, who fought in the Trojan War along with his cousin Glaucus (both of them grandsons of Bellerophon), is placed in the late thirteenth century BC. These traditional dates are not reliable, of course, but they are in general agreement with modern historical and archaeological research. Archaeologists have uncovered evidence of human habitation dating back to the Bronze Age at a number of Lycian sites. Hittite archives of the mid-fourteenth century BC refer to a rebellious people in the general area of south-western Anatolia called the Lukka, who must certainly be the Lycians. And tablets of about the same period, found at Tel-el-Amarna in Egypt, refer to a nation of sea-raiders called the Lukki who would undoubtedly be the same people. This evidence has led modern authorities to agree generally that south-western Anatolia was inhabited as early as c. 1400 BC by the people whom the Greeks knew as Lycians, and scholars now tend to agree with the tradition established by Herodotus that the Lycians came from Crete in a great population movement that began in the second half of the second millennium BC and probably passed through Caria on its way down to the Mediterranean coast and the mountains of Lycia. These people retained their ethnic identity even in historical times and, though they were later Hellenized, the inhabitants of south-western Anatolia were distinguished as Lycians up until the Roman period. They were always renowned as a nation of warriors, and Herodotus gives a fascinating glimpse of how they appeared at the beginning of the historical era as he describes the Lycian contingent in the army of Xerxes in 480 BC:

The Lycians contributed fifty ships. They wore greaves and corslets; they carried bows of cornel wood, cane arrows without feathers, and javelins. They had goatskins slung around their shoulders, and hats stuck around with feathers. They also carried daggers and rip-hooks. The Lycians are of Cretan origin; their old name was Termilae.

In Strabo's time (64 BC–AD 25) the Lycians were still a distinct people, although by then thoroughly Hellenized. Though under Roman rule they still had considerable national autonomy and settled their own affairs as members of the Lycian League. This was founded in 167 BC, though it probably perpetuated an ancient ethnic union of the Lycian people. 'There are twenty-three cities that share in the vote', Strabo writes. 'They come together from each city in a general congress after choosing whatever city they approve of. The largest of the cities control three votes, the medium-sized two, and the rest one'. Strabo then lists the six largest cities in the Lycian League as Xanthus, Patara, Pinara, Olympus, Myra, and Tlos, after which he writes that 'since they lived under such a good government they remained ever free among the Romans, thus retaining their ancestral usages'.

Kurdoğlu Burnu is surmounted by a 1,400-foot peak named Kapı Dağ, the Mountain of the Gate, for the headland does indeed seem to form the gateway to the Bay of Glaucus at its western end. The headland is the southernmost point of a dolphin-shaped peninsula that is connected to the mainland at an extremely narrow isthmus, making it virtually an island. At the dolphin's tail the peninsula breaks off into a little archipelago whose nearest islet is Domuz Adası, the Donkey's Isle, and whose farther one is Tershane Adası, the Isle of the Arsenal. The peninsula and its archipelago form the seaward barrier for a long and very beautiful bay called Skopea Limanı.

We had been told that there were a number of superb places to anchor here for a swim or to explore the surrounding coast, along which there are several interesting ruins and rock-hewn Lycian tombs and sarcophagi. George Bean, in his *Lycian Turkey*, identifies this headland as the site of Lydae, a little-known Lycian town of which the most interesting remains are two large mausolea and an exceptionally well-preserved stretch of an ancient paved roadway leading up to the town from the isthmus.

Bean has also identified two other Lycian towns that lie some distance inland, best approached from the village of Göçek at the north-western corner of Fethiye Körfezi; these are Daedala, which is about two and a half miles to the north-east; and Calynda, which is the same distance to the east, just south of the road to Dalaman near the new international airport.

After passing Kurdoğlu Burnu we headed eastward across Fethiye Körfezi, which takes its name from the port-town of Fethiye, hidden away in its own secluded bay on the eastern side of the gulf. Fethiye has been identified as the ancient Telmessus, whose name was changed in Byzantine times to Macri, the gulf thenceforth also being known by that name. The Gulf of Fethiye is one of the most magnificent harbours on the western shores of Turkey, rivalling Marmaris in the beauty and splendour of its setting. Then finally we came into the harbour of Fethiye, a pleasant town standing at the foot of the rugged mountains that ring the gulf, the jagged cliffs behind it pock-marked with the tombs of the necropolis of ancient Telmessus.

We had decided to spend the night in Fethiye, but first we set off for the necropolis, stopping on the way to look at the splendid Lycian sarcophagus that is displayed outside the town hall; this is mounted on a high stone pediment and its sculptured lid is carved like a Lycian cottage or tent with a pitched roof. The eternal home of the deceased thus resembled his earthly home. The magnificent Lycian sarcophagi displayed in the Istanbul Archaeological Museum are temples in miniature, the homes of deified royalty. The necropolis itself is just outside the town, where the cliff is honeycombed with rock-hewn tombs carved out of the sheer face of the precipice. The grandest funerary monuments are designed in the form of temple façades, and most splendid of all is the Tomb of Amyntas, dating from the fourth century BC. It is a huge rock-hewn chamber whose façade is that of an Ionic temple *in antis*. These strange Lycian tombs have a haunting and sombre beauty about them, and there is nothing else quite like them in the world. The fact that they are modelled on the actual structures in which the ancient Lycians lived and worshipped makes them all the more evocative, as Charles Fellows first observed when he examined the tombs above Fethiye.

We climbed up into the doorway of one of the tombs and from there commanded a dramatic view of Fethiye, the ancient Telmessus, looking out over the vast indentation of the Bay of Glaucus. This bay may be taken as the coastal boundary between Caria and Lycia, and early historians sometimes included Telmessus in one region, sometimes in the other. But George Bean reports that five inscriptions in the ancient Lycian language have been found in Fethiye, and that means Telmessus was in fact Lycian. It was certainly included in the Lycian League in Roman times, and was considered part of that region throughout the remainder of antiquity.

Telmessus was renowned for its soothsayers, who are mentioned by Herodotus in connection with King Croesus. He twice sought their advice concerning omens, and one of them predicted the fall of Sardis in 546 BC. The most celebrated of the seers was Aristander of Telmessus, whose fame was so great that he was hired by King Philip of Macedon for his own court, and afterwards served Alexander the Great as interpreter of dreams and omens. Aristander would have been with Alexander when the Macedonians marched into Lycia after the siege of Halicarnassus and captured his native town. As Arrian writes of Alexander's conquests in this part of his campaign: 'On entering Lycia he took over Telmessus, the people agreeing not to resist him, after which he crossed the Xanthus and accepted the surrender of Pinara, Xanthus, Patara, and about thirty smaller places'.

After Alexander's time the history of Telmessus is much the same as that of the other Graeco-Roman cities in Asia Minor until the end of antiquity. The town probably fell to the Turks early in the thirteenth century, when the Lycian and Carian coasts were controlled by the Menteşeoğlu *beylik*. But then early in the fifteenth century the Knights Hospitallers of St. John appear to have established a foothold here, building the fortress whose ruins still give something of a medieval atmosphere to the old quarter of Fethiye. After coming down from the necropolis we looked at this old fortress, which probably dates to the same time as the castle of St. Peter in Bodrum, although it was rebuilt in the Ottoman period.

That evening we had supper down by the harbour, reminiscing about our first visit to Fethiye aboard the *Tarih* in January 1961 when we had stopped for lunch in this same *lokanta*. At that time I noticed some interesting paintings in the restaurant, and the waiter introduced me to the artist, a bearded young Turk who called himself Texas—dressed appropriately as he was in boots, spurs, and ten-gallon hat. Texas told us that he was only the second-best painter in Fethiye, and pointed out an excellent landscape that he thought was better than anything he had done; it was painted by a friend now in the local prison. Texas wanted us to meet his friend and so we went with him to the prison, just outside the town, and there the artist arranged an impromptu exhibition of his works for us in the yard outside his cell block. Afterwards Texas had shown us to the necropolis and then walked us back to the pier, waving goodbye as a boatman rowed us back out to the *Tarih*.

Texas stood there waving on the pier even as the *Tarih* sailed down the gulf, and we thought of him now, nearly a quarter of a century later, wondering what had become of him. We asked the owner of the restaurant if he knew our friend Texas, but he had never heard of him, nor had anyone else to whom we spoke. But he remains at any rate in our memories, striding through the cobbled streets of the village in his boots and spurs as he talked excitedly to us about art and the great world outside this once-remote port on the south coast of Turkey.

18

THE XANTHUS VALLEY
AND THE TOMB OF
BELLEROPHON

The following morning we began our journey along the Lycian coast. Once out of the harbour at Fethiye, Hüseyin steered us around the enormous headland that forms the eastern arm of the Bay of Glaucus and, after we rounded the cape at Ilbis Burnu, we headed into the deeply indented bay to its south. There we were suddenly and dramatically confronted with the sight of the Anticragus mountains.

As a great bastion of the Lycian coast for nearly ten miles, the Anticragus mountains stretch to the next headland to the south, where the Cragus range extends seaward in a promontory known in antiquity as Hiera Acra, the Sacred Cape. This is the more western of the two capes of that name, the other one being the south-westernmost promontory of Lycia. The two Sacred Capes together form the turning-points for the vast extension of the Anatolian subcontinent into the Aegean to the south. The western rampart of this sub-continental bulge is one of the eight peaks of Mount Cragus, a landmark noted by Strabo in his description of the coast between the Bay of Glaucus and the western Sacred Cape.

After rounding Ilbis Burnu we sailed along the shore towards the north-eastern corner of the bay below the northern end of the Anticragus mountains, an almost completely land-locked cove called Ölü Deniz, the Dead Sea. This inlet—a lagoon of pink-white sand around a little turquoise bay fringed with trees—was one of the most stunningly beautiful spots along

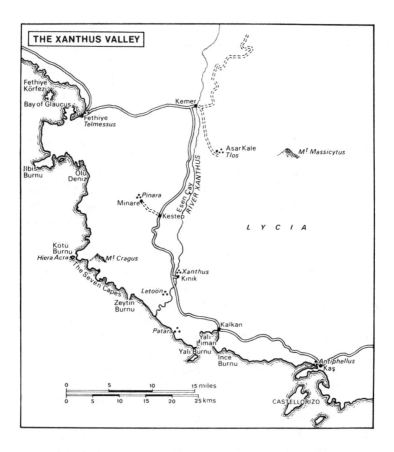

THE XANTHUS VALLEY

Fethiye
Körfezi
Bay of Glaucus
Fethiye
Telmessus
Kemer

Asar Kale
Tlos
Mt Massicytus

Ilbis
Burnu
Ölü
Deniz

Pinara
Minare
Kestep

L Y C I A

Esen Çay
RIVER XANTHUS

Kötü
Burnu
Hiera Acra
Mt Cragus

Xanthus
Kınık

The Seven Capes

Letoön

Zeytin
Burnu

Kalkan

Patara
Yalı
Liman
Yalı Burnu
İnce
Burnu

Antiphellus
Kaş

CASTELLORIZO

| 0 | | 5 | | 10 | | 15 miles |
| 0 | 5 | 10 | 15 | 20 | | 25 kms |

the whole of the western shores; but the boom in tourism in recent years has completely ruined Ölü Deniz, whose once-pristine beach has been polluted by the armadas of yachts and charter boats that anchor in the cove. The result is that it has now been closed to the public. An effort is being made to restore the cove and open it up to visitors again, but under carefully controlled conditions.

From Ölü Deniz we headed southward along the coast, with the Anticragus mountains towering off our port side. Nine miles south of Ölü Deniz we rounded Kötü Burnu and headed south-east as the serrated coast now turned in that direction. This brought us first past the treacherous coast called Yedi Burunlari, the Seven Capes, which, together with Kötü Burnu, are the seaward extensions of the eight peaks of Mount Cragus mentioned by Strabo. After we passed the last of these capes, Zeytin Burnu, the Promontory of the Olives—which is the southernmost projection of Mount Cragus—we came to a long sandy beach that stretches for eight miles to the next prom-ontory, Yalı Burnu. Half-way along this stretch lies the mouth of Esen Çay, the great river that in antiquity was known as the Xanthus. Beyond the mouth of the Xanthus, along toward the end of this beach, we could see the ruins of Patara, one of the sites we were going to visit from Kalkan. There we planned to spend two nights. Then we rounded the cape at Yalı Burnu and entered Yalı Liman, a deep indentation of the Aegean in the south-western corner of Lycia, its eastern arm formed by Ince Burnu, the Cape of the Pearl. We headed directly across the bay toward its north-eastern corner, and entered the harbour of Kalkan, a small town huddled under the great mountain-wall behind it.

After supper that evening we asked around to find transport to the Xanthus valley over the next two days, eventually coming across a young man named Osman who agreed to take us in his jeep. We arranged to meet him the following morning at eight o'clock, after which Dolores and I joined Hüseyin for a night-cap at a waterfront cafe. Relishing two days of idleness ashore, he had already made some boon companions among the local boatmen.

At eight o'clock sharp next morning Osman drove us westward from Kalkan on the modern coastal highway, a tremendous improvement over the cliff-hanging dirt tracks along which we had driven on our first land-journeys along the Lycian coast. Our first stop was at Patara, the final approach to which took us along beside a stream that widened as it approached the sea at the inner end of the ancient harbour, silted up since the early Byzantine period. We drove on until we could gain our first view of the ruined city, whose nearest structure was a splendid triumphal arch standing grandly by itself in the middle of the fields. That had been erected *c.* AD 100 as the ceremonial entrance to Patara.

Patara was renowned in antiquity for its oracle, of which Herodotus writes, ' ... the Lycian town of Patara, where the priestess who delivers the oracles ... is shut up in the temple during the night'. The oracle, which was housed in the Temple of Apollo, is believed to have been the one consulted by King Telephos of Mysia after he was wounded by Achilles. One authority for this tradition is Pausanius, who writes that 'the Lycians at Patara show you a bronze urn in the temple of Apollo which they say was dedicated by Telephos and made by Hephaistos'. The shrine of Apollo at Patara is referred to by Ovid in his *Metamorphoses*, where Apollo tells of how one of Cupid's arrows struck him and caused him to fall in love with Daphne. At the end of this tale Apollo, who here refers to himself as 'lord of Delphi, of Claros, Tenedos, and royal Patara', exclaims in mock sadness, 'Ah me! for no herb can remedy love; the art which heals all but cannot heal its master!'

The Temple of Apollo at Patara has never been identified, although some authorities have suggested that its site may be the low hillock just to the south-east of the monumental gateway where some Attic pottery of the classical period has been unearthed. Patara has never been systematically excavated, and the only temple that survives is a small Corinthian edifice about a quarter of a mile to the south-west of the monumental gateway; this has sometimes been described as the famous sanctuary of Apollo and the site of his oracle, but the structure is far too small for such a renowned building, and it is also much too late, dating to the second century A D.

The theatre is set into the northern side of a hill that rises above the sandy beach. Dunes have drifted into its cavea, a scene of great romantic beauty when viewed from the hilltop above, with the whole ancient city of Patara spread out below. On the eastern side of the city we could see the ruins of three structures arrayed between the theatre and the monumental entrance about half a mile to the north-west: first some baths erected by the emperor Vespasian (A D 69–79); then a basilica, identified as either more baths or a shipwright's building; and then yet more baths consisting of two side-chambers flanking a vaulted structure. On the western side of the city, on the opposite side of the ancient harbour, we could see the enormous granary built by the emperor Hadrian who visited Patara in A D 1 30 along with his wife Sabrina; this is a vast structure more than 200 feet by 80 feet, still virtually intact except for its roof and one of the most impressive structures on the Turkish coast. A short way to its north on the shore of the old harbour there are the ruins of a large and extremely well-built Roman tomb designed in the form of a temple.

We now descended to the beach and walked along the sand to the western side of the harbour. There a vaulted structure can be seen half-buried in the dunes, the remains of what was probably an ancient lighthouse which stood on a mole projecting from the western side of the harbour entrance. Patara was always the principal harbour of Lycia, serving as the port of Xanthus, and during the Hellenistic period the city's importance was enhanced by its strategic position at the southernmost point of Asia Minor with access to both the Aegean and the Mediterranean. It continued as the principal port of Lycia throughout antiquity, and early in the Byzantine era it achieved the rank of metropolis, renowned as the birthplace, *c.* A D 300, of St. Nicholas Thaumathurgos, the Miracle-worker. Patara is also mentioned in the Acts of the Apostles, which records that St. Paul stopped there in A D 57 to change ships on the homeward voyage of his third missionary journey.

We walked back to where Osman was parked in his jeep and, after returning to the main highway, we turned left to head westward once again. A short way along we crossed what Homer describes as 'the whirling waters of Xanthus', the principal river of Lycia. The river takes its name from the Greek word for 'yellow', a colour given to its stream by the alluvial soil it carries down to its delta. This reminded me also of the lines that Alcman of Sparta wrote twenty-five centuries ago: 'She sings like a swan, beside the yellow stream of Xanthus'.

After crossing the Xanthus we drove on for a short way and then turned left on to a side road that took us to the Letoön, the Xanthian shrine of Leto, mother of Apollo and Artemis, which was the central meeting-place and sanctuary of Lycia. This sanctuary eluded Charles Fellows during his exploration of Lycia, and it was first identified by Hoskyn in 1840-1. A French archaeological team under Professor Henri Metzger has been excavating the site since 1950 and, in addition to the theatre, has now unearthed the remains of three temples in the centre of the site; just to the south of these a Roman nymphaion and an early Byzantine church with a fine mosaic pavement; a small section of the west portico of the sanctuary; and a much larger section of the north portico and an exedra. The very well-preserved theatre is on the northern side of the site, much of which lies below the water-table of the Xanthus.

The heart of the Letoön is the triad of temples in the centre of the site, the central one of which is dated to the fifth or fourth century B C and those to the east and west to the second century B C. The central temple has been identified as a sanctuary of Artemis and the eastern one was dedicated to Apollo. This has led to the surmise that the central shrine was sacred to their mother Leto. The identification is supported by the discovery nearby of a trilingual inscription—an exceedingly important carving in Greek, Lycian, and Aramaic—telling the story of Leto and her three children and the nymphs. The Roman nymphaion, just to the south-west of this temple, appears to have replaced an earlier water-sanctuary of the nymphs, whose fountain would have had as its source the sacred spring of which Ovid writes in the *Metamorphoses*. According to Ovid's version, Leto stopped here on her flight from the wrath of Hera after bearing Apollo and Artemis. Leto was exhausted and parched, and she paused to rest and drink at the spring with her divine infants. But the local peasants tried to drive her away, jumping into the pool and dancing there to foul the water, so Leto took her revenge by turning them all into frogs, leaving them there to croak away for the rest of time.

The site of Xanthus is some five and a half miles inland from the mouth of the river as the eagle flies, and is perched grandly in the Lycian hills overlooking the fertile Xanthus valley. The final approach is made via the old road through the village of Kınık, which leads directly to the archaeological site. This road undoubtedly follows the course of the original roadway that led up to ancient Xanthus from the plain below. As we entered the site we passed the fragmentary remnants of the south gate of the Hellenistic city, with an inscription of the Seleucid king Antiochus III, the Great (223–187 BC), behind which was a Roman arch dedicated to the emperor Vespasian (AD 69–79). The road then brought us to the centre of the archaeological site, to the theatre and agora of the Roman city.

Although the River Xanthus is mentioned several times in the *Iliad*, along with the river of the same name in the Troad, there is no mention of a city of Xanthus, and so perhaps the Lycians who were led in battle by Sarpedon and Glaucus lived in scattered farming communities in the vicinity, gathering together for shelter on the fortified Xanthian acropolis hill when threatened by invaders as happened so often in their history. The first such episode on record is reported by Herodotus in Book I of his *Histories*, when, following the fall of

Sardis in 546 BC, the Persian general Harpagus marched south to subdue Caria and Lycia.

> When Harpagus advanced into the plain of Xanthus, they met him in battle, though greatly outnumbered, and fought with much gallantry; at length, however, they were defeated and forced to retire within their walls, whereupon they collected their women, children, slaves and other property and shut them up in the citadel, set fire to it and burnt it to the ground. Then having sworn to do or die, they marched out to meet the enemy and were killed to a man. Most of the Lycians who now claim to be Xanthians are foreign immigrants, except eighty families who happened on that occasion to be away from home, and consequently survived.

The men of Xanthus fought just as valiantly in defence of their city in 42 BC, when it was besieged by Brutus. Then, when all hope of deliverance was gone, the Xanthian warriors set fire to their city and committed suicide *en masse*. As Plutarch completes the story in his *Life of Brutus*:

> It was so tragical a sight that Brutus could not bear to see it, but wept at the very mention of the scene ... Thus the Xanthians ... repeated by their desperate deed the calamity of their forefathers, who ... in the Persian Wars had fired their city and destroyed themselves.

This was not the end of Xanthus, for the survivors returned to rebuild their city on the same site, so that in imperial Roman times it once again became the leading community in Lycia, and indeed survived on into the Byzantine era as a bishopric under the Metropolitan of Myra. But by the time that Xanthus was rediscovered by Charles Fellows, in 1838, the site had been long abandoned, the nearest settlement being the Turkish village of Kınık. Fellows excavated Xanthus in three campaigns between 1839 and 1844, shipping all of the important antiquities he found back to England, where they are now on exhibit in the British Museum, most notably the Nereid Monument. The site of Xanthus then lay undisturbed until 1950, when a French team of archaeologists began their work here. The French excavations have unearthed structures covering the entire span of the existence of Xanthus, ranging from the original Lycian fortress-town of the eighth century BC to the medieval Byzantine bishopric of the twelfth century AD. Here, as elsewhere in Lycia, the most interesting remains are the funerary monuments, although all of these are now stripped of their original sculptural decoration.

The two most important of these monuments stand side by side next to the Roman theatre. One of them is a Lycian pillar-tomb, a handsome sarcophagus of the fourth century BC standing on a tall platform. Beside this is the famous Tomb of the Harpies, a tall monolith supporting a sarcophagus in the form of a chest decorated with sculptures in low relief. (The relief *in situ* is a plaster copy of the original which is in the British Museum.) The so-called harpies from which the tomb takes its name are actually sirens, half birds and half women: they are shown conducting the souls of the dead to the Underworld.

Beside the road near the Roman agora is the famous Xanthian Stele, a pillar-tomb with an inscription of over 250 lines written in both Greek and Lycian. This has been one of the most important sources for the decipherment of the Lycian language, and it also records information about the history of Lycia in the last third of the fifth century BC. The Greek text apparently refers to an incident which Thucydides describes in his account of the second year of the Peloponnesian War, 430–429 BC.

The theatre, which dates from the mid-second century AD, is built in against the north face of the acropolis, the site of Lycian Xanthus. The oldest ruins there are of a palace of the Lycian kings, destroyed at the time of the Persian conquest, *c.* 540 BC. All of the Lycian buildings on the acropolis, including a temple dedicated to Artemis, were eventually replaced by the Byzantine structures one sees today.

Xanthus was enclosed by a defence wall which is still standing along its eastern side, where the fortifications extend northward to join those slanting down from the northern acropolis, the second eminence which was the centre of Xanthus during the Hellenistic, Roman, and Byzantine periods. The south-eastern slope of this acropolis was apparently the principal necropolis of Lycian Xanthus, as evidenced by the number of sarcophagi and rock-hewn tombs one sees there. The most splendid of these is an almost perfectly preserved pillar-tomb of the fourth century BC; this stands just above the ruins of the famous Payuva Tomb whose reliefs are now in the Lycian Room of the British Museum. The ascent of the acropolis is rather difficult because of the dense undergrowth, but it is well worth the effort for the superb view it affords of the ruins and their surroundings, with the great massif of Ak Dağ, the White Mountain, to the north-east. To the south the River Xanthus winds its way to the sea through its fertile valley, Homer's 'rich countryside of Lycia'.

Making an early start the following day, we had retraced by sunrise our trip of the day before, passing the turn-offs to Patara, the Letoön, and Xanthus. Then we continued north-wards as we headed up the Xanthus valley and deeper into the Lycian hills towards Pinara and Tlos, with the Anticragus mountains rising to the left above the coast, and ahead to the right the towering massif of Ak Dağ, the ancient Massicytus, with its peak over 10,000 feet high. Its summit glistened in a plume of snow in the golden light of the brilliant June morning.

Soon after passing Kestep we turned off the main Kalkan–Fethiye highway on to a side road that took us to the village of Minare, which means Minaret, a corruption of the name of the ancient Lycian city of Pinara. As we did so we could see the site of Pinara—one of the most spectacularly situated ruins in Asia Minor. The ancient city perched on the flat top of a 1,500-foot high table-rock, an enormous truncated cone very much like the giant mesas of the south-western United States, except that here in Lycia the foreground is fertile and even heavily wooded.

Pinara was one of the principal cities of ancient Lycia, represented in the Lycian League by the maximum number of three votes. A Xanthian historian of the fourth century BC attributes the founding of Pinara to people from Xanthus, who were forced to leave their own lands because of over-population and settled on a round mountain-top in the Anticragus range, which in the Lycian language they called Pinara. The original settlement would have been on the upper acropolis, with the town later spreading out on to the terraced hillside to the east of the precipice, whose sheer face is honeycombed with tombs. But there may have been a settlement at Pinara long before the Xanthian colony was founded, perhaps in the late Bronze Age. This supposition is based on Strabo's statement that at Pinara there was a shrine to the hero Pandaros, the famed archer from Lycia mentioned by Homer as one of the great warriors among the Trojan allies. Aeneas addresses him in Book V of the *Iliad*:

Pandaros, where now are your bow and your feathered arrows;
where your fame, in which no man here dare contend with you,
nor can any man in Lycia claim he is better?

The ruins of the classical city of Pinara are clustered on the plateau or saddle below the ancient acropolis to the east, and the remains of a much lower fortified acropolis stand on an eminence rising from the south-western corner. The best-preserved edifice remaining from the ancient city is the theatre, dating from the late second century BC, which is outside the walls to the north-east, with its cavea cut into the side of the hill and facing westward towards the city and the old acropolis.

Pinara is known principally for its rock-hewn tombs. The most interesting of them is the so-called Royal Tomb, hollowed out of the rock-face of the lower acropolis at its south-eastern corner. This is of particular interest because one of its reliefs shows the houses, towers, and battlements of an ancient city. Charles Fellows believed it to be a representation of Patara itself.

After lunching at a shady spot beneath the acropolis, we drove back through Minare to the main highway; there we turned north to drive farther up the valley of the Xanthus, heading for Tlos, which is nine miles south of the town of Kemer. After turning off the main highway on to the approach road we drove on to the hamlet of Asar Kale, where we finally saw the ruins of Tlos looming above us on the acropolis of the ancient city. Charles Fellows wrote when he came upon this dramatic site in 1839: 'The whole ride down this upper valley is beautiful, and varies continually; its scenery, on approaching the bold and Greek-like situation of the ancient city of Tlos, is strikingly picturesque'.

The site of Tlos is indeed picturesque, its ancient acropolis dominated by a medieval fortress perched on the summit nearly 1,650 feet above the Xanthus valley, with the river three miles to the west and Massicytus rising to its snow-covered peak just nine miles to the east. They create a stunning background. The original settlement at Tlos was on this acropolis; in Lycian it was known as Tlawa, so that it has been identified as the city of Dalawa in the Lukka lands mentioned in Hittite archives of the fourteenth century BC. This is probably one of the oldest places of settlement in all of Lycia. Tlos was always one of the most important cities in the region, and was one of the six entitled to three votes in the Lycian League. Nevertheless, it is seldom mentioned by ancient historians, probably because its remote location on this hilltop deep in Lycia kept it out of the mainstream of events.

Virtually no trace remains of the prehistoric fortress-town that must once have stood on the acropolis hill. The building of its medieval castle obliterated all earlier structures except the Lycian defence walls which can still be seen on the mountain-top along with the Byzantine fortifications and numerous rock-hewn tombs in the side of the cliff. The Roman town stands on the level area below, its monuments including a stadium, an agora, a gymnasium with a palaestra, two baths, an unidentified temple, an early Christian basilica, and a theatre, this last dated by an inscription to the reign of Antoninus Pius (A D 138–61).

The most remarkable of the funerary monuments carved into the side of the acropolis cliff is the one known as the Tomb of Bellerophon. The tomb takes its name from the relief in the porch of the funerary monument which shows the Corinthian hero Bellerophon riding on his winged horse Pegasus, given to him by his ancestor Poseidon. This sepulchre was probably built for a prince of the royal line at Tlos who claimed descent from Bellerophon, known in Greek as Bellerophontes and a grandfather of Sarpedon and Glaucus. According to mythology, Bellerophon first came to Lycia during the reign of King Iobates, who set him the series of tasks described in Book VI of the *Iliad* where Sarpedon tells of his ancestry:

First he sent him away with orders to kill the Chimaera
none might approach; a thing of immortal make, not
    human,
lion-fronted and snake behind, a goat in the middle,
and snorting out the breath of the terrible flame of bright
    fire.
He killed the Chimaera, obeying the portents of the immortals.
Next after this he fought against the glorious Solymoi,
and this he thought was the strongest battle with men that
    he entered;
but third he slaughtered the Amazons, who fight men in
    battle.
Now as he came back the king spun another entangling
treachery; for choosing the bravest men in wide Lycia
he laid a trap, but these men never came home thereafter
since all of them were killed by the blameless Bellerophontes.
Then when the king knew him for the powerful stock of
    the god,
he detained him there, and offered him the hand of his
    daughter,
and gave him half of all the kingly privilege. Thereto

the men of Lycia cut out a piece of land, surpassing
all others, fine ploughland and orchard for him to administer.
His wife bore three children to valiant Bellerophontes,
Isandros and Hippolochos and Laodameia.
Laodameia lay in love beside Zeus of the counsels
and bore him Sarpedon of the brazen helmet.

The myth of Bellerophon undoubtedly perpetuates the folk-memory of the first Greek heroes who settled in Lycia toward the end of the Bronze Age, carving out for themselves a kingdom in the Xanthus valley. Inscriptions found at Tlos record that the people of the city were formed into demes named for Bellerophon, his grandson Sarpedon, and his father-in-law Iobates, whom he succeeded as king of Lycia. But Bellerophon ended his days in sadness, for he fell from favour with the gods who, in their divine displeasure, killed two of his children. Sarpedon tells the tale, concluding the account of his heroic ancestry:

But after Bellerophontes was hated by all the immortals
he wandered alone about the plain of Aleois, eating
his heart out, skulking aside from the trodden track of
    humanity.
As for Isandros his son, Ares the insatiate of fighting
killed him in battle against the glorious Solymoi,
while Artemis of the golden reins killed the daughter in anger.
But Hippolochos begot me, and I claim that he is my father;
he sent me to Troy, and urged upon me repeated injunctions,
to be always among the bravest, and hold my head above
    others,
not shaming the generation of my fathers, who were
the greatest men in Ephyre and again in wide Lycia.
Such is my generation and the blood I claim to be born from.

Such is the myth of Bellerophon, which we recalled when standing before the tomb that bears his name in Tlos, an ancient city that still dominates the surrounding valley of the

Xanthus. As Captain Spratt remarked of Tlos in 1839, coming upon these ruins just shortly after they were discovered by Fellows, 'a grander sight for a great city could scarcely have been selected in all Lycia'. So we felt ourselves, as we looked out over the beautiful countryside in what was once the heart of the Lycian kingdom, the land of Bellerophon.

19

THE WESTERN LYCIAN SHORE

The first part of our journey the following morning took us out
of the harbour at Kalkan and south through Yalı Liman, after
which we rounded Ince Burnu and headed east-south-east,
past the islets of Sarıbelen and Oksuz Adası. Soon we were
heading directly toward a narrow strait between a long and
narrow promontory of the mainland, Çukurbağ Yarımadası,
and the Greek island of Castellorizo, known in Turkish as Meis
Adası. Castellorizo is the most distant from Athens of all the
inhabited Greek islands, and its remoteness, plus its isolation
so close to the Turkish coast, has led to the migration of most
of its population, although some have now begun to return
from places as far distant as Australia. Almost all of the remaining islanders live in the Chora, the main town of Castellorizo.
It nestles in a bay at the north-eastern corner of the island,
facing the Turkish town of Kaş across only three miles of water.
The Chora is a typical cubistic Greek island town, with tiers of
whitewashed houses clustering around a medieval Frankish
fortress. But there were few signs of life as we sailed by into
Kaş Liman; it looked a veritable ghost town. By contrast, as
we approached the pretty white town of Kaş at the end of the
bay, we could see that it had developed tremendously since
our last visit nearly a quarter of a century before. There was
a yacht marina in the port and, as we approached the dock,
we noticed other evidence of the boom in tourism that has
taken place along the southern coast of Turkey—the water-

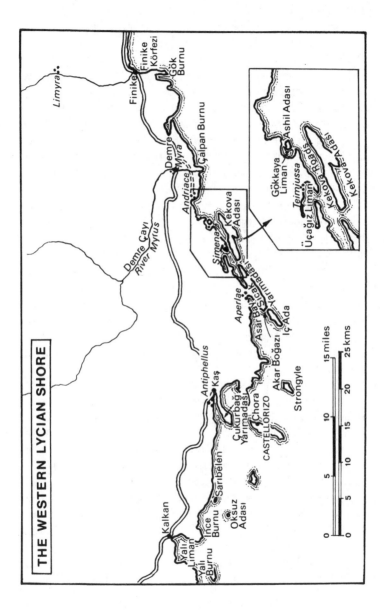

THE WESTERN LYCIAN SHORE

front lined with motels, restaurants, and cafes—creating a modern resort very different from the sleepy fishing-village we had first seen from the deck of the *Tarih*.

Kaş has a uniquely beautiful setting, with the crescent-shaped port opening out on to an immensely long fiord ringed with undulating pine-clad hills of sensuous outline, while the village itself spreads across the neck of the Çukurbağ peninsula and over on to the end of the deep inlet known as Bucak Deniz. Looming up behind is the dramatic backdrop of Felendağı, the southernmost of the Lycian mountains, culminating in a sheer 1,500-foot precipice which adds to the drama of the setting. Rock-hewn tombs in its cliff add a note of mystery.

Kaş has been identified as the ancient Antiphellus, which archaeological finds indicate was occupied as early as the sixth century BC. Antiphellus was originally just the port for the inland town of Phellus, whose site has been identified on Felendağı above the village of Çukurbağ. However, Antiphellus developed into a prosperous shipping town during the Hellenistic and Roman periods, and became one of the most important harbours on the southern coast of Asia Minor. In fact it eclipsed the mother town.

The principal monument of Antiphellus is its Hellenistic theatre, which is some 500 yards to the east of the port, built into the hillside above the sea. We walked out there as soon as we went ashore, taking along a picnic lunch and a bottle of wine. On the way we stopped to look at the ruins of a little temple, built originally in the first century BC, its identity unknown. Beyond the temple along the shore there are fragmentary remnants of the Hellenistic sea-wall, the only fortifications built to defend Antiphellus, which had neither land-walls nor a fortified acropolis. Its citizens apparently depended on the Lycian mountains for protection. The theatre is set into the side of the hill above the northern end of these walls, and we climbed up through an olive-grove to reach it. The theatre is remarkably well-preserved except for the loss of its proscenium, and the sturdy retaining wall to its rear still holds up the cavea, with twenty-six tiers of seats arrayed continuously in somewhat more than a semicircular arc without an intervening diazoma, or aisle. We climbed to the uppermost tier and enjoyed our picnic there, commanding a view of the entire bay across to the island of Castellorizo, where we could see the white houses of the Chora shining in the late afternoon sun, looking more than ever like a ghost town.

We next set out to explore some of the Lycian funerary monuments, beginning with a rock-hewn tomb on the hillside some 200 yards to the north-east of the theatre. This is known as the Doric Tomb, a cubic mass of living rock carved into the shape of a house-mausoleum with sides some sixteen feet long. It has pilasters in low relief on the corners, and a portal with a moulded frame that was once closed by a sliding door. Inside the burial chamber there is a fascinating relief showing a line of small female figures with their hands linked in a dance, a scene evocative of the folk-dances that one still sees today in Anatolia and the Greek islands. Yet this sculpture dates to the fourth century BC, a haunting reminder of the deep roots of the culture along this coast.

There are other rock-hewn Lycian tombs on the hillside to the north of the town, including one with a Gothic arch and inscriptions in both Lycian and Latin indicating that the ancient burial-chamber was reused in Roman times. On the eastern side of the town there is a remarkable free-standing tomb in the form of a sarcophagus shaped like an ancient Lycian house. Pairs of lion-heads project from either side of the Gothic arches on the lid, and there is an undeciphered Lycian epitaph, another haunting evocation of Antiphellus.

The next stage of our journey took us out of Kaş Liman and around the succession of headlands to its south, passing on our starboard first Castellorizo and then its tiny satellite of Strongyle, the most remote possession of Greece. From my classical atlas I saw that we were now rounding the southernmost promontory of Lycia, with the open sea off to our south identified on the map as the Mare Lycium.

We turned eastward along the coast. As we did so we then saw the elongated transverse extrusion of the Lycian coast known as Sıcak Yarımadası, the Hot Peninsula, and just off its nearest point the islet called Iç Ada with the narrow but navigable channel called Akar Boğazı passing between them. We planned to pass through Akar Boğazı later that day but first we intended to visit the site of Aperlae, on the mainland near the inner end of Asar Bükü, the long and narrow bay inside the eastern extension of Sıcak Yarımadası. As we entered Asar Bükü we began scanning the mainland coast from close in and finally, when we came to within 500 yards of the inner end of the bay, we spotted some ruined walls on a low ridge just above the shore. This was the site of Aperlae and, as Hüseyin manœuvred us in to the shore, we could see under-water the ruins of a pier and what had been the maritime quarter of the ancient city, submerged in some subsidence of the Lycian coast in times past.

Aperlae is mentioned by a number of ancient geographers, though Ptolemy wrote it as Aperrae and Pliny as Apyrae. The first European traveller to place Aperlae at the inner end of Asar Bay was C. R. Cockerell, who identified the town from an inscription on a sarcophagus he found here on the mainland shore in 1811. The underwater ruins of the harbour quarter of Aperlae were discovered in recent years by the American yachtsman Robert Carter and his wife, who first observed them when sailing along the Aegean coast and later examined the site in detail. Besides the underwater ruins the principal remains of Aperlae on the mainland are the defence walls which extend up from the shoreline in two lines that converge at the little acropolis on the hilltop, with fragmentary towers and gates still visible. But the unforgettable experience here is swimming underwater to look at the ruins of the harbour quarter of Aperlae. The quay and a number of the port build-ings are still visible in the ultramarine light at depths of only six to eight feet; it is a view that evokes visions of Atlantis.

Coins as early as the fifth century BC have been identified as belonging to Aperlae. Aperlae was a member of the Lycian League, the principal town in a sympolity, a group of three or four local communities that together were entitled to but a single vote. Apart from that distinction, Aperlae was of little note, as far off the beaten track in antiquity as it is today.

We now retraced our way through Asar Bay, after which Hüseyin steered a careful course through the narrow channel at Akar Boğazı, the southernmost arc of our journey around the Lycian coast. We then followed the shore of Sıcak Yarımadası to its eastern tip and there passed through the western channel between the peninsula and Kekova Adası, the four-mile-long spit of an island that parallels the mainland like a great barrier reef and creates the inland waterway known as the Kekova Roads. This labyrinthine succession of bays, coves, channels, and offshore islets, with the ruins of several ancient Lycian communities lying along their shores, some of them submerged and visible underwater, makes this a most extraordinary and exciting stretch of coast.

The first European traveller to mention Kekova Adası was Sir Francis Beaufort, who charted the coast of southern Turkey in 1811–12; as he writes in his *Karamania*: 'Kekova is altogether unnoticed by Strabo; but there is no doubt that this is the Dolichiste of Ptolemy. The name implies its long and narrow shape; and it is placed by him next in order to Megiste, which was certainly the ancient name of Kastelorizo island'. The two channels that lead into the Kekova Roads are divided by a pair of tiny islets called Kara Ada and Toprak Ada, which from their honeycombed appearance seem to have long served as quarries. Immediately to the west inside the channel is the entrance to the long and narrow inlet called Polemos Bükü. The name of the bay is derived from the Greek word for 'war', probably because this secluded waterway served as a hide-out for ships, most recently for British submarines in the Second World War. Polemos Bay leads in as far as the narrow isthmus which joins Sıcak Yarımadası to the mainland, with Asar Bay and the ruins of Aperlae on the far side.

The main stretch of the Kekova Roads comprises two water-ways, with Xera Cove forming the channel between Kekova and the mainland, and opposite the eastern end of the island an almost completely land-locked and serpentine cove named Üçağız Liman opening up just inside the coast. Its name in Turkish is a direct translation of the Greek Tristomo, the 'Three Mouths', so called because of the three narrow channels that lead into it through a maze of islets, its outer end known as Ölüdeniz, the Dead Sea. The shores of Ölüdeniz and Üçağız are littered with ruins, ancient, medieval, and of more recent date. At the western end of Kekova island just inside the east channel at the entrance to the Roads one sees the apse of a large Greek church, which once served the Greek community of the village of Tershane, abandoned after the 1923 population exchange.

Two ancient Lycian communities have been identified on the shore of Ölüdeniz and Üçağız Liman. The first of these is at Kale Köy, Castle Village, a seaside hamlet that takes its name from the splendidly preserved medieval fortress that dominates the promontory at the eastern entrance to Üçağız. The local houses blend in imperceptibly with the Lycian, Greek, Roman, and medieval ruins to create one of the most picturesque spots on the Turkish coast. Kale Köy has been identified as the Lycian town of Simena, and coins and inscriptions record its existence as far back as the fourth century BC. Simena was a member of the Lycian League, part of the sympolity headed by Aperlae, and its citizens were referred to as Aperlites from Simena. Ruins of some Roman baths stand close to the landing-stage, with an inscription recording that they were dedicated to the emperor Titus (AD 79–81) by the council and people of Aperlae and the other communities of the sympolity. This would have included Simena, although it was little more than a village in antiquity, just as it is today. As we made our way up from the landing-stage to the fortress we passed two large sarcophagi with Gothic arches, as well as the fragmentary portico of an unidentified temple just under the castle walls. The fortress itself is one of the best-preserved and most attractive along this coast; its walls still stand to their full height and are topped with battlements. Inside the fortress there is a charming little odeion with its seven tiers of seats carved out of the rock on the acropolis hill. It has a seating capacity of perhaps 300, which gives one a good idea of just how small Simena was. But what a pearl of a place it must have been, perched on the promontory at the head of this secluded and surpassingly beautiful inland waterway!

The other ancient site in the Kekova Roads is just to the east of Üçağız Köy, the little village on the north shore of Üçağız Liman. This has been identified by an inscription as the ancient Lycian village of Teimiussa, which was apparently of too little importance to be a member even of the Aperlaean sympolity. The village had no defence walls, and its only fortification is a tiny citadel on a rocky eminence above the cove that appears to have served as the acropolis. Teimiussa does not seem to have had any public buildings, probably because it was a suburb of the nearby Lycian towns of Cyanea and Myra. Inscriptions upon the numerous sarcophagi with Gothic lids that lie scattered around the site, all of them written in Greek and dating from the Hellenistic and Roman periods, indicate that this was probably so. There are also a number of rock-hewn tombs in the form of house façades with ornate portals. One of them is decorated with the figure in low relief of a naked youth, undoubtedly the deceased, who is identified in a Lycian inscription over the entrance as Kluwanimi. Another inter-esting structure surviving from ancient Teimiussa is its rock-hewn quay, which lies along the shore of the cove at the eastern end of the site.

As we continued sailing through the Kekova Roads, we passed a medieval fortress on the mainland near the eastern end of the channel. Then, at the end of the Kekova Roads, we found Gökkaya Liman, a fiord-like inlet between an indentation of the mainland and an offshore archipelago, the largest of the isles being Ashil Adası. Our course took us north-north-east

across the bay beyond Gökkaya Liman and the eastern tip of
Kekova island, heading toward a promontory on the other side
known as Çalpan Burnu. Hüseyin brought us into a cove just
under the promontory to its north. There we anchored off a
shingle beach at the mouth of a river which entered the sea
in a pair of channels on either side of us. We had arrived at
the site of Andriace, the ancient port of Myra, whose ruins lay
some three and a half miles upstream.

Andriace has now become a popular summer resort, connected by a good road to Demre, the site of ancient Myra, and
thence to the coastal highway. In imperial Roman times it
became an important port, particularly after Hadrian built a
huge granary there similar to the one he erected in Patara.
The impressive ruins of this enormous building, some 200 feet
in length, are on the south side of the harbour, and busts of
Hadrian and his wife Sabrina are still visible over the main
entrance. Directly opposite the granary on the right bank of
the river are the ruins of a nymphaion, and farther upstream
are the remains of a water-mill. The water for both of these
was brought to the port along the Roman aqueduct whose
remnants can still be seen in the valley leading inland from
the port. There is also a well-preserved sarcophagus that must
have been removed from the necropolis on the hillside to the
north of the port. The ruins of a watch-tower can also be seen
on a hill overlooking the harbour on its southern side.

The watch-tower was probably built in the Hellenistic era,
and so it would have been one of the landmarks that St. Paul
saw when he stopped here c. AD 60 to change ships, while
being taken to Italy as a prisoner following his arrest by King
Agrippa. As one reads in Acts 22:1–7: 'And when we had
sailed over the sea of Cilicia and Pamphylia, we came to
Myra, a city of Lycia. And there the centurion found a ship of
Alexandria sailing into Italy; and he put us therein. And when
we had sailed slowly many days, and scarce were come over
against Cnidus, the wind not suffering us, we sailed under
Crete ... unto a place which is called Fair Havens'.

After lunch we hired a taxi for the short ride to Demre, a village near the site of ancient Myra. Before going on to Myra, we stopped to visit the Church of St. Nicholas. The present church, which was abandoned by its Greek congregation in 1923 after the population exchange, is a heavily restored eleventh-century structure built on the site of an earlier sanctuary of the same name. It has an inscription recording that it was also restored by the emperor Constantine IX in 1043. The original structure seems to have been a basilica erected above the tomb of St. Nicholas, who died in the late fourth century; the edifice was restored and perhaps enlarged by Justinian in the second quarter of the sixth century. St. Nicholas was bishop of Myra and represented Lycia at the First Ecumenical Council of the Church at Nicaea in AD 325. He is said to have slapped the heretic Arius so hard there that his bones rattled. Numerous miracles were attributed to Nicholas during his lifetime, one of them known as that of the Pickled Boys. Three poor youths had been murdered by a villanous butcher, cut up, pickled, and placed in a tub to be sold as meat, but when the saint learned of this he restored them to life. He was also noted for his philanthropy and once surreptitiously presented dowries to the three unmarried daughters of a poor ınan of Myra. He threw three purses of gold into their house during the night while they slept, and this story gives rise to the legend of Father Christmas, with whom the saint came to be identified in the Western world. The miracles continued after the death of St. Nicholas, who is buried in a sarcophagus now in the south aisle of the church. The church became one of the most famous shrines in Byzantium, but in 1087 some merchant adventurers from Bari stole the bones from his sarcophagus and brought them back to their native city, where they remain to this day.

After visiting the Church of St. Nicholas in Demre we went on to see the ruins at Myra, a short distance away. The site is a very dramatic one, with the ancient acropolis on the lofty ridge of a rocky crag. The south-east and south-west sides of the precipice are pockmarked with Lycian tombs, and a splendid Graeco-Roman theatre stands below the citadel to the south-west at the foot of the hill.

The tombs at Myra can be divided into two groups; the first necropolis comprises those in the cliff-face flanking the theatre; and the second those on the cliff below the acropolis to the south-east. Most of the tombs are of the house type, and some of them are decorated with splendid sculptures in relief. Two tombs possess notable mourning scenes; in one, the Painted Tomb, there are eleven almost life-sized figures; and in the other is a relief showing two warriors in combat. But only faint traces now remain of their original painted decoration, which is known mostly from its description by Charles Fellows. There are also a few tombs of the temple type, as well as some of much humbler form, little more than rectangular cavities carved out of the rock-face of the precipice. On one such simple tomb Texier found the following graffito, possibly an epitaph: 'Moschus loves Philiste, daughter of Demetrius'.

The oldest part of Myra is the acropolis, which is approached by a stepped path that ascends to the western edge of the walled enclosure on the ridge above. The oldest walls date to the fifth century BC, the earliest extant remains of the Lycian settlement. Myra was always one of the most important towns in Lycia, and during the Hellenistic period it was one of the six cities in the Lycian League that had the maximum quota of three votes at meetings of the federation. During the imperial Roman era Myra attained the status of metropolis, and it retained the title during the Byzantine period when the renown of St. Nicholas made it one of the most famous cities in Asia Minor. The emperor Theodosius II (AD 408–50) in fact made it capital of Lycia. During the Arab invasions that began in the seventh century Myra suffered terribly; the city was even occupied by Arab forces for a time in 809, during the reign of the caliph Haroun el-Raschid, and again in 1034. These invasions, and the incursions of the Turkoman tribesmen following the Selcuk victory at the Battle of Manzikert in 1071, led to the abandonment of Myra in the late Byzantine period, so that the city fell into ruins. The once-renowned metropolis was lost to the Western world until it was rediscovered by the first European travellers who passed this way. One of these was Charles Fellows, and the thrill of his discovery is evoked by his journal. 'The fatigue of excitement, from the beauty and singularity of the scenery, made me rejoice at reaching this ancient city', he wrote on 26 April 1840.

After leaving Myra we returned to Andriace, where Hüseyin was waiting for us on the caique. As soon as we were aboard he cast off and took us out of the harbour, rounding Çalpan Burnu as we continued our voyage along the Lycian coast. We headed due east at first, passing the mouth of the Demre Çayı, after which Hüseyin gradually began changing our course towards the north-east, as the coast curved in that direction. We continued on that course until we came to Gök Burnu, the Heavenly Cape, where the shoreline suddenly veers due north at the beginning of the great bight that curves from there to Cape Chelidonia, the south-easternmost point of Lycia. We could now see it in the blue distance. Rounding Gök Burnu, we turned into Finike Körfezi, and soon there hove in sight the next port-of-call on our journey, the town of Finike, ancient Phoenicus.

20

THE EASTERN LYCIAN SHORE

When we first saw the little port of Finike in January 1961, stopping there for a few hours aboard the *Tarih*, the town was almost completely isolated. The coastal highway was still far from complete, and the road from the coast through the high mountains of the interior was primitive. The monthly visit by the *Tarih* was Finike's main link with the outside world. Now the coastal highway has been completed and, as a result, the town has prospered, for the local farmers can ship to Izmir and Istanbul the fruits and vegetables that grow in such abundance in the valley that leads inland from the coast. The town has also profited from tourism, as travellers now stop there while driving around the southern coast or cruising along the Lycian shore in yachts or chartered caiques. Finike is one of the regular ports-of-call on the Mavi Yol, the Blue Journey.

Hüseyin steered us in to a mooring at the yacht quay along the southern arc of the port, an artificial harbour that has been created by constructing two long breakwaters out into Finike Körfezi. There is absolutely nothing left of ancient Phoenicus, the Lycian town from which Finike takes its name, nor is there anything else of interest to be seen in the modern port, but the following morning we hired a taxi to take us to Limyra, an ancient Lycian city in the hills some four miles to the north-east of Finike and near Demirciköy, the Village of the Iron-worker. When Fellows passed this way in 1840, fording two rivers on his way to Limyra on horseback, he found that

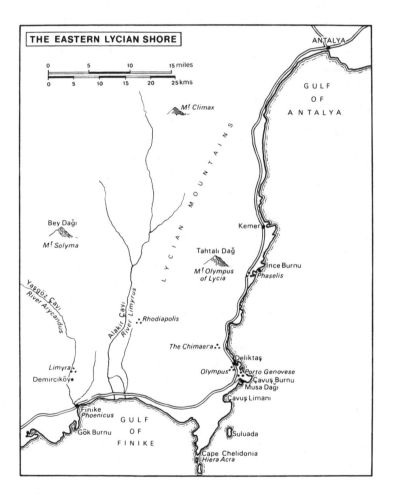

THE EASTERN LYCIAN SHORE

0   5   10   15 miles

0   5   10   15   20   25 kms

Mᵗ Climax

GULF
OF
ANTALYA

Bey Dağı

Mᵗ Solyma

Kemer

Tahtalı Dağ

Mᵗ Olympus
of Lycia

Ince Burnu

Phaselis

Yaşgöz Çayı,
River Arycandus

Alakır Çayı,
River Limyrus

Rhodiapolis

The Chimaera

Deliktaş

Olympus

Porto Genovese

Çavuş Burnu

Musa Dağı

Limyra

Çavuş Limanı

Demirciköy

Finike
Phoenicus

GULF

Gök Burnu

OF

Suluada

FINIKE

Cape Chelidonia

Hiera Acra

Demirciköy was inhabited by gypsies, in Turkish Çingane, whom one often sees along the south coast of Turkey serving as migrant workers during the farming season, or occasionally making their way as itinerant musicians, sometimes with a dancing bear in company.

The rivers that Fellows forded were the Yaşgöz Çayı, to the west, and the Alakır Çayı, to the east; these two streams flow parallel to one another a few miles apart and empty into the sea just to the east of Finike, watering one of the most fertile valleys in Lycia. The first of these rivers has been identified as the Arycandus, while the second is generally agreed to be the Limyrus, taking its name from Limyra itself, which we were now approaching, evidenced by the numerous Lycian tombs we could see around us.

The site of Limyra is at the foot of Mount Tocat, which rises above the surrounding plain to an altitude of nearly 4,000 feet. The acropolis is on the crest of a steeply sloping hill at the foot of this mountain, with the necropolis on the hillside and the Roman city on the plain below to the south, at the source of the River Limyrus. Some fragments of the acropolis wall survive on this eminence, and archaeological evidence indicates that there was a settlement on the summit of the hill dating back to the first half of the fourth century BC. That was the period when Limyra was the capital of a principality ruled by a local warlord named Pericles, who managed to maintain his independence both from the Persians and from Mausolus, ruler of Caria, who in the second quarter of the fourth century BC extended his dominions down into Lycia.

The most prominent structure in the lower city is the theatre, which stands just to the right of the road that passes through the archaeological site. The present theatre replaced an earlier structure destroyed by an earthquake in AD 141, which apparently levelled most of the town. An inscription records that the theatre was rebuilt that same year by Opramoas, a wealthy citizen of the nearby town of Rhodiapolis, who may have financed the reconstruction of the other public buildings of

Limyra that had been destroyed. Across the road from the theatre there is a stretch of the late Roman defence wall, the other structures in the surrounding area ranging in date from the imperial Roman era into the Byzantine period, with several branches of the River Limyrus meandering through the ruins from its source at a spring. According to Pliny, there was a fish-oracle at Limyra, and so it is possible that it may have been located at this spring. One structure of interest among these ruins is a funerary monument in the north-western corner of the site. This has been identified as the cenotaph of Gaius Caesar, grandson and adopted son of Augustus, who died in Limyra on 21 February in the year AD 4, succumbing to the grievous wound inflicted by an assassin during a revolt by the Parthians in the Araxes valley. The cenotaph was erected by the people of Limyra and by Augustus, who twenty years earlier had made Gaius his heir, for the boy was the eldest son of his daughter Julia.

The finest of the tombs in the lower part of the necropolis is a Lycian funerary monument behind the theatre to its west; it consists of a sarcophagus with a Gothic lid standing on a pedestal with a relief depicting a funeral banquet and the judgement of the deceased in the Underworld, and is reproduced by Fellows in his *Travels and Researches in Asia Minor*. This tomb is dated to the fourth century BC and is a memorial to a Lycian nobleman named Catabura, a brother or close relative of King Pericles.

Of all the funerary monuments in the necropolis the most interesting, however, is a newly discovered structure high up on the western end of the hillside at the edge of the lower terrace of the acropolis. There archaeologists have unearthed the foundations of a splendid mausoleum standing on a platform some sixty feet on each side. The monument was surrounded by a frieze, now in the museum at Antalya, showing a ruler riding in a war-chariot at the head of his troops. This structure, dated to the first half of the fourth century BC, may have been erected as a memorial to King Pericles himself, who died *c.* 370 BC. Certainly the monumental scale of the mausoleum and its decoration would have been appropriate for a great warrior like Pericles, as would the grandeur of its setting, looking out over the most fertile valley in the lands that had once comprised his kingdom. His capital at Limyra was just eighteen miles south of Bey Dağı, the ancient Mount Solyma. Its snow-capped summit soars more than 10,000 feet above sea-level and is the highest peak in Lycia. Mount Solyma gave its name to the people who dwelt there at the dawn of history, warriors referred to in the *Iliad* as 'the glorious Soly-moi'. Mount Solyma is also referred to in the *Odyssey*, for this was where Poseidon stood when Odysseus on his raft neared 'the shadowy mountains of the Phaikian land', as the god peered at him from 'far on the mountains of the Solymoi'.

After visiting Limyra we returned to Finike, where Hüseyin was waiting to begin the next stage of our journey. This took us straight across the Gulf of Finike to Cape Chelidonia, at the south-eastern tip of Lycia, which is continued seaward by the little archipelago known as the Chelidonian Isles. The ancient Greeks called this point Hiera Acra and the Romans Pro-montarium Sacrum. Both mean Sacred Cape, and this is the more eastern of the two promontories that bore that name.

Cape Chelidonia, I could see on my classical atlas, formed the coastal boundary between the Mare Lycium and the Mare Pamphylium. The ancient land of Pamphylia extended to the east of Lycia from the modern town of Antalya onwards. Cape Chelidonia has been known as a maritime graveyard since the beginning of history. Pliny wrote that it is 'fraught with disaster for passing vessels'. One of the earliest wrecks known to under-water archaeologists was discovered here in recent years, dated to *c.* 1200 BC, and its artefacts are now on exhibit in the Bodrum Museum.

After rounding Cape Chelidonia the shore now veered off sharply north-north-east, and ahead we could see the massed peaks and ridges of the coastal mountains as they marched tier on tier towards Antalya, some twenty-eight miles to the north. About three miles beyond Cape Chelidonia we passed between the mainland and Suluada, an islet known to Strabo as Crambousa and to Scylax and Pliny as Dionysia. Then we rounded the first of two promontories that jut out from the south-eastern corner of Lycia above Cape Chelidonia, passing the bay known as Çavuş Limanı, the Port of the Sergeant. As we did so, heading toward the northern promontory, we could see a long sandy beach at the inner end of Çavuş Limanı, and just north of it towered Musa Dağı, the Mountain of Moses, which rises almost directly from the coast to its peak of 3,250 feet. Fifteen miles north of that stands the magnificent Tahtalı Dağ, the Wooded Mountain, with its snow-capped conical summit at 7,800 feet. These were the landmarks for the last two ancient cities we would be visiting along the Lycian coast; Olympus is on the shore beneath Musa Dağı, and Phaselis below Tahtalı Dağ.

Local legends abound about these two mountains, and when Beaufort explored the coast of eastern Lycia he heard stories particularly about Tahtalı Dağ, which has been identified with some certainty as the ancient Mount Olympus of Lycia: 'The Aga of Deliktaş assured us, that every autumn a mighty groan is heard to issue from the mountain, louder than the report of any cannon, but unaccompanied by fire or smoke ... he believed it was an annual summons to the Elect to make their way to Paradise.' And concerning Musa Dağı, Beaufort writes that 'They have also one tradition, that, when Moses fled from Egypt, he took up his abode near this mountain, which was thenceforth called Moosa-dagh, or the Mountain of Moses ...'

Musa Dağı was known in times past as Adrasan, a name also applied to the promontory now known as Çavuş Burnu which forms the northern arm of Çavuş Limanı, and even to its offshore islet. We rounded this promontory and then headed north-west to follow the coast as it veered back in that direction. We held to this course for about two and a half miles until we headed in to the almost land-locked cove called Porto Genovese and dropped anchor at the inner end of the inlet.

This is the most spectacular sight on the Lycian coast, as the great mountain wall plunges down in almost sheer grey cliffs to the shore of the cove, fringed by two narrow crescent beaches intersecting in an ogival headland clad in the dark green of dwarf pines, and the great massif of Musa Dağı looms directly above the cliffs. The cove takes its name from the fact that it was used as a port by the Genoese, probably in the later centuries of Byzantine rule in Asia Minor. Beaufort was the first European traveller to come upon this extraordinary cove, and wrote that 'Beyond Adrachan island we found a snug little harbour called Porto Genovese, but without inhabitants, and with only a few scattered ruins of houses. Small deer were browsing among the thorny bushes; but they were too shy to admit of our approach'.

We anchored in Porto Genovese for an hour or so, taking a late afternoon swim in the cove and then walking along the beach, already perceptibly cooler in the penumbra of the shadow now cast by Musa Dağı. Then we resumed our voyage, as Hüseyin took us out of the cove and around the craggy headland that forms its northern arm. We turned north-east there and continued along the coast for another two miles or so, Tahtalı Dağ looming ahead with slanting sunlight blazing golden on its snowy summit. We headed in toward Çıralı Liman, an open anchorage off the southern end of a long shingle beach, and landed at Deliktaş, a coastal hamlet on the site of ancient Olympus whose ruins we could see flanking a river that flowed into the beach, the silted-up harbour of the Lycian town.

Tahtalı Dağ, the Mount Olympus of Lycia, is one of a score of mountains known to the Greeks by that name, the most famous, of course, being Mount Olympus in Thessaly, the Home of the Gods. The name Olympus was also given to the ancient city that we were now exploring at Deliktaş, some ten miles to the south of the main peak of Tahtalı. Virtually nothing is known of the early history of Olympus, but by *c.* 100 BC it was an important city in the Lycian League, one of the six communities that had the maximum quota of three votes at meetings of the federation. During the First Mithridatic War (89–85 BC), the pirates of the Cilician and Pamphylian coasts had formed much of the Pontic navy and, after the first stage of the revolt against Rome ended, they maintained their independence. One of the pirate captains, Zenicetes, held Olympus, Corycus, and Phaselis. Within a few years he made Olympus the capital of a principality that extended from Mount Solyma through eastern Cilicia and along the Pamphylian plain. In 78 BC, however, the Romans mounted a campaign against him under P. Servilius Vatia, the governor of Cilicia, with the young Julius Caesar serving as a junior officer. Servilius led his army into the Lycian mountains and trapped Zenicetes at Olympus, whereupon the pirate captain immolated himself and his household.

Olympus, which prospered during the first two and a half centuries of the imperial Roman period, was honoured in AD 129 by a visit from the emperor Hadrian, after whom it was for a time re-named Hadrianopolis. During the reign of Antoninus Pius (AD 138–61), it was adorned with a number of edifices endowed by Opramoas of Rhodiapolis, the plutocrat who rebuilt the theatre at Limyra after the earthquake of AD 141. But in the following century Olympus seems to have fallen to corsairs once again, after which it fades into the obscurity of the Middle Ages. The port was fortified by the Genoese during the latter centuries of Byzantine rule in Asia Minor, but then, after the Ottoman conquest of Anatolia, seems to have been abandoned.

The ruins of Olympus flank the river as it flows between steep banks to the shingle beach, which has filled up what was once the city's harbour. The surviving edifices of Olympus are heavily overgrown with bushes and trees that make much of the site impenetrable. On the south bank of the river there is a well-preserved stretch of the quay, as well as the remains of a large building that was probably a warehouse. Directly across from this, on an eminence above the north bank of the stream near its mouth, are the ruins of the acropolis, probably where Zenicetes and his followers committed suicide.

Farther inland on the south bank of the stream are the remains of several structures, including a basilica that was used as a church in the early Byzantine period. Just upstream from the basilica one can see an abutment of the bridge that once crossed the river between the southern and northern halves of the city, the main residential quarter being on the north bank. Set into the hillside above the southern bank is the theatre, ruined and completely overgrown with wild trees and shrubs, most of its seats removed for building material. Directly across from the theatre on the northern bank are the remains of a gymnasium-baths complex. Farther inland, on the shores of a swampy pond that feeds into the river, there stands a splendid portal with its frame and side walls completely intact along with its sculptured lintel, the most impressive monument in Olympus. Beside the door there is a statue base with an inscription recording that it was dedicated to the emperor Marcus Aurelius, dated to the years AD 172–5. There is no inscription to identify the deity to whom the temple was dedicated, but it was probably Hephaestus, god of the forge. Hephaestus was the patron deity of the city, associated with it because of its proximity to the unquenchable fire which, since the beginning of history, has burned on one of the hilltops above. At least since the fourth century BC ancient writers have associated this phenomenon with the Chimaera, that mythological beast described in the *Iliad* as 'lion-fronted and snake behind, a goat in the middle, and snorting out the breath of the terrible flame of bright fire'. Pliny wrote: 'In Lycia, therefore, after leaving the promontory of Mount Taurus, we have ... Mount Chimaera, which sends forth flames at night, and the city-state of Hephaestum, which also has a mountain range that is often on fire. The town of Olympus stood here'.

The site of the Chimaera, known in Turkish as Yanar, or the Fire, lies up in the hills to the north-west of Olympus, a hike of about an hour and a half from Deliktaş although it is now possible to hire a tractor to drive one to the base of the hill just below it. The site has been described both by ancient geographers and by modern travellers, but none does so better than George Bean in *Turkey's Southern Shore*. He locates it in a burned-out area about fifty yards in diameter on the heavily wooded hillside. At the centre of this the fire burns in a deep hole two or three feet wide, hardly rising above the mouth of the hole, 'its volume ... about that of a small bonfire'. Bean also reports that, in 1967, a team of Turkish scientists studied the Yanar and found traces of methane. The source of the methane is apparently inexhaustible and it emerges under pressure already on fire, re-igniting itself within seconds of any attempt to extinguish the flame.

The unquenchable fire of the Yanar is visible at night far out to sea, burning like an active volcano on the heights just south of Tahtalı Dağ, even though for all of its glow the flame itself is no greater than a shepherd's bonfire. But this is the ancient hearth of Lycia, the fire-breathing monster that Beller-ophon was sent off to kill by King Iobates. Bellerophon was the first Greek hero to venture into these wild mountains on the southern coast of Anatolia, from whose crags passing mariners had seen 'the terrible flame of bright fire'.

The next leg of our journey took us some ten miles up the coast from Çıralı, the shoreline slanting out to the north-north-east as Tahtalı Dağ towered above our port bow, until we finally headed into the shore at Tekirova, a bow-shaped cove under a promontory called Ince Burnu, the site of Phaselis.

According to tradition Phaselis was founded in 690 BC by Dorian colonists from Rhodes, who were led by an Argive hero named Lacius. The men of Phaselis were renowned traders, and theirs was one of the nine Greek cities which together founded Naucratis, the 'Queen of the Sea'. Otherwise, Phaselis had much the same history as the other cities of the region in antiquity, liberated from the Persians by Alexander the Great in 333 BC, then under Roman rule allowed some local auton-omy as a member of the Lycian League.

The beach where we landed, under the promontory, is noted in archaeological plans as the South Harbour. The Central Harbour is a smaller and almost land-locked cove directly across the headland on its north-eastern side, while the bay to the east of the isthmus forms the North Harbour, partially protected from the open sea by a breakwater that once extended between the two offshore islets. Most of the surviving edifices of Phaselis lie between the South and North Harbours, which are joined by two stretches of a paved avenue that meet in an agora at the centre of the peninsula. There the theatre stands, facing inland across a complex of ruined baths, agoras, and structures that may have been market buildings and warehouses. The theatre and most of the other structures date from the imperial Roman era, and an inscription in one of the agoras records that it was dedicated to the emperor Domitian (AD 81–96). A gate near the South Harbour likewise honours the emperor Hadrian, and was erected at the time of his visit to Phaselis in AD 130. Other inscriptions found on the eminence across the avenue from the theatre indicate that two temples stood there; one of them was dedicated to Athena Polias, the patron goddess of Phaselis, and founded in the fifth century BC; the second was a sanctuary of Hestia and Hermes, dating from the third century BC. The Temple of Athena is mentioned by Pausanius, who says that the bronze spear of Achilles was exhibited there; he concluded from this and from battle scenes in the *Iliad* that warriors in Homeric times used bronze weapons. Apparently there was also a citadel on this hill, and water was carried to it by the aqueduct whose remnants can still be seen between the city centre and the North Harbour.

Archaeologists have recently unearthed an ancient settlement on the heights above the North Harbour, with remains of the defence walls that enclosed it during the Hellenistic period. The necropolis of Phaselis was burrowed into the sides of this hill, with funerary monuments in the form of structured tombs as well as mausolea and sarcophagi. These have all been looted by grave-robbers, some of the sarcophagi having been dragged elsewhere in the process, including one that now lies on the beach of the North Harbour.

After exploring the site, we had a picnic lunch at a beautiful spot in Phaselis looking out through a bower of trees, with a view of the three harbours of the ancient city and the tumbled ruins of its public buildings. From here we took our last long look at the ruins of Phaselis, for this was also the last Lycian site we would see on this voyage. As we did so I recalled what Charles Fellows wrote in his journal for 28 April 1840, expressing his exhilaration upon discovering the magnificent ruins along the Lycian coast: 'What a wonderful people the ancient Greeks were! This mountain country was literally strewed with cities and stately towers, which stand uninjured and unoccupied two thousand years after their builders are removed!'

Back on the *Hürriyet*, we continued up the coast, rounding the next promontory to the north, and after that we headed in to the harbour at Kemer, a coastal village which has now become a popular resort. From Kemer to Antalya, a voyage of about twenty miles, took us the rest of the afternoon, as we sailed past the most magnificent stretch of coast in all of southern Turkey with its continuous wall of mountains extending from Tahtalı Dağ in the south to Mount Climax in the north, just before the beginning of the Pamphylian plain at Antalya. Alexander took his army through and around these mountains on his way from Phaselis to Perge in Pamphylia, at one point leading a detachment of his best troops along a narrow stretch of beach which was passable only when favourable winds kept back the sea. As Strabo describes it, 'Alexander came when there was a storm, and trusting generally to fortune, set out before the sea had receded, and the soldiers marched during the whole day up to the middle of the body in water.'

By the time we reached the head of the gulf the sun had fallen below the massif of the Lycian mountains, casting a vast shadow over the sea. Spears of light glinted from the jagged peaks of Mount Climax, with the Taurus mountains now looming ahead above the Pamphylian plain. Then, as we approached the dramatic cliffs that flank the port, once the principal harbour on the pirate coast of Pamphylia, the houses of Antalya began to take shape before us.

21

THE PAMPHYLIAN PLAIN

Antalya is a magnificent sight from the sea. The old town clusters around its medieval port below the cataract cliffs at the western end of the great Pamphylian plain; the Taurus range rises up behind it and, beyond the endless white beach to its left, Mount Climax and the other serried peaks of Lycia form the western ramparts of the immense gulf down which we had sailed, the ancient Mare Pamphylium.

After we had tied up at the pier, Dolores and I took our bags ashore and said goodbye to Hüseyin, thanking him for having skippered us on a wonderful voyage around the Lycian coast, and promising that we would come to see him again in Bodrum, *inşallah*, God willing. Then we strolled down into the medieval quarter around the port, which is now being transformed into a modern tourist complex, with only the ancient Roman walls and the fluted minaret of Yivli Minare Camii to remind us of the Antalya we had first known.

Originally Antalya was named Attaleia, for Attalos II of Pergamum (159–138 BC) who founded the town in the first years of his reign. Attalos intended the town to be the main Pergamene port on the Mediterranean coast, enclosing it with a line of powerful defence walls and towers which were rebuilt in Roman times and still survive today. Attaleia was the principal port of Pamphylia throughout antiquity and on into the Byzantine era, when it was known in Europe as Adalia. During the Crusades Adalia often served as a port for the Latin armies

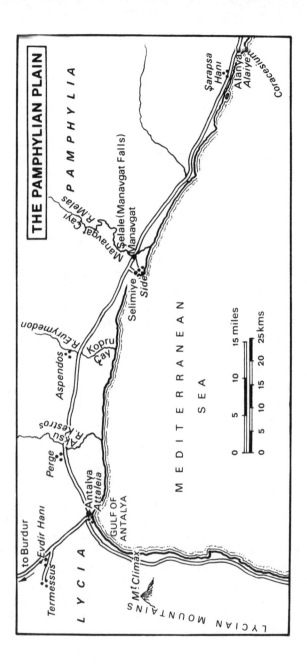

THE PAMPHYLIAN PLAIN

PAMPHYLIA

Şarapsa
Hanı

Alanya
Alaiye

Coracesium

Selale (Manavgat Falls)
Manavgat
Manavgat Çayı = R. Melas

Selimiye
Side

R. Eurymedon

Aspendos

Kopru
Çay

Aksu
R. Kestros

Perge

Antalya
Attaleia

GULF OF
ANTALYA

to Burdur

Evdir Hanı

Termessus

LYCIA

Mt Climax

LYCIAN MOUNTAINS

MEDITERRANEAN
SEA

0   5   10   15 miles

0   5   10   15   20   25kms

who sailed from there to the Levant, in many instances to avoid the long and difficult march across southern Asia Minor. In 1207 the town was captured by the Selcuk Turks under Sultan Giyaseddin Keyhüsrev I, and it was after this that its name became Antalya.

In the late thirteenth century Antalya fell to the Hamitoğlu Turkoman tribe, and soon afterwards was taken over by their vassal, the emir of the Tekke *beylik*. The Tekke emirs held Antalya up until 1361, when the town was captured by Peter de Lusignan I, king of Cyprus. He took as a trophy the great chain that had barred the port and sent it back to Rome, where it was hung in the Church of St. Peter. Thus began the brief but colourful period of Lusignan rule in Antalya which ended with the assassination of King Peter I on 17 January 1369. As Chaucer writes of him in *The Monkes Tale*, referring to his conquest of Alexandria: 'O worthy Petro, king of Cypre, also/ That Alisaundre wan by heigh maistrye ... '

The oldest part of Antalya is the quarter in and around the port. Its monuments range in date from ancient Roman to late medieval Turkish and include a number of lovely old Ottoman wooden houses. The morning after our arrival we spent re-exploring this picturesque quarter, which we knew well from our earlier trips.

There are still some fragmentary remains of the defence walls of ancient Attaleia, as well as the lordly remnants of a few of the watch-towers that once stood along its landward side. These fortifications were originally built in Hellenistic times, though much of what now survives is Roman, along with considerable parts dating from a thorough reconstruction of the city's defences undertaken by the emperor Manuel I Comnenus (1143–80). The best-preserved stretch of the walls of ancient Attaleia stands along Atatürk Caddesi, the main avenue that runs south from the city centre and then curves around to the cliff south of the port. A short way along this avenue on the right stands the Gate of Hadrian, the monumental entrance built to celebrate Hadrian's visit in AD 130.

The gateway itself consists of three coffered arches of equal height, flanked by two older towers of the original Hellenistic wall, with Corinthian columns standing on detached pedestals in front of the pier of each gate. When we first saw this gateway in 1961 it was beginning to fall into picturesque ruin, but now, completely restored, it lends a touch of Roman splendour to the town.

At the seaward end of Atatürk Caddesi there is another splendid monument of Roman Attaleia, the huge tower known as Hıdırlık Kulesi. This massive structure, which probably dates from the second century A D, consists of a cylindrical drum on a square base, and a poorly built parapet perhaps added in the medieval period. The tower resembles Hadrian's mausoleum in Rome, and it is believed to have been built as a sepulchre for a local notable, perhaps a Roman senator from Attaleia.

We next went to visit Yivli Minare Camii, the Mosque of the Fluted Minaret, which stands a short distance below the main square of modern Antalya. The minaret is the principal land-mark of the town, virtually its symbol, and so we had no trouble finding it. The fluted shaft is made of pink-red bricks into which have been set blue-green tiles of the Selcuk period. The minaret was erected in 1219 for the Selcuk sultan Alaed-din Keykubad I, and originally it was attached to a mosque that had been a Byzantine church before the Selcuk conquest of Attaleia in 1207. This mosque was replaced in 1373 by the present structure, which is covered by three pairs of domes supported by twelve columns in three rows of four each, some of them surmounted by ancient Ionic and Corinthian capitals. The second founder of the mosque, and builder of the 1373 structure, was Mehmet Bey, emir of the Hamitoğlu *beylik* in the years just prior to the Ottoman capture of Antalya in 1389. Mehmet Bey also built the *türbe*, or tomb, which stands in the garden above the mosque, a distinctive Selcuk structure with a pyramidal roof; this was erected in 1377 and is the finest example of medieval Turkish funerary architecture on the Anatolian coast. The other building in the upper courtyard is an eighteenth-century *tekke*, or monastery, which once housed a community of Mevlevi dervishes.

Directly across the courtyard from the mosque there are the ruins of two Selcuk *medreses*, or theological schools. The isolated portal to the right is all that survives of a *medrese* built in 1239 by Sultan Giyaseddin Keyhüsrev II; on the other side are the more substantial ruins of a theological school founded *c.* 1220 by his father, Sultan Alaeddin Keykubad I.

We left the courtyard of Yivli Minare Camii and strolled down through the old neighbourhood toward the port, where there are a number of Ottoman and Selcuk edifices. The most ancient of these is the Karatay Medresesi, founded in 1250 by the vizier Celaleddin Karatay. We also visited the oldest structure surviving from the Byzantine period, Kesik Minare Camii, the Mosque of the Broken Minaret, formerly the Church of the Panayia. This once-splendid basilica, now an utter ruin, was originally constructed in the fifth century A D, and it served as the cathedral of Byzantine Attaleia up until the Selcuk conquest of 1207.

Later we visited the new Antalya Archaeological Museum, which is on the main highway above the long stretch of white pebble beach to the north of the town. This museum has one of the most attractive and interesting displays of any local institution in Turkey: it has exhibits from the whole spectrum of civilization in Anatolia, concentrating chiefly on sites in the Antalya region, including Pamphylia and Lycia. The oldest artefacts here are from the Karain Cave, a Stone Age site on the upper level of the Pamphylian plain under the southern foothills of the Taurus, approached by the road north to Burdur and Isparta.

The archaeological museum now houses the ethnological collection formerly displayed in Yivli Minare Camii. Most of these fascinating exhibits are artefacts of the nomadic Yürük tribes that live in the Taurus and in the Lycian mountains above the Pamphylian plain, still making their annual trek between the lowlands and their *yayla*, summer encampments in the highland meadows that they have used for centuries. Their way of life has remained virtually unchanged since they first wandered into Anatolia in the wake of the victorious Selcuk warriors after the Battle of Manzikert in 1071. The museum has an extremely interesting collection of objects used by the Yürüks, particularly of the Tahtacı people, the Wood-cutters, who inhabit the coastal mountains of Anatolia. The objects include finely carved wooden household articles and musical instruments, as well as their beautiful and colourful *kilims* and the native costumes still worn by the nomads one sees along the coastal plain, living in the black goat-hair tents that have been their mobile dwellings since the beginning of civilization.

The next day we drove north from Antalya to Termessus, in the mountains north-west of Antalya. There is now a good road there off the highway to Burdur, twenty miles from Antalya. On our way, about four miles after leaving the highway, we stopped to see the Evdir Hanı. This is a well-preserved Selcuk caravanserai built in the period 1210–20 by Sultan Izzedin Keykavus I, son of Keyhüsrev I, the conqueror of Attaleia. Between the caravanserai and the main road there are the remains of an unidentified ancient town, probably a dependency of Termessus.

Termessus is perched on a peak of Güllü Dağ, the Rosy Mountain, whose summit is more than 3,250 feet above sea-level. The new road now brings one to a parking-lot at the base of the acropolis hill; from there a steep path leads up to the ancient city, which is set in a scene of wild beauty at the top of the mountain. Its ruins are completely overgrown with trees and underbrush, and ancient walls and sarcophagi are tumbled about in romantic disorder.

Although Termessus is often included within Lycia, it was actually located in Pisidia, the mountainous region to the north of both the Lycian mountains and the Pamphylian plain. The people of Termessus always referred to themselves as Solymoi, the warrior race that lived in these mountains before the coming of the Lycians and who are referred to in the *Iliad* as 'the glorious Solymoi'. Termessus first appears in history when Alexander's army passed this way in 333 BC. As Arrian describes the site of Termessus: 'The town stands on a lofty and precipitous height, and the road which leads past it is an inconvenient one.... The two cliffs make a natural gateway on the road, so that quite a small force can, by holding the high ground, prevent an enemy from marching through'. Alexander, frustrated by the impregnable position of Termessus, eventually marched on without taking the city.

The path to the mountain-top site of Termessus follows the course of an ancient road known as the King's Way, dating from the second century AD. This road passes through the remains of the outer defence wall that closed off the valley here, continuing through the inner fortifications above, where the city centre was enclosed. The principal buildings of ancient Termessus are the agora, a gymnasium, some temples, arcaded shops, houses, and (most impressive of the surviving structures) the theatre. We sat there for an hour, eating our lunch and looking out over the ruins, and then we climbed the slopes of the surrounding hills to explore the vast necropolis with tombs and sarcophagi tumbled on every side amidst the impenetrable thicket that has overgrown the ancient city.

The following morning we left Antalya and began our long drive along the southern coast of Turkey. As we drove through the outskirts of the town we were thrilled to see the Pamphylian plain opening up before us once again, stretching off to the east in subtropical lushness between the Mediterranean and the Taurus mountains. Camel caravans of Yürük nomads were strung out along the road in their immemorial march to their summer encampments, their black goat-hair tent-villages visible among the olive-groves and banana plantations. Soon the road veered inland and brought us deeper into the plain as it crossed the Duden Çayı, which flows into the sea at the site of ancient Magydus. Then, some eleven miles east of Antalya, we turned left on to the approach road to the site of Perge.

Perge was one of the most important cities of ancient Pamphylia. According to tradition, it was one of the places founded by the 'mixed multitudes' of Hellenic people who migrated to the southern coast of Anatolia after the Trojan War. Most of them settled in Pamphylia, but some went on to Cilicia and even as far as Phoenicia and Syria. Legend has it that the leaders of this population movement were the famous seers: Mopsus, Calchas, and Amphilochus. The first two of these seers, Mopsus and Calchas, were recognized in later times as the 'founders' of Perge.

Like Termessus, Perge first appears in history in 333 BC, when the city surrendered to Alexander immediately after the Macedonians marched into Pamphylia. The city is renowned as the birthplace of Apollonius of Perge, one of the greatest mathematicians of the Hellenistic age, who was born here c. 260 BC. It was also famous for its shrine of Artemis Pergea, which the orator Polemo, speaking in the time of Hadrian, called 'a marvel of size, beauty, and workmanship'. The shrine is mentioned by Strabo, who writes that 'near Perge, on a lofty site, is the temple of Artemis Pergea, where a general festival is held every year'. Despite its fame, no trace has ever been found of this shrine, though Turkish archaeologists continue to excavate for it.

The road to the archaeological site at Perge brought us first to the theatre, where we parked our car and started to explore the ruins of the ancient city. The theatre was built in the Hellenistic period and reconstructed in the imperial Roman era, with a seating capacity of 14,000. The stage building is still largely intact, and at its southern end, near the present entrance, there are some fine sculptures in relief, principally scenes from the life of Dionysus.

We walked next to the city centre of ancient Perge along the road that had brought us to the site. Beyond the theatre, this road branches off to wind around the curved northern end of the great stadium, the best-preserved in Asia Minor after that at Aphrodisias, with a seating capacity of about 12,000.

Next we arrived at the main gate of Perge, a structure built in the fourth century A D, when the city spread along the plain south of the ancient acropolis hill rising up half a mile to the north, with defence walls studded with watch-towers enclosing a rectangular area below it. Within this outer gate on the right can be seen the remains of a Byzantine church. Continuing through the enclosed area, we came then to the older gate in the Hellenistic walls, which had enclosed the city to the east, south, and west, while the northern side was protected by the steep slope of the acropolis hill. This inner gate is the most impressive structure at Perge; together with the defence walls of which it forms a part, it is the only surviving monument of the Hellenistic city, for the remainder of the ruins date from imperial Roman times. The inner gate is flanked by two huge round-towers, through which we passed into a semi-elliptical courtyard, built in A D 120–2. We paused here to survey the ruins of the ancient city which now lay spread out before us.

The main entrance to the inner city of Perge opens out through this courtyard on to the beginning of a colonnaded street that was the main thoroughfare of the ancient city, its marble paving still showing the ruts of wagon-wheels. The street is divided down its middle by a water-channel, an arrangement that is still used in modern Antalya and many other towns throughout Anatolia. At Perge, this main avenue was the great showpiece of the ancient town, a monumental way flanked by statues of prominent citizens, lined by the usual arcaded shops of a market street in the Graeco-Roman world, and with an agora opening off to the right at its southern end. At its upper end the main street ends in a monumental nymphaion at the base of the acropolis hill, with water issuing from behind a reclining figure of the river-god Kestros, to flow from there down through a series of cascading pools and along the watercourse.

After visiting Perge we returned to the main highway and continued eastward through the Pamphylian plain. Then some twelve or thirteen miles beyond Perge we reached the turn-off for Aspendos, the next stop on our itinerary. This very pleasant drive, about three miles up the fertile valley of the Köprü Çay, the ancient River Eurymedon, passes on the way a handsome Selcuk bridge dating from the thirteenth century. After this one reaches Aspendos, whose acropolis hill we could now see rising up from the plain before us with the great theatre directly below it.

Aspendos was another of the ancient Pamphylian cities founded by the seer Mopsus and his 'mixed multitudes' of Greeks after the Trojan War. Archaeological evidence has in general confirmed this tradition, showing that the acropolis hill was occupied as early as the late Bronze Age, with a second wave of settlers arriving during the dark ages of the Hellenic world. Inscriptions indicate that they were Greeks from Arcadia. But another interesting possibility is that the dark age settlement at Aspendos was a neo-Hittite colony sent out from Cilicia or Phoenicia, where there was a twilight revival of Hittite culture after the fall of that great Anatolian empire at the end of the Bronze Age, c. 1200 BC. This is a fascinating theory now being explored by Turkish archaeologists excavating the site.

The theatre at Aspendos is the most magnificent edifice of its type that has survived from the ancient world. It was built by the architect Zenon during the reign of Marcus Aurelius (AD 161–80), and inscriptions in Greek and Latin over the entrances to the stage building record that the theatre was a gift of the two brothers, Curtius Crispinus and Curtius Auspicatus, who dedicated this splendid monument 'to the gods of the country and to the Imperial House'. The stage building is an imposing structure—80 feet high and 360 feet wide across the front of the theatre—with the five major tiers of windows corresponding to the different levels of the interior. The tower-like entrance is not an original part of the structure, but was erected by the Selcuks early in the thirteenth century, when Sultan Alaeddin Keykubad I used the stage building as a palace.

The interior of the theatre is as splendid and as perfectly

preserved as the exterior, lacking only the columns and other architectural elements and sculptures that once adorned the inner façade of the stage building. This was on three storeys, with the uppermost façade being used principally to support an awning-like roof that projected out over the stage, erected more for its acoustical effect than for the shade it provided. The two lower levels of the façade were adorned with a double colonnade and their entablatures, with ten pairs of columns on each level (Ionic capitals on the first level and Corinthian on the second). The central quartet of columns on the upper level was surmounted by a pediment with a relief of Dionysus, and there were statues, portrait busts, and reliefs in the other panels.

The auditorium is estimated to have had a capacity of about 20,000 spectators. The seats are divided horizontally by a diazoma, with twenty tiers of seats below and twenty-one above. Ten radial stairways rise from the semicircular orchestra to the diazoma, while twenty-one more stairways ascend to the uppermost tier, which is backed by an arcaded gallery with fifty-nine vaults. Special seats in the front row were reserved for high-ranking city officials such as senators and magistrates, and the priestesses of Vesta sat in private boxes in two tower-like structures that flank the stage building.

From the theatre we walked north beside the acropolis hill to the stadium, an immense structure more than 700 feet long and almost 100 feet wide. Just to the east of the stadium is a rock-hewn tomb, and beyond this a number of sarcophagi, plus another tomb to the south of the stadium, all of them part of the necropolis of Aspendos.

We now climbed the acropolis hill and entered the upper city through what was once its north gate. The path then brought us around through the civic centre of ancient Aspendos, where there are the impressive remains of the bouleterion, a market hall with arcaded shops, a basilica, an exedra, and a nymphaion, with the remains of an unidentified building just inside what was once the south gate of the upper city. But by far the most impressive site we saw there was the magnificent aqueduct, which carried water to the city from the mountains to the north; a long line of stately Roman arches march across the plain to the northern side of the acropolis, at two points rising up to a height of 100 feet at water-control towers on double arches. This is the finest ancient aqueduct that has survived in Asia Minor, a monument to the extraordinary prowess of Roman engineering.

Back on the main highway we continued our journey eastward along the Pamphylian plain. As we did so we crossed the Köprü Çay, the ancient Eurymedon, whose mouth in antiquity would have been close to the present highway, while today it is some two miles seaward. This was the site of the Battle of the Eurymedon, which took place in 466 BC, when Cimon of Athens led the Greeks to a great victory over the Persians on both land and sea. A funerary monument was afterwards erected at the mouth of the Eurymedon to honour the Greek heroes who had died there, and this epitaph is inscribed upon it: 'These are the men who laid down the splendour of their manhood beside the Eurymedon; on land and on the swift-sailing ships alike they fought with their spears against the foremost of the bow-bearing Medes. They are no more, but they have left the fairest memorial of their valour'.

About fifteen miles past the Eurymedon we turned off the highway to the right on to the approach road to Selimiye, the site of ancient Side, two and a half miles distant. As we approached we could see, in the fields to our left, stretches of a Roman aqueduct. It had once carried water some fifteen miles from the Taurus mountains to Side, whose outlying ruins lay scattered in the fields on both sides of the road. Then we passed through the outer walls of Side and entered the ancient city.

According to Strabo, Side was founded by settlers from the Aeolian city of Cyme, a colony that modern historians date to c. 750 BC. Strabo also says that a slave-market was established here by the infamous pirates of Cilicia, writing that 'In Side, a city in Pamphylia, the dockyards stood open to Cilicians, who would sell their captives at auction there, though admitting that these were freemen'.

Side was inhabited up until the end of the tenth century A D, when it was abandoned after a great fire and the surviving population resettled in Antalya. The site was utterly deserted for more than nine centuries thereafter, as sand driven in by the south wind piled up dunes over the ruined city. At the beginning of the present century Greek-speaking Muslim refugees from Crete were resettled at Side, founding the little fishing-village of Selimiye, and their descendants still live there. Beginning in the early 1960s Side was 'discovered' by a few foreigners, and a hotel and restaurant were built there by Suat Şakir, younger brother of the Fisherman of Halicarnassus, so that soon the picturesque fishing-village became an extremely popular seaside resort. This has to a certain extent spoiled the natural charm of Side, but those who love the place still find it the most beautiful and romantic spot on the southern coast of Turkey. It was thus with a renewed sense of pleasure that we drove into the village, finding a room to rent in one of the local houses, and setting out to explore once again the ruins we already knew so well from having discovered this place ourselves nearly a quarter of a century earlier.

Side is still ringed by its ancient defence walls, which sealed off the peninsula on which the city was founded. These superb fortifications are among the finest extant examples of Hellenistic defence walls on the southern coast, and probably date from the second century B C. The approach road to the site brings one up to the main gate, with an outer and inner portal flanked by two massive towers in the city walls. Inside the main gate, the road continues westward along what was once one of the main streets of Side, a colonnaded way that led to the agora, the theatre, and other public buildings at the city centre. Some of the columns that once lined this avenue have recently been re-erected by Turkish archaeologists. At the western end of the colonnaded way is what was once the main square of ancient Side, with the agora and the great theatre to the left, the gate to the inner city straight ahead and, to the right, the Roman baths. The baths have now been restored and are used to exhibit antiquities discovered in the excavations at Side, including some of the finest Roman statuary in Asia Minor. The setting is so superb that the old Roman building seems to be a shrine rather than a museum.

Once again we walked over to the theatre, by far the most important and impressive monument in Side. We had spent many happy hours in this theatre on our first visit in January 1961, studying its architecture while our three children played among the ruins, and the memory of that happy time now made us feel a bit nostalgic, as we sat in the uppermost tier with an incomparable view out over the ruins and the long white sand beaches that flank the ancient city to east and west.

The theatre at Side was built in the second century AD, and was designed along the same general lines as the theatre at Aspendos. The only difference between the two structures is that here the auditorium has been extended beyond the exact semicircle of the classical Roman theatre, and so the vaulted passages of the paradoi, or entrances to the orchestra, stand at an oblique angle to the proscenium. The stage building must have been splendidly adorned, as one can see from the fragments of reliefs among the ruins that tumbled into the orchestra, a dramatic jumble that has only recently been cleared up by Turkish archaeologists. The most striking relief we saw was that of a star and crescent, the symbol of Islam, except that here, in ancient Side, it was an emblem of Cybele, and symbolized that she was a moon goddess. There are also poorly preserved frescoes which reveal that the theatre was converted to a Christian sanctuary in the fifth or sixth century AD.

After visiting the theatre, we continued to explore Side, beginning with the large complex to the south-east of the theatre recently identified as the State Agora. This comprises a central courtyard surrounded on all four sides by an Ionic colonnade. It has a complex of three large chambers opening off the eastern side, which was apparently an area reserved for the use of the emperor of Rome on ceremonial occasions when he might visit Side. Along the back and side walls of the central hall there are niches for statues, some of which are now in the Side museum. One remains in place at the south-east corner of the hall. This is a headless statue of Nemesis, one of the relentless goddesses who eventually spelled out the doom of this beautiful city.

After seeing the State Agora, we returned to the colonnaded way and walked past the theatre to the western end of the road, where we came to the inner gate of the city. This was a monumental entrance surmounted by a marble quadriga, in which an imperial figure once stood driving the four-horse chariot. This chariot gave its name to the neighbourhood just inside the gate, called the Quarter of the Quadriga. The gate has recently been reconstructed to make it safer for the villagers who pass through it each day, but in the process it has lost much of its picturesque grandeur.

We passed through the inner gate and turned left to follow the main street of the village, which runs in a straight line from behind the theatre out to the end of the peninsula. It follows the course of the ancient colonnaded way that was the main avenue in the inner city. At the beginning of the road to the left, in behind the rear wall of the theatre, there are the ruins of a late Roman temple, probably a sanctuary of Dionysus.

After examining the temple, we continued along the village street, where the local houses share the ground with ruined edifices of the Graeco-Roman period. The whole area is as yet unexcavated precisely because it is occupied by the community of Selimiye. Half-way along the street we turned right on to the street that leads down to the harbour, once a tiny fishing-port, now lined with restaurants, cafes, and boutiques, with little to remind us of the old Side that we once knew. So we returned to the main street of the village and continued out to the end of the peninsula, where we walked over to the promontory to the right to look at the ancient harbour. Half of its area is silted up and the rest is a stagnant pond, with bits and pieces of ancient stonework lying along its shore. We found the ruins of two sanctuaries side by side, one of them dedicated to Athena and the other to Apollo, both of them peripteral temples of the second century A D. The promontory on the southern horn of the harbour must have been a sacred spot, for behind the sanctuaries of Athena and Apollo are the ruins of an early Byzantine church, as well as the remnants of a temple dedicated to the Anatolian god Man—an ancient lunar deity whose cult seems to have survived into the imperial Roman period here in Side since his shrine also dates to the second century A D.

Late in the afternoon we walked out to the beach that seems to stretch to infinity east of Side, enjoying a swim there, then sitting out on the seaward end of the defence walls, which are half-buried in sand-dunes, and watching the sun set. That evening at supper in one of the restaurants down by the port, we reminisced about the good times we had enjoyed there in the past with Suat Şakir and his family, particularly his madcap son, the painter Cem Kabaağac. Both of them are now dead and buried far away from their beloved Side. We drank to their memory.

The following morning, after taking one last look out over the ruins from the top tier of the theatre, we left the town and drove back out to the main highway. A short way along, going eastward on the Pamphylian plain, we crossed the Manavgat Çayı, the River Melas of antiquity, and came to the village of Manavgat. We stopped there for a short excursion upstream to the Manavgat Falls at Şelale. Beyond Manavgat the Pamphylian plain begins to narrow inexorably as the Taurus mountains approach tangentially the Mediterranean. The highway, now coming closer and closer to the sea, passes a succession of sandy beaches and secluded coves, a few of them still untouched by the tourism that has exploited most of the

Turkish coast. Farther along we began to notice orange-groves and banana plantations beside the road, as we entered the subtropical region west of Alanya where the narrow coastal plain is protected from the cold northern wind by the great wall of the Taurus.

About an hour's drive east of Manavgat we passed on the left a superb old Selcuk caravanserai called the Şarapsa Hanı, another of the medieval Turkish hostelries that still adorn the highroads of Anatolia. This *han* was built by the Selcuk sultan Giyaseddin Keyhüsrev II, who reigned from 1236 to 1246. At that time the port at Alanya was booming, as Selcuk trade with Egypt was at its peak, stimulating an unprecedented economic revival in Anatolia. During those prosperous times in the middle of the thirteenth century the Şarapsa Hanı would have been packed with travellers, merchants, and drivers as camel caravans made their way over the final stretch of the road that took them from Konya over the Taurus mountains to the Pamphylian plain, with just a few more miles to go before they reached the Selcuk port at Alaiye, modern Alanya.

As we were talking about this we suddenly came within sight of Alanya itself, the great peninsular rock looming like a Levantine Gibraltar above the Mediterranean, crowned with the crenellated battlements of the great Selcuk rock-fortress. Its walls and towers glowed brick-pink in the brilliant morning light. This was the stronghold that the Greeks called Kalonoros, the Beautiful Mountain. In antiquity it used to indicate the maritime boundary between Pamphylia and Cilicia; for us it marked where one stage of our journey along the southern coast of Turkey ended and another began.

22

THE CILICIAN SHORE

The great rock-fortress at Alanya, the Greek Kalonoros, was known to the Selcuks as Alaiye. The name was still in use in 1811–12 when Sir Francis Beaufort charted the southern Turkish coast, and described this landmark in his *Karamania*:

> The promontory of Alaya rises abruptly from a low sandy isthmus, which is separated from the mountains by a broad plain; two of its sides are cliffs of great height, and absolutely perpendicular: and the eastern side, on which the town is placed, is so steep that the houses seem to rest on each other; in short it seems a natural fortress that might be rendered impregnable: and the numerous walls and towers prove how anxiously its former possessors laboured to make it so.

The port on the northern side of this peninsular rock, the modern Alanya, was called by the Greeks Coracesium. It was first mentioned by the Milesian geographer Hecataeus, who flourished in the sixth century BC. Coracesium was of only minor importance in the classical and Hellenistic periods, and served as a haven for the pirates who ravaged the Pamphylian and Cilician coasts. The most infamous of these corsairs was Diadotus Tryphon, the Voluptuary, who in the mid-second century BC became so powerful that he tried to seize the Seleucid throne in Syria; he was eventually put down and killed by Antiochus VII (139–129 BC). The Romans finally put an end to piracy in the eastern Mediterranean when they

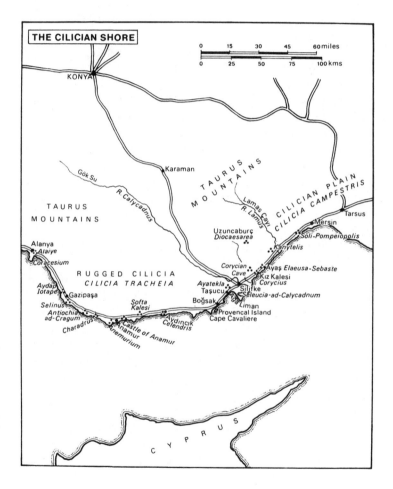

THE CILICIAN SHORE

0	15	30	45	60 miles

0	25	50	75	100 kms

KONYA

Karaman

Gök Su

R. Calycadnus

TAURUS MOUNTAINS

TAURUS
MOUNTAINS

Lamas Çayı
R. Lamus

CILICIAN PLAIN
CILICIA CAMPESTRIS

Tarsus

Uzuncaburç
Diocaesarea

Mersin
Soli-Pompeiopolis

Alanya
Alaiye
Coracesium

Kanytelis

Corycian
Cave

Ayaş *Elaeusa-Sebaste*

RUGGED CILICIA
CILICIA TRACHEIA

Ayatekla

Kız Kalesi
Corycius

Aydap
Iotape
Gazipaşa

Taşucu

Silifke
Seleucia-ad-Calycadnum

Selinus
Antiochia
ad-Cragum

Softa
Kalesi

Boğsak

Liman
Provencal Island
Cape Cavaliere

Charadrus

Aydıncık
Celendris

Castle of Anamur
Anamur
Anemurium

C Y P R U S

assumed control of the southern coast of Asia Minor. In a lightning campaign in 67 BC, Pompey completely cleared the corsairs from this coast, destroying their fleet in a final battle off Coracesium. 'Thus', as Plutarch concluded his account of this campaign in his *Life of Pompey*, 'was this war ended, and the whole power of the pirates at sea dissolved everywhere in the space of three months, wherein, besides a great number of other vessels, he took ninety men-of-war with brazen beaks; and likewise prisoners of war to the number of no less than twenty thousand'.

Coracesium remained under the control of the Roman governor of Cilicia until 34 BC, when it became part of the vast eastern territory that Antony turned over to Cleopatra, the so-called 'Donation of Alexandria'. But these dominions reverted to Rome after Antony and Cleopatra were defeated at Actium in 34 BC.

During the Byzantine period the name Coracesium fell into disuse and the town came to be called Kalonoros, but it was known to the Latins as Candiloro or sometimes Scandelore. Part of the army of the Third Crusade, led by Richard the Lionheart and Philip II Augustus of France, made their way along this coast in the spring of 1191, one of their chroniclers remarking that Scandelore was the frontier between Byzantine Pamphylia and the Armenian kingdom of Cilicia. The Armenians were in control of the town when the Selcuks attacked it in 1221, but the commander of the garrison surrendered it to Alaeddin Keykubad I after a short siege. The sultan renamed the town Alaiye, erected the magnificent fortress one sees today on the great peninsular rock, and also built the harbour works necessary to make this the principal port in the sultanate of Rum, surpassing Antalya throughout the remainder of the Selcuk period.

But before we made the climb to explore the Selcuk fortress once again we walked down to the southern end of the port to visit Kızıl Kule, the Red Tower. This is a second Selcuk fortress, also of red brick, and it towers over the inner end of the breakwater which forms the northern arm of the harbour. Octagonal in shape it is more than 100 feet high and nearly 100 feet in diameter, with a crenellated parapet and projecting machiolations. It was built in five storeys each of a different design, and has a water-storage tank rising through the lower four floors. This was undoubtedly the first edifice built by Alaeddin Keykubad I when he captured the city in 1221, and it served not only to defend the town but also to anchor the land-walls to the maritime wall.

Then we walked around the periphery of the harbour to look at the Selcuk *tershane*, or naval arsenal, the only one of its type still extant in Turkey. This medieval dockyard is a long building that has five vaulted galleries opening directly on to the sea side by side and arched portals in the walls between them. It is guarded on the south side by a tower known as Tophane, the Cannon House, a storehouse for arms and ammunition. The *tershane* was the most important of the harbour works constructed by the Selcuks after their capture of the town. When Ibn Battuta, the Arab traveller, landed in Alaiye in 1333, he found that the harbour was one of the busiest on the southern coast of Anatolia and that the town served as the main port of entry for Egyptian and Syrian merchants engaged in inland trade across the hinterland of Anatolia. Marshal Boucicault of France took the town briefly in 1403, heading a Crusader force that had been directed there by the grand master of the Knights Hospitallers on Rhodes. In 1448, when Alaiye was held by the Tekke emir Lutfi Bey, it was besieged by Ibrahim Taj-ad-Din, the emir of Karaman. Lutfi Bey was at the time allied with the Hospitallers on Cyprus and Rhodes, whose grand master sent a fleet to break the Karamanid siege of Alaiye and to retake the fortress at Corycius in Cilicia, which had also fallen to the emir of Karaman. Later in the fifteenth century the whole of the southern coast of Anatolia was taken permanently by the Ottoman Turks, after which Alaiye declined in importance as a port, its *tershane* eventually falling into ruins.

The main line of the land fortifications climbs steeply uphill from the Kızıl Kule; since this was the most vulnerable side of the rock, the walls and towers in this section are the most massively built of the fortifications. There is a good road from the lower town that winds uphill and passes through Kale Kapısı, the main gate in the outer wall. This is a handsome double portal with two entrances at right angles to one another; a Persian inscription above the outer gate dates it to 1226, and the one above the other one reads 1230–1; both dates fall within the reign of Alaeddin Keykubad I, the conqueror of Alanya, who undoubtedly had his imperial residence up here within the inner citadel of the fortress. During his reign, 1219–36, Keykubad extended his dominions all along the southern coast of Antalya to Silifke in Cilicia, in the process absorbing the Armenian kingdom of Cilicia. It was at this time that the city of Alanya reached the peak of its prosperity.

Once inside Kale Kapısı the road runs out toward the tip of the peninsular rock, after which it cuts back sharply and winds uphill to the entrance to Iç Kale, the Inner Fortress. Although this is the quicker way to reach the top of the peninsular rock, it is far less interesting than walking, and so we decided to leave our car by the outer gate. The path brought us up through the castellated enceinte known as the Ehmediye, where the Turkish quarter of Alanya was located in Selcuk and early Ottoman times. The non-Muslims lived down by the port, their population being principally Greek but also including Armenians, Jews, and European merchants. The Ehmediye still shelters an exceptionally picturesque hamlet of old wooden houses clustering amidst the remains of an ancient *bedesten*, a mosque, and the tomb of a Muslim saint, Akşebe Türbesi, whose sacred well continues to be a place of pilgrimage.

Iç Kale, the Inner Citadel, stands on the almost flat top of the peninsular rock, and offers views of the extraordinarily beautiful coastline and the interior mountains, a maritime landscape of breath-taking loveliness and grandeur. Three sides of the citadel are bordered by vaulted galleries and the fourth side by a defence wall running along the sheer edge of the cliff. Within the grounds bounded by these walls there is virtually nothing standing except a cistern and a pretty little Byzantine church which somehow survived the seven centuries of Selcuk, Turkoman, and Ottoman rule in Alanya. From the absence of other buildings it appears as if the only other structures within the citadel may have been shed-like barracks built up against the defence walls as housing for the garrison. At the far end of the İç Kale we climbed up on to the patrol walk of the outermost defence wall and walked out on to a platform at the very edge of the cliff to admire the magnificent view of Pamphylia stretching away to the west, and of Cilicia to the east. This spectacular spot at the north-western corner of the citadel is known in Turkish as Adam Atacağı, the Place From Which Men are Thrown; so named, according to tradition, because condemned prisoners were hurled down on to the rocks below. That baleful thought always drives me away from this perilous perch.

We then walked over to the south-western corner of the citadel to look down on Cılvarda Burnu, the tongue-like promontory which juts out some 450 yards into the sea from that corner of the peninsular rock. A short way out along this almost inaccessible extrusion of craggy rock there is a Selcuk structure known as the Darphane, or Mint; but this seems an unlikely identification, and more probably it was a defence-post to keep off sea-borne invaders from approaching the stronghold from below. Farther out on the promontory there are the ruins of a Byzantine chapel and some fragments of a monastery, once the residence of some hermits who chose to renounce the world by isolating themselves on this sea-pounded rock, where few of the temptations of life in Byzantium could ever reach them.

We hired a boat to take us around the peninsular rock to explore its seaward sides, which are honeycombed with

335

grottoes, in one of which we enjoyed a wonderful swim. Then our boatman took us around to the western side of the rock, where one of the most beautiful beaches in all of Turkey stretches off to the west. At the eastern end of the beach an immense cave called Damlataş penetrates deep into the peninsular rock, and we followed a guide who took us into the cathedral-like gallery below. Its humid atmosphere draws arthritics from all over Turkey, but soon drove us back out into the fresh air of a splendid June day.

The following morning we resumed our drive eastward, passing a camel caravan of Yürüks who were heading for the cattle fair opening that day in Alanya. Then, as we left the outskirts of Alanya, we entered the land which in ancient times was called Cilicia, a region which extended from Pamphylia to the borders of Syria. Cilicia comprises two regions, each different in its character and topography. The western section was known as Cilicia Tracheia, or Rugged Cilicia, for there the Taurus mountains march right down to the sea, leaving hardly any level land for cultivation as well as making it extremely difficult to build roads for communication with the hinterland. The eastern part was called Cilicia Campestris, the Cilician Plain, where the Taurus mountains retreat far inland leaving an immense and fertile plain along the coast, one that has been a cradle of civilization and a highway of history since the beginning of human existence on the subcontinent of Asia Minor.

The coastal scenery changes dramatically just east of Alanya, as the corniche road winds around a succession of heavily wooded headlands and deep fiords, with wild cliffs plunging sheer into the sea. The coast of Rugged Cilicia was sparsely inhabited in antiquity and still is today, although the coastal highway is beginning to change this and the area is already showing signs of population growth. When we first travelled along the coast from Alanya to Silifke the only settlements were poor fishing villages, most of them former pirate havens, barely eking out a living from their fisheries and through shipping timber out from the Taurus, just as they did in antiquity.

The coast of Rugged Cilicia is littered with the ruins of ancient fortress-towns, most of them dating from the Hellenistic and Roman periods and none of them of any great importance. The first is some twenty-one miles east of Alanya, a headland known locally as Aydap, which has been identified tentatively as the site of ancient Iotape. Iotape was one of three fortress-cities established in Cilicia Tracheia by the Seleucid king Antiochus IV (175–163BC), who named the town after his wife, Iotape Philadelphus. All that now remains are some huge column drums scattered beside the roadway and the ruins of defence walls and towers on a promontory above the sea. Francis Beaufort, who was the first to describe this site in his *Karamania*, was undecided as to whether the ruins on the promontory were those of Iotape or Hamaxia, another ancient city known to have been located in this region. George Bean thought that the site of Hamaxia was five miles to the northwest of Alanya, where there are ruins on a hilltop above the village of Elikesik. My own opinion, although unverified, is that Hamaxia was on the coast east of Alanya, and my theory is based on the following passage from Strabo's *Geography*, where he describes the Cilician shore eastward from Coracesium:

After Coracesium one comes to ... Hamaxia, a settlement on a hill, with a harbour, where ship-building timber is brought down. Most of this timber is cedar; and it appears that this region beyond others abounds in cedar-wood for ships; and it was on this account that Antony assigned this region to Cleopatra ...

From Aydap we soon came to the village of Gazipaşa, the first settlement of any size east of Alanya. Up until recent years the name of the village was Selinty, a corruption of the ancient Selinus, whose ruins are about half an hour's walk towards the sea. Selinus was founded by Antiochus IV at about the same time as Iotape, the second of the three fortress-towns that he established along this pirate-infested coast. The emperor Trajan died here in the first week of August in AD 117, and for a while the town was called Trajanopolis in his honour. Here again Beaufort was the first to identify the site, and among the edifices he found there, most of which have disappeared, was one that he believed to be the mausoleum of Trajan.

After Gazipaşa the road follows a course that takes it inland for about twelve miles; then it returns to the coast and to scenery even more spectacular than before. We were now driving high above the Mediterranean under towering vertical cliffs which plunged dramatically into the sea, with the magnificent ramparts of the Taurus looming on the northern horizon. Then, off to the right, I spotted ruins on the summit of a sea-girt promontory and identified them from my classical atlas as the site of Antiochia-ad-Cragum (literally 'on a crag'), the third and easternmost of the three fortress-towns founded by Antiochus IV. This site was also identified by Beaufort:

> We next came to the ruins of an antient town, which, I apprehend, must have been the Antiochia-ad-Cragum of Ptolemy.... Several columns were observed, whose shafts were single blocks of red granite. A square cliff, the top of which had been carefully fortified, projects from the town into the sea; flights of steps cut in the rock lead from the landing place to the gates; and, on the other side, there is a singular arch in the cliffs, with a sloping channel, as if intended for boats.

The highway descended to a river valley at the inner end of a magnificent fiord. We passed Kaledıran, above which we could see the ruins of an ancient fortress on a craggy hilltop. This Beaufort says was the site of ancient Charadrus, 'a fort and harbour placed by Strabo between Cragus and Anemurium, on "a rough coast, called Platanistus"'. Beaufort also observes that here 'The great arm of Mount Taurus, which proceeds in a direct line from Alaya toward Cape Anamour, suddenly breaks off abreast of Karadran, and was probably the Mount Andriclus which Strabo describes as overhanging Charadrus'.

The highway now took us up into the hills once more before bringing us down into a broad and fertile valley at the end of which we could see Anamur, the only town of any size between Alanya and Silifke. Then we turned off the highway on to a dirt road that led us seaward to the site of ancient Anemurium, which stands on a promontory at the southernmost point of Asia Minor. Beaufort was also the first foreign traveller to come upon this site, describing the defence walls, aqueducts, theatre, and odeion, as well as the necropolis, an enormous city of the dead with sepulchres in the form of detached houses, far exceeding in area any present living town on the coast of Rugged Cilicia.

At Anamur we stopped to have lunch, but there is absolutely nothing of interest to see there, for Anamur has no association with ancient Anemurium other than its name, being merely a later resettlement on a nearby site after the destruction of the Graeco-Roman city on the promontory. And so we drove on quickly to Mamure Kalesi, nearly four miles farther along the coastal highway, where we were suddenly confronted with the sight of a magnificent medieval fortress standing dramatically on the seashore, a splendid survivor from Crusader days.

Mamure Kalesi, the Castle of Anamur, is the largest and best-preserved medieval fortress on the Mediterranean coast of Turkey, with all of its walls and thirty-six towers still standing. It is believed to have been built in the late twelfth century by the kings of Lesser Armenia, the Christian realm that flourished in Cilicia during the twelfth and thirteenth centuries. After the fall of the Armenian kingdom in the mid-fourteenth century the castle was held for a time by the Lusignan kings of Cyprus, but it fell in turn to the Selcuks, the Karamanid Turkoman *beylik*, and finally to the Ottoman Turks.

When Beaufort came to Anamur he found that the fortress was still occupied by a garrison of Turkish soldiers, commanded by an Ağa; as he writes:

Anamour Castle, though in a very ruined state, has a resident

Ağa.... It stands on the edge of the sea, about six miles to the eastward of the cape: and in its general appearance resembles some of the antient castles of Great Britain. Its keep or citadel is placed on a small eminence and commands two open courts, which are surrounded by a chain of towers of all shapes—dodecagonal, octagonal, square, triangular, round, and half-round. The extreme dimensions are about 800 by 300 feet, the walls and towers are everywhere embattled, and in some parts of the ramparts, apertures have been made for cannon.... There are three arched gateways, the principal of which is through a square tower on the western side ...

The castle of Anamur was the last Anatolian residence of Prince Jem, who held out there for a month in the summer of 1482 after he was defeated by his older brother, Beyazit II, in a war of succession following the death of their father, Sultan Mehmet II, the Conqueror. After Jem's defeat he turned to the Knights Hospitallers on Rhodes, who negotiated with Sultan Beyazit II to have his rebellious brother shipped off to one of their castles in France. Jem died in captivity in 1495, and was generally supposed to have been poisoned on the orders of his brother. His remains were returned for burial in the old Ottoman capital at Bursa, and thus ended the remarkable career of the most romantic figure in all of Ottoman history, whose exploits are still celebrated in Turkish folklore and whose poems are still recited by Anatolian bards. The seventeenth-century Turkish chronicler, Evliya Çelebi, writes of Jem's burial in his *Narrative of Travels*:

> The corpse of Jem, together with his property, amongst which was an enchanted cup which became brimful as soon as delivered empty into the cup-bearer's hand, a white parrot, a chess-playing monkey, and some thousands of splendid books, were delivered up to Said Çelebi and Haider Çelebi, that they might be delivered to the Sultan ... Beyazit ordered the remains of Jem to be buried at Bursa, beside his grandfather Murat III. While they were digging the grave there was such a thunder-clap and tumult in the sepulchral chapel, that all who were present fled, but not a soul of

them was able to pass its threshold till ten days had passed when, this being represented to the Sultan, the corpse of Jem was buried by his order in his own mausoleum, near to that of his grandfather.

We spent an hour wandering through and around Anamur Castle, which to my mind still seemed deeply immured in the late medieval world, always associated with the romance of the ill-fated prince. Even after we left and drove on I turned round for one last look at its majestic towers silhouetted against the Cilician landscape behind it, seeing Prince Jem sailing off from Anatolia for the last time on 20 July 1482 on a Crusader galley, to return only in death. As Jem wrote in the last couplet of his only surviving poem: 'Ah, for the time when your threshold was residence, also, for Jem!/ How good a time it was we never knew until lost without trace.'

From the castle to Silifke the road wound up and down a succession of promontories and coves, sometimes bringing us so high above the Mediterranean that we could see far off to the south the faint outlines of Cyprus. We passed a number of ruined castles and fortress-towns, beginning with Softa Kalesi, the remains of which crown a crag high above the road some seven miles beyond Anamur Castle. This fortress is believed to have been built at the same time as that at Anamur, erected by the kings of Lesser Armenia, later occupied by both Latins and Turks before falling to the Ottomans. The story of all the medieval castles along the Cilician coast is much the same.

Farther along we saw the remains of a medieval fortress-town at Aydıncık, a pretty little village on a sandy cove at the head of a deeply cut indentation of the sea. The former name of this place was Gilindere, a corruption of the Greek Celendris whose ruins stand on a promontory above the village. This was one of the most ancient towns in Rugged Cilicia, founded in the late fifth century BC as a colony of Samos. Beaufort identified the site as well as some interesting islets off the coast, an archipelago called Papadoula, or Butterfly Islands, writing that 'Their only inhabitants are eagles, who, unaccustomed to the intrusive sound of human voices, quitted their aeries on the lofty cliffs, and hovered over the boats with amusing surprise and uneasiness'.

Driving on from Aydıncık, we followed the highway as it climbed up into the hills and out along the last stretch of the mountainside corniche road above the sea. We were now approaching the eastern limit of Rugged Cilicia, where the Taurus sends down its last spur to the sea to form Cape Cavaliere, as it was known to the Latins. The ancient Greeks knew it as Zephyrium and today it is called Ovacık Burnu.

The highway brought us down to the shore just beyond Cape Cavaliere, where there is a crescent cove called Boğsak with a beautiful sandy beach. On our first trip along this coast, twenty years before, we had camped out on the floor of an old shack on the beach, which was romantic but very uncomfortable. Now we were pleasantly surprised to find that an excellent motel had been built on the beach, and so we checked in there and took a late afternoon swim before supper. It was a lovely evening, the sea and the mountainous shore still glowing in the last faint tints of twilight, and I was struck by how little this scene had changed since Beaufort first saw it from his campsite on one of the hills above in the autumn of 1811:

> The evening was clear, and this spot afforded a beautiful prospect: we could trace the coast that had already been explored to an immense distance; the plain, with its winding rivers and ruins, was spread out like a map at our feet, and behind all, a prodigious ridge of mountains, whose black sides, having already lost the evening sun, formed a singular contrast with their snowy tops. We had also a distinct view of the island of Cyprus rising from the southern horizon, though more than 65 ... miles distant.

The next morning I rose early and swam out to the offshore islet that Beaufort had called Provençal Island. I had explored this twenty years before, but now I was pleased to find that it had completely escaped tourism, for nothing of its unique and bewitching quality had changed. It was still a haunted isle of the dead, as every square foot of the place is littered with broken sarcophagi, tombstones, and the ruins of medieval buildings, the most striking of which is a Crusader chapel with Gothic arches. According to Beaufort, this island once belonged to the Armenian kingdom of Cilicia, but in 1196 it was given to the Knights Hospitallers of St. John, after which it was named for the highest-ranking group of knights in that order, the Langue de Provence.

After breakfast on the motel terrace, we walked along the beach to the promontory that forms the eastern arm of the bay at Boğsak, where there are the ruins of a late medieval fortress called Liman Kalesi. This was built in the fourteenth century by the Armenians, and in the sixteenth century it was held for a time by the Pisans before it finally fell to the Turks. A short distance inland from the castle, near the highway, are the ruins of a small rock-hewn Christian chapel, probably dating to the early Byzantine period.

As we drove away from Boğsak the scenery changed perceptibly, for we were reaching the eastern limit of Rugged Cilicia and approaching the Cilician plain. As Beaufort writes of this transitional region: 'To the eastward of Cape Cavaliere the higher mountains recede from the coast; a succession of low points takes place of the rude outline that we had so long pursued, and the general aspect of the country materially changes'.

The highway brought us around the periphery of the large bay called Taşucu Körfezi, and then at the head of the bay we came to Taşucu, the port of Silifke. Up until recent years Taşucu was just a sleepy little village, but now a large commercial harbour has been developed there, with a ferry service to Cyprus.

Taşucu Körfezi used to be known as Ağa Liman, the Ağa's Port, once infamous as a pirate's haven. Beaufort found the remains of a small medieval fortress there, but this has now all but vanished. This would seem also to have been the pirate stronghold mentioned in Grimstone's *General Historia of the*

Turks, which is the earlier Ottoman history of Knolles brought up to 1638. One reads there, in a paraphrase of Plutarch's *Life of Pompey*: 'From this haven in former times, has come forward a powerful army of pyrats with a thousand sayle, so proudly rigged, as many of them had their sayles of purple, the tacking of gold thread, and the oars garnished with silver; marks of the spoyles of above four hundred cities ruined by these pyrats'.

Driving on for a few miles past Ağa Liman, we came to an archaeological signpost directing us to the site of Ayatekla, which is a short distance down a side road to the left. There we found the ruins of a huge Byzantine basilica, of which only the apse remains. This was built by the emperor Zeno the Isaurian, who reigned A D 474–91. Before coming to the throne his name had been Tarasicodissa and he had been chieftain of the Isaurians, wild tribesmen who dwelt in the Taurus above Cilicia. He changed his name to Zeno in 466 when he married Princess Ariadne, daughter of Leo I. When Zeno succeeded to the throne eight years later he built this church in thanksgiving to his patron saint, St. Thecla. Thecla had been converted to Christianity by St. Paul in Iconium, the modern Turkish town of Konya, and afterwards accompanied the Apostle on his missionary journeys. Thecla's life became the subject of the apocryphal Acts of Paul and Thecla, which was widely circulated throughout both the Latin West and Greek East and which made her one of the most popular saints in the early Byzantine world. This ruined church in Cilicia is the only surviving monument to her, and when I looked upon it I was reminded of the words that she spoke to the Apostle when they first met, according to the Acts of Paul and Thecla: 'I shall cut my hair and follow thee whithersoever thou goest'.

We returned to the main highway and moments afterwards we were within sight of Silifke, the second and more eastern of the two modern towns on the coast of Rugged Cilicia. The town is on the banks of the Gök Su, the Calycadnus of antiquity, which the highway crosses on an ancient bridge of six graceful arches. This river was known in times past as the Saleph, and under that name it played an important part in the history of the Third Crusade. The German emperor Frederick I Barbarossa, led his army down along the upper valley of the Saleph in the spring of 1190, reaching Karaman on 30 May, then heading southward along the river towards Silifke. But on 10 June Barbarossa was drowned while crossing the river on horseback, a tragedy that shattered the morale of his army so that some of them returned to Europe after they reached Silifke and the others continued in despair on to Antioch under the Duke of Swabia. The duke had the emperor's corpse carried at the head of the army, pickled in a cask of vinegar, so that he might be buried in the cathedral in Antioch. Some of the emperor's bones were set aside at the burial and taken on the campaign to the Holy Land by the remnants of his army, 'in the vain hope', as Sir Steven Runciman puts it, 'that at least a portion of Frederick Barbarossa should await the Judgement Day in Jerusalem'.

Silifke stands on the site and preserves the name of Seleucia-ad-Calycadnum, founded at the beginning of the third century BC by Seleucus I Nicator, founder of the Seleucid dynasty. During the Hellenistic and Roman periods Seleucia was the most important city in Rugged Cilicia, for then, as now, it stood at the junction of the coastal highway and the road which led up through the Taurus into the central Anatolian plateau. Despite its antiquity, the present town of Silifke has little of interest apart from the fragmentary ruins of a Roman temple, dedicated to Zeus, and its impressive medieval citadel. The original fortress was built by the Byzantines in the seventh century AD, probably on the foundations of the Hellenistic defence walls. In 1098 the town was taken by the Crusaders, but in 1204 it was recaptured by the Byzantines, at which time the present fortress was built. Subsequently the fortress was taken in turn by the Armenians, Byzantines, Crusaders, Selcuks, Karamanids, and Ottomans, who finally captured the town and its citadel permanently in 1471.

We stopped only briefly in Silifke on this visit. After looking

345

at the castle once again, we drove north for some nineteen miles to Uzuncaburç, the site of ancient Diocaesarea. These are the most impressive ruins on the Cilician coast, particularly the great Temple of Zeus Olbius. This immense sanctuary is believed to have been erected by Seleucus I at the beginning of the third century BC, about the same time as his foundation of Seleucia-ad-Calycadnum; and it has the distinction of being the oldest known temple built in the Corinthian order.

We returned to the main highway and, after crossing the marshy delta of the Calycadnus, arrived by the sea again at Susanoğlu, where we stopped to have a swim on the pretty sand beach. Some three miles farther on we came to the tiny fishing village of Narlı Kuyu, the Pomegranate Well, where we stopped to have lunch at a restaurant supported on stilts over the sea, and to look at the interesting remains of some Roman baths that are preserved under a shed in the village square. These are known locally as Kızlar Hamamı, the Bath of the Maidens, from the three female figures depicted in the mosaic pavement. They are believed to represent the Three Graces, the beautiful daughters of Zeus and Eurynome. As Hesiod wrote of them in his *Theogony*: 'And Eurynome, the daughter of Ocean, beautiful in form, bore him three fair-cheeked Graces: Aglaea, Euphrosyne, and lovely Thaleia, from whose eyes as they danced flowed love and unnerves the limbs; and beautiful is their glance beneath their brows'.

A modern sign outside Kızlara Hamamı asserts that this is the legendary Fountain of Knowledge, a place mentioned by Pliny. Beaufort sought this fountain in vain, along with the nearby Corycian Cave mentioned by Strabo, which is just over a mile inland from Narlı Kuyu. A road leads directly from the village to the cave, or caves, for there are actually two of them. One is called Cennet Deresi, the Vale of Paradise, and the other Cehennem Deresi, the Vale of Hell.

Cennet Deresi is a most extraordinary sight, and it is a pity that Beaufort missed it. The chasm is more than 650 feet wide at the top and 230 feet deep from the edge of the sheer cliff which overlooks it on the far side. A flight of steps leads down to the cave itself. The place has been sacred since antiquity, as evidenced by the legends and monuments that surround it. On the north-east edge of the chasm there is an abandoned church that was originally a sanctuary of Zeus Korkios, erected in the third or second century BC and converted into a Christian house of worship in the fifth century AD. And within the chasm there is another abandoned church, originally built in the fifth century AD, with surviving frescoes indicating that it was dedicated to the Blessed Virgin Mary. This church was probably built at the mouth of the cavern to assure early Christians that the Virgin had destroyed or put to flight the monster who was reputed to live there in pagan days, for in mythology the Corycian Cave of Cilicia was the birthplace of the Giant Tryphon, one of the pre-Olympian deities of the ancient Greek religion. Thus the evil reputation of the Corycian Cave was changed in Christian times to a benevolent one, and it has remained so under the Muslim Turks who still refer to it as Cennet Deresi, the Vale of Paradise.

Nevertheless we still found the Corycian Cave to be an ominous place and our sense of foreboding deepened as we descended the long flight of steps from the level of the sunny earth to the dark entrance of the actual abyss, following from there a slippery path for another 200 feet into the bowels of the cavern. Then finally we came to the heart of the grotto—a veritable Cave of Darkness which looked like a subterranean cathedral dedicated to some frightening plutonic deity. We could hear his roaring increasing in intensity as we neared the far end of the cave. Local tradition, however, holds that the roaring sound is only that of a great underground torrent, undoubtedly in fact the one mentioned by Strabo, which emerges at the Fountain of Knowledge on the shore below, supplying water to the Bath of the Maidens in Narlı Kuyu.

The pathway leading off to the right from the parking area at Cennet Deresi leads to Cehennem Deresi, the Vale of Hell. This second chasm of the Corycian Cave is apparently imposs-

347

ible of access except for experienced rock-climbers, for it looku as if it was indeed an entrance to the Underworld. According to both Christian and Muslim tradition, this is one of the entrances to Hell, and superstitious locals have tied little rag pennants to the branches of the surrounding trees as talismans to ward off the evil spirits who dwell below.

Another path leads off from the car-park at Cennet Deresi to Dilek Magarası, the Cavern of Wishes, another part of the Corycian Cave complex. Here again the trees around the mouth of the cave have dedicatory rags tied to their branches, except that in this case they are talismanic petitions, placed there by locals who have asked for very specific favours from the benevolent spirits who inhabit the cavern.

After seeing these fabulous caves we returned to the main highway, and three miles farther along we came to Kız Kalesi, the Maiden's Castle, one of the most beautiful sights on the Turkish coast. Kız Kalesi is actually made up of two castles, one of them crowning a promontory at the end of a superb beach of white sand, and the other built on an islet about a hundred yards out to sea, looking like the setting for a medieval romance. In the Turkish version of this romance a maiden is sequestered in the sea-girt castle by her father, the king, who has been told by a seer that his daughter is doomed to die from the bite of an asp. In this legend, which is associated with virtually every medieval fortress in Turkey, she eventually does die according to Fate's decree. The two castles here were originally connected by a causeway, to create an artificial port for the medieval town of Corycius. An inscription in Armenian on the sea-girt castle records that it was constructed in the year 1151, and the other fortress was presumably built at the same time. This dates them to the early years of the Armenian kingdom of Cilicia.

The story of this medieval Cilician kingdom is one of the most interesting episodes in the history of the Levant. Its history begins in the aftermath of the Battle of Manzikert in 1071, when the Selcuk invasion forced many Armenians to leave north-western Anatolia and settle in increasing numbers along the Cilician coast, where at first they were subjects of the Byzantine emperor. During the first half of the twelfth century the Rubenid dynasty succeeded in creating an independent Armenian principality in Cilicia, and by the middle of that century they had established their independence from Byzantium, as evidenced by their construction of the Corycian castles. The Rubenid kings maintained their independence largely through close alliances with the various Crusader kingdoms in the Levant, strengthening their ties through dynastic marriages between Armenian princesses and Frankish nobles. Thus the kingdom of Lesser Armenia, as it was called, came to combine the richest elements of Armenian civilization with the Latin European culture of the early Renaissance, and created a wondrous flowering of Western chivalry on the shores of Levantine Cilicia. A contemporary description of the medieval Armenian court evokes a glimpse of that vanished age, as the chronicler writes of the 'gilt throne on which the King is seated in elegant majesty, surrounded by brilliant-faced young men, attendants of his rejoicings, also by groups of musicians dancing in an admirable manner'.

But at the beginning of the fourteenth century the Mongol advance into south-eastern Anatolia ended Crusader rule in that region, and the Turkoman tribes moved in to take their place. The Armenians now were left alone to face numerous enemies who threatened their very existence. As the Venetian historian Marino Sanudo wrote at the time: 'The King of Armenia is under the fangs of four ferocious beasts: the lion, or the Tatars, to whom he pays a heavy tribute; the leopard, or the Sultan, who daily ravages his frontiers; the wolf, or the Turks, who destroy his power; and the serpent, or the pirates of the sea, who worry the very bones of the Christians of Armenia'.

The onslaught of these numerous enemies forced the Armenians to retreat to their coastal castles and mountain-top strongholds. But even there the forces arrayed against them were too strong. In 1360 the people of Corycius invited King Peter I of Cyprus to be their ruler, but after his assassination in 1369 the town and its two castles were taken by the Turks, and virtually disappear from history.

The extensive ruins of the ancient town of Corycius are scattered over the countryside beyond the landward castle, including the remains of several churches and an enormous number of sarcophagi and rock-hewn tombs. In his time Beaufort described the scene along the coast past Corycius:

> From Korghos to Ayash, and for several miles beyond it, the shore presents a continued scene of ruins, all of which being white, and relieved by the dark wooded hills behind them, give to the country an appearance of splendour and populousness, that serves only, on a nearer approach, to heighten the contrast with its real poverty and degradation.

The Cilician shore is now far more prosperous than it was in Beaufort's time, for the new highway along the shore has put its coastal towns and villages in communication with outside markets. But the landscape beyond Corycius is just as ruin-haunted today as it was when Beaufort saw it in 1811, and during the drive from there to Tarsus we went by a succession of ancient cities, each with a vast necropolis representing many centuries of human occupation.

The first of these sites that we passed was Ayaş, a village two miles east of the Corycian castles. (This Ayaş should not be confused with the more famous port of the same name farther east in Cilicia.) Ayaş stands on the site of ancient Elaeusa which, early in the imperial Roman era, was renamed Sebaste, Greek for Augustus, in the emperor's honour. The original settlement was an islet, now connected to the shore, and the Roman town was built on the mainland just opposite. Among the monuments of the ancient town that have survived are a Roman temple, the remnants of a theatre, and stretches of three aqueducts, all of which are described by Beaufort.

After Ayaş the highway is flanked for a long distance by

sarcophagi and tombs which were once part of the necropolis of Elaeusa-Sebaste. Two and a half miles past Ayaş we turned off to the left for a brief diversion to Kanlıdıvane, a village near the site of ancient Kanytelis. The ruins of Kanytelis are quite extensive and even more impressive than those of Elaeusa-Sebaste, with which it may have been administratively associated in the imperial Roman period.

A little farther along we crossed the Lamas Çayı, the River Lamus of antiquity. Strabo considered the Lamus to be the natural boundary between Rugged Cilicia and the Cilician plain, for here the rocky coast finally ends and gives way to the flatlands which extend inland to the foothills of the Taurus, now receding into the northern distance. After we crossed the Lamas Çayı, we paused for a moment, remembering that at one point during the Crusades this had been an armistice line while an exchange of prisoners was arranged, with the liberated Christians and Muslims passing one another on the bridge as they rushed to freedom on the opposite sides of the river, after which the fighting resumed.

On our left we now saw a Roman aqueduct with two tiers of arches, part of the hydraulic system that brought water from the Taurus mountains to Kanytelis, Elaeusa-Sebaste, and Corycius. Three miles farther on is the seaside resort of Limonlu, with the ruins of a medieval fortress standing on the heights to the left of the highway. Next we passed through Erdemli, the largest town between Silifke and Mersin. Then we drove on for fifteen miles until we came to Mezitli, where a road to the right leads to Viranşehir, a village near the site of ancient Soli.

Soli was one of the oldest cities in Cilicia Campestris, founded as a Rhodian colony *c.* 700 BC. Some of the settlers must have been Athenians, for long afterwards their descendants in Soli spoke a corrupt Attic dialect that gave rise to the word 'solecism', an offence against grammar or idiom. Soli was renowned in antiquity as the birthplace of Chrysippus (*c.* 280–207 BC), one of the founders of the Stoic school of philosophy. In 83 BC it was captured by Tigranes the Great, king of Armenia, who resettled the entire population in the Armenian capital of Tigranocerta. Shortly after 67 BC the city was repopulated by Pompey following his victory over the Cilician pirates, as he resettled the surviving corsairs here and renamed the town Pompeiopolis. The principal remnant of Soli-Pompeiopolis is a splendid colonnaded street some 500 yards long; this once led down to the harbour, which is now almost completely filled in with sand. Only a score of columns remain standing, about a tenth of those that used to flank this once-magnificent avenue where Alexander the Great reviewed his troops in 333 BC, just before the Battle of Issus.

Here again the first traveller to give a detailed description of the site was Beaufort, and as we stood there by the Roman harbour I read from his description of the ancient city:

At length the elevated theatre and tall columns of Soli, or Pompeiopolis, rose above the horizon, into view; and appeared to justify the representations which the pilots had given of its magnificence. We were not altogether disappointed. The first object that presented itself on landing was a beautiful harbour, or basin, with parallel sides and circular ends; it is entirely artificial, being formed by surrounding walls, or moles, which are fifty feet in thickness, and seven in height.... Opposite to the entrance to the harbour, a portico rises from the surrounding quay, and opens to a double row of two hundred columns, which, crossing the town, communicates with the principal gate towards the country; and from the outside of that gate, a paved road continues in the same line to a bridge over a small river. At the end next to the harbour there are some indications of the two rows of columns having been united by arches, and possibly the whole colonnade was once a covered street, with which the avenue, the portico, and the harbour, must have formed a noble spectacle; even in its present state of wreck, the effect of the whole was so imposing, that the most illiterate seaman in the ship could not behold it without emotion.

We returned to the main road and continued driving eastward, coming out to the sea again after cutting across the base of the promontory we had just explored. Across the way we could now see the massed houses of Mersin, the largest port on the Mediterranean coast of Turkey, where we would be spending the night. Here we had left Rugged Cilicia behind and were about to enter the Cilician plain.

23

TO THE 'FAIR CROWN
OF THE ORIENT'

Mersin's origins date back to the Old Hittite Kingdom (1700–1450 BC); but the modern city has little to offer in the way of history, architecture, or archaeology, so most travellers, as we did, merely stop there for the night when driving across the Cilician plain.

After breakfast the following morning we returned to the main highway and continued driving eastward. We now emerged fully into Cilicia Campestris, the Cilician plain, which the Turks now call Çukurova. From Alanya past Silifke we had driven along the rocky coast of Cilicia Tracheia, Rugged Cilicia, entering Cilicia Campestris after we crossed the River Lamus, and from there to Mersin the plain had gradually widened as the Taurus mountains gave way and receded from the sea. But now, beyond Mersin, the Taurus mountains cut back sharply to the north-west, leaving below them to the south the vast and fertile lowland. This great plain is watered by three rivers which we would pass in our journey eastward: the Tarsus Çayı, the Seyhan, and the Ceyhan, which in antiquity were known, respectively, as the Cydnus, the Sarus, and the Pyramus. The main entrance to this plain from the north is through the Cilician Gates, the mountain pass through the Taurus that leads down to Tarsus and then out on to Cilicia Campestris, bounded to the east by the Amanus mountains, in the south-eastern corner of coastal Turkey called the Hatay. That would be the course of our journey over the next two days.

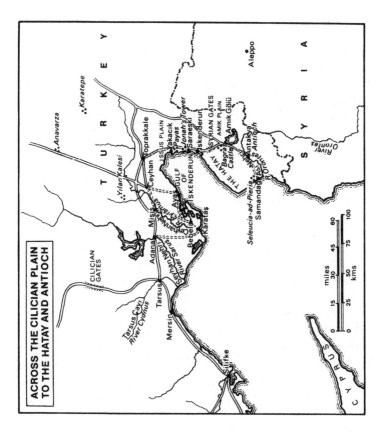

ACROSS THE CILICIAN PLAIN
TO THE HATAY AND ANTIOCH

A drive of seventeen miles from Mersin brought us to Tarsus, a nondescript town on the Tarsus Çayı, the ancient River Cydnus. Its origins go back as far as those of Mersin, to the Old Hittite Kingdom, but here again there is very little left standing to give evidence of the town's antiquity. The principal monument of ancient Tarsus is Kancık Kapısı, the Gate of the Bitch, once one of the main entrances to the Roman city. This is sometimes called St. Paul's Gate, though it has no known connection with the Apostle.

Although Tarsus has no other monuments its historical associations are very rich. During the second millennium BC it may have been the capital of the Hittite state of Kizzuwatna, and in 698 BC it was captured by Sennacherib. Alexander the Great stopped here in 333 BC, after passing through the Cilician Gates, and he almost died of a fever after a chilling swim in the Cydnus. Cicero lived in Tarsus in 50 BC when he was governor of Cilicia, and Julius Caesar visited the city in 47 BC to meet a deputation of Cilician representatives. Mark Antony came to Tarsus in 41 BC and exempted the city from taxes as a reward for its resistance against Brutus and Cassius. Later that same year Antony summoned Cleopatra from Alexandria to meet him here, and her arrival in Tarsus was one of the most spectacular moments in the history of Graeco-Roman Asia Minor, as the Queen of Egypt came sailing up the Cydnus in her royal barge, a scene described by Plutarch in his *Life of Antony*. Sir Thomas North's translation of this passage was Shakespeare's inspiration for the description of this royal meeting in his *Antony and Cleopatra*, beginning with the memorable lines:

The barge she sat in, like a burnish'd throne
Burned on the water; the poop was beaten gold,
Purple the sails, and so perfumed that
The winds were love-sick with them; the oars were silver,
Which to the tune of flutes kept stroke, and made
The water which they beat to follow faster,

It is intriguing that, amongst those who watched the royal progress, may have been the family of Saul of Tarsus, for the Apostle's mother and father were probably living there in 41 BC. Paul himself was born in Tarsus, and his family belonged to the large Jewish community which dated back to at least the time of Antiochus the Great. As Paul himself once said, 'I am a Jew, from Tarsus in Cilicia, a citizen of no mean city'.

After stopping briefly in Tarsus we drove on twenty-five miles to Adana, the largest city on the southern coast of Anatolia and the fourth most populous in Turkey, its population now numbering over half a million. We stopped for a lunch of the renowned Adana kebab, and then we checked into a hotel, for we intended to use Adana as a base to visit a number of sites in the Cilician Plain.

Adana stands on the banks of the Seyhan Nehri, the ancient River Sarus, in the very centre of the vast Cilician delta, and it is the wealth of that great plain that has made it the most prosperous provincial city in the country. The history of Adana goes back to the beginning of the first millennium BC, and, like most other Turkish cities, it has been fought over by all of the great powers that have marched across Anatolia. Here again, little evidence of its historic past remains in the modern town, although there is an interesting museum with exhibits from the many archaeological sites in the Cilician plain. The most prominent ancient monument in Adana is the Taş Köprü, a bridge across the Sarus built by Hadrian and repaired by Justinian. The principal Turkish monument is Ulu Cami, built in 1507 by Halil Bey, the emir of the Ramazanoğlu Turks who ruled in Cilicia before the region was conquered by the Ottomans under Selim I, the Grim, who took Adana in 1517. The tiles in the mosque and in Halil Bey's *türbe* are among the finest ceramic decoration in Turkey, products of the kilns at Iznik in its greatest period.

The main highway runs eastward from Adana to a crossroads north of the Gulf of Iskenderun, with one branch extending eastward into Anatolia and the other going south along the gulf to Iskenderun itself. The first stretch of the highway from Adana to the crossroads bypasses Misis and Ceyhan to the north. So on our excursion from Adana we chose to drive on the old road, which goes through both Misis and Ceyhan, as well as leading to interesting diversionary routes into the Cilician plain.

One such diversion is to the great delta south of Adana, whose western part is formed by the Seyhan and the eastern by the Ceyhan. A secondary road leads from Adana to Karataş, a small port at the southernmost point of the delta; a second road goes south from Misis—the ancient Mopsuestia, known to the Crusaders as Mamistris—leading from there to Bebeli, which is thought to be the site of ancient Serrapolis; and a third road leads from Ceyhan to Yumurtalık Liman and Ayaş, the ancient Aegae, which in the Middle Ages was known to the Latins as Lajazzo. We used all three of these roads in exploring the eastern part of the delta, which forms one side of the Gulf of Iskenderun, looking across to the Hatay.

The most intriguing site on the delta was Ayaş. Virtually nothing remains of the medieval town, though it was once the most important seaport on the Mediterranean. Marco Polo, who first visited Ayaş in 1271, described it as 'a city good and great and of good trade', adding that 'all the spicery and the cloths of silk and gold and of wool from inland are carried to this town'. But this wealth attracted the attention of the Mamluk sultan of Egypt and Syria, Baybars I ('al-Bunduqdari'), who invaded Cilicia in 1275, the first in a series of attacks that eventually brought about the downfall of Ayaş and the other cities in the Armenian kingdom of Cilicia. Within a century, they would disappear from history.

After seeing the delta we drove on from Adana to Misis, which is fifteen miles to the east on the banks of the Ceyhan. According to tradition Misis, or ancient Mopsuestia, was one of the places founded after the Trojan War by the legendary seer Mopsus. The settlers were the 'mixed multitudes' who are credited with the establishment of so many towns along the

358

Mediterranean coast of Anatolia and down as far as Syria and Phoenicia. Archaeological excavations on the acropolis hill at Misis indicate that the town dates back to the middle of the second millennium BC, and was probably founded during the Old Hittite Kingdom. Mopsuestia remained a place of considerable significance throughout antiquity and on into the medieval Byzantine era, when it came to be known as Mamistra. Mamistra was of strategic importance since it stood astride a bridge over the Pyramus in the middle of the Cilician plain, and during the late Byzantine period it was held in turn by the Greeks, Armenians, Crusaders, Turkomans, Mamluks, and finally by the Ottomans under Sultan Selim I who took it *en route* to his conquest of Syria and Egypt in 1517. The only traces of antiquity to be seen in Misis now, however, are its acropolis hill, the remains of the Roman theatre, and a late Roman mosaic depicting Noah's Ark.

Driving on from Misis toward Ceyhan on the old road, one comes after about six miles to Sirkili, on the left bank of the Ceyhan. At the approach to the village there is a rock-hewn relief representing the Hittite king Muwatalli, who ruled the Hittite Empire in the early thirteenth century BC. In May of 1285 BC, Muwatalli led the Hittite army to victory over the Egyptian forces under Rameses II at the Battle of Kadesh in Syria, and this relief may commemorate that triumph. The conflict between the Hittites and the Egyptians was settled in 1269 BC by the Treaty of Kadesh, the earliest known peace agreement in history, the pact being signed by Rameses II and Hattusili III, younger brother and successor of Muwatalli. One of the two surviving copies of the Treaty of Kadesh is now preserved in the Museum of the Ancient Orient in Istanbul.

Continuing on from Misis towards Ceyhan, we turned north on a side road that led us to within sight of Yılan Kalesi, the Castle of the Snake, a medieval fortress perched high on the peak of a rocky crag above the Pyramus. The castle takes its name from the carving over the main gateway, in which an imperial figure is shown holding a pair of sceptre-like objects resembling serpents. The local Kurds call this figure Shah Meran, the King of Snakes, and refer to the castle by the same sinister name. The figure is believed to represent Leon III, who ruled as king of Lesser Armenia from 1270 to 1289.

We returned to the main road and drove on to Ceyhan, a large town on the banks of the Pyramus. We used Ceyhan as our base for two interesting excursions: to Anavarza and Karatepe, both of which are approached by the road leading north to Kozan and Kadırlı. Anavarza, which is also known as Anazarbus, was founded in the first century BC, and it became a flourishing town during the imperial Roman period. The city's advanced position on the south-eastern frontiers of Asia Minor put it in the path of every invading army that marched through Cilicia, and it was sacked and changed hands a number of times from late antiquity up to the medieval period, serving as capital of the Armenian kingdom during the reign of Thoros I (1102–9) and also under his successors until c. 1162. Anavarza remained in the hands of the Armenians until 1375, though during that time it was sacked on several occasions by the Mamluks. After the downfall of the Armenian kingdom in 1375, Anavarza was abandoned and fell into ruins. The town has never been systematically excavated, although the archaeologist Michael Gough made exploratory studies there in the years 1949–51.

Karatepe has been identified as the Neo-Hittite city of Asit-wanda, founded in the twelfth century BC. A number of monumental sculptures and reliefs have been restored and replaced *in situ*, making this one of the most interesting outdoor museums in Turkey. Both Karatepe and Anavarza can be visited in a single excursion from Adana via Ceyhan.

In Adana we paid another visit to the local archaeological museum. It has exhibits from sites all over the Cilician plain, which is one of the cradles of Anatolian civilization. A survey published in 1951 by the British School of Archaeology in Ankara has identified 150 ancient settlements in the region between Mersin and Toprakkale, at the highway crossroads above the Gulf of Iskenderun, with sites ranging in date from the neolithic and chalcolithic periods through the Bronze Age and the Hittite era up to Graeco-Roman times. This vast plain was formed by alluvial deposits brought down principally by the Ceyhan and Seyhan rivers. The Ceyhan, the more easterly, flows down from the Anti-Taurus range which bounds the Cilician plain to the north, while the Seyhan has its sources in the Taurus mountains above Rugged Cilicia. Medieval Arab geographers called these two rivers the Streams of Paradise.

The following morning we travelled eastwards once again, this time driving along the new highway and turning south at the crossroads above the Gulf of Iskenderun. At the cross-roads we turned off to see Toprakkale, a village dominated by a medieval fortress atop the huge mound from which it takes its name: Toprak-Kale (Earth Castle). The fortress first appears in history during the reign of Nicephorus II Phocas (963–9), who used it as a base for his victorious campaigns against the Arabs. Then he was known in the West as the Pale Death of the Saracens. Here again, the fortress was fought over and held in turn by all those who contended for power in this region during the medieval period. It was known to the Turks as Toprakkale, to the Crusaders as Tilium, and to the Arabs as Tell Hamdun (a name of Syriac or even Aramaic origin); and it was used as a fortress by the Armenians until 1377, after which it seems to have been abandoned. The old castle is a very evocative sight, a reminder that this is one of the great crossroads of history. The fortress on its ancient mound guards the route which leads south from Cilicia into Syria, the plain now narrowing down into a converging strip of land between the north-east corner of the Mediterranean and the Amanus mountains. This strip was known in antiquity as the Plain of Issus, the gulf then called the Sinus Issicus; and it was the scene of Alexander's great victory over Darius III in 333 BC, a triumph that enabled the Macedonians to penetrate south into Syria and thence deep into the heart of Asia.

After passing the Plain of Issus, the highway brought us

down the eastern shore of the Gulf of Iskenderun. The first place we passed was Yakacık, the former Payas, a village surrounded by gardens on the shore of the gulf. In the olive-groves south of the village there are numerous fallen columns and squared stones, the remains of the Seleucid town of Baiae. On the shore there is a ruined Crusader castle dating from the beginning of the thirteenth century and repaired in Ottoman times. There are also the remains of a mosque and a cara-vanserai erected in the middle of the sixteenth century by Süleyman the Magnificent. These Ottoman buildings and their associated pious foundations date from the time when Payas was an important port and the terminus of the caravan route from Mesopotamia to the eastern Mediterranean.

About five and a half miles south of Yakacık we came to Saraeski. Here, beside the sea, we saw the ruins of another fortress called Kız Kalesi, the Maiden's Castle, and also the remains of a sea-girt ruin called Baba Yunus Kulesi, the Tower of Father Jonah. The tower, which appears to date from the Seleucid period, takes its name from a local legend that this is the place where the prophet Jonah finally was spewed out by the whale, having survived in the leviathan's stomach for three days. Evidently the tower was considered to be a holy place by Christians and Muslims alike who associated it with Jonah and the sign that Christ speaks of in *Matthew* 12:39–40:

An evil and adultrous generation seeketh after a sign; and there shall be no sign given to it but the sign of the prophet Jonah: for as Jonah was three days and three nights in the whale's belly; so shall the Son of man be three days and three nights in the heart of the earth.

Then, another six miles south of Saraeski, we came to Isken-derun, Turkey's southernmost port. Formerly known as Alex-andretta, the town is named after the original port on this site, Alexandria-ad-Issum, founded by Alexander the Great after his victory at the Battle of Issus in 333 BC. This port was soon eclipsed by Seleucia-ad-Pieria, the port of Antioch, which was founded *c.* 300 BC somewhat farther to the south. After the First World War the town here became part of the Sanjak of Alexandretta, a French mandate, until the Hatay was annexed to Turkey in 1939. It was after this that its name was changed to Iskenderun. Iskenderun was the most important port on the Mediterranean coast of Turkey up until the late 1950s, but since then it has been surpassed by the development of Mersin. Iskenderun has a pleasant seafront promenade that gives it a Mediterranean atmosphere lacking in Mersin, and we relaxed at a cafe there before starting to drive inland through the Hatay.

We started off for Antakya, ancient Antioch, as the highway left the shore and headed inland toward the Amanus mountains. After passing the village of Belen we went through the pass known in ancient times as the Porta Syriae, the Syrian Gates, where a medieval fortress still stands guard over the ancient route between the Mediterranean and the Amık plain. This historic pass was of particular importance during the Crusades, since it controlled the main route from Antioch down to the sea.

We went through the pass and reached the Maraş–Antakya highway, where we turned left and headed south through the Hatay, with the Amanus mountains to our right and to our left the Amık plain. After about two and a half miles we turned on to the approach road that took us to Bagras Castle, the greatest of all the medieval fortresses in the Amanus mountains. Bagras was another strategic point on the medieval road between Antioch and the Mediterranean, guarding the southern approach to the Syrian Gates. The fortress is believed to have been built by the Byzantines in the tenth century, perhaps during the campaigns of Nicephorus II Phocas. During the siege of Antioch in 1097–8 it was occupied by the Crusaders, who called it Gaston. The fortress then became the property of the Crusader kingdom of Antioch which, in 1153, turned it over to the Knights Templar. Bagras was besieged and captured by Saladin in 1188, but two years afterwards he dismantled it on the approach of the German Crusade, not knowing that its leader, Frederick Barbarossa, had been drowned. The Armenians stole a march on the Latins by occupying Bagras in 1191, and King Leon II used the fortress as a base in his diplomatic campaign to add Antioch to his kingdom. In 1194 he lured the Antiochene king Bohemund and his family to the castle and captured them as hostages, sending them back to his capital at Sis. But the scheme did not work, and in 1211 the Armenians were forced to return Bagras to the Templars. It was abandoned by the Templars after Antioch fell to the Mamluks under Sultan Baybars in 1268. After that the fortress was held by the Mamluks throughout most of the period up until 1517, when Selim the Grim conquered the whole of south-eastern Anatolia along with Syria and Egypt and added these regions to the Ottoman Empire.

After seeing Bagras Castle we continued heading south along the western side of the vast Amık plain. This was once a great corridor of civilization, for through it passed all of the land-traffic between southern Anatolia and the coastal regions of Phoenicia and Syria, as well as the caravan trade between northern Mesopotamia and the eastern Mediterranean. Early on, both nomads and permanent settlers were attracted by this fertile plain so that in time it became densely populated, as evidenced by the many mounds of ancient settlements that we had noticed when we first passed this way in the spring of 1962. We had been travelling then in a *dolmuş*, which brought us from Aleppo to Iskenderun via Antakya, and our car seemed to be the only one crossing the Amık plain that day for the ancient traffic that used this route has been almost totally cut off by international boundaries. There was considerably more traffic at the time of our most recent trip, but almost all of it was Turkish. The civil war in Lebanon has severely limited travel between Turkey and the countries to its south.

After passing the huge lake at the southern end of the Amık plain we came within sight of the Asi Nehri, the River Orontes of antiquity, coming closer to its right bank as we approached

Mount Silpius, the splendid eminence that rises to 1,660 feet above sea-level directly behind Antakya. Then we drove on into the town, which is mostly on the left bank of the river, on the comparatively level ground between the Orontes and Mount Silpius. This finally brought us to the centre of Antakya, the ancient Antioch on the Orontes.

Here again we were impressed by change, for it was our first visit since 1962 and Antakya had developed from a small and isolated border town into a thriving commercial centre for the surrounding region in the Hatay, with a population of over 100,000. As we walked through the streets we noticed that many people were speaking Arabic, and in fact this is now the first language of the majority of the population in this area, part of the Arab borderlands of Turkey. We also heard a number of people speaking Süryani, the Syriac language used by the majority of the numerous Christian people in south-eastern Turkey. They are mostly members of the Jacobite Church, a schismatic branch of the original Patriarchate of Antioch. Other sects are represented too, including Nestorians and Chaldeans, further adding to the interest of this old town.

Antioch and its sister-city of Seleucia-ad-Pieria were founded by Seleucus I Nicator, both of them dedicated within a year after his victory over Antigonus at the Battle of Ipsus in 301 BC. Seleucus, who already controlled Babylonia, now gained Syria and Mesopotamia as well, and thus reigned over a vast and heterogeneous realm. He therefore abandoned his former capital of Seleucia-on-the-Tigris and built a new one closer to the centre of his empire.

Seleucus laid his first foundations on the Syrian coast in April of 300 BC, when he established the port city of Seleucia-ad-Pieria just north of the Orontes. The following month he founded Antioch-ad-Orontes some eighteen miles inland. Seleucia-ad-Pieria served as the capital until 281 BC, when the old emperor was assassinated, after which his son and successor Antiochus I Soter moved the capital to Antioch. For the next two centuries Antioch remained the capital of the Seleucid

Empire which, at its peak, included most of what is now Turkey and Iran. The Seleucid realm collapsed after the conquest of Syria by Tigranes the Great in 83 BC, and two years later it was annexed by the Romans. In 64 BC Pompey made Antioch capital of the Roman province of Syria, and for the next three centuries it was surpassed in the Hellenistic world only by Rome and Alexandria, with a population that may have exceeded half a million; the historian Ammianus Marcellinus, himself an Antiochene, called it 'the fair crown of the Orient'.

Despite its splendours, the site of Antioch had two serious flaws, and these eventually brought about its downfall. First, it was subject to frequent and devastating earthquakes. Second, the site was difficult to defend and, as the power of Rome began to wane, Antioch became increasingly vulnerable to attack by its enemies to the east and south. In the middle of the third century A D the city was twice taken and sacked by the Persians, and on the latter occasion it was almost totally destroyed by fire. In the year 540 Antioch was captured and burned down again by the Persians, and shortly afterwards it was rebuilt on a reduced scale by Justinian. Early in the seventh century the Persians completely overran Asia Minor and Syria and almost brought about the downfall of the Byzantine Empire. They captured Antioch in 611 and held it until the Byzantines managed to regain the city in 628. But in 636 the Byzantine army was annihilated on the River Yarmuk by the Arabs, who then reconquered all of Syria, taking Antioch in the same year. It remained in Arab hands until it was recaptured in 969 by Nicephorus II Phocas. For more than a century it then served as an outpost of the Byzantine Empire, until in 1084 it was captured by the Selcuks. In 1098, after a long and bloody siege, the city was taken by the Crusaders under Bohemund and became the capital of the Latin principality of Antioch. This Crusader state lasted until 1268, when the city was totally destroyed by the Mamluks under Sultan Baybars. Antioch never recovered from this disaster, and during the Ottoman period travellers reported that it was little more than a broken-down village, with a few hundred houses scattered among the vast ruins of the ancient city.

After the First World War Antioch was part of the territory placed under French mandate by the League of Nations, until in 1939 a referendum resulted in the Hatay being annexed to the Republic of Turkey. The name of Antioch was then officially changed to Antakya, and since then it has become an apparently typical Turkish provincial town, with little evidence today to indicate that it was once one of the great cities of the world.

Excavations in the 1930s revealed, however, that the main street of Antakya, Kurtuluş Caddesi, follows the course of the famous colonnaded street of ancient Antioch. Two Roman miles in length, more than thirty feet wide, flanked by a splendid colonnade with triumphal arches at both ends and a nymphaion in the central forum, this was probably the first and grandest of such monumental thoroughfares in the Roman world. It is thought to have been constructed in 30 BC by King Herod of Judea, who thus honoured Octavian on his triumphal visit to Antioch following his victory over Antony and Cleopatra at Actium the previous year.

During the same excavations a large number of superb mosaic pavements were discovered in Antioch and its vicinity, particularly in what was once the shrine of Daphne. These are now on exhibit in the archaeological museum of Antakya, along with antiquities from other sites in the Hatay. The mosaics date from the second century AD to the sixth, filling in what had been a serious gap in the history of mosaic decoration in the late Roman period. The most important and interesting is the Yakto Mosaic, whose border is believed to depict scenes from the life of Antioch in the fifth century AD, when the city was coming to the end of its golden age.

The site of ancient Daphne is near Harbiye, a village about five miles south of Antakya on the highway that leads south from Turkey to Syria and the Lebanon. About half a mile south of the village one finds the springs and waterfalls for which Daphne was celebrated all over the ancient world, a beautiful and sacred place that was the subject of legends. According to one myth, Apollo's pursuit of Daphne occurred here, and the laurel (*daphne*, in Greek) into which she was transformed was shown to travellers in Seleucid times. Here also stood the mournful cypress into which the youth Cyparissus was changed when he died of sadness after accidentally killing a pet stag. Because of its surpassing beauty, the gods are said to have used this vale for the Judgement of Paris. The sacred springs were reputed to be the abode of nymphs; and in one of them, the Castalia, there resided an oracle of Apollo. The emperor Seleucus I Nicator was inspired by these and other legends and miracles to establish here a sanctuary of Apollo, which became the principal adornment of his empire, the centre of a shrine and pleasure-dome which was celebrated throughout the ancient world. The Seleucid rulers and, later, several Roman emperors built temples and palaces here, and still later the Byzantine emperors added churches and monasteries, making this a shrine whose fame rivalled that of Ephesus. It was probably in Daphne that Antony married Cleopatra in 40 BC, and here he received King Herod and confirmed him as ruler of Judea. Here also were held the Olympic Games of Antioch, the late antique successor to the games of Peloponnesian Olympia. They were a series of athletic and cultural contests which were part of the most famous festival in the Roman world.

But all of these splendours eventually vanished, as Daphne was engulfed in the catastrophes which ultimately destroyed Antioch, and today only a few scattered columns remain of the once-great shrine. The lovely springs and waterfalls remain, shaded by laurels and mourning cypresses, and the place is a favourite resort of the residents of modern Antakya.

The most famous Christian monument in the Hatay is the Church of St. Peter, which is reached by taking the road that leads toward Aleppo and turning off to the right just over a mile outside the town. The church is in a grotto on a hillside overlooking the fields and orchards on the left bank of the

Orontes. The present church was constructed in the thirteenth century by the Crusaders, though local tradition holds that this was one of the very first Christian sanctuaries in Antioch, founded by St. Peter himself. Peter is known to have been in Antioch between AD 47 and 54 together with Paul and Barnabas, and their efforts led to the establishment of the first Christian community there. This was also the first congregation that included Gentiles as well as Jews, and was particularly important in establishing the ecumenical character of the early Church. As one reads in Acts 13:25–6: 'Then departed Barnabus to Tarsus, for to seek Saul: and when he found him he brought him unto Antioch. And it came to pass, that a whole year they assembled themselves with the church, and taught much people. And the disciples were called Christians first in Antioch'.

About a hundred yards beyond the Church of St. Peter there is a curious relief carved into the cliff-face. According to Ioannes Malalas, an Antiochene chronicler writing in the sixth century AD, this figure was carved as a talisman on the order of Antiochus IV, who thus tried to rid his capital of the plague. The relief is presumably named for Charon, the legendary boatman who ferried souls across the River Styx into the Underworld. This was one of two famous talismans which were placed outside Antioch, the other having been set up by Apollonius of Tyana to drive scorpions and gnats out of the city.

We now began the last stage of our journey, driving from Antakya to Samandağ, the site of ancient Seleucia-ad-Pieria, now a resort village on the Turkish coast just north of the Syrian border. On the way to Samandağ we saw to the south the peak of the mountain known as Saman Dağ, the Miraculous Mountain of the Middle Ages. On the summit of this mountain there are two ruined churches dedicated to St. Simeon Stylites the Younger who, in the year 521 at the age of 7, ascended a column there to spend the rest of his life on top of its capital in fasting and prayer. This ascetic saint was named for and emulated the original St. Simeon Stylites, first and foremost of the pillar-sitting saints. St. Simeon the Elder was born c. 390, and at the age of 27 he ascended a column some thirty miles east of Antioch and began a life of asceticism there, living atop a series of columns each taller than the one before until his death in 459. As his fame grew, numerous pilgrims from all over the Christian world flocked to see Simeon on top of his pillar, and from his perch he exerted an enormous influence which at times bent to his will several patriarchs and emperors of Byzantium. After an earthquake in the year 458, the entire population of Antioch camped around his pillar for fifty days, praying to the saint to intercede with God for their salvation, but when he died the following year they took it as a sign of divine disapproval and believed that their world was coming to an end.

Shortly after passing the Miraculous Mountain we reached Samandağ, which is on the coast just north of the mouth of the Orontes. From there we made our way to Magaracık, the actual site of Seleucia-ad-Pieria, now a hamlet overlooking the long beach which stretches north from the mouth of the Orontes. Little now remains of Seleucia, save for numerous tombs and the fragmentary remains of the defence walls and harbour works, along with a remarkable water-tunnel some 240 yards long and 30 feet in width, with a maximum height of 70 feet. An inscription bearing the names of Vespasian and Titus dates it to AD 79.

Seleucia-ad-Pieria was one of four sister cities founded in 300 BC by Seleucus I Nicator, the others being Antioch, Apamaea, and Laodiceia-ad-Marem. These were designed as two linked pairs of seaports and inland towns, with Seleucia serving as the port for Antioch and Laodiceia (modern Laddik) for Apamaea (Qalaat el Moudiq). The latter two are now across the border in Syria. Seleucia, the north-westernmost of the four cities, served as the capital of the Seleucid Empire from the time of its founding until 281 BC, when Seleucus I was assassinated by Ptolemy Ceranus. Antiochus I then succeeded to his father's throne, burying Seleucus at Seleucia in a splendid tomb called the Nikatoreion, in keeping with the ancient custom of interring a king in the capital of his realm. But Antiochus immediately thereafter shifted the Seleucid capital to Antioch, where it remained till the end of the empire. Seleucia continued to be the seaport of Antioch until Antioch's last days, then the two of them together were eventually abandoned and fell into ruins. Remains of the ancient harbour of Seleucia can still be seen, including a ruined pier and part of a mole, the sight of which reminded me of the passage in Acts 12: 4, which tells of the first missionary journey of Paul and Barnabas: 'So they, being sent forth by the Holy Ghost, departed into Seleucia; and from thence they sailed to Cyprus'.

The Turkish province now known as the Hatay was in antiquity the north-western corner of Syria, which was, according to Strabo, 'bounded on the north by Cilicia and Mount Amanus'. Strabo also says that among those whom Seleucus I Nicator settled here were the 'mixed multitudes' who followed the seers Calchas and Mopsus after the fall of Troy, and also 'descendants of Triptolemos', the corn-god of Eleusis, who 'was sent by the Argives in search of Io', wandering through Cilicia and on into northern Syria, where his followers 'gave up in despair, and remained with him in the river-country of the Orontes'. The settlers mentioned by Strabo represent a tradition that was already perhaps more than a thousand years old when he wrote about these events, the myths here again enshrining folk-memories of the great population movements that took place at the end of the Bronze Age.

We had been reminded of these ancient migrations constantly on our journeys along the Turkish coast, particularly whenever we saw the Yürük tribes on their annual marches between the Taurus and the coastal plain, still wandering even though more than nine centuries have passed since they first entered Anatolia after the Battle of Manzikert. And down on the great plain of Antioch, one begins to see the camel caravans of Arab nomads along the roads that lead inland towards places like Harran, the ancient Turkish village on the Syrian border south of Urfa, where the family of Abraham settled four millennia ago. As one reads in the Book of Genesis:

> And Terah took Abram his son, and Lot the wife of Haran his son's son, and Sarai his daughter-in-law, his son Abram's wife; and they went forth with them from Ur of the Chaldees, to go into the land of Canaan; and they came unto Harran and dwelt there.

And so life passes in the ancient land of Turkey. We had now traversed its coast from the Hellespont to the Syrian border, following the tides of history as they ebbed and flowed along the immemorial shores that divide Europe from Asia, evoking memories of the Old Testament and of the fall of Troy even here in this remote corner of the Hatay. We talked of all this as we took one last walk along the beach at Samandağ, reflecting on our travels along the western shores of Turkey. These had begun for us with our three children aboard the old post-boat *Tarih* a quarter of a century before, a long odyssey in space and time that had taken us through history and the middle years of our lives, leaving us together in this forgotten port above Phoenicia. And now even that last Anatolian journey has passed from the real world into the haunted landscape of memory, and the sunlit coastline of Aegean and Mediterranean Turkey has faded into the deepening shadows of what Homer, in the last book of the *Odyssey*, called 'the country of dreams'.

But what dreams they are, and what memories!

CHRONOLOGY

Palaeolithic Period (Old Stone Age) (prior to 7000 BC)

?–7000 BC — Cave-dwellings at Karain; primitive stone implements and weapons

Neolithic Period (New Stone Age) (c. 7000–5000 BC)

c. 7000 — First settlement at Hacilar; earliest evidence of agriculture in Anatolia

c. 6500–5500 — Çatal Hüyük becomes first cultural centre in Anatolia; earliest known religious shrines, pottery, statuettes, and frescoes

c. 5800 — Earliest evidence of human habitation at Aphrodisias

Chalcolithic Period (Copper Age) (c. 5500–3000 BC)

c. 5500 — Sophisticated painted pottery and figurines at Hacilar and Çatal Hüyük

5000–3000 — Settlements at Hacilar and Çatal Hüyük continue; new settlements at Alacahüyük, Alişar, Canhasan, Beycesultan, and Aphrodisias

Bronze Age (c. 3000–1200 BC)

3000–2500	Troy I
2500–2200	Troy II
2200–2050	Troy III
2050–1900	Troy IV

1950	Assyrian merchant colony at Kültepe; first written records in Anatolia
1900	Founding of Hattusa by Hittites
1900–1800	Troy V
1800–1300	Troy VI
1700–1450	Old Hittite Kingdom
1450–1200	Hittite Empire
1300–1260	Troy VII
c. 1260	Fall of Troy
c. 1200	Fall of Hattusa
c. 1200–1100	Foundation of Neo-Hittite states in south-eastern Anatolia at Carchemish, Karatepe, and Zincirli
c. 1100–1000	Migration of Aeolian and Ionian Greeks to Aegean coast of Anatolia
c. 800	Foundation of Panionic League and rise of Greek culture in Anatolia
757	Cyme establishes colony at Cumae in Italy
717	Carchemish and other Neo-Hittite states fall to the Assyrians

Anatolia's Dark Age (c. 700–490 BC)

c. 700	Birth of Homer in Smyrna
667	Foundation of Byzantium
650–600	Miletus establishes colonies at Sinope, Amisus, and Trebizond
c. 650	Cimmerians destroy most cities in western and central Anatolia
600–650	Beginnings of Greek science and philosophy in Ionia
561–546	Reign of King Croesus of Lydia
546	Fall of Sardis; Croesus defeated by King Cyrus of Persia; Ionia subjugated by the Persians
512	Byzantium taken by Darius
499	Ionian cities revolt against Persia
494	Ionians defeated at Battle of Lade and revolt against Persia crushed
490	Persians defeated at Marathon
c. 484	Herodotus born at Halicarnassus

480	Xerxes crosses Hellespont and invades Greece; Persians defeated at Salamis
479	Persians defeated at Plataea and Mycale; Persians evacuate Greece and Ionian cities regain their freedom

Classical Period (479–323 BC)

478	Ionian cities join the Delian Confederacy
431	Beginning of the Peloponnesian War
401	Xenophon and the Ten Thousand begin their expedition
386	Ionia subjugated once more by Persia
356	Birth of Alexander the Great
336	Accession of Alexander
334	Alexander crosses the Hellespont and defeats the Persians at the Battle of the Granicus
333	Alexander conquers western Asia Minor
323	Death of Alexander

Hellenistic Period (323–130 BC)

323	Outbreak of war between the Diadochi, Alexander's successors
318–317	Antigonus controls Asia Minor
301	Battle of Ipsus and death of Antigonus; Lysimachus rules Anatolia and Seleucus gains northern Syria
281	Battle of Corupedium; Seleucus defeats Lysimachus and occupies Anatolia; assassination of Seleucus
276–275	Gauls invade Anatolia and are defeated by Antiochus
261–241	Reign of Eumenes I and rise of Pergamum
230	Alliance of Rome and Pergamum; Attalos I defeats the Gauls
223–187	Reign of Antiochus III, the Great
189	Antiochus defeated by Romans and Pergamenes at the Battle of Magnesia
188	Treaty of Apamea ends Seleucid rule in Anatolia; expansion of Pergamene kingdom

| 133 | Death of Attalos III of Pergamum; Rome inherits his kingdom |

Roman Period (130 BC–AD 330)

129	Organization of Roman Province of Asia
88	Mithridates, king of Pontus, begins his first revolt against Rome; slaughter of Roman colonists in Asia Minor
83	End of Seleucid Empire
67	Pompey defeats the Cilician pirates
64	End of the Mithridatic Wars; Romans control most of Asia Minor
40	Antony and Cleopatra marry in Antioch
34	Octavian defeats Antony and Cleopatra at the Battle of Actium
27	Octavian becomes Augustus

AD

14	Death of Augustus
44–56	Missionary journeys of St. Paul; establishment of first Christian churches in Anatolia
117–38	Reign of Hadrian
263–70	Goths invade Asia Minor
324	Constantine defeats Licinius and becomes sole ruler of Roman Empire; begins to build new capital at Byzantium
330	Constantinople dedicated as capital of Roman Empire

Byzantine Period (AD 330–1453)

392	Edict of Theodosius I banning paganism
524–65	Reign of Justinian the Great; zenith of Byzantine power
616	Sardis and other cities in western Asia Minor sacked by the Persians under Chosroes II
636	Arabs defeat Byzantines at the Battle of the Yarmuk and penetrate deep into Asia Minor
677	Arab fleet attacks Constantinople

717–18	Arabs besiege Constantinople
813	Bulgars besiege Constantinople
923	Bulgars take Adrianople and besiege Constantinople
963–9	Nicephorus Phocas victorious over Arabs; Byzantines regain Cilicia, Cyprus, and Crete
1071	Byzantines defeated by Selcuks at Battle of Manzikert; Turks overrun Anatolia
1071–1283	The Sultanate of Rum; Selcuks dominant power in Anatolia
1096	Beginning of First Crusade; Latin armies enter Anatolia for the first time
1176	Selcuks annihilate Greeks at Myriocephalon
1203	Beginning of the Fourth Crusade; Latins attack Constantinople
1204	Latins take Constantinople; dismemberment of the Byzantine Empire
1204–61	Latins rule in Constantinople; Lascarid dynasty rules remnant of Byzantine Empire from Nicaea; beginning of Byzantine renaissance
1240	Ottoman Turks make first appearance in western Anatolia as minor vassals of Selcuks; Mongols invade eastern Anatolia
1242	Mongols defeat Selcuks at Kösedag and destroy their power in Anatolia
1261	Michael VIII Palaeologus retakes Constantinople and restores Byzantine Empire
1324	Death of Osman Gazi, founder of Ottoman dynasty
1326	Ottomans under Sultan Orhan take Prusa (modern Bursa) and establish their first capital there
1336	Karasi *beylik* conquered by Sultan Orhan; the Troad becomes part of the Ottoman realm
1354	Prince Süleyman leads Ottoman force across the Hellespont, establishing first Turkish foothold in Europe
1363	Turks under Sultan Murat I capture Adri-

	anople and establish Ottoman capital there
1396	Ottoman force led by Beyazit I defeats Crusader army at Nicopolis
1397	First Ottoman siege of Constantinople
1402	Tamerlane defeats Ottomans under Beyazit I at Ankara; the sultan dies in captivity. Mongols overrun Anatolia and Ottoman power in the subcontinent is temporarily crushed
1402–13	Interregnum in the Ottoman Empire
1413–21	Reign of Mehmet I; revival of Ottoman power in Anatolia
1421–51	Reign of Murat II; Ottoman armies sweep through the Balkans and also regain lost territory in Anatolia
1451–81	Reign of Mehmet II, the Conqueror
1453	Turks under Mehmet II conquer Constantinople, which then becomes capital of Ottoman Empire under the name of Istanbul

Ottoman Turkish Period (1453–1923)

1481–1512	Reign of Beyazit II
1512–20	Reign of Selim I
1517	Selim I captures Cairo and adds the title of caliph to that of sultan
1520–66	Reign of Süleyman the Magnificent; zenith of Ottoman power
1566–74	Reign of Selim II, the Sot
1571	Turks conquer Cyprus; Christian powers defeat Turkish fleet at Battle of Lepanto
1578–1666	'The Rule of Women', ineffectual sultans give up control of the Ottoman Empire to their women and grand viziers
1666–1812	Period of intermittent wars between Turks and European powers; Ottoman Empire loses much power in southern Europe
1821	Greeks begin War of Independence
1826	Mahmut II destroys Janissary Corps
1832	Greece achieves independence; Ibrahim Pasha

	of Egypt invades Anatolia
1839–76	The Tanzimat Period; programme of reform in the Ottoman Empire
1876–1909	Reign of Abdül Hamit II
1877	Establishment of first Turkish parliament; dissolved the following year by Abdül Hamit II
1908	Abdül Hamit forced to accept constitutional rule; parliament restored
1909	Abdül Hamit deposed; Young Turks take power
1912–13	Balkan Wars; Turks lose Macedonia and part of Thrace
1914	Turkey enters First World War as ally of Germany
1915	Turks repel Allied landings on Gallipoli peninsula
1918	Turks surrender to Allies; Istanbul occupied by Anglo-French army
1919	Sivas Congress; Atatürk leads Turkish Nationalists in beginning of struggle for national sovereignty; Greek army lands at Smyrna
1920	Establishment of Grand National Assembly of Turkey with Atatürk as president; Greek army advances into Asia Minor
1922	Turks defeat Greeks and drive them out of Asia Minor; sultanate abolished
1923	Treaty of Lausanne establishes sovereignty of modern Turkey, defines its frontiers, and arranges for exchange of minorities between Greece and Turkey

Modern Turkish Period (1923–Present)

1923	Establishment of the Turkish Republic with Atatürk as its first president
1924	Abolition of caliphate
1925–38	Atatürk's programme of reforms to modernize Turkey
1938	Death of Atatürk

1945	Turkey enters Second World War on side of Allies
1946	Turkey becomes charter member of United Nations
1950	Turkey enters Korean War as part of United Nations force
1973	Bosphorus Bridge built between Europe and Asia; opened on fiftieth anniversary of the founding of the Turkish Republic

TURKISH GLOSSARY

The following is a glossary of Turkish words used in the text, most of them geographical or topological terms. It should be noted that the words *camii, medresesi, türbesi,* and similar forms are used when a noun is modified by a preceding noun; thus Sultan Ahmet Camii, the Mosque of Sultan Ahmet, but Yeni Cami, the New Mosque. In the glossary the modified forms are shown in parenthesis. The ending *'lar'* is the plural form, as in *adalar,* or 'islands', which is the plural of *ada,* or 'island'. (To preserve vowel harmony, the plural ending may instead be *'ler'.*)

ada (adası)   island
bakkal   grocery shop
beyaz   white
beylik   Turkoman principality
boğaz (boğazı)   strait, channel
bozca   grey
bulvar (bulvarı)   boulevard
burun (burnu)   cape, promontory
büyü   bay
büyük   big
cadde (caddesi)   avenue
camı (camii)   mosque
çay   tea; but it also means a small stream, in which case the modified ending is *çayı*
çayevi (also *çayhane*)   tea-house
dağ (dağı)   mountain
deniz   sea
dolmuş   public taxi

eski   old
göl (gölü)   lake
hamam (hamamı)   Turkish bath
han (hanı)   caravanserai; an inn for travellers
hisar (hisarı)   castle, fortress
imaret   soup-kitchen
irmak   river
iskele (iskelesi)   landing-place
kale (kalesi)   castle, fortress
kapı (kapısı)   gate
kara   black, or earth
kaza   local administrative centre
kırmızı, kızıl   red
köprü   bridge
körfez (körfezi)   gulf
köy   village
küçük   small, little
kule (kulesi)   tower
liman (limanı)   port
lokanta (lokantası)   restaurant
medrese (medresesı)   theological school
melteme   northerly breeze
mescit (mescidi)   small mosque
meydan (meydanı)   main square in town
nehir (nehri)   river
ova (ovası)   plain
panayir   festival; from the Greek *panegyri*, or religious festival
saray (sarayı)   Turkish palace
şehir   city
sokak (sokağı)   street
su   water; also stream, in which case the modified ending is *suyu*
tekke (tekkesi)   dervish monastery
tepe (tepesi)   hill, mound
türbe (türbesi)   Turkish tomb
yarimada (yarimadası)   peninsula
yeni   new
yol (yolu)   road, journey
Yürük   Turkish nomad

ARCHITECTURAL GLOSSARY

agora   market-place; the civic centre of an ancient Greek city

andron   a room reserved for men in a Greek house or temple, particularly a dining-room

apse   the circular or polygonal termination of a church sanctuary

architrave   a lintel carried from the top of one column to another; the lowest member of an entablature

atrium   the entrance court of a Roman house, roofed over at the sides but open to the sky at the centre

barrel vault   a continuous vault of semicircular cross-section

basilica   the Roman exchange and court of law; an oblong rectangular building usually with aisles around and an apse at one end

bouleterion   senate house of an ancient Greek city

capital   the crowning feature of a column or pilaster

cavea   auditorium of a Greek theatre; so-called because originally it was dug out of the side of a hill

cella   the inner sanctuary of a temple; also called the naos

cornice   the crowning or upper portion of the entablature

crenellations   the indentations in the parapet of a fortress wall

cunei   the wedge-shaped sections into which the parts of a theatre are divided by the radial aisles

curtain-wall   a defence wall linking the towers in a fortress

decastyle   temple front with ten columns

diazoma (pl. diazomata)   aisle of a Graeco-Roman theatre

dipteral   a temple surrounded by a double row of columns; a double colonnade

distyle-in-antis   temple front with two columns between antae, or *in antis*

383

entablature   the upper part of an order of architecture, comprising architrave, frieze, and cornice, supported by a colonnade

exedra   a rectangular or semicircular recess

exonarthex   the outer vestibule of a Byzantine church

frieze   the middle division of a classical entablature, often decorated with carvings in low relief

gymnasium   a school for physical education and training

hippodrome   the course provided by the Greeks for horse and chariot racing

hypaethral   a temple, the naos of which was partly or wholly open to the sky

intercolumniation   the distance between the columns in a colonnade

lesche   an assembly room

lintel   the horizontal beam covering a door or window opening or spanning the opening between two columns of piers

megaron   the principal hall of a Mycenaean palace

naos   the inner sanctuary of a temple; also called the cella

narthex   the inner vestibule of a Byzantine church

nymphaion   a fountain or fountain-house; so called because such places were sacred to the nymphs

odeion   a roofed building in which rehearsals and musical performances took place; sometimes used for meetings of the town council in an ancient Greek city

opisthodomus   the recessed porch in the rear of a Greek temple, sometimes enclosed with bronze grilles and serving as a treasury

orchestra   the 'dancing-place' and hence the place of action for the chorus and at first even for the actors in the Greek theatre; generally circular in plan

order   an order in ancient Greek architecture usually comprised a column (but not in the Doric order) with base, shaft, and capital, the whole supporting an entablature

palaestra   a training-school for physical exercises; in a gymnasium usually a large open area surrounded by a colonnade

paradoi   side entrances to a Greek theatre, passing between the stage building and the auditorium

pediment   the triangular termination of a ridge roof

peripteral   a temple, the cella of which is surrounded by a peristyle

peristasis   another term for peristyle

peristyle   a covered colonnade which surrounds a temple

pier   a mass of masonry, as distinct from a column, from which an arch springs

pilaster   a rectangular feature in the form of a pillar, but projecting one-sixth of its width from a wall

plinth   the supporting member for a statue or an honorific column

portico   a colonnaded space, with a roof supported on at least one side by columns

pronaos   the porch in front of the naos or cella of a temple

propylaeum   the entrance gate-building of the temenos or sacred enclosure of a temple, when there is one doorway only; when there is more than one doorway the plural form propylaea is used

propylon   a very simple building of the propylaeum type

proscenium   a colonnade between the orchestra and the stage building

prostyle   a temple with a portico of columns in front

prytaneion   the state dining-room and senate committee building in a Greek city

quadriga   the ancient four-horse chariot

respond   the wall pilaster behind a column

skene   the stage building which formed the back scene of a theatre

stoa   a building with its roof supported by one or more rows of columns parallel to the rear wall

stylobate   the upper step of a temple, which formed a platform for the columns

temenos   the sacred enclosure or precincts of a temple

BIBLIOGRAPHY

Ekrem Akurgal, *Ancient Civilizations and Ruins of Turkey*. Istanbul, 1973.

Treasures of Turkey. Geneva, 1966.

Bahadir Alkım, *Anatolia I*. Geneva, 1968.

Metin And, *Dances of Anatolian Turkey*. Ankara, 1959.

Apollonius of Rhodes, *The Voyage of Argo*, translated by E.V. Rieu. London, 1959.

Arrian, *The Campaigns of Alexander*, translated by Aubrey De Sélincourt. New York, 1971.

Oktay Aslanapa, *Turkish Art and Architecture*. London, 1971.

Ibn Battuta, *Travels, 1325–1354*, translated by H.A.R. Gibb. Cambridge, 1951.

N.H. Baynes and H.St.L. Moss, *Byzantium: An Introduction to East Roman Civilization*. Oxford, 1948.

George Bean, *Aegean Turkey*. London, 1966.

Turkey's Southern Shore. London, 1968.

Turkey Beyond the Maeander. London, 1971.

Lycia. London, 1973.

Francis Beaufort, *Karamania*. London, 1818.

Everett C. Blake and Anna G. Edmonds, *Biblical Sites in Turkey*. Istanbul, 1977.

Carl W. Blegen, *Troy* (3 vols.). Princeton, 1950–3.

The Mycenaean Age. Cincinnati, 1962.

Troy and the Trojans. London, 1963.

J. Boardman, *The Greeks Overseas*. Baltimore, 1964.

T.S.R. Boase (ed.), *The Cilician Kingdom of Armenia*. Edinburgh and London, 1971.

T.S.R. Boase, *Castles and Churches of the Crusading Kingdom*. London, 1967.

Carl Brockelmann, *History of the Islamic Peoples*. New York, 1960.

John Burnet, *Early Greek Philosophy*. New York, 1952.

J.B. Bury, *A History of the Later Roman Empire* (2 vols.). London, 1889.

J.M. Cadoux, *Ancient Smyrna*. Oxford, 1938.

Claude Cahen, *Pre-Ottoman Turkey*. New York, 1968.

R. Carpenter, *Folk-Tale, Fiction and Saga in the Homeric Epic*. Berkeley, 1946.

M. Cary, *The Greek World from 323–146 BC*. London, 1963.

Evliya Çelebi, *Narrative of Travels*, translated by Joseph von Hammer, 1834. Reprinted, New York, 1968.

Richard Chandler, *Travels in Asia Minor, 1764–1765*. Reprinted, London, 1971.

Marshall Clagett, *Greek Science in Antiquity*. New York, 1963.

C.R. Cockerell, *Travels in Southern Europe and the Levant, 1810–1817*. London, 1903.

John M. Cook, *The Troad: An Archaeological Study*. London, 1973.
The Greeks in Ionia and the East. London, 1966.

F.M. Cornford, *Greek Religious Thoughts from Homer to the Age of Alexander*. New York, 1923.

Covel, *Early Voyages and Travels in the Levant*, edited by Th. Bent. London, 1893.

Edward S. Creasy, *History of the Ottoman Turks*. London, 1854.

H.M. Denham, *The Ionian Islands to the Anatolian Coast*. London, 1982.
Dardanelles, A Midshipman's Diary, 1915–16. London, 1986.

Aubrey De Sélincourt, *The World of Herodotus*. Boston, 1966.

William Bell Dinsmoor, *The Architecture of Ancient Greece*. London, 1902.

Glanville Downey, *Antioch in the Age of Theodosius the Great*. Norman, Okla., 1962.
A History of Antioch. Princeton, 1961.

T.J. Dunbabin, *The Western Greeks*. London, 1948.
The Greeks and their Near Eastern Neighbours. London, 1957.

Kenan T. Erim, *Aphrodisias, the City of Venus Aphrodite*. London, 1986.

Benjamin Farrington, *Greek Science*. Baltimore, 1953.

Charles Fellows, *A Journal Written During an Excursion in Asia Minor*. London, 1839.

Discoveries in Lycia. London, 1841.

George Finlay, *History of Greece* (7 vols.), edited by H.F. Tozer. Oxford, 1877.

M.I. Finley, *The World of Odysseus*. New York, 1954.

Clive Foss, *Byzantine and Turkish Sardis*. Cambridge, Mass., 1976.

Ephesus After Antiquity. Cambridge, 1979.

Robin Lane Fox, *Alexander the Great*. London, 1973.

P.M. Fraser and G.E. Bean, *The Rhodian Peraea and the Islands*. Oxford, 1954.

John Freely, *The Companion Guide to Turkey*. London, 1979.

John Garstang, *The Land of the Hittites*. London, 1910.

The Hittite Empire. London, 1929.

Prehistoric Mersin. Oxford, 1952.

H.A.R. Gibb and H. Bowen, *Islamic Society and the West*. London, 1950.

Edward Gibbon, *The History of the Decline and Fall of the Roman Empire*. Edited by J.B. Bury. London, 1900.

H.A. Gibbons, *The Foundation of the Ottoman Empire*. Oxford, 1916.

Godfrey Goodwin, *A History of Ottoman Architecture*. London, 1971.

Mary Gough, *The Plain and the Rough Places*. London, 1954.

Michael Grant, *Cleopatra*. London, 1974.

From Alexander to Cleopatra. New York, 1982.

Peter Green, *Alexander of Macedon*. London, 1970.

O.R. Gurney, *The Hittites*. London, 1968.

W.K.C. Guthrie, *A History of Greek Philosophy*, vols. I and II. Cambridge, 1962–5.

The Greeks and Their Gods. Boston, 1965.

William J. Hamilton, *Researches in Asia Minor* (2 vols.). London, 1842.

N.G.L. Hammond, *A History of Greece to 322 BC*. Oxford, 1967.

G.M.A. Hanfmann, *Letters from Sardis*. Cambridge, Mass., 1972.

Esther V. Hansen, *The Attalids of Pergamon*. Ithaca, NY, 1947.

F.W. Hasluck, *Christianity and Islam Under the Sultans*. Oxford, 1929.

Sybille Haynes, *Land of the Chimaera*. London, 1974.

T.L. Heath, *A History of Greek Mathematics*. Oxford, 1931.

Rod Heikell, *Turkish Waters Pilot*. London, 1985.

388

Herodotus, *The Histories*, translated by Aubrey De Sélincourt. New York, 1954.

Hesiod, *Theogony* and *Works and Days*, translated by Dorothea Wender. New York, 1973.

D.G. Hogarth, *Excavations at Ephesus*. London, 1908.

Accidents of an Antiquarian's Life. London, 1910.

Homer, *The Iliad*, translated by Richmond Lattimore. Chicago, 1951.

The Odyssey, translated by Richmond Lattimore. New York, 1965.

The Homeric Hymns, translated by Hugh G. Evelyn-White. Cambridge, Mass., 1914.

Joan Hussey, *The Byzantine World*. London, 1957.

G.L. Huxley, *The Early Ionians*. London, 1906.

Halil Inalcık, *The Ottoman Empire: The Classical Age, 1300–1600*. London, 1973.

J. Inan and E. Rosenbaum, *Roman and Early Byzantine Portrait Sculpture in Asia Minor*. London, 1961.

Norman Itzkowitz, *The Ottoman Empire and Islamic Tradition*. New York, 1972.

L.H. Jeffery, *Archaic Greece*. London, 1976.

A.H.M. Jones, *Cities of the Eastern Roman Province*. Oxford, 1937.

The Greek City from Alexander to Justinian. Oxford, 1940.

The Later Roman Empire. Oxford, 1964.

The Decline of the Ancient World. New York, 1966.

Evelyn Lyle Kalças, *Bodrum Castle and its Knights*. Izmir, 1984.

Lord Kinross, *Europa Minor; Journeys in Coastal Turkey*. London, 1956.

Atatürk, The Rebirth of a Nation. London, 1964.

The Ottoman Centuries. London, 1977.

G.S. Kirk and J.E. Raven, *The Presocratic Philosophers*. Cambridge, 1960.

Richard Knolles, *A General Historie of the Ottoman Empire*. London, 1603.

Richard Krautheimer, *Early Christian and Byzantine Architecture*. London, 1965.

Aptullah Kuran, *Ottoman Architecture in its First Period*. Ankara, 1964.

The Mosque in Early Ottoman Architecture. Chicago, 1968.

Walter Leaf, *A Study in Homeric Geography*. London, 1912.

W.M. Leake, *Journal of a Tour in Asia Minor*. London, 1824.

Bernard Lewis, *The Emergence of Modern Turkey*. London, 1951.

BIBLIOGRAPHY

Geoffrey Lewis, *Turkey.* London, 1965.

Raphaela Lewis, *Everyday Life in the Ottoman Empire*. London, 1971.

Seton Lloyd, *Early Anatolia*. London, 1960.

Seton Lloyd and Rice D. Storm, *Alanya*. Ankara, 1958

Emil Ludwig, *Schliemann of Troy*. New York, 1931.

G.H. Macurdy, *Hellenistic Queens*. Baltimore, 1932.

D. Magie, *Roman Rule in Asia Minor*. Princeton, 1950.

Cyril Mango, *Byzantine Architecture*. New York, 1976.

Otto F.A. Meinardus, *St. Paul in Ephesus and the Cities of Galatia and Cyprus*. Athens, 1973.

    St. John of Patmos and the Seven Churches of the Apocalypse. Athens, 1974.

James Mellaart, *Çatal Hüyük*. London, 1967.

Henri Metzger, *Anatolia II*. Geneva, 1969.

W. Miller, *The Latins in the Levant*. London, 1908.

    Essays on the Latin Orient. Cambridge, 1921.

    The Ottoman Empire and its Successors. Cambridge, 1936.

Alan Moorhead, *Gallipoli*. London, 1956.

Mark P.O. Morford and Robert J. Lenardon, *Classical Mythology*. New York, 1971.

H.V. Morton, *In the Steps of St. Paul*. New York, 1935.

W. Müller-Weiner, *Castles of the Crusaders*. London, 1965.

Serapie der Nersessian, *The Armenians*. London, 1969.

C.T. Newton, *Discoveries at Halicarnassus, Cnidus and Branchidae* (2 vols.). London, 1861.

    Travels and Discoveries in the Levant. London, 1865.

Donald M. Nicol, *The Last Centuries of Byzantium, 1261–1453*. London, 1972.

M.P. Nilsson, *Greek Popular Religion*. New York, 1940.

    History of Greek Religion. Oxford, 1949.

Georg Ostrogorsky, *History of the Byzantine State*, translated by Joan Hussey. London, 1968.

Ovid, *Metamorphoses*, translated by F.J. Miller. Cambridge, Mass. 1946.

Pausanius, *Guide to Greece*, translated by Peter Levi (2 vols.). New York, 1971.

L. Pearson, *Early Ionian Historians*. Oxford, 1939.

John G. Pedley, *Sardis in the Age of Croesus*. Oklahoma, 1968.

    Ancient Literary Sources on Sardis. Cambridge, Mass., 1972.

F.E. Peters, *The Harvest of Hellenism*. New York, 1970.

Plutarch, *Lives of the Noble Romans*, edited by Edmund Fuller. New York, 1959.

The Rise and Fall of Athens, Nine Greek Lives, translated by Ian Scott-Kilvert. Baltimore, 1960.

Marco Polo, *The Description of the World*, edited by A.C. Moule and P. Pelliot. London, 1938.

J.E. Powell, *The History of Herodotus*. Cambridge, 1939.

William M. Ramsay, *Letters to the Seven Churches*. London, 1901.

The Historical Geography of Asia Minor. London, 1907.

The Cities of St. Paul. London, 1907.

David Talbot Rice, *Byzantine Art*. Baltimore, 1935.

Tamara Talbot Rice, *The Seljuks in Asia Minor*. London, 1961.

Everyday Life in Byzantium. London, 1967.

D.S. Robertson, *Greek and Roman Architecture*. Cambridge, 1971.

Charles Alexander Robinson, *Ancient History, from Prehistoric Times to the Death of Justinian*. New York, 1951.

C. Roebuck, *Ionian Trade and Colonization*. New York, 1959.

H.J. Rose, *Gods and Heroes of the Greeks*. London, 1957.

Handbook of Greek Religion. New York, 1960 (sixth ed.).

M. Rostovtzeff, *The Social and Economic History of the Hellenistic World* (3 vols.). Oxford, 1956.

Steven Runciman, *Byzantine Civilization*. London, 1933.

A History of the Crusades (3 vols.). London, 1952–4.

The Last Byzantine Renaissance. Cambridge, 1971.

Paul Rycaut, *The History of the Present State of the Ottoman Empire* (3 vols.). London, 1670.

Heinrich Schliemann, *Troja: Results of the Latest Researches and Discoveries on the Site of Homeric Troy*. London, 1881.

Dux Schneider, *The Travellers' Guide to Turkey*. London, 1975.

Gerschom Scholem, *Sabbetai Sevi, the Mystical Messiah*. Oxford, 1984.

K.M. Setton (ed.), *A History of the Crusades* (3 vols.). London, 1969–75.

Stanford J. Shaw and Ezel Kural Shaw, *History of the Ottoman Empire and Modern Turkey*. London, 1976–7.

Philip Sherrard, *The Greek East and Latin West*. Oxford, 1959.

Michael Llewellyn Smith, *Ionian Vision; the Greeks in Asia Minor, 1919–23*. New York, 1973.

BIBLIOGRAPHY

T.A.B. Spratt and E. *Forbes*, *Travels in Lycia, Milyas and the Cibyratis* (2 vols.). London, 1847.

Freya Stark, *Ionia, A Quest*. London, 1954
The Lycian Shore. London, 1956.
Alexander's Path. London, 1958.

J. Starr, *The Jews in the Byzantine Empire*. Athens, 1939.

Strabo, *The Geography*, translated by Horace Leonard Jones. Cambridge, 1971.

W.W. Tarn, *Alexander the Great* (2 vols.). London, 1948.
Hellenistic Civilization. London, 1952.

Thucydides, *The Peloponnesian War*, translated by Rex Warner. Baltimore, 1954.

Behçet Ünsal, *Turkish and Islamic Architecture in Seljuk and Ottoman Times*. London, 1959.

A.A. Vasiliev, *History of the Byzantine Empire* (2 vols.). Madison, Wis., 1961.

Cornelius Vermeule, *Roman Imperial Art in Greece and Asia Minor*. Cambridge, Mass., 1966.

Emily Vermeule, *Greece in the Bronze Age*. Chicago, 1964.

Virgil, *The Aeneid*, translated by Robert Fitzgerald. New York, 1951.

Speros Vryonis, Jr., *The Decline of Medieval Hellenism in Asia Minor and the Process of Islamization from the Eleventh to the Fifteenth Century*. Los Angeles, 1971.

Gwyn Williams, *A Travellers' Guide and History*. London, 1867.

Paul Wittek, *The Rise of the Ottoman Empire*. London, 1938.

J.T. Wood, *Discoveries at Ephesus*. London, 1877.

Michael Wood, *In Search of the Trojan War*. New York and London, 1985.

R.E. Wycherley, *How the Greeks Built Cities*. New York, 1962.

Xenophon, *The Persian Expedition*, translated by Rex Warner. Baltimore, 1949.

S. Ximines, *Asia Minor in Ruins*. London, 1925.

Eduard Ziller, *Outlines of the History of Greek Philosophy*. New York, 1955.

INDEX

INDEX

398

INDEX